SPORT, THE MEDIA AND IRELAND: INTERDISCIPLINARY PERSPECTIVES

Neil O'Boyle would like to dedicate the book to Ronan and Eoin, his all-time favourite sportsmen

Marcus Free would like to dedicate the book to the memory of his parents and their many happy shared hours of armchair television sports; and to Helen and Ezra for their love, support and tolerance of their many shared hours of armchair television sports

Sport, the Media and Ireland: Interdisciplinary Perspectives

EDITED BY

NEIL O'BOYLE AND MARCUS FREE

CORK UNIVERSITY PRESS

First published in hardback in 2020 by
Cork University Press
Boole Library
University College Cork
Cork
T12 ND89
Ireland

Library of Congress Control Number: 2019955524
Distribution in the USA: Longleaf Services, Chapel Hill, NC, USA

British Library Cataloguing in Publication Data
A CIP record for this book is available from the British Library.

ISBN HB: 978-1-78205-392-7

Printed by BZ Graf in Poland.
Print origination and design by Carrigboy Typesetting Services,
www.carrigboy.com
Cover images courtesy of shutterstock.com, vecteezy.com
and Studio 10 Design.

www.corkuniversitypress.com

Contents

Notes on Contributors

ALI BOWES is currently a lecturer in the sociology of sport at Nottingham Trent University. Her PhD, completed at Loughborough University in 2013, focused on the relationship between women's sport and English national identity. This research has been published in the *International Review for the Sociology of Sport* and the *Journal of Sport and Social Issues*, as well as featuring in two edited collections. Her research interests centre on feminist analyses of women's sport, and most recently she has been researching women's professional golf. This research has specifically focused on the experiences of professional golfers, as well as on their media representations.

JOHN CONNOLLY is an associate professor at Dublin City University. His research interests include sports, the sociology of organisations, and habitus formation and change. His most recent work has examined generational tensions and relations. He is a member of the editorial board of the *European Journal for Sport and Society*. His work has been published in *Current Sociology*, *Sociological Review*, *Sociology*, *Organization* and *Theory, Culture & Society*, among others.

MIKE CRONIN is the academic director of Boston College in Ireland. He has worked extensively on the history of Irish sport, and in particular has concentrated on questions of sport and identity. He was one of the directors of the Gaelic Athletic Association Oral History Project (2008–12), which can be viewed at https://www.gaa.ie/the-gaa/oral-history/.

SEÁN CROSSON is the co-director of the MA in sports journalism and communication, and leader of the Sport & Exercise Research Group at National University of Ireland, Galway. His principal research interest is the relationship between film, visual media and sport, the subject of a wide range of publications, including *Gaelic Games on Film: From silent films to Hollywood hurling, horror and the emergence of Irish cinema* (Cork University Press, 2019), *Sport and Film* (Routledge, 2013), and the co-edited collection *Sport, Representation and Evolving Identities in Europe* (Peter Lang, 2010).

CONOR CURRAN is an Irish Research Council postdoctoral research fellow in the School of Education at Trinity College, Dublin. He has taught sports history at the International Centre for Sports History and Culture at De Montfort University, Leicester and at the University of Giessen and University of Marburg. He is the author of *The Development of Sport in Donegal, 1880–1935* (Cork University Press, 2015) and *Irish Soccer Migrants: A social and cultural history* (Cork University Press, 2017). He is also co-editor of *New Perspectives on Association Football in Irish History* (Routledge, 2018), and has published numerous articles on the history of sport.

PADDY DOLAN is a senior lecturer in sociology and social policy at Technological University, Dublin. His research interests include figurational and historical sociology, sport, childhood, emotions, and organisational change. His work has been published in *Sociology, British Journal of Sociology, History of Education* and *Sociological Review*, among others. He serves as secretary-treasurer of the Historical Sociology Research Committee (RC56) of the International Sociological Association.

CIARÁN DUNNE is an assistant professor in the School of Applied Language and Intercultural Studies at Dublin City University. He lectures across several disciplines, including sociology, Spanish language, social entrepreneurship, and intercultural studies, as well as creative and future thinking. He is the chairperson of the BA in social sciences and cultural innovation, and his research outputs have been published in top-ranking international journals relating to intercultural studies, creativity studies, the sociology of sport, qualitative-research methodology, and international education.

DAN DWYER teaches media studies through the Irish language at undergraduate and postgraduate level at Acadamh na hOllscolaíochta Gaeilge in the National University Ireland, Galway. He is currently completing a PhD with the Huston School of Film and Digital Media at the same university. The focus of his research is the relationship between media-audience practices and identity construction among the Irish in Britain.

RODDY FLYNN is an associate professor at the School of Communications, Dublin City University, where he is chair of contemporary screen industries studies. He has written extensively on media policy in Ireland, and is co-author (with Professor John Horgan) of the second edition of *Irish Media: A critical history* (Four Courts Press, 2017).

MARCUS FREE is a lecturer in media and communication studies at Mary Immaculate College, University of Limerick. He has published widely in peer-reviewed journals and scholarly collections on the interrelationships between sport, national identity, gender and race in film, print and broadcast media. He is co-author (with John Hughson and David Inglis) of *The Uses of Sport: A critical study* (Routledge, 2005).

COLM KEARNS is a post-doctoral researcher at Dublin City University. He completed his PhD on sport sponsorship and national identity in 2019. He currently contributes to projects on deliberative democracy (with FuJo, the Institute for Future Media and Journalism) and climate change (with the Insight Centre for Data Analytics). His present research focuses on how social media has affected the relationship between major football clubs and their supporters with regard to the neoliberalisation of top-level football.

NIAMH KITCHING is a lecturer in physical education at Mary Immaculate College, University of Limerick. She has a wealth of experience of golf environments and settings, having represented Ireland at amateur level and having worked in Junior Golf Ireland and the Professional Golfers' Association in England and Ireland. Her research interests include the sociology of sport and PE, sports pedagogy and coaching, elite sport, sports development and coach education. Her published research focuses on gender equality and sport, with a particular emphasis on female athletes and coaches, and their presence, participation and presentation in sports and sports media. She has published in a number of sociology-of-sport outputs and edited collections.

KATIE LISTON is senior lecturer in the social sciences of sport at Ulster University (Jordanstown). Her research interests include gender, national identity, and pain and injury in sport. She has published widely in these areas, including a recent co-edited four-volume collection titled *The Business and Culture of Sports: Society, politics, economy, environment* (Gale, 2019). She is a regular contributor to media on these issues. She has All-Ireland honours in athletics, Gaelic football (including All-Stars), soccer and rugby, and international honours in the latter two.

ANTHONY P. MCINTYRE is a teaching fellow in film and media studies at University College, Dublin. He is co-editor of *The Aesthetics and Affects of Cuteness* (Routledge, 2017) and book-reviews editor of *Television and New Media*. He has published chapters and articles in numerous scholarly edited collections and journals, and is currently finishing a monograph, *Transnationalism, Diaspora and Regionality in 21st Century Irish Popular Culture* (Palgrave Macmillan, 2020).

NEIL O'BOYLE is a communications lecturer and associate professor at Dublin City University. His work examines the relationship between media, popular culture and collective identities, a topic he explored in his book *New Vocabularies, Old Ideas: Culture, Irishness, and the advertising industry* (Peter Lang, 2011). More recently, he has written about the overlapping fields of sport, media and tourism, with his work published in journals such as *Sport in Society* and *Television and New Media*.

MARY O'CONNOR is CEO of the Federation of Irish Sport. She holds a masters in voluntary and community sector management from University College Cork (UCC). Prior to her current role, she worked with the Camogie Association as director of technical development and participation. She is a regular contributor to sports media, notably on the 20x20 campaign launched in 2018. Mary holds All-Ireland honours in camogie and Gaelic football and All-Star awards in both codes. She was awarded an honorary doctorate from UCC in recognition of her contribution to sport in Ireland.

LANCE PETTITT has been a part-time lecturer at Birkbeck, University of London since 2016, where he is also an associate research fellow, and is chair of Irish Film Festival London Ltd. He has published widely on Irish cinema, television and cultural history. Since 2011 he has been a founding co-editor of 'Ireland on Film', a screenplay critical edition whose fourth volume will be *Maeve* (1981) by Pat Murphy (UFSC, 2020 forthcoming). He has published essays in *Éire-Ireland* (2015, 2017), an essay on Pat Murphy for a forthcoming collection on Irish women in film (Cork University Press, 2020) and is preparing a monograph, *The Last Bohemian,* on the films of Brian Desmond Hurst for Syracuse University Press.

PAUL ROUSE is associate professor of history at University College, Dublin. He has written extensively on the history of Irish sport. His books include *Sport & Ireland: A history* (Oxford University Press, 2015) and *The Hurlers: The first All-Ireland championship and the making of modern hurling* (Penguin UK, 2018).

CIARÁN RYAN is a member of the Department of Creative Arts, Media and Music at Dundalk Institute of Technology. He was awarded his PhD by Mary Immaculate College, University of Limerick in 2015 for his research on Irish music fanzines. He has previously lectured at Mary Immaculate College, National University of Ireland, Galway and the University of Limerick.

Acknowledgements

FIRST AND FOREMOST, our sincere thanks to the contributors to this collection. We thank them for sharing their excellent work and for their professionalism throughout the editorial process. We also offer our thanks to Tyrone Productions Ltd for the use of images in Seán Crosson's chapter, which is based on an earlier version published in *Review of Irish Studies in Europe*. Second, we thank the participants at our symposium in May 2018 (some of whom are contributors here), where the idea for the present collection was born. Our sincere thanks also to the speakers at our round-table discussion on women, media and sport for their generosity, honesty and commitment to this project, and to Mike Cronin for providing the facilities at Boston College, Dublin, and for making the arrangements for the recording of the discussion. Third, we are immensely grateful to Maria O'Donovan and her colleagues at Cork University Press, and to the reviewers of the manuscript for their time and expertise, and for their helpful and encouraging feedback. Finally, we thank our families for their constant love and support, and for putting up with our regular email exchanges in the early hours of the morning.

NEIL O'BOYLE
Dublin City University

MARCUS FREE
Mary Immaculate College, University of Limerick

Introduction

NEIL O'BOYLE AND MARCUS FREE

SPORTING IRELAND

IN JANUARY 2018 a nine-week criminal trial began at Belfast Crown Court involving two Ulster province and Irish international rugby players, Paddy Jackson and Stuart Olding. The trial, the acquittal of the players involved, and the subsequent controversy surrounding the publication of ignominious WhatsApp messages sent by the players illustrate numerous facets of the sports–media relationship, the subject of the present collection of essays. Our interest here is in how the media report, shape and *enter into* sport, and how 'media sport' (new and old) in turn reflects the values, politics and social processes at work in contemporary Irish society.

Sport is sometimes regarded as mere light entertainment. Indeed, sports journalists are sometimes condescendingly described as working in the 'toy department' of media organisations. Yet we argue that the importance of sport is manifold, not only because of the many people worldwide who participate in it (or are excluded from it) but also because of the many more who 'consume' it (in a media sense). To offer an example: on 20 January 2017 Donald Trump – a celebrity businessman without any political or military experience – was sworn in as the forty-fifth president of the United States, sparking at least 261 protest marches internationally and the largest single-day protest in American history.[1] On 14 June of the same year, Leo Varadkar of Fine Gael became the youngest and first openly gay Taoiseach (prime minister) of Ireland. Amidst these two hugely significant and newsworthy happenings, it is instructive to note that the three 'most-viewed' television broadcasts in the United

States in 2017 were American-football games. Indeed, according to Nielsen ratings, American-football games accounted for thirty-seven of 2017's top fifty broadcasts, or nearly three-quarters of the most-watched programmes on US television.[2] Likewise, figures from Nielsen and Television Audience Measurement Ireland indicate that sporting fixtures accounted for four of the top five 'most-watched' programmes on Irish television in 2017, and eleven of the top twenty programmes. These included the All-Ireland football and hurling finals and two of the Republic of Ireland's World Cup soccer qualifiers (against Denmark and Wales).[3]

Such figures offer some indication of the significance of sport internationally and its particular importance in Irish social and cultural life. Among other things, sport has been studied as a site of myth-making and heroism, gender displays and tribalism, and national self-realisation. For example, Roman Horak and Georg Spitaler have demonstrated that urban soccer and alpine skiing played a crucial role in the development of national identity and self-awareness in Austria.[4] Similarly, Mark Falcous has discussed how the New Zealand rugby team, known internationally as the All Blacks, was central to attempts to rebrand national identity in a manner that reconciled Maori culture with decolonised settler culture.[5] Such works highlight how sport is both a site of cultural continuity and a site of cultural change and contestation. For Messner, sport and the broader culture of which it is part and to which it contributes 'is a dynamic social space where dominant (class, ethnic, etc.) ideologies are perpetuated as well as challenged and contested'.[6]

In the Irish context, sports scholarship has also emphasised this duality. Whether examining Irish sport narrowly or broadly, Rouse's *Sport and Ireland* (2015), Cronin et al.'s *The GAA: A people's history* (2014), and Curran's *Irish Soccer Migrants* (2017) each consider sport in Ireland against the backdrop of a changing Irish society. Irish scholars have similarly used sport as a lens for investigating shifting discourses surrounding Irish culture and the changing nature of 'Irishness'. For example, Aidan Arrowsmith has examined the successes of the Republic of Ireland international football team under Jack Charlton (1986–96), and has argued that the team – which included a number of British-born players – was representative of a more inclusive, modern Irish identity that stood in contrast to an outdated, essentialist and somewhat parochial conception of Irish identity characterised by the Gaelic Athletic Association (GAA).[7]

However, as Ireland's economic fortunes improved throughout the 1990s and immigration overtook emigration, a discourse of 'embarrassment' about Irish football's over-reliance on the diaspora began to take hold. In contrast to the football team, the Irish rugby union team was quickly deemed more 'authentically' Irish, given that the majority of its players were Irish-born and played for professional province-as-clubs in European competition in rugby's post-1995 professional era. Equally, the team's success on the international stage was suddenly championed as symbolic of a new, confident Celtic Tiger Ireland. Marcus Free has argued that the perceived 'professionalism' of the management of the Irish rugby team, provinces and feeder academies was in some respects conflated with the projected political and media image of Celtic Tiger Ireland as a national achievement – a 'happy ending' outcome of successful economic management despite the over-reliance on foreign direct investment and, latterly and disastrously, an unsustainable property boom fuelled by a poorly regulated financial sector.[8] Moreover, he suggests that this association persists to the present day, that the continued success of the team has acted as an ideological balm for the country's economic woes following the financial crisis of 2007–8, with celebrity rugby players depicted as paragons of entrepreneurial virtue investing in their own higher education and post-playing careers in a hegemonic political and media narrative of economic 'recovery'.[9] As an index of the impact of media on the popularity and symbolism of sport, despite rugby's lagging some way behind Gaelic football and soccer in terms of participation and live attendance,[10] TV3's television audience for Ireland's game against England in the 2018 Six Nations Championship peaked at 1,328,000 – more than a quarter of the population of the Republic of Ireland.[11]

The above examples highlight how sport plays both internal and external roles for nations, insofar as all nations increasingly compete for attention, reputation, tourism and inward investment. Sport invariably incorporates both culture and commerce, and resultant economic gains are often of important symbolic value, too. For example, Rowe's analysis of three East Asian Olympic Games (Tokyo 1964, Seoul 1988 and Beijing 2008) demonstrates the

perceived connection between hosting international sporting events
and a country's standing in the global symbolic order.[12] Rowe argues
that, in different ways and with varying degrees of success, each of
these Olympic Games demonstrated that the various host nations
had 'arrived' on the global stage. As he puts it:

> It is argued that each was subjected to a test that extended well
> beyond the event to a measure of whether, in the context of
> Asia after the middle of the twentieth century, the host could be
> said to have matured and joined a 'club' founded in the West.[13]

Rowe's analysis also points to the close connection between sport
and tourism. Like film and television-inspired tourism, sport often
drives tourism, and sporting events can yield significant economic
returns for host nations. Apart from attending events, tourists
commonly travel to see signature stadia like London's Wembley
Stadium or Barcelona's Camp Nou, or to visit attractions like the Old
Trafford Museum. In Ireland, sports tourism has grown significantly
in recent decades, and the country has enjoyed a strong record of
hosting international sporting events, such as the Ryder Cup (2006)
and Solheim Cup (2011) in golf, and the Heineken Cup final (2013)
in rugby. Just as significant, however, is the number of visitors who
partake in non-competitive sporting activities, as acknowledged by
Ireland's Department of Transport, Tourism and Sport:

> The sports tourism industry is worth an estimated €450bn
> globally and is the fastest growing tourism sector. During 2014,
> overseas activity/sport tourism was worth €900m to Ireland.
> Tourists engaged in a range of non-competitive sporting
> activities such as cycling, golf, hiking, walking, angling and
> water-based pursuits. Ireland's strong position as a destination
> for these outdoor activities assists in the regional diversification
> of tourism, and supports Ireland's overall reputation as a clean,
> green country...Sports Tourism is a high yield sector with the
> adventure or sports traveller spending on average 40% higher
> than the average overseas holiday maker.[14]

However, despite the frequently expressed political optimism
regarding the economic and cultural benefits of sports tourism,
it is essential to turn a critical eye to the confluence of political

interests, media hype and economic arguments in such cases. The failed Irish government-backed bid to host the 2023 Rugby World Cup is an interesting case of how sport may be seen to function ideologically at specific historical conjunctures. When launched in 2014 as an initiative to host the tournament on the island of Ireland, it was presented by the Republic's then minister of state for sport and tourism (and subsequent Taoiseach) Leo Varadkar as key to the 'tourism strategy on both sides of the border'.[15] Emergency legislation was rushed through the Irish parliament in July 2017 to ensure that the Irish government would pay the host fee of €138 million and guarantee estimated tournament running costs of €200 million. Although the 2015 Rugby World Cup in England was hailed as a huge direct and indirect boost to the economy, with the cost of the event partly restrained by the use of existing stadia,[16] the 2011 New Zealand tournament involved substantial stadium and infrastructure investments. Steve Jackson and Jay Scherer have questioned the extent to which this expenditure was recovered through ticket sales and visitor spending.[17] Arguably, Ireland's bid was more comparable to New Zealand's than England's due to the necessity to upgrade several stadia and to secure permission to redevelop another. The GAA's planned provision of all but three stadia contributed to the general theme of 'sporting ecumenism' in Irish media, dating from the first use of its Croke Park stadium for rugby internationals in 2007.[18] However, the bid failed partly because the independent assessment deemed the promised upgrades a substantial risk factor given the timescale, and also considered one of the recently completed upgrades inadequate for tournament needs.[19] There was an overwhelming sense of grievance in the Irish media with the decision to award the tournament to France.[20] Yet despite the failed bid, arguably Taoiseach Leo Varadkar and his right-of-centre coalition government benefitted from his highly vocal and visible backing at the bid presentation in London in September 2017, and from the bid's contribution to the political and media narrative of economic recovery.

While the global significance and popularity of sport and sports media are clear, academic scholarship must focus on the ways in which sports media variously contributes to, obscures and helps negotiate or contest collective identities, solidarities, divisions and hierarchies within and across nation states. If the economic benefits of mega sports events are debatable, equally the cultural impact of sport's development is not necessarily straightforwardly 'positive', 'negative' or easily understood. In 2017, for example, the Department of Education confirmed that physical education would be available to students as a Leaving Certificate subject for the first time during the 2018–19 school year. Education Minister Richard Bruton presented this as a validation of sport's contribution to 'our overall wellbeing, not just our physical fitness' but 'our mental health too…in line with this government's overall emphasis on promoting healthy lifestyles'.[21] This development might be alternatively viewed as an illustration of how, in an age of financial austerity and 'lean' government, successive Irish governments have heightened and repeatedly promoted the 'neoliberal' discourse of self-discipline and individual responsibility[22] that emerged in the Celtic Tiger years.[23] And yet the growing popularity of fitness-tracking applications, such as Strava and Runkeeper, suggest that new-media technologies are playing an ever-more important role in building a sense of community among enthusiasts and audiences across local, national and global contexts.[24] These technologies may also be considered as part of a more widespread 'quantified self' movement[25] or 'bottom up governmentality'[26] in contemporary Western societies that 'cannot be simplistically reduced to the work of discursive formations on passively acquiescent participants'.[27]

Such complexities in, and mutually contradictory readings of, sport are such that it is worthy of extensive academic inquiry. Although sport continues to occupy a relatively marginal position within the academy, sports scholars have drawn attention to the social, cultural and economic aspects of sport, and – as we explore in this collection – increasingly are investigating the interrelationship of sport and media. Attending live sporting events remains a passion for some people, and one cannot deny the deep affective significance of physical sites of sport. However, for the vast majority of people, sporting contests are experienced and enjoyed far away from the playing field, as members of a widely dispersed global media audience.[28] Media are not just carriers of sport content but, more importantly, are also shapers of meanings about and around sport; indeed, they sometimes shape the practice of sport itself, such as the controversial use of the Video Assistant Referee (VAR) in the English Premier League.

To our knowledge, there are currently no collections or monographs devoted to the interrelationship of sport, the media and Ireland, a gap we hope the present collection of essays will go some way towards redressing. The title of this collection signifies an attempt to place the 'interrelationships' of these domains at the heart of our analysis; however, it is to the particular significance of media that we now turn.

THE MEDIATISATION OF SPORT

As David Rowe notes in his 'Sports and Media' entry in Oxford Bibliographies, the sports–media nexus became a significant object of scholarship from the mid-1980s, with many media-sports scholars arguing that media are both important ideological vehicles and key agents in the commercialisation of sports.[29] Seminal anthologies edited by Lawrence Wenner, including *Media, Sports, and Society* (1989) and *Mediasport* (1998), gave shape to this emerging field, and charted the complex and sometimes ambivalent relationship between sport and media. Nowadays, media have infiltrated the material spaces of sport, from microphones on cricket stumps and in NFL helmets to cameras in the corners of boxing rings. Documentaries such as *From Fat to Finish Line* (Media Meld Studios, 2015) extol the physical, emotional and relational benefits of sport and exercise, while others, such as *Dementia, Football, and Me* (BBC, 2017) and *League of Denial: The NFL's concussion crisis* (Frontline, 2013), draw attention to health risks and fuel social anxieties. Likewise, complex social issues such as racism, sexism, nationalism and ableism are often debated in the context of sport. For example, American football player Colin Kaepernick's refusal to stand for the US national anthem in 2016 – which he insisted was an act of protest against racial injustice – sparked a media firestorm and led to President Donald Trump calling for his suspension from the NFL. If the Kaepernick scandal centred on issues of racism, patriotism and political activism, the so-called 'sandpapergate' ball-tampering scandal that rocked Australian cricket in March 2018 centred on questions of sporting integrity and honesty, and played out across Australian and global media as the fall from grace of national hero Steve Smith.[30] On a much smaller scale, journalist Kevin Myers sparked considerable controversy in 2004 when he wrote in *The Irish Times* that 'we [Irish people?] don't want to watch women playing sports'.[31]

Such examples demonstrate the complex interdependences of sport and media, but they also offer a clear sense of how sport can activate ideological debate and division. Further, they demonstrate that sport is especially well-suited to the increasingly format-driven nature of media. For example, Stauff argues that sport's 'seriality' creates a continuously evolving and recursive storyworld that spans myriad media forms (texts, movies, photos, and so on) and different media platforms (television, social media, and so on). Consequently, Stauff considers sport a paradigmatic example of what he calls 'transmedia world-building'.[32]

As noted above, sports scholars have long observed the myth-making powers of sport, which are radically enhanced by media, especially during international events. In particular, scholars have drawn attention to the myth-making powers of media sport in relation to national identity. For example, Rowe et al. argue that 'there is surely no cultural force more equal to the task of creating an imaginary national unity than the international sports–media complex'.[33] Emma Poulton and Joseph Maguire similarly suggest that sport continues to be among the most potent and visible symbols of national identity, and that international sporting contests function as forms of 'ritualised war'.[34] Such media sporting events also exhibit what Gary Whannel describes as a 'vortextual' character. Whannel's invented term 'vortextuality' means the ways in which certain events so dominate the media landscape that they have a whirlpool-like quality, sucking in the media and their consumers to such an extent that it seems almost impossible to discuss anything else for a time.[35]

While there are international patterns to be observed in these respects, there are also national and cultural specificities to the mediatisation of sport. The smallness of Ireland as a country and the ways in which print, broadcast and social media can feed into and from each other on a national scale are such that some sporting events have attained 'vortextual' status in Ireland in recent years. When Irish soccer captain Roy Keane was dismissed by manager Mick McCarthy immediately prior to the 2002 World Cup in Japan and South Korea following an *Irish Times* interview in which he criticised the team's preparation, the Irish media was dominated by acrimonious discussions for over a week, with the metaphor of the Irish civil war repeatedly invoked as 'McCarthyites' and 'Keanites' debated the decision and speculated as to whether or not Keane would apologise and be invited back. Marcus Free has analysed how, despite being a working-class emigrant footballer whose entire professional career was spent in Britain, Keane became, for his supporters, an 'attractive symbol of fantasised collective achievement' in an economic bubble fuelled by foreign direct investment and the ultimately catastrophically unsustainable construction boom of the Celtic Tiger.[36] Nonetheless, despite – or paradoxically, because of – the seemingly all-encompassing 'civil' war, Keane's vortextuality exemplified how the physicality of sport and the emotional intensity of supporters' investment in athletes and contests generates 'moments when an affective unity can be posited against the grain of structural divisions and bureaucratic taxonomies' in the lived experience of national identity.[37]

Central to this saga, too, were fantasies of 'hard', competitive and implicitly heterosexual masculinity as the embodiment of national identity. Conversely, the spectacle and consumption of 'live' sport and details of the lives of sporting celebrities can provide vehicles for the challenging of hegemonic gender and cultural constructions, but this may occur in contradictory ways, as illustrated by another recent Irish example.

Patrick McDevitt argues that Ireland's largest sporting organisation, the GAA, was explicitly informed at the outset by the aspiration to repudiate the colonial image of the feminised Celt and to promote an ideal of Irish 'manhood' through games whose codification and interpretation negotiated several conflicts in pre-revolutionary Ireland. 'Civilising tendencies', discipline and 'intellectual control' would ideally be balanced with 'a determination to present an impression of incipient revolution' and 'the paramountcy of muscular stature'.[38] Despite the GAA's atypical adherence to amateurism as an ethical code in a global sporting context, when Cork hurler Dónal Óg Cusack came out as gay in his 2009 autobiography,[39] such was the rarity of openly gay athletes in sport that it was reported internationally. In their analysis of the book's critical reception, Debbie Ging and Marcus Free observe that it was overwhelmingly positively received both by Cusack's fellow players and by Irish and international media commentators, perhaps surprisingly given a 'torrent of radio-show call-ins' and a 'death threat to the offices of the Irish Advertising Standards Authority' following a GAA-themed *Gay Ireland* magazine launch poster as recently as 2001.[40] They suggest that, while Cusack's coming out was a significant event in Irish sport and society (and, indeed, Cusack later became a prominent figure in campaigns against homophobic bullying), part of the book's appeal lay in its downplaying 'the personal and political significance of his sexual orientation in undoing assumptions of heteromasculinity embedded in sport and in Irish society more generally'[41] in favour of a rather conservative, if playful, eulogising of hurling's inherent violence and the construction of 'hard' masculinity associated with it.

Such a case illustrates how the reading of sport and its representation must be sensitive to the intersection of gender, sexual orientation and national identity at specific historical conjunctures. Cusack's book preceded the legalisation of gay marriage in Ireland in 2015, despite strong opposition from the Catholic Church. Its widespread positive reception may well have contributed to the wider acceptance of homosexuality in Ireland, but its simultaneously provocative revelation and conservative form reflect an enduring logic in Irish society that 'coming out' has often additionally entailed unthreateningly 'fitting in'[42] with assumptions of a culturally conservative environment.

Free's study of how 2012 Olympic boxing gold-medallist Katie Taylor was represented in Irish media traces a related combination of transgression and conservatism, albeit in a different context. Theoretically, Taylor's achievements exemplified how women's boxing, introduced to the Olympics for the first time in 2012, might, as Kath Woodward has argued, 'offer women a means of challenging patriarchal constraints and of subverting hegemonic masculinities' and, thus, sport itself as a key cultural site in which supposedly visible gender differences are actively policed.[43] However, despite her evident physical strength and technical prowess, such that she regularly sparred with the Irish male boxers, Taylor repeatedly attributed her victories to divine inspiration and protection, thus evincing an unthreateningly 'humble', 'softly spoken' Irish femininity. This proved attractive to conservative religious commentators, while her success having being achieved despite her training in spartan conditions was rhetorically appropriated by some economic and political commentators at the very moment the post-Celtic Tiger discourse of 'public service waste' became widespread in Irish media as a justification for successive 'austerity' budgets.[44]

These cases indicate that there is a national specificity to the ways in which Irish sports celebrities are both represented and represent themselves in the media that invokes what Tom Inglis (drawing on French sociologist Pierre Bourdieu) calls a cultural and corporeal 'habitus', a learned predisposition towards 'humility', 'self-deprecation' and 'self-denial' peculiar to Irish society and which reflects the extensive influence of the Catholic Church.[45] The historical connections between the GAA, Catholicism and Irish cultural nationalism are well documented. The amateur ethos of the GAA is often celebrated as something uniquely 'Irish' for going against the grain of professionalism in contemporary sport, and by its evincing of a voluntarist, anti-individualist and communitarian spirit. The accusations by 'anti-Keanites' in the 2002 Irish 'civil war' of Roy Keane's self-serving abandonment of his country through the incendiary critical comments that led ultimately to his dismissal may also be evidence of this habitus at work. While the brashness and arrogance of 'notorious'[46] Irish MMA fighter Conor McGregor might be seen as contradictory evidence, he might equally be seen as the 'exception that proves' the rule, even as he capitalises on a stereotypical 'fighting Irish' image in the US in particular.[47]

However, in contemporary Irish society the insistence on the cultural purity of the amateur ethos has its contradictions. As Mike Cronin has shown, the paradox of the GAA's insistence on amateurism is that it has made its teams and players more attractive to commercial sponsors.[48] Debbie Ging has shown how representations of the GAA in Irish media, and particularly in advertising, have tended to both naturalise and fetishise the image of the games as 'rooted' in national soil through such visual devices as the literal merging of the male body, the playing field and equipment.[49] In each area of sport and its media representation in Ireland we find variants of what Tom Inglis calls 'global Ireland: same difference', the title of his book[50], which seeks to identify the particularities of how the global and local intersect in modern Ireland. The commodification of the amateur GAA may follow the same economic logic as elsewhere, but it feeds off the uniqueness of the organisation to do so.

These cases also illustrate the frequent ambiguities or 'polysemy', the potential for multiple meanings in sporting events and athletes' actions and utterances – a potential that has greatly increased with new media technologies. In this context, Hutchins and Rowe have introduced the term 'media sport content economy'. This term describes the recent shift that has taken place in the transmission of sports content, from a period of television dominance to a new, convergent and complex multimedia environment characterised by digital plenitude.[51] In particular, Hutchins and Rowe draw attention to how the rise of digital technologies, such as social media and video-hosting sites like YouTube, are impacting traditional sports coverage and commentary, and effectively 're-mediating' it. Moreover, these scholars argue that video streaming, download technologies and online distribution mechanisms have resulted in myriad new content providers in a 'do-it-yourself' digital media culture that produces unanticipated ways of relating to and using media content.[52]

This new environment has direct implications for sports organisations, many of which are restructuring due to the perceived importance of digital media. For example, Frandsen has found that Danish national sports federations now typically spend about 50 per cent of their communication budgets on maintaining their websites, and a further 20 per cent on social media and 'push communication'.[53] New platforms and online channels offer new routes for advertising and enable greater levels of interactivity and relationship-building between sports organisations and fans. However, new media also present difficulties in terms of relational and reputational management when dealing with critical feedback and, sometimes, with fan activism.[54] In short, new-media technologies are changing the ways in which sport is played, promoted, viewed, analysed and 'participated' in, broadly conceived. Indeed, wearable devices such as Fitbit and Polar Loop can be viewed as part of an 'expanding media sport ecosystem'.[55]

A useful example of the workings of this new ecosystem is provided by O'Boyle and Kearns' study of how the mediated performances of Irish football fans at Euro 2016 became central to the 'eventness' of the tournament.[56] O'Boyle and Kearns' study focuses on fan footage taken on smartphones and uploaded to YouTube (mostly by Irish fans themselves), and examines how this fed into the wider media coverage of the tournament, which relied heavily on long-standing representational tropes about Irishness. This study tells us much about the meaning-making activities of sports fans in the context of digital media. However, changes in media are not just important because of the 'new' social practices around sport that they activate; they also have implications for many of the traditional concerns of sports scholars, such as issues of identity relating to race, nation, gender and class.

For example, as already noted, much has been written about the gendered nature of sports media, the underrepresentation of women's sports, the objectification of women's sporting bodies, and the trivialisation of women athletes. 'Sport has long been and continues to be a masculine purview. Women may be welcomed as sexy cheerleaders, supportive mothers and wives, and well-behaved fans, but they are less welcome as fierce competitors and capable athletes.'[57] Barnett argues that gender differences in sport are reinforced by the mass media, which often works to reinscribe traditional gender roles. However, her research also finds that female athletes are sometimes complicit in this process. For example, in her analysis of the personal websites of athletes such as tennis players Serena Williams and Maria Sharapova, Barnett concludes that women use websites to construct an 'apologetic identity' that emphasises the time and energy they have sacrificed for their sport but which also communicates strongly that they have not abandoned traditional feminine roles (such as sex object, mother and caretaker).[58] Similarly, Holly Thorpe has found that female athletes, such as professional surfer and model Alana Blanchard, 'self-subjectify' by using a combination of online and social-media platforms such as Instagram and Facebook to post glamorous and revealing images of their muscular, toned bodies. Thorpe argues that self-subjectification of this sort is most likely financially motivated, and is actively encouraged by corporate sponsors. For example, she notes that Alana Blanchard remains the highest-paid female surfer, earning more than US$1.8 million in 2014 from her various sponsorships, which included Rip Curl, Sony and T-Mobile.[59]

The various examples of research just cited highlight how media-focused sports scholarship is evolving. These studies demonstrate the intersections of sport, media and the cultural industries; they open up new lines of inquiry while at the same time demonstrating the continued relevance of long-standing concerns of sports scholars, including issues such as sport and soft power, nation, race, gender and class in the sports-media industries, and sports-media representations of athletes and non-athletes.

It may be impossible for scholars to take into account the intersections of various dimensions of social and cultural relations and identity, and the interplay between 'old' and 'new' media in single studies, but there are great complexities in all regards that require extended academic research. One of the most widely covered stories in 2018 across Irish media, North and South, illustrates the complex intersection of 'old' and 'new' media, the ways in which sport can crystallise issues in contemporary cultural politics, both on and off the field of play, and the relationships between representation and the political economy of sport. The unfolding details of the nine-week trial of Ulster-province and international rugby players Paddy Jackson and Stuart Olding for the rape of a woman in 2016 were extensively covered in all Irish print and broadcast media. Although they were acquitted, the men's boasts regarding their sexual prowess and their sexual objectification of the woman in question as a 'spitroasted' piece of meat in their WhatsApp messages were widely condemned in media commentaries and during protests in Belfast and Dublin.[60] Following a comment by Republic of Ireland Senator Aodhán Ó Ríordáin using the widely circulated #Ibelieveher Twitter hashtag, Jackson's lawyer threatened to sue Ó Ríordáin and anyone else he considered to have made 'defamatory' comments about Jackson. In response, the #suemepaddy hashtag quickly gained traction on Twitter, highlighting the extent of the outrage at the documented exchanges, the legal efforts to control publicly voiced reaction, and the difficulty or impossibility of doing so.[61] Two crowd-funded advertisements appeared in the *Belfast Telegraph*, the first demanding that the players never be allowed to play for Ulster or Ireland again, the second from a supporters' group demanding their immediate reinstatement following their acquittal and subsequent 'cyber prosecution' via social media.[62] Ulster's decision to terminate the players' contracts (both later moved to French clubs) followed widespread reports of sponsors' 'concerns over the "serious behaviour and conduct issues"' raised by the case, and prompted extensive speculation – denied by the club[63] – that the decision was at least partly informed by the financial consideration arising should a key sponsor withdraw support. In the Republic, the minister for education announced that the relationships and sexuality education programme in schools would be reviewed in order to take account of issues of consent, prompting calls for a similar review in Northern Ireland.[64]

There is insufficient space here to explore the various dimensions of this case and its media representation or its implications for the understanding of sexual consent across Irish society. The bare details, however, serve to highlight how sport is enmeshed in social processes, and how, as David Andrews and Steven Jackson argue, media representations of sport celebrities can provide a vehicle for understanding 'contemporary debates about identity politics (gender, race, sexuality, [dis]ability, national), social policy (including those associated with health), and consumer capitalism'.[65]

SPORT, THE MEDIA AND IRELAND: INTERDISCIPLINARY PERSPECTIVES

The present collection of essays grew initially from a symposium on Sport, Media and the Cultural Industries in Ireland at Dublin City University (DCU) on 22 May 2018, which was organised jointly by DCU's School of Communications and the Department of Media and Communication Studies at Mary Immaculate College, University of Limerick. As organisers of the symposium and as editors of this collection, our intention has not been to impose a uniform point of view on which aspects of sport are worthy of investigation, but rather to represent a variety of approaches and viewpoints on the subject. The original symposium brought together sports scholars from across the humanities and social sciences in Ireland, and sought to examine the current 'state of play' of sports-media research in the Irish context, the contemporary and historical cultural significance of the sports–media nexus, and the lived experience of sports media as popular culture. Most contributors focused on the interrelations of sport and media in Ireland, but some papers extended this focus to British-media representations of sport in Ireland, Irish sports fans' engagement with British-produced sports media, Irish emigrants' or emigrant descendants' engagement with Irish sports media, or transnational sports celebrities who could not be straightforwardly identified as 'Irish'. For these reasons this volume has been titled *Sport, the Media and* [rather than 'in'] *Ireland*.

This collection of essays represents, we believe, an important milestone in the development of sports research in and about Ireland, and is unique in its foregrounding of the media. We hope that it will stimulate and invigorate sports research in Ireland and, just as importantly, act as a helpful resource for future scholars in the field. The book has been organised into five sections. The chapters are organised more or less according to the chronological order of the themes they address. Ranging from the tightly focused to the broad span in scope, they do not offer a progressive narrative of the interrelations between sport and the media in Ireland, but rather a series of research studies that show the complexity and variation of these interrelations at specific historical conjunctures.

The opening section presents two contrasting historical perspectives on the interconnections between sport and the media in Ireland. Chapter 1, by Conor Curran, addresses the theme of the Irish emigrant voice and sensibility in soccer, a sport with a long history of emigration of Irish-born players to the more widely supported and – since the advent of professionalism – lucrative leagues of England and Scotland. Examining the life and career of Buncrana-born Irish international Charlie O'Hagan, Curran notes that while O'Hagan's playing career has been reasonably well documented within non-academic online articles, less has been written about his term as editor of the short-lived newspaper *Football Sports Weekly* in the mid-1920s. Curran examines O'Hagan's career and his views on the state of professional football in the early twentieth century through an analysis of his editorial writing. Approaching the subject as a historian rather than as a media scholar, Curran illustrates how this source can shed light on the lives of some of Ireland's first football migrants in a pre-celebrity era. His chapter also highlights the challenges facing the historian in attempting to piece together a coherent biography and sense of self-identity for an athlete of that era, even with access to columns written in the first person. This contrasts markedly with the proliferation of self-disclosure in the contemporary era.

In chapter 2, John Connolly and Paddy Dolan explore the changing relationship over time between the media and the GAA, an association formed in 1884 that has since become a major influence not only in Irish sporting life but also in the lives of Irish people globally. The chapter considers the sometimes contentious relationship between the GAA and the Irish media during the association's early years, their growing interdependence, and some of the GAA's own publications, which were often aimed at integrating young people into the association. Applying a more theoretical figurational-sociological approach, and focusing on the GAA's changing perspective as an institution, Connolly and Dolan explain how the media activities of the GAA were connected to the increasing fear of other sports, the perceived functional importance of television, an advance in individualisation processes throughout Irish society, and an evening-up of intergenerational power relations.

The book's second section, 'Sport and Representation in Television and Print Media', comprises four studies of the representation of Irish sport and sporting figures in a range of media, including advertising, popular television-entertainment formats and journalism. The chapters demonstrate considerable variety in their disciplinary approaches and methods.

Indirectly offering an interesting illustration of the growing power of media that so worried the GAA in the 1960s, particularly in its promotion of 'foreign' sports such as soccer and rugby, Lance Pettitt (chapter 3) explores how, through his participation in emerging British documentary and early popular television-entertainment formats in the late 1960s and early 1970s (which were available both in Northern Ireland and along the east coast of the Republic), Northern Ireland international and Manchester United footballer George Best was a conscious agent in the shaping of his own popular celebrity off the field of play. Through his innovative recourse to archived television recordings and contextual production-related material, Pettitt traces how different facets of the Best persona – emigrant Belfast Protestant dislocated from his original cultural context as an elite professional player in Britain, entrepreneur seeking to capitalise on his 'star' image through branded offshoots, and 'ladies' man' object of desire and admiration – were cultivated through a variety of television appearances. Best remains an enigmatic figure who, as a Belfast-born Protestant emigrant to England, was both an early exemplar of the celebrification of football players and an instance of a historically neglected section of the 'Irish' diaspora in Britain.

Explicitly addressing the growing intersections of Irish and British sport and media, and the political context within which these intersections must be situated, in chapter 4 historian Mike Cronin examines media reaction in Ireland and Britain to the infamous riot by a section of England supporters at an Ireland–England international soccer friendly held at the old Lansdowne Road stadium in 1995. The game was staged a year before the Euro 96 football tournament was due to take place in England. Cronin contends that the dominant media narrative that emerged, and that was widely reiterated on the twentieth anniversary in 2015, was that this was not a typical hooligan riot but was instead orchestrated by a far-right organisation, Combat 18, with an explicitly anti-Irish agenda. He juxtaposes the endurance of this narrative with prominent English hooligan figures' own recollections of events in which they deny extensive Combat 18 involvement and orchestration, and with an Irish government-commissioned report that does not blame English political extremists. The narrative, he argues, was convenient for the British and Irish media and for the English Football Association in its depiction of the event as an aberration from the more typical containment of hooliganism by the early 1990s and the new image of soccer as a luxury commodity in the all-seater stadia in the satellite-subscription era.

Among other things, Cronin highlights the role of media in reiterating mythic narratives that it has been instrumental in creating, especially through anniversaries. Demonstrating the complex interplay between documentary record, live television and the form and aesthetics of film, Seán Crosson (chapter 5) examines how sport and media interact in spectacles of public commemoration. Crosson suggests that commemoration is part of what defines nations and their configurations, a suggestion that is supported by the considerable investment of the Irish state and various sporting organisations during 2016 in commemorating the events of 1916. Crosson notes, however, that processes of commemoration are neither straightforward nor uncomplicated; on the contrary, they are rife with contradictions, unresolved tensions and paradoxes. Commemoration involves a constant process of writing and rewriting, an ongoing renegotiation of the past in response to contemporary developments and future aspirations in a process that is intrinsically political. In this chapter Crosson considers the mediatisation of one of the largest and most viewed sporting commemorative events in Ireland, the 2016 *Laochra* pageant organised by the GAA and broadcast live by the Irish-language broadcaster TG4 on Sunday 24 April, exactly one hundred years to the day since the first shots were fired in the Easter Rising. The process through which Irishness was 'textualised' through the performance and mediatisation of *Laochra* is the key concern of Crosson's chapter. While *Laochra* may have been primarily a televisual experience, he argues that the cinematic has now been incorporated into major sporting events.

Finally in this section, Colm Kearns (chapter 6) analyses recent advertisements centring on Irish rugby in order to trace how the sport has been rendered more appealing to the wider Irish public. Despite rates of participation far lower than Gaelic games or soccer, rugby has become a major television sport in Ireland since its professionalisation in 1995. The international dimensions of the annual Six Nations Championship and Champions Cup, in which the Irish national and provincial teams, respectively, have been highly successful, have given rugby a distinct advantage over the GAA in particular. Kearns draws on studies that suggest that the values of the Irish rugby team became synonymous with the perceived virtues of Celtic Tiger Ireland while at the same time causing a degree of cultural anxiety because of the sport's 'foreign' roots. Kearns' chapter demonstrates how commercial sponsors of Irish rugby have negotiated this difficult cultural terrain in recent advertising. Connecting with later chapters' concerns with the limits of national corporatism in a geographically divided island in which access to games through live attendance or, in some cases, subscription-only is increasingly expensive, his analysis suggests that recent advertisements have successfully balanced tradition and modernity in their appeals, highlighting some of the ways in which the cultural anxieties of post-Celtic Tiger Ireland are being resolved. Indeed, the commercial sponsors' advertisements are closely related in form and content to the government-sponsored promotional video for the ultimately unsuccessful bid to host the 2023 Rugby World Cup.[66]

At the peak of his success and fame, George Best was a classic example of media projections of 'having it all' masculinity that stems from sporting achievement, an economically successful star player able to capitalise on his off-field erotic appeal in his business ventures and non-sports-media appearances. Kearns' study suggests that the adverts and related online material featuring Irish rugby players entail the projection of sport and masculinity as inextricably linked, and facilitate the players' celebrity profiles and off-field earning power. By contrast, section 3, 'Women, Media and Sport in Ireland', addresses the enduring role of popular media in neglecting and undervaluing the sporting achievements of women athletes.

In chapter 7, Katie Liston and Mary O'Connor provide a framing chapter for the section. They highlight the contrasting fortunes of women, both within Ireland and internationally, whose achievements as elite athletes have been marginalised or downright ignored within various media. Women remain underrepresented as sports journalists, but also as managers and coaches and as key sports-policy decision-makers. They argue that 'more' – more women participating in sport and sports media – does not necessarily further the aims of gender equality and challenge male hegemony in sport. Highlighting the profound social and cultural changes currently taking place in Irish society (recently represented by the marriage-equality (2015) and abortion (2018) referenda, and by the resurgence of the feminist movement in various spheres), they give consideration to the aim of the 20x20 campaign, launched in 2018, to increase media coverage of women in sport by 20 per cent, and its connections with Sport Ireland's recently launched (2019) 'Women in Sport' policy. While these are welcome and potentially groundbreaking developments, they also stress the structural conditions and cultural obstacles – principally constructions of gender – that lie in the way of progress.

In chapter 8, Ciarán Dunne reiterates many of the findings in international research reviewed by Liston and O'Connor. Dunne further notes that while there has been much anecdotal evidence of underrepresentation of women in sport in Ireland, there has been relatively little formal research carried out to explore the phenomenon. With this in mind, Dunne's chapter presents a quantitative study examining the coverage of sportswomen over a four-month period in *The Irish Times*. The findings, which are based on a data set of almost 1,700 images contained within 500 pages, reveal that less than 4 per cent of photographs were of sportswomen. Dunne argues that these findings indicate that the Irish situation mirrors international research findings, and reflects a continuation of the status quo in terms of how sportswomen and women's sports are (under)valued and (under)reported in the media.

Niamh Kitching and Ali Bowes (chapter 9), in their case study of Irish media representation of Leona Maguire, the former world number-one international amateur golfer who has recently turned professional, explore the extent to which such gendering practices are reproduced or superseded by a more 'gender-neutral' approach in current constructions of women in sport. Like Dunne, they focus on Irish print-media coverage, but undertake a partly quantitative and partly qualitative analysis of Maguire's discursive representation. While highlighting the relative absence of the gender markers in coverage of women in sport evident in international research, the emphasis on Maguire's legitimacy as an athlete and on her status as a 'model citizen' through, for example, reports of her education at Duke University in the US and representation as a 'teacher's daughter' is indicative of golf's enduring associations with social class. In an individual sport where national representation on the international stage does not have the same status as other sports, it is also interesting to note the frequency with which her county of origin (Cavan) is prominent in media reports, thus, perhaps, connecting her representation with patterns in coverage of GAA players, male and female.

Chapter 10, the final chapter in this section, is unique in the book. It takes the form of a recorded 'round-table' discussion in which high-profile Irish women sports journalists (Sinéad Kissane, Cliona Foley and Jacqui Hurley) engage in an extended debate with Federation of Irish Sport CEO Mary O'Connor and academics Katie Liston and Niamh Kitching concerning a number of the issues that emerge from the previous chapters regarding women, media and sport in Ireland. Taking place in May 2019, the discussion was organised in order to explore the ways in which academic research can engage in a productive dialogue with sports-media practitioners with the aim of promoting greater gender fairness in both the quantitative distribution of sports coverage and the quality of that coverage. The discussion ranges from a review of the current state of play in Ireland with regard to gender in sports media to the experiences of women journalists working in the area of sports media, and to the issue of whether 'more' is necessarily better if male hegemony in sport and the gendered constructions of 'women' athletes endure.

In section 4, 'Broadcasting and the Political Economy of Sport', authors consider some of the important economic and political forces shaping sport in Ireland, and in particular the role and influence of public-service broadcasters and commercial media organisations. Both chapters in this section highlight the limits of the rhetoric of national corporatism in Irish sporting and political spheres by stressing the tensions between sporting organisations' claim to integrative national representation and their profit-driven commercial actions. They also show that developments in Ireland are both nationally specific and inextricably linked to international developments. Rupert Murdoch has described the securing of television sports rights as a 'battering ram'[67] with which to penetrate national broadcasting systems around the world. The actions of Irish sporting organisations such as the GAA and IRFU (Irish Rugby Football Union) may facilitate the aspirations of transnational media corporations while impacting negatively on Irish public-service broadcasting.

In chapter 11, Paul Rouse examines the relationship between the GAA and Sky Sports, and the ongoing controversy that surrounds the sale of broadcasting rights beginning in April 2014. Rouse reflects on the manner in which a so-called 'amateur' sporting organisation like the GAA engages with issues around media rights, and he is deeply critical of the official rhetoric surrounding the association's arrangement with Sky. For Rouse the sale of Gaelic games broadcasting rights to a commercial broadcaster epitomises a disconnection between the grass-roots community ethos of the GAA and the profit-driven reality.

In chapter 12, Roddy Flynn historicises such current controversies by examining the context in which Irish sport rights were negotiated up until 2002, when Sky Sports sought to acquire all television rights to the Republic of Ireland's home and away, competitive and friendly soccer matches, and how this has changed since. While Rouse's chapter focuses on the GAA as a national institution, Flynn focuses on the plight of Ireland's public-service broadcaster RTÉ, a pioneer in the 1920s and 1930s in radio broadcasting of sport, and a key vehicle for the promotion of sport as a symbol of post-independence national identity in Ireland. RTÉ is now largely unable to compete in broadcasting's increasingly marketised environment for the rights to screen such events as rugby's Six Nations Championship, rights it held for decades. Flynn traces how both subscription-based and 'free-to-air' competitors are backed by global corporate owners with resources that dwarf those of RTÉ and other public-service broadcasters across Europe. While national sporting organisations such as the GAA, IRFU and FAI (Football Association of Ireland) are keen to maximise the market value of their events, Flynn considers the implications and future for RTÉ both as a public-service broadcaster and as a national institution.

In the final section, 'Media, Geography and the Negotiation of National and Local Identities', authors consider how sport and place interact in the formation and maintenance of identities – cultural, professional, fan-based and political – and how media (new and old) are both resources for identity formation and maintenance and central to the everyday practices of identity work. This section completes the book's 'circuit of culture',[68] from its concern with sport and media-industry interrelationships and regulation, through the cultural and national situation of sport and sports media, to issues in media representation of sport, and to supporters' (and athletes') consumption of sport and investment of sport with individual and collective meanings.

In chapter 13, Ciarán Ryan explores the impact of new media on a decades-old phenomenon: Irish football-supporters' fascination with English clubs. Historically this was fuelled by interest in Irish emigrant players attached to these clubs. Since the 1960s this phenomenon has been enhanced through Irish audiences' exposure to English league games via British television and, from the 1980s, RTÉ television. Ryan examines Liverpool Football Club fandom through a uniquely modern lens: The Anfield Wrap (TAW), a multi-award-winning podcast and website created and hosted by fans of Liverpool for fellow supporters. Ryan argues that TAW provides uncensored and subjective accounts of supporting the club, and has given a strong sense of place to an audience that may have no tangible link to Liverpool. In particular, his chapter examines how TAW has fostered a sense of familiarity for its Irish listeners – a familiarity with the club, the city, its local supporters and, quite significantly, its language – in the wider context of increasingly globalised football fandom. While Liverpool has long-standing Irish associations as a first port of call and settlement for Irish emigrants since the nineteenth century, this phenomenon is less associated with 'Irish' cultural links, either mediated or forged through familial connections. Rather, supporters are imaginatively engaging with the 'sounds' – accent and dialect – of Liverpool as a place. The audio medium offers a form of involvement very distinct from the image focus of film and television and the journalistic discourse of the press.

Conversely, mediated sport offers the possibility for emigrants to connect with and imagine the 'home' they have left behind. In chapter 14, Dan Dwyer first notes the significance of sport in the formation and maintenance of an Irish cultural identity within Irish emigrant populations. His chapter then draws on interviews with members of the Irish media audience in Britain to highlight the significance of media sport in their everyday media practices and significant memories. His study highlights how everyday media use, which includes high levels of Irish sports coverage across a number of different platforms, coexists with emotive memories of specific sporting occasions for his interviewees. Dwyer argues that media sport therefore offers a sense of belonging and connection to a wider Irish community in Britain. In this case affective attachment is inextricably linked with national identity, geographical displacement, and the search for a sense of vicarious presence or 'being thereness' through 'live' consumption rather than before/after-the-event interaction with fellow supporters. The contrast between Ryan's and Dwyer's studies may also indicate a generational as well as geographical specificity to media engagement, given the different age profiles of their respondents.

Anthony McIntyre, in chapter 15, examines Derry-born Republic of Ireland and West Bromwich Albion player James McClean's refusal, in recent years, to wear the Earl Haig poppy in the November games proximate to Remembrance Sunday. McIntyre notes that this action by McClean is in defiance of an increasingly conformist public pressure in Britain regarding the symbol that has seen a variety of public figures castigated for not wearing or somehow disrespecting the poppy. Far from being the 'apolitical' symbol that some have claimed, McIntyre argues that the Remembrance poppy is an ideologically charged symbol that articulates a particular civic-military positioning and construction of nationalism that resonates deeply within Britain at a time when ideas of nationhood are in flux, a resonance that is highly ambivalent to settled diasporic communities within the UK. Characterising the wearing of the Remembrance poppy as an instance of what Svetlana Boym has termed a 'restorative nostalgia',[69] McIntyre's chapter examines how, both through his related social-media postings as well as through popular news coverage of his yearly refusal, McClean crystallises notions of non-conformism and diasporic non-assimilation in ways that bear fruitful analysis in terms of both post-Troubles Irish diasporic positionings and also pluralistic subjectivities within the UK more broadly.

McIntyre's concerns appropriately conclude the book in several ways. First, they illustrate the necessity in contemporary sports-media scholarship to track the complex interplay between 'old' and 'new' media in the construction, negotiation and circulation of such sports celebrities, not least through their own interventions in attempting to control or influence their interpretation. Second, Derry-born McClean, in his 'mediatised' form, embodies the enduring tensions between unionism and nationalism in Northern Ireland, and between Northern Ireland and the Republic of Ireland as distinctive geographical-political entities; the historically vexed relationship between Ireland and Britain; and the involvement of Irish soldiers in the First World War and the contestation of the poppy as an ideologically charged rather than neutral commemorative symbol. The chapter thus resonates with the many themes addressed elsewhere in the book. Finally, it illustrates the value of sport and sports media as vehicles for critically investigating 'conjunctural' moments of historical, cultural and social change. The furore over McClean's actions has taken place in the context of the 2016 Brexit referendum and its fraught and as yet unresolved aftermath, the consequences of which for the UK and Ireland are unpredictable. Rather than constituting a hermetically sealed apolitical sphere, this and the other chapters show how sport and sports media are enmeshed in, and provide vehicles for illuminating, the cultural politics of social formations at specific historical conjunctures.

PART I

೮ဝ

Historical Perspectives on the Interconnections of Sport and the Media in Ireland

Ex-professional Footballers and Sports Journalism: Charlie O'Hagan's careers as a migrant professional footballer and writer in the early twentieth century

CONOR CURRAN

NEVER SHORT OF SELF CONFIDENCE, Buncrana-born Irish international footballer and inside-left Charlie O'Hagan – who earned eleven caps in the pre-First World War years and had spells at Everton, Tottenham Hotspur, Middlesbrough, Aberdeen, Greenock Morton and Third Lanark between 1902 and 1913 – claimed in 1926 that his football and travel experiences were 'perhaps unrivalled in the history of the game'.[1] While his playing and managerial careers have been reasonably well documented within non-academic online articles, much less has been written about his term as columnist and editor of the short-lived Dublin-based newspaper *Football Sports Weekly* in the mid-1920s after he had retired from playing.[2] In this way his post-playing career was somewhat unique among Irish-born football migrants of his day. Following an examination of Charlie O'Hagan's career as a footballer and his initial dabbling in journalism in Britain, this chapter places his term as editor of *Football Sports Weekly* within the context of other professional-footballers' post-playing careers at that time. It discusses his views on the state of professional football in the early twentieth century through an analysis of his columns and editorial writing in *Football Sports Weekly*. It also illustrates how his writing sheds light on the lives of some of Ireland's first football migrants and other professional players at that time. However, it also highlights how undertaking research through the use of newspaper sources can at times also raise further questions for the historian, given the fragmentary nature of the evidence.

CHARLIE O'HAGAN'S PROFESSIONAL FOOTBALL CAREER

Like most footballers of his day, O'Hagan did not leave behind an autobiography. It is nevertheless possible to construct a profile of O'Hagan's career and to explore why he was attracted to, and academically capable of, a career in sports writing at a time when other Irish professional footballers generally did not follow this route.

O'Hagan was born in Buncrana in 1881 and was one of seven children.[3] His eldest brother, Philip, was a solicitor based in Derry city.[4] His father died reasonably young, which meant his mother, Anne, took charge of the family business, a shop. By 1901 Charlie was still living at home, and is described in that year's census as a scholar aged nineteen.[5] There is some evidence of how he may have learned to play soccer, with a number of Buncrana club men said to have been involved in assisting him with this, according to the *Derry Journal*.[6] Both he and his nephew Billy had played the game (or at least some form of football) at St Columb's College in Derry before joining English and Scottish clubs, according to Joyce's *Football League Player Records*.[7] O'Hagan himself wrote that 'he studied for one of the professions before embracing football in Liverpool and London'.[8] He claimed that he had played for Derry Celtic as a fifteen-year-old in the Irish League before moving a year later to Liverpool (to work in a fruit shop) and playing for Xaverians, said to be one of the leading Catholic clubs in the area.[9] This chronology is somewhat patchy as it means he was no longer living in Donegal by 1896, and contradicts the census material mentioned earlier. However, it does indicate that he was from a middle-class background and had some second-level education, which probably went some way to preparing him for his later career in football writing.

As noted by Matthew Taylor, the English Football Association had been founded in 1863, with professionalism legalised in 1885, and by the late nineteenth century both the FA Cup, inaugurated in 1871, and the Football League championship, founded in 1888, were becoming well-established.[10] As Tony Mason has stated, there was an increase in the number of professional footballers in England from the four registered with the Nottingham Football Association in 1885 to 448 Football League players in 1891, and the majority of these were 'almost certainly part or full-time professionals'.[11] By 1910 the English Football Association had 6,800 players.[12]

Given the scarcity of coverage of O'Hagan's playing career in the Irish provincial and national newspapers, players' appearance records can help to piece together his early professional career; he also received attention in the British press. O'Hagan was signed by Everton in 1902, having also had a trial at Preston North End,[13] although he did not play for Everton in the English Football League. He later joined Tottenham Hotspur, playing twenty-one league games and scoring five goals between 1904 and 1906. He then had a short spell at Middlesbrough, playing only five times. He enjoyed more success in terms of appearances in Scotland, having joined Aberdeen in 1906, making ninety-nine league appearances and scoring twenty-two goals. In 1910 he joined Greenock Morton and spent two years there before signing for Third Lanark of Glasgow in 1912.[14] Having played only three times there, he was suspended by the club over a wage dispute and was said to be leaving in December 1912.[15] One newspaper noted how he had not settled down at either Greenock Morton or Third Lanark after leaving Aberdeen, while another stated that he 'was in business at Greenock' at the start of the war.[16]

O'Hagan's football career ended prior to the First World War, which began in September 1914. He actively participated as a soldier, although how long he spent in the military is not clear. Even reports of the names of the regiments he was part of do not match his own fleeting testimony.[17] Although his career was generally not widely covered in Irish newspapers, according to the *Derry Journal* he served with the Cameron Highlanders and Highland Light Infantry.[18] By January 1915 it was noted in the British press that he was seriously ill with bronchitis in a Surrey hospital having served with the Irish Guards.[19] One provincial Irish newspaper highlighted that by April 1915 he had been 'gazetted second-lieutenant, and attached to the Leinster Regiment', which was then based in the

Curragh.[20] Unfortunately, O'Hagan wrote little in *Football Sports Weekly* about his time in the First World War other than to state that he was 'regaled in the kilt of the Cameron Highlanders'.[21] He also mentioned that his nephew, Irish international goalkeeper Billy O'Hagan, had served with the 13th Black Watch at Gallipoli, Salonika, Egypt and France before returning to Ireland in 1918.[22] It is therefore likely that some newspapers confused the two men's military-career paths.

Throughout his football career and afterwards, Charlie O'Hagan was never far from controversy within the media. In March 1920 he issued a public apology for having the previous month accused nine Aberdeen players of accepting bribes before a 1908 Scottish Cup semi-final versus Celtic.[23] He apparently gained some coaching experience in Germany and a number of other countries, and became Norwich City manager in 1920.[24] He left this position the following year, with problems with directors at the club and inadequate funds evident, as he described it as 'the most trying experience of my football career'.[25] In June 1923 he was said to have been appointed as manager of a team in Verviers, Belgium, although, again, this was for only a brief period.[26] Around that time he was described in the *Derry Journal* as 'an able writer', having 'contributed extensively to the sporting newspapers in England and Scotland'.[27] He was appointed manager of Seville later in 1923, where he claimed to have trained a nephew of the bullfighter Jose Belmonte, but he said little of the club's progress on the field at the time.[28] However, he did have some success in winning the Copa de Andalucia, a major competition in the days before La Liga was formed.[29] The following year he was reportedly appointed as player-manager at Irish League club Ards, but did not remain in this position for very long, and by the second half of the 1920s was focused more on journalism.[30]

FOOTBALL SPORTS WEEKLY AND EARLY SOCCER JOURNALISM IN IRELAND

Portrayed by cultural nationalists as 'the garrison game' since the early twentieth century, soccer has been a hugely popular pastime in Ireland, despite efforts to prevent its growth in many villages and towns, and the Gaelic Athletic Association's (GAA) 'ban' on its members' involvement in 'foreign games', lifted only in 1971.[31] Initiated in Belfast in the 1870s after a number of experimental matches, soccer had become a popular game in Ireland by the early twentieth century.[32] Developments in the establishment of clubs and competitions mirrored those in Britain to some extent, but were hindered by local factors, such as a lack of progress in schools, particularly after the partition of Ireland in 1921, and by the strong parish and county identity fostered by the GAA. In addition, internal conflict within the Irish Football Association (IFA), founded in Belfast in 1880, saw a number of its Dublin-based member clubs withdraw, and in 1921 the Football Association of Ireland (FAI), which later was briefly known as the Football Association of the Irish Free State (FAIFS), was set up. This meant that by the mid-1920s there were two national governing bodies for soccer in Ireland in existence.[33]

Despite tensions between governing bodies of the game in Britain and Ireland, and the development of two national professional soccer leagues in Ireland by the early 1920s, professional football in England and Scotland proved to be a major attraction for Irish players and supporters. Visits by British clubs, players and coaches also helped foster the game's growth throughout the twentieth century. By the time the Irish Free State was established in 1922, Irish soccer players aspiring to play the game at the highest levels had been moving to Britain for more than three decades, with English and Scottish clubs having scouting networks in place in Belfast and Dublin. In addition to annual inter-league fixtures, British clubs visited Ireland to play friendly matches, while Irish clubs also travelled to Britain, thereby strengthening cross-channel soccer links.[34]

Naturally, the popularity of the game meant that it attracted attention in the newspapers. As Neal Garnham has stated, newspapers specialising in sport in Ireland had been initiated by the early 1900s, with the *Irish Sporting Chronicle* established in 1840.[35] In addition, 1880 saw the first publication of *Sport*, although it was not until 1887 that the first newspaper dedicated to soccer coverage, the *Ulster Football and Cycling News*, was operational.[36] In 1894 *Ulster's Saturday Night* was published for the first time, and this later became known as *Ireland's Saturday Night*. By the last decade of the nineteenth century, the number of sporting and athletic news publications had reached double figures, and, as Garnham states, 'as commercial ventures these newspapers must have been launched to cater for a perceived existing demand'.[37] He also notes that 'at the same time they acted to familiarise readers with the finer points of sports, to make them aware of the wider dimensions of games, and to expose them to the likeness and exploits of men who were to emerge as sporting heroes'.[38] By the early 1900s, many provincial newspapers had evolved from simply publishing results and snippets of matches to having regular columns dedicated specifically to covering particular sports, although in some areas, such as west Donegal, there was a failure to consistently report on what was taking place on the sports field.[39]

National and provincial newspapers also raised awareness of how Irish soccer players were progressing at British clubs. By 1904, a reporter in *Ireland's Saturday Night* noted that 'the migration of Irish players has set in', while writers such as the *Belfast Telegraph*'s 'Ralph the Rover' opined on cross-channel clubs' signing of Irish players and their progress.[40] The first newspaper to be published in Dublin that focused mainly on soccer, *Football Sports Weekly*, was up and running by the late summer of 1925, with its first issue published on 29 August that year.[41] This meant that the progress of aspiring Irish soccer migrants was also covered. By April of the following year, it was said to be selling out regularly, and claimed to 'cater for the huge and growing army of footballers and the best interests of the game' without bias to 'any particular side, club or body'.[42] It ran until 4 February 1928, but its weekly publication meant that soccer had a dedicated newspaper for at least some of the then FAIFS's early years.[43] According to Conor McCabe, 'the newspaper was the *de facto* voice of the Football Association of the Irish Free State', and 'its desire to equate soccer with Irish identity was done partly to counter the more rabid mutterings of the GAA, and partly to distance the FAIFS from the IFA'.[44] By the 1920s, the playing of soccer was being regularly attacked in some sections of the nationalist press such as the *Gaelic Athlete*, while some provincial newspapers, such as the *Donegal Democrat* – the mouthpiece of the Donegal GAA county board at that time – were more eager to propagate the activities of that sporting body than those of organisers of other codes.[45]

O'HAGAN AND SPORTS WRITING AS A POST-PLAYING CAREER

From 1888 until 1939, 286 Irish-born footballers played league football in England.[46] Charlie O'Hagan appears to have been unique among Irish soccer migrants in the pre-Second World War era in editing a newspaper, albeit briefly, and his motivations varied from the simple desire to earn a basic wage as a writer, to promoting his own talents within professional football, as he had ambitions to stay in this field in Ireland but could not find a satisfactory long-term position at a club.[47] It is possible to establish how O'Hagan's post-playing career pathway fits into the occupational choices of a number of the other 285 Irish-born football migrants in English League football from 1888 until 1939 by drawing on work undertaken for the book *Irish Soccer Migrants: a social and cultural history*.[48]

A few other Irish-born football migrants tried their hand at journalism, including Lawrie Cumming, who had spells at English and Scottish clubs, and later, in 1965, became a founder member of the Scottish Football Writers' Association.[49] Early Irish football migrants differed from more general Irish migrants in showing a tendency to return to the country of their birth, as returning home was 'rare' in the nineteenth century, although Irish seasonal workers in Britain were more inclined to do so than migrants who moved to the US.[50] Writing in 1904 of those who had moved to cross-channel clubs, one Belfast reporter felt that 'the majority will, I am certain, return'.[51] Of the 286 pre-Second World War Irish football migrants who played in English League football, 133 were identified as having returned to Ireland, although they did not all continue to play the game on arriving home. Some, such as Billy Gillespie, who took over as Derry City manager in 1932, stayed only temporarily before returning to live in England.[52]

Mason has noted in his major study of English football that, after retiring, early professional footballers generally took up positions as shopkeepers, public-house licensees or football managers, or 'whatever job the player held before he became a professional'.[53] Irish football migrants appear to have been no different. A few players became managers (Peter Doherty, Johnny Carey, Elisha Scott), coaches (Alex Stevenson) and scouts (Bob Fullam, Jimmy Ferris, Billy Behan), while some availed of new positions created within the Irish Free State in the post-1922 years. On his return

in 1932, Southport player Paddy Clarke became an employee
with the Electricity Supply Board, established in 1927.[54] Former
New Brighton, Sheffield United, Arsenal and Southampton player
Jimmy Dunne became a coach with Bohemians after ending his
playing career with Shamrock Rovers; he died suddenly aged forty-
four in 1949.[55] Some players, such as Newton Heath's John Peden
and Derby County and Reading player Sid Reid – who both ran
sweetshops – took up positions in retail. Jack McCandless ran a
shop in Coleraine before succumbing to the eventual effects of a
gas attack sustained while he was serving in the First World War.[56]
Micky Hamill ran a pub, The Centre Half, on the Falls Road, before
drowning in the River Lagan in 1943.[57] Matty Reilly also ran a pub,
in Dublin.[58] Tom Priestly, who joined Chelsea from Linfield in 1933,
became a school principal in Lambeg, while Hugh Blair, who had
spells at Manchester City, Swansea and Millwall, became a teacher
in Liverpool. However, only a very small number took up positions
in education.[59] Although Mason has noted a few players taking up
coaching positions in colleges in the pre-First World War period,
'the number of openings in football itself was not very large' at that
time, and this continued for much of the twentieth century.[60] Patrick
O'Connell is the most famous Irish-born player to take charge of
a continental club. The former Manchester United captain is said
to have saved FC Barcelona from folding during the Spanish Civil
War by taking the club on a tour of Mexico and New York. He also
managed Racing Santander, Real Oviedo and Real Betis.[61]

Mason has noted how former England internationals George
Wall and Micky Bennett returned to industrial work after retiring
from the game and has stated that 'individual personality' was also
a factor in the post-playing career choices of early professionals.[62]

Charlie O'Hagan appears to have penned his first newspaper
pieces in Scotland. In October 1908 he began writing for the *Bon
Accord*, an Aberdeen newspaper.[63] His work as a part-time writer
from 1908 gave him some experience to later dabble in editorial
work upon retiring from the game. Following post-playing-career
managerial spells with Norwich City and Seville, he had become a
columnist in *Football Sports Weekly* by June 1926. He was noted
initially as being available to give advice to clubs that summer,
but it appears his appeal for work in the game in Ireland went
unanswered.[64] Having begun writing in June with a rather potted

autobiographical piece, he temporarily left to take up a coaching position in Rotterdam in August 1926, having been unable to secure satisfactory employment in Dublin.[65] Returning to Ireland after only a short spell in Rotterdam, he again wrote regularly for *Football Sports Weekly* and became editor of the paper by 20 August 1927.[66] On his appointment as editor it was noted that 'his ambition is not only to help clubs and players, but to render, at all times, whatever assistance he can to the governing body – the Free State Football Association'.[67] He maintained this role until 21 January 1928, by which time his position was stated in the newspaper to have been 'terminated'.[68]

From an analysis of his writing, his hints that he might end up in Liverpool or New York, and his claim that 'football is a great game, but travel-tramping – if you prefer it – has a charm all on its own', it is clear that he was a restless character, so his short spell as editor, which ended a few weeks before the newspaper folded, was no great surprise.[69] Despite this, his writings offer an insight into the state of professional football in Ireland, Britain and continental Europe at that time. He was one of only a few former players in this decade who took up positions within newspapers in Ireland or as a coach in continental Europe, although a few, such as Joseph Stynes of Bohemians, also contributed pieces, or at least provided the necessary information for ghost-writing.[70]

O'Hagan discussed contemporary players and offered advice on playing positions, lifestyle, management, training and debates within the game, as well as penning biographies of players he was familiar with, such as Patsy Gallagher, who apparently 'could play football like a master' despite being small in stature; Billy Gillespie, whose Kerrykeel home was only ten miles from O'Hagan's; and Bobby Walker, 'the idol of Edinburgh, prince of forwards'.[71] His writing is quite descriptive and could be described as a mixture of football analysis, travel writing and self-promotion, as at times he is almost too keen to show his experience in the hope of being offered a coaching role in Ireland, and he was certainly not immune to embellishment. Frustratingly for the researcher, there are at times only tantalising glimpses of key events in a career of which Charlie O'Hagan says little. For example, the death of his father while he was still young goes unmentioned, and it is unclear how much education he received prior to moving to England. In addition, he reveals little about his role in the First World War or his failed venture as a coach in Holland.

O'Hagan's actual playing lifestyle is reasonably well discussed in his columns, and it is in these that we learn most about life as a professional footballer in Britain in the early 1900s. O'Hagan maintained a disciplined routine, and considered the human body to be 'the machine that wants tending and keeping in order' with the player himself responsible for its upkeep. He was in favour of 'a few short sprints on the Friday morning – an exercise known to the cross-channel professionals as "muscle-looseners"', while players needed to train at least three times per week. A proper recovery from training and matches included hot baths to relieve aches and stiffness, while a massage was apparently 'the most important injunction of all' in aiding this. Players would, he felt, also benefit from a Turkish bath, to be taken once every two weeks.[72]

As Mason has shown, many English clubs neglected ball-work in the early part of the twentieth century.[73] Although O'Hagan provided little information on team training or ball-work drills, he recommended that players 'don't ever ask to see or kick a football from one Saturday till the next'.[74] By the early 1880s, English teams were participating in specialised training for cup matches. By the time O'Hagan was appearing in the Football League, in the early 1900s, professional players were requested to be at their clubs by 10 a.m. before undertaking a variety of training methods, including sprinting, walking, ball practice, weight training, skipping and ball-punching.[75] O'Hagan undoubtedly would have had experience of this, and he alluded to his own regimen when still a professional footballer.

O'Hagan felt that 'the players must also be regular in all things'.[76] His disciplined routine included stretching in the morning and the taking in of fresh air through an open window after awakening, and he felt that players should be out of bed by 8 a.m. at the latest.[77] On getting up in the morning, players should engage in skipping and shadow-boxing, and later take a cold bath. Before the day of a match, they needed to get ten to twelve hours' sleep, with just one meal to be taken prior to the game, and not after 12.30 p.m. when the kick-off was at 3 p.m.[78] Before going to bed, a player would benefit from 'a brisk walk in the country', and O'Hagan recommended that this should take place shortly after supper, which should not be later than 8 p.m. He also noted that, on return to digs, they should drink hot milk to benefit sleep, and the saying of prayers was also recommended.[79]

Unlike many Irish football migrants after their careers abroad have ended, he did not return to a club in Ireland as a player or coach in any significant capacity. He was highly critical of the lack of structures in Ireland for the game to develop, and claimed that those running the game were to blame for this, although he acknowledged that Ireland did not have the population to support professional football as a spectator sport.[80] Writing in 1926 about the system of professional football in Ireland, he claimed that 'the lack of training and coaching has been responsible for more failures than what may appear to the man about town. Without it, no man can hope to succeed.'[81] While the conflict between organisers of the GAA and Association football over which code was appropriate for nationalists was raging in provincial newspapers by the late 1920s, O'Hagan surprisingly offers little on this given that his native Donegal was a key area in this debate.[82]

O'Hagan's career illustrates the precarious nature of professional football and the difficulty in securing full-time work after a playing career in Britain. While he did have the benefits of second-level education, he was more interested in travel from his teenage years onwards, and enjoyed a colourful career wandering around Europe, claiming prior to his departure to coach the Young Hollanders of Rotterdam in 1926 that Russia and Holland were the only countries across the English Channel where he had not 'previously kicked a football or wielded a towel' as a masseuse.[83]

Some of O'Hagan's writing helps illuminate his views on professional football and the consumption of alcohol, and he returned to this topic on more than one occasion in his columns. He felt that 'an occasional drink of stout or beer is to be commended', and that he would have more faith in a player who drank than one who was 'a staunch exponent of the Discipline of Temperance'.[84] However, he also recommended that players 'keep far adrift from the entrancing sounds of corks that are being extracted behind the inner enclosures of the pubs' as it was necessary to 'keep the interior running machinery of the body in perfect working order'.[85] Mason has shown how some pre-First World War footballers, such as Tom Brandon of Blackburn and England, were quite fond of alcohol, while some of Aston Villa's poor performances in the 1892–3 season were said to be caused by a drinking culture among their players at that time.[86]

O'Hagan never stayed long enough in any place to make this work his life, and his health was not good. Upon his death in 1931 in New York, he was described in the Scottish press as having 'a style peculiarly his own. He was an expert dribbler and a capital shot, but his forte was in making openings for others.'[87] His death went largely unnoticed in Ireland's newspapers at the time. There was later a rumour that O'Hagan's fondness for alcohol had led to his early death, yet this appears to contradict his devotion to the game.[88]

O'Hagan pined for the opportunity to travel to the US, although he warned Irish players against moving to the American Soccer League when recruitment of Irish players was underway in earnest in the latter half of the 1920s.[89] With his insider information within the game, he was well capable of assessing how things might develop. He wrote that 'all is not milk, honey and dollars for the professional footballer who decides (in his dreams of new El Dorados) to take up residence and the continuance of the game in Uncle Sam's land'.[90] He also noted that 'a few old Scottish internationalists' had become 'deeply disillusioned, and set forth in the direction of the nearest booking office in New York city in order to book a return passage'.[91] O'Hagan was not unique among Irish writers at that time in attempting to put Irish players off, and his views were borne out the following year when a number of Irish-born players were stranded in the US after the owner of the Philadelphia Celtic club, Fred Maginnis, left them without pay or accommodation.[92] However, O'Hagan also admitted that he was somewhat jealous of those who had the opportunity to experience the game there, and stated in 1927 that it was one of the ambitions of his life to get to the US.[93] This he achieved, but like so many positions in his careers, his spell there lasted only briefly, and he died in Brooklyn in the summer of 1931.[94] The *Aberdeen Press and Journal* recalled his life fondly, stating that he was 'of a bright and breezy disposition, typically Irish, Charlie was a great favourite with football enthusiasts', but 'in recent years he had not enjoyed the best of health, and some time ago he went to America'.[95]

CONCLUSION

Through O'Hagan's journalism with *Football Sports Weekly*, we are able to gain an insight into professional football in Britain, Ireland and the rest of Europe in the 1920s, although admittedly his writing is sometimes quite vague and his recollections do not always add up when compared to other contemporary sources. While professional footballers' lives are of course linked to travel and the occupation's migratory nature, O'Hagan's failure to settle at any one club for very long is indicative of his personality and his appetite for new adventures, particularly abroad. His other writings and editorial experiences in the English and Scottish press require further research, but it is safe to say that he failed to gain a full-time position. While he was an advocate of a healthy lifestyle among footballers, it is unclear how his own death came about before he had reached the age of fifty.

O'Hagan's career pathway also illustrates the precarious nature of professional football, and how there were few choices for players upon retirement other than to stay involved in the game, while the public house was never too far from the minds of some players. In some respects, little has changed, although in the early twenty-first century there are more opportunities for footballers who have played at the highest level to become involved in the media. Some of the early players later became involved in retail or other business interests, but few were capable of or given the opportunity of editing a weekly newspaper. O'Hagan's insider information on the running of clubs and professional football in general were no doubt of benefit to his work at *Football Sports Weekly*, although it is not obvious why he lost his position at the newspaper. Given the lack of player autobiographies from the period in question, O'Hagan's comments on other Irish-born football migrants, such as Patsy Gallagher, and the short biographical pieces on individual players he penned are of value.[96] While much publicity has been afforded recently to Patrick O'Connell – with a documentary broadcast and a plaque recently unveiled at his early home – perhaps it is time that another pioneer of Irish and British soccer coaching is remembered more publicly, one who, though not as successful as a coach, also left his mark on the professional game in a rather unique way.[97]

CHAPTER TWO

National Identity, Media and the Promotion of Gaelic Games

JOHN CONNOLLY AND PADDY DOLAN

HISTORIANS OF THE GAELIC ATHLETIC ASSOCIATION (GAA) and indeed, of other sports bodies have identified how GAA activists (and others, such as national and local politicians) sought to conflate 'true' national identity with membership of the GAA in the years following its foundation and in the early decades of the twentieth century.[1] Within this broad narrative were several tropes that fused to serve the function of promoting Gaelic games and the GAA while simultaneously attempting to delegitimise competing sports and their representative organisations. The media were perceived as central in this process from the outset,[2] with media outlets castigated or praised for their representations of various sports. After the formation of the Irish Free State, the relationship between the GAA and media became more functionally interdependent, yet media coverage of sport remained a central point of tension. The linking of national identity with Gaelic games was seen by many GAA activists and administrators as important in integrating people into the GAA. Thus, the GAA, in contradistinction to other sports bodies, was to be presented as the embodiment of 'true' Irishness. That the media, in the view of GAA officials, failed to do this, or sought to represent other sports in a national light, became a persistent source of antagonism. Significantly, and the focus of this chapter, is the fact that after the 1960s the use of this narrative by GAA activists began to fade, as did the tendency to decry the media on these grounds. Instead, the individual needs and motivations of young people became the primary focus, while the media came to be perceived as more important to integration processes. Drawing on the theoretical insights of Norbert Elias,[3] we examine why this change occurred.

THEORETICAL APPROACH

Our study is informed by the figurational sociological approach developed by Norbert Elias.[4] Elias explains, through theoretical and empirical interplay, the relationship between changing social structures and the changing social habitus of people. By social habitus Elias was referring to the 'second nature' way in which people think, feel and act (embodied learning that feels natural and operates more or less automatically and unconsciously). For Elias the social habitus is always in process, and an important driver of habitus change is the change in how people are bonded to, and dependent upon, one another – the structure of interdependency and power. Elias demonstrated how lengthening chains of social interdependences in conjunction with a developing state monopoly over the control of violence exert a growing social constraint on people to exercise greater self-restraint over their emotions and behaviour. This gradually becomes internalised to the extent that it becomes second nature. This shift in the balance between social constraint and self-restraint also reflects an individualisation process (though social constraints remain important in underpinning self-steering capacities). For people to adjust their behaviour, they must have both awareness of others and of their own behaviour and level of emotional expression. Consequently, the compelling pressure to exert greater self-restraint involves greater reflection and consideration of one's own behaviour; it enhances the feeling of individuality. A greater sense and experience of self-observation develops.

Elias also developed the concept of the I-we balance, which he maintained is an integral part of the social habitus of people and open to individualisation. Elias used the concept to explain how (and the extent to which) people are always, from the moment they are born, integrated into groups of interdependent people. He used the concept of figuration to encapsulate this; a figuration refers to the network of interdependent people, such as a family, organisation, town and even global society bonded through mutual relations of dependency and power. Elias used the concept of I-we identity to illustrate how individuals always simultaneously form groups and the extent of the emotional identification with such (we) groups. Yet he also stressed that this relationship has a processual aspect: 'There is no I-identity without we-identity. Only the weighting of the I-we balance, the pattern of the I-we relation, are variable.'[5]

As has been well recognised by historians, it is the we-identity of the nation state, and the emotional charge connected with it, that became one of the strongest forms of we-identification in the twentieth century. This, of course, has varied over time and space. Thus, when one speaks of national identity, one is essentially referring to a form of we-identification – a feeling of belonging and a set of characteristics one shares with others. Individuals of particular geographical territories come to share extra-individual characteristics and feelings that are deep-rooted in the social habitus of these people. However, its deep-rooted nature is not unchanging in structure or intensity – we-images and we-feelings formed around the nation can weaken or intensify. One of the drivers of this change, as Elias sought to illustrate, can be a change in the specific structure of interdependences enveloping people within a nation[6] and between nations. In this chapter we discuss how the I-we identity balance of people in Ireland shifted over the course of the twentieth century, and how this came to shape and change the narratives and strategies deployed by GAA administrators as they sought to integrate young people into the GAA.

THE GAA, NATIONAL IDENTITY AND MEDIA RELATIONS

Prior to and in the immediate period following the GAA's foundation, those seeking to promote Gaelic games deployed a blame gossip[7] that fused competing sports with the labels of Englishness and inferiority.[8] The genesis of this discourse was the social context generated by the coloniser–colonised figuration within which the GAA was established in 1884.[9] As the power balance between the native Irish middle classes and Anglo-aligned landed classes shifted and became less unequal, the greater confidence experienced by the rising native Irish social groups manifested itself in the formation of the GAA and other cultural-nationalist organisations and movements. A further feature of this was the more fervent expression of antipathy towards the Anglo-orientated established groups and their ways and mores. Sports and sporting organisations became increasingly aligned and ascribed with 'national' associations based around the coloniser–colonised figuration of Ireland and Britain. This process was interwoven with a series of different yet interrelated social tensions that included the inter-organisational contest for the control of athletics and other sports.

Newspaper coverage of sports and sporting encounters was already an established feature in Ireland by that time, with specialist newspapers such as the *Irish Sportsman* and *Sport*[10] in circulation. In that regard, the newspaper media provided one strand through which sport was 'defined' and represented. Just as important was the perception for many that the media was central to both the promotion of sport and sports-participation levels. This belief added to the growing tension and anxiety over how to influence and shape media representations. Indeed, one manifestation of this was the efforts by some to create their own media outlet to fulfil such a function. For instance, Michael Cusack, one of the founding members of the GAA, established his own newspaper, *The Celtic Times*, for that very purpose:

> [contrast] the publicity given to the proceedings of clubs which engage in foreign games, with the supercilious treatment of those who cultivate the Gaelic games. We have started this journal for the purpose of publishing in its columns full and accurate reports of the meetings of the Association, and as we have arranged for its circulation in all parts of the Island, it will afford a constant and satisfactory medium, in harmony with the people, for acquainting the country with the position and prospects of the Gaelic movement.[11]

As the internecine conflict in the GAA subsided by the late 1890s,[12] the efforts of GAA activists to convert those involved in other sports to Gaelic games was reignited and swiftly intensified. Soccer and rugby remained popular in many parts of Ireland – they were the dominant sports in some areas – and were quickly targeted by GAA activists. For example, at the 1901 GAA annual congress, the Kerry GAA official and strident nationalist Thomas O'Sullivan called 'on the young men of Ireland not to identify themselves with Rugby or association football or any other form of imported sport'.[13] As before, the insecurities generated by the fact that many young men continued to play other sports, combined with a strong belief in the efficacy of the media in this process, led GAA activists to produce their own publications such as the *Gaelic Athletic Annual*. The tenor of many articles in this publication was the stigmatisation of those remaining loyal to or adopting other sports:

> A large number of our population are afflicted with that disease called 'classy notions,' the Johnny, the toff, the well dressed cad, the shoneen, the ape, the jelly fish and similar fry love to despise everything belonging to their own country and are anxious to adopt the games and manners of their conquerors.[14]

The animosity underpinning such contentions also extended towards sections of the media, centring around two perceptions: that the GAA was not receiving a fair share of coverage relative to other sports, and that the GAA deserved more, and better, reporting given its credentials as the embodiment of true Irishness. For instance, in an article titled 'The Press and the G.A.A.' in the *Gaelic Annual* 1908–9, the author claimed that the 'space allotted to some of our most important games by the National press is disgraceful'. The same author goes on to say:

> There are papers in Dublin which on Saturdays print a special football issue, giving the latest soccer news. Then Dalymount and Lansdowne get lauded to the skies, column after column is filled with details of play and players, photographs are given of prominent (sometimes 'very prominent') exponents of the garrison games.[15]

After partition and the creation of the Free State, the vilification of rugby and soccer as unGaelic (incapable of embodying true national identity) continued. Nor were such polemics restricted to GAA activists: many national and local politicians, as well as newspaper journalists, also expressed such views.[16] The virtues of the Irish 'race' and Gaelic games were conflated and placed in contradistinction to so-called foreign sports, which was essentially code for British. Notwithstanding this, soccer and rugby remained popular in many parts of Ireland. The capacity of their respective sporting organisations to field 'national' teams and to participate in international competitions certainly contributed to their profile. It gave these sports another level of representation in the national media, one that amplified their status as 'nationally' representative of 'Ireland' – the Free State or 'Ireland'[17] in international sporting competitions. This contributed further to the insecurities of GAA activists, who sustained an equally ambivalent attitude towards the media.

Both local and national media continued to be perceived as essential in popularising and legitimising Gaelic games, and this brought GAA activists into both cooperative and conflictual relations with journalists and the media as a whole. While some activists admonished the media for continuing to patronise other sports in their reporting, those at the apex of the GAA sought greater cooperation with media functionaries – journalists and editors. They appealed to and instructed GAA units to furnish local and regional newspapers with relevant material, such as match reports and fixture lists, as a means to promote Gaelic games.[18] Yet media coverage remained a vector for the expression of hostility towards various media outlets. The strength of we-feeling experienced by some GAA administrators was often inseparable from that of the nation, and the generated emotive charge led to ambivalent responses to media coverage. For example, in 1930, when several British-based newspapers that distributed Irish editions in Ireland began incorporating reports of Gaelic games, one GAA official demanded 'that any member of the G.A.A. writing Gaelic notes or giving information on Gaelic matters to foreign newspapers, shall be expelled from the Association'.[19]

State functionaries had established a national radio broadcasting service in 1926 in response to developments in Britain.[20] Leading GAA functionaries had initially embraced the service, viewing it as a means to promote Gaelic games; the ideals of cultural nationalism underpinning the state service contributed to this benign response. However, that state representatives occupying specialist functions in delivering the service took a more pluralistic conception of national sports soon led to condemnatory pronouncements from GAA administrators. For instance, in 1936 the GAA's national secretary took exception to 'the linking up of Gaelic results with reports of foreign games'. This was considered 'an insidious method of introducing non-Gaelic pastimes to the attention of the Irish public at large'.[21] The economic and cultural policies of the Irish state in the 1930s were often in tandem with the beliefs and motivations of some GAA activists who desired what they referred to as an 'Irish-Ireland'. That several state functionaries and media outlets adopted a more inclusive conception of national sport, and saw it as their functional responsibility to do so, continued to bring them into conflict with elements of the GAA. Perhaps the most high-profile example of these encounters involved the expulsion from the GAA in 1934 of the then president of the Irish Free State and patron of the GAA, Douglas Hyde, for attending an international soccer match in his role as president.[22]

The expanding coverage of sport (and of increasing varieties and levels) by Irish media organisations was impelled and constrained by competitive interdependences; those comprising media organisations made decisions and took actions based on what others in competing organisations did. For instance, when *The Irish Press* began to dedicate a greater percentage of total newspaper space to sport – not just Gaelic games – the proprietors and editors of competing newspapers were compelled to emulate this and to innovate their coverage of sport in response to these competitive pressures. Consequently, the percentage of newspaper space given over to sport by the three Irish national dailies expanded significantly during the period, while sports-related programming on radio also increased.[23] That sport was increasingly perceived to be a means to attain customers and market share was underpinned by the fact that the social significance of sport in Ireland was increasing.[24] And while coverage of Gaelic games expanded across the different media, so, too, did that of other sports. This remained a source of tension for GAA administrators at all levels of the organisation. Implicit in the verbal attacks by GAA activists on the media was a belief in the capacity of the media to normatively shape the meaning of 'national' sport. For instance, in 1939 the chairperson of the Armagh County Board stated:

> At the present moment in two parts of Ireland one saw two different methods being adopted to weaken the national games.

The great national daily newspapers were doing their utmost to cause a split in the ranks of the players, and some papers were working might and main to give foreign games equal stature and further more to make British games sport in this country.[25]

The persuasive powers attributed to the media also meant GAA officials found themselves in a double-bind: despite their sense of grievance and animosity towards the media, the perception that media coverage could increase participation meant they also needed to develop cooperative and harmonious relations with the media. It was this constellation of processes that contributed to the often conflicting and contradictory responses emanating from GAA officials. On one hand, the media were regularly and publicly lambasted by some leading GAA officials, while on the other hand they were on occasion lauded – deserving 'our thanks', as the GAA national secretary noted in his annual report of 1953.[26] These conflicting responses to media coverage (both national and local) persisted through the 1960s and 1970s.

THE DE-AMPLIFYING OF 'TRUE' NATIONAL IDENTITY IN MEDIA RELATIONS

The focus on, and perceived importance of, the integration of young people into the GAA had remained an important consideration for GAA administrators up to the 1960s. Equally, the conflation of Gaelic games with true national identity as a means of achieving this remained a dominant aspect of their approach. For example, addressing the province's annual convention of 1953, the president of the Ulster Council stated:

> …we reject the idea of our games being an apprenticeship for our young men so that they may later perform for the recreation of another people. Our games are meant to foster an Irish youth on its native soil, healthy in mind and in body, and the glory of a united nation Gaelic and free.[27]

In the 1950s a hostile approach was still being taken against those – including elements of the media – deemed to be responsible for the organisation or promotion of foreign games. However, by the 1960s the primary narrative conflating Gaelic games with 'true' national identity, so as to encourage youth to partake in Gaelic games, had lost some of its potency. For example, in 1969 the president of the Ulster Council of the GAA argued: 'We must provide more appeal... [and get involved in] any other type of social activity that will attract the youth in our clubs so that they will become imbued with a pride in our traditions handed down to us by our predecessors'.[28] Three years later the president of the Ulster Council in his annual address declared that 'youth is influenced to a decreasing degree by the tenets of traditions', and that 'games and pastimes of other lands can be seen from the fireside'. He went on:

> In the years ahead I believe the G.A.A. cannot rely solely on the traditional appeal it had for our youth. It must, as an Association, show itself to be actively interested in the youngsters if it is to have any hope of winning their allegiance.[29]

The drivers in changing how youth were understood and communicated with were a constellation of interwoven social processes, including inter-organisational competition, the increasing mediatisation of sport, and advancing individualisation (we will return to the latter point later in this chapter). The increasing mediatisation of sport in the 1960s – propelled in part by the increasingly important medium of television and its specific characteristics – amplified the sense of competition with other sports and leisure activities. Television broadcasts from the BBC were available to approximately 40 per cent of the population of the twenty-six counties at the time,[30] and this included *Match of the Day*, covering English soccer. Furthermore, from 1962 RTÉ presented a weekly sports programme, *Sports Desk*, and in 1966 the station broadcast the soccer World Cup in England.[31]

For many GAA activists there remained a strong belief in the potential power of the media in determining the sporting preferences of people. For instance, in his report to the GAA's annual congress in 1961, the most senior administrator, the general secretary, warned of the effects of the increasing mediatisation of sport, noting:

> We in Ireland have not as yet felt the full impact of these varied and powerful forces of publicity. We are as yet sheltered from the

winds that have greatly altered the pattern of sport elsewhere. We have seen how traditional pastimes have been assailed and how sports common to the countryside are threatened by the mass media of entertainment.[32]

Notwithstanding this, several GAA activists were more sanguine in their appraisal of television.[33] The GAA remained, if not the predominant sporting organisation in Ireland, at least one of the leading ones, and this contributed to the confidence felt by many GAA administrators in how television might be exploited to benefit Gaelic games. Still, some GAA activists were both fearful and insecure about television in particular. These insecurities found expression in the rebuke of the television media for both the level and nature of coverage given to Gaelic games. In that sense the view among many GAA activists that Gaelic games did not receive a fair share of coverage from the national media certainly persisted throughout the 1960s and 1970s, as did the articulation of this by GAA administrators. However, whereas before this assessment was often framed around the idea that Gaelic games were reflective of 'true' national identity and that other sports were less Irish, there was now a more pronounced reluctance to denounce competing sports in that or any other way. As one columnist for a GAA magazine wrote, 'Now I am not campaigning against soccer, rugby, golf or boxing. All of them deserve their share of publicity. But they get it, and Gaelic games do not.'[34] The 'national' association with Gaelic games could still be invoked, but a more restrained approach to criticising other sports was taken:

> Positive encouragement of the national ideal, in an unrestricted environment, will now be the mode of operation. We believe that G.A.A. members and supporters, and perhaps, many others, will respond gladly to the new challenge. Gaelic games are *the national games* [original emphasis] and not only must their traditional motivation not be lost, it must not be diluted.[35]

The ban on foreign games was removed in 1971, and this, perhaps, further fuelled concerns about attracting young people to Gaelic games. Such concerns about how 'youth' were to be attracted and communicated with were expressed by a range of administrators and commentators at the time. Writing in the GAA annual *Our Games* in 1972, one commentator suggested:

> It is no longer sufficient to say that you must play Gaelic games because they are Irish. Today's youth seeks better reasons than that. They have alternative games to turn to and if they find in these the things missing in the G.A.A., the haemorrhage will continue.[36]

So alongside the wider feeling among many GAA administrators and activists that GAA affiliation could not simply be sustained by claims to national identity, there was a growing concern about the need for greater publicity and media coverage. Certainly, throughout the 1970s, 1980s and beyond, the media could still be subject to rebuke by GAA administrators for the nature of coverage. However, demands for better and expanded coverage were no longer couched in terms of 'true' national identity.

By this time the bonds of interdependency between the GAA and the media had tightened further; the functional importance of each to the other had increased. This, in conjunction with the lengthening and expansion of competitive interdependences between sports organisations, also impelled greater functional specialisation within the GAA. The de-amplification of true national identity in discursive pronouncements about media coverage of Gaelic games was largely replaced by recognition of the importance of the media and the development of more cooperative activities to address this. In addition to specialist media-training courses, GAA functionaries sought to accommodate and facilitate the media as the means to enhance coverage:

> The competition for space in the media is now intense. Daily decisions are made in newspapers about the news value of different items. All sports are in competition here…To provide a proper system of information each county should have its own PRO…The PRO must work with the County Committee and the main task is to provide information re county activities to national and provincial papers and to train clubs in the value and use of publicity.[37]

The changes we have illustrated, including the de-amplification of national identity in both the narrative of attracting 'youth' and in relation to media coverage, were, as we now explain, connected to several interwoven processes, including the wider social dynamic of expanding social interdependences and advances in individualisation.

EXPANDING SOCIAL INTERDEPENDENCES AND INDIVIDUALISATION SPURTS

Following Elias, we argue that an expansion and lengthening of social interdependences involving the figuration of Ireland and the wider international structure of nation states impelled an advance in individualisation processes in the 1960s in particular, when the social habitus of people became more individualised. This was part of a longer-term process stretching back centuries.[38] Commercial and industrial activities expanded and lengthened the bonds of competition and cooperation between people in Ireland and those of other nations. Dependence on Britain as the main export market declined as economic and commercial bonds with industrialists and commercial functionaries in other nation states were initiated and expanded. Agriculture as a source of employment continued to decline, while industrialisation, through a state policy of encouraging foreign investment, became more significant. State services also expanded, as did urbanisation processes, as more people migrated to cities and towns in search of economic and social opportunities. These developments meant that more people from different social classes came to exert greater pressure on one another as they became more interdependent in more varied ways. Consequently, individuals were forced to exercise greater awareness of others, to take greater consideration of others' needs, and to become more willing to compromise. This process of moving from smaller and tightly knit communities to a more complex society with greater levels of specialisation and differentiation, and the changed requirements in behaviour and thinking it propels, also contributes to a process of increasing individualisation. There is a greater range of choices, one is 'freer' to make them, and these choices must be made. It is the extent and pattern of this feeling and belief that becomes habit – second nature. Of course, social structures (and psychic structure or social habitus) are processual in that societies can and do become more complex through the development of longer and denser chains of interdependences. In parallel with this, processes of individualisation advance – there is no end point to individualisation.[39]

Expanding industrialisation, commercialisation and monetisation of the economy, growing state services, and urbanisation are examples of the development of social interdependences that give rise to individualisation spurts.[40] For instance, by the 1960s the more localised, patriarchal social structures and the more autarkic economic structures throughout much of Ireland – which had pertained through the early decades of the twentieth century and which had more tightly bound women and younger generations to older male generations – had declined significantly. The expansion of state services and of industrial and commercial employment led to a decline in dependence on more familial and localised social networks for one's economic and social needs. It simultaneously created opportunities for individuals to give greater expression to their needs and desires freer from the social observances of the familial and community ties in which they were enmeshed. The I-we identity balance of people tilted, and the I-identity of people took on a greater emotional charge. In such circumstances, the emotional charge connected with 'we' national identity weakened relative to the I-identity of people.[41]

Furthermore, more advanced individualisation meant people felt less compelled to partake in or follow the norms and traditions of their parents, while parents and people more generally felt compelled to be less doctrinal in how they spoke to or advised others. Thus, people of all generations, though to varying degrees, came to express and expect a more tolerant attitude towards the making of more varied choices in life. This, we argue, was reflected in the realm of sport. It was becoming clearer that demanding younger generations to take up specific sports – including on the grounds of 'national identity' – was losing potency. Their 'individual' needs were to be understood, and they were to be encouraged and given greater scope to choose.[42]

The felt need to show tolerance towards others – to their needs, desires and motivations – is also reflected in the changed discourse of GAA administrators towards competing sports and media outlets. Media organisations were subjected to less critique on the grounds of true national identity. Many of the wider social changes we have alluded to – urbanisation, more individualised behaviour and thinking – did not go unnoticed among GAA administrators at the time. Leading GAA administrators commissioned sociologists and other specialist researchers, such as the Economic and Social Research Institute, to examine the changes.[43] Such knowledge and perhaps personal experience or observation also acted as a compelling pressure on GAA functionaries to instigate changes – for instance, greater specialisation around communications and better consideration of youth.

CONCLUSION

From the 1960s the espousing of the trope of national identity as a mechanism through which youth could be commanded and encouraged to play Gaelic games was de-amplified. This development also found expression in relation to media organisations. In the past 'true' national identity was often invoked and stressed by GAA administrators and activists in denouncing media organisations for the scale and nature of their reportage of Gaelic games. As illustrated, after the 1960s this had subsided. This was an unplanned and unintended development underpinned by a myriad of intertwined social processes that reinforced each other. It included the dynamic of inter-organisation competition involving both sporting and media organisations, the increasing functional importance of sport in society, and, as we sought to explain in this chapter, the lengthening of social interdependences and advances in individualisation. By the late 1960s this more individualised way of thinking, acting and behaving, which was more acutely evident in younger generations, became more transparent to many within the GAA. One consequence of this was that the principles underpinning the use of national identity as an integrating mechanism or means of stigmatising others became subject to greater scrutiny within the GAA. And while it did not disappear, it was gradually de-amplified and superseded by a more individualised-oriented narrative. The focus shifted more towards the individual's motivations and needs, and became less centred around pronouncements based on national identity. This change was mirrored in media relations, too. Media organisations were no longer subjected to claims that they were supporting 'less national' sports and games. Certainly, the media was still accused of not giving the GAA a 'fair share' of coverage, but this was no longer couched in terms that suggested the GAA was entitled to it on the grounds of its being the embodiment of 'true' national identity.

PART II

෯

Sport and Representation in Television and Print Media

CHAPTER THREE

Best on the Box: George Best, television and the making of celebrity

LANCE PETTITT

The work of the media in selecting, in framing, in focusing, and, above all, in narrativising the lives of sports stars, is a work of construction and production.[1]

THIS ESSAY EXAMINES A formative episode in British television's construction of the Northern Irish sports celebrity George Best (1946–2005) by analysing the relationship between television, sport and popular culture from the mid-1960s to the early 1970s. It includes a preliminary section that acknowledges the local press formation of Best through a 'local lad making good' biographical narrative, due largely to the influential sports writing of Malcolm Brodie. This section also highlights material that complements existing studies of the English press coverage of Best in London and Manchester.[2] Turning to social and television history, Best is routinely presented as an emblematic figure of 'Swinging Sixties' Britain, but this is based on a very narrow selection of audio recordings and film footage.[3] Although commentators have asserted the significance of television to Best's celebrity,[4] few have provided any detailed analysis of his televisual presence off the field, especially during his playing career.

The main body of the essay examines Best in four networked-TV programmes between 1969 and 1973. *Frost on Saturday* (1969), *The World of Georgie Best* (1970), *This Is Your Life* (1971) and an appearance on *Parkinson* (1973) are seen as early examples of

Best as chat-show subject moulded by television's myriad formats. Best became, in his latter appearances in the 1990s, almost a kind of penitent evangelist on the evils of celebrity. I seek to demonstrate how Best's sports celebrity is figured into larger national imaginings and identities in early-to-mid-1960s Ireland. The sources available for this archive-based approach to an analysis of celebrity include Belfast Central Library's newspaper-clippings collection, Ulster TV's archive, the BBC's radio archive in Cultra, the National Film and Television Archive at the BFI in London, and the BBC Written Archives Centre in Caversham, Berkshire. All have been used to view or listen to extant audio-visual material, to read scripts or programme transcripts, and to follow the 'paper trail' of notes, the BBC's own audience research data from the period, and the letters and memoranda associated with TV production in a pre-digital age.[5]

THE BUSINESS OF BEING BEST: 'FRAILTY ANIMATED INTO INTENSELY PERSONAL ENTERPRISE'[6]

Leaving his native Belfast aged fifteen, Best's professional football career at Manchester United (1963–74) ended prematurely due to alcoholism. He did play for some lower-league clubs and had a spell in the US in the 1970s, but essentially Best took up residence in Chelsea, a fashionable district of London, and survived over the next three decades (including two marriages, jail and major liver surgery) through after-dinner speaking, media appearances, charity work and living off his celebrity status, including several 'ghost-written' books.[7] Turning a talent for football into the business of your life, of mediating one's individuality, expressed an entrepreneurial and spiritual mode deep within Best's working-class Ulster Protestant formation. It is captured in the description of his 1963 debut performance against West Bromwich Albion as 'frailty animated into intensely personal enterprise'.[8] Increasingly transformed under conditions of exile in a secular, rapidly commodified and media-saturated society, he became, from 1969, a serial talk-show guest, a confessor testifying to the exuberance and excesses of celebrity. It is important to note that Best's 'business ethic' operated from early on and was integral to his playing career. He rarely discussed his faith, and failed to remain effectively connected with his home/class formation despite a brief attempt in later life to 'return' to live in Portavogie, County Antrim.[9] But as a sports celebrity his life was as allegorical a tale as the Bible could provide, and closer to his local Presbyterian roots than many in Britain appreciated. Business and the Bible are far from incompatible, and it is in these contexts that Best's prodigal return, his televised, quasi-state funeral, and the subsequent celebrity commodification in his native city should be viewed.

Sport, like other social and cultural activities, underwent significant changes in the course of the 1960s, and Best's playing career at its peak between 1966 and 1968 (1968 European Footballer of the Year) captures the key features of this transitional phase. Much of what we now routinely discuss – as fans, TV viewers, casual observers and academics – about sports celebrity can be discerned in the figure of Best. I argue that his case shows succinctly how his generation recast relationships between sports, media and celebrity. The social, political, technological and organisational conditions concerning football zeroed in on a young Irishman who was distinctive because he was out of place at the right time in Manchester, and who became a 'dislocated footballing hero'[10] cut off from locale as well as class. Although Rojek has suggested that 'celebrity and notoriety [are] a response to the absence of religion and the practical limitations of democratic culture',[11] others have argued that Best retained penitent responsibility for his actions: his comment 'I built my own image up first of all...and then I was sorry for it'[12] is evidence of a lingering Presbyterian mindset.[13] In this essay, to understand the workings of sports celebrity we need to attend to 'celebrity as a field of production, representation and consumption'.[14] We can do this by first examining some of the news-press material, specifically that generated in Belfast, and then four early television programmes that shaped his image.

FROM THE 'STARLET OF CREGAGH' TO IRELAND'S 'HUMAN TELESTAR'

The growth of football on network television fed off print journalism's changing coverage of sport in general and football in particular. The extent of Best's 'life in the news'[15] has been chronicled and perceptively analysed by Whannel. He identifies his youth, facial 'prettiness', non-muscular build and teenage tastes in haircuts, clothing and music as key features in the press' re-inscription of Best.[16] By early 1964, Best is 'the thin-faced Beatle', a 'boy among men', and a celestial technological phenomenon: for the Irish he is 'their human telestar'.[17] Back on earth, the impact of Best's aura on the pitch makes an explicit connection between sport and the business of entertainment: 'They gasped, they marvelled. They smiled. They shuddered. For it was all there. The magic and the mystery...It was wonderful stuff. Soccer showbusiness and it came from one of the "with it" boys.'[18]

Like the association with telecommunications, the link between sport and show business is not merely a metaphor, it had material existence, as illustrated in the pages of *Ireland Saturday Night*. Indeed, Best saw himself as an entertainer from early in his career: 'I like to think of myself as an entertainer. I like to feel that the fans have gone away after the hour and a half, have really enjoyed it and I've entertained them fully.'[19]

Best's re-inscription (as a 'boy with magic feet') in the English press was built on the sparse details of the teenager's recent, short past and the effect of his increasingly mediated sporting performances in words and images. But it is important to note that this was preceded in print locally in Northern Ireland with its own unfolding. In the pages of 'The Pink' (the nickname of the *Irish Sports News* because of its dirty 'pink' newsprint dye), he was the subject of 'The Best Story', a six-part biography in weekly 'episodes' bannered by a photo of his face and which traced his development in text and accompanying images from fourteen-months old, through youth teams, news headlines, with pet dog, holding baby sisters, to shots of him at his Manchester boutique.[20] His accelerated football achievement is linked to consumer celebrity ('he buys shirts weekly') and to a worldliness beyond his years or housing-estate birthplace in Belfast. The photogenic Best and the local journalist ensured an intimate, sympathetic representation. There was tremendous familial, local and, indeed, civic pride in his achievements: 'despite the idolatry and Mod clothes [he] remains the same...[he] realizes that family is the real basis of his life...George Best never forgets himself. He has no big head.'[21] This early biography of Best appeared alongside weekly profiles of each of the Beatles. Although a sports paper, the *Irish Sports News*' pages provided inside columns on 'Film Fare', 'TV Time', amateur drama, and arts reviews/features, as well as cinema listings and dances. Crucially, Brodie's 'Soccer Page' provided 'Up to-the-minute views *and gossip*' (my italics). The linking of entertainment with sports talk, gossip and celebration of success appears in the Northern Ireland newspaper the *Belfast Telegraph*, whose Friday column 'The Groove' featured, for example, the emergence of Van Morrison, Stephen Rea, Best and the snooker player Alex Higgins.[22]

The reporting of Best exemplifies the pivotal moment when a sports star becomes a celebrity through multiple media connections, linking local/national press and radio, amplified through television whose media events achieve international recognition, thus exerting a supercharging effect. He became a highly telegenic sports celebrity, 'effectively a multi-textual and multi-platform promotional entity'.[23] Competing in football competitions from the mid-1960s, he became a highly recognised face to *non*-football fans across Europe. What one journalist called Best's 'instinctive gift for self-publicity'[24] emphasises charisma over the effect of having a full-time agent whose purpose was 'to make him money and to look after his image'.[25] Best himself was already astute enough of a businessman to know he was his own best advert: 'I mean to show that the clothes I wear are good advertisement for my boutique.'[26] Between 1964 and 1969, he consciously built an image, a public 'media self', using the press on occasion to conduct his personal relations with women, and TV shows to express views and 'confess' his sins with sympathetic journalists such as Michael Parkinson and Hugh McIlvanney. It is to these late-1960s TV shows that we now turn.

SPORTSMAN, SHOW BUSINESS AND TV CELEBRITY, 1969–73

[He] is arguably the most handsome footballer in Britain, certainly the highest paid and probably the most talented. He is the first man to bring together the worlds of sport and pop culture.[27]

Together, the programmes discussed in this section represent a crucial juncture in the transformation of Best's TV image, whose story moved from sports star to penitent media celebrity. We compare four appearances on networked BBC and ITV channels from peak-time evening chat and variety shows to, for contrast, a high-profile arts feature in the BBC's *Omnibus*, 'The World of Georgie Best' (BBC, 1970). In the earliest of these shows, *Frost on Saturday* (1969), Best appears in a red tracksuit, demonstrates his ball skills in the studio (playing with members of the audience), and talks with insider knowledge about his profession with a track-suited David Frost as compère/interviewer. His guest spot is part of an evening's live entertainment during which Frost fluffs his lines, another guest's costume hat falls off, and technical limitations linking with filmed footage are apparent. These elements give the programme a quaint, amateur-night feel, and Frost indicates it is a 'celebration' of ITV's first transmission in colour. The theme music, the audience, the guest line-up in smart casuals, and Frost as host are typical of the content and mode of address for TV variety in the period. It combines light interview, humorous chat (Frankie Howerd, Dame Edna Everage), singing (Dusty Springfield) and Spanish guitar (Manitas de Plata). Best as sportsman is cued-in showman style: 'And so to another form of wizardry – the wizardry of the one and only, George Best!'

Despite his obvious liking of Best and his own interest in the game (he demonstrates passable keepy-up skills), Frost's questions demonstrate a revealing mix of reverence and probing about the modern game (high transfer fees) and Best's status within it: 'How much would this body, we see here before us, be worth?' (Gestures, stands back.) Best deflects good-naturedly: 'After the way I played today, not very much.' (Laughter.) But Frost persists: 'But you're rated, what, two hundred, two hundred and twenty thousand pounds, aren't you?' Best becomes serious: 'I dunno, the whole thing's got a bit out of hand at the moment with the money. They've got to stop sometime, but they reckon around two hundred thousand. But I wouldn't give it for anyone.'

On the ethics of the game, its toughness, professional fouls and dirty play, Best opines: 'They don't normally get away with it, unless you're a good actor, which a lot of footballers are.' (Best touching his nose. Frost off camera: 'Yeah.' Then cut to Frost.) 'You're pretty good at the – at that, too [eyes up] "what Ref?"' (Mimics 'innocent' gesture. Best laughing. Cut to him.) 'Of course, everybody's good at it.' (Studio laughter.) The tone lightens with a matey, jocular have-a-go invitation. (Frost to audience:) 'Who'd like to come and have a shot at George Best? Fire away at George, give it a bang.' (Frost promises:) 'We'll give you an autographed ball.' Frost and Best's interaction is friendly and good-humoured but with an undertow of the serious; the mode of address is to a non-specialist audience in the studio and at home ('That, for soccer fans, is a marvellous example of ball control', says Frost).

Though the time and activities were planned, it is unlikely that it was rehearsed beyond running order and technical requirements. With live transmission and studio-audience participation, the frisson of the unpredictable can be sensed: on some shots we lose sound, see boom mics in shot, footballs bounce awkwardly. To allow Best to show off his body swerve, a track-suited Frost adopts a role ('I am your lumbering defender') and shows acute awareness of camera-use to suture the TV viewer into this simulation ('Which camera are we shooting this on?'): 'Okay, great, running straight into this camera...so let's try... Could *you* [meaning us] get the ball off George Best? Watch the body swerve... oh, bea-u-ti-ful. I think that deserves a round of applause [audience complies].' Frost's patter, attitude and mode of address to those in the studio and fans at home, his drawing-in of the non-expert TV viewers, combines with Best's engaging banter and evidence of a controlled performance of his celebrity.

In stark contrast, Scottish sports journalist Hugh McIlvanney of *The Observer* scripted a 'serious' documentary portrait for the BBC's innovative *Omnibus* arts programme that was transmitted two months later, in early 1970. Using the familiar form of his name in 'The World of Georgie Best', its impact then and over the years is significant. It 'aroused a good deal of interest among the sample audience even if, in the event, not a few appear to have found the programme less rewarding than they had hoped'.[28] Despite this equivocal response to its first broadcast, the fifty-minute film remains the seminal TV Best document. Snippets of its footage, sound and music appear in almost all later non-fiction compilations, the film was repeated for the 'Best Night' in 1998, and its visual style is referenced in Mary McGuckian's feature film *Best* (1999). For all its undoubted structural flaws, partiality and failure to deliver its own intended approach of 'observing him [Best] in everyday life rather than setting up special scenes', it gives a fascinating contemporary insight into the phenomenon of Best's celebrity.[29] With a commentary that states that 'at twenty-three Best is accepted by worshipping fans and professional experts alike as the most lavishly gifted player in Europe, if not the world',[30] it is ironic that the panegyric to Best's genius simultaneously signalled the moment at which his football career went off-kilter. In 1969 he was disciplined for incidents such as throwing mud at a referee, voicing dissent and fighting. Off the field he was banned for drink-driving and became dissatisfied with his club's direction, while his personal/social life became increasingly spotlighted. Although acknowledged by McIlvanney in a *Radio Times* article previewing the film,[31] none of these subjects were included, but the film's director expressed concern that its lead-in to broadcast (January 1970) coincided with Best being on a twenty-eight-day match suspension.

   Shot on 16mm film, directed by 'fellow Irishman' John Gibson with a generous £7,500 budget (£1,000 of which was Best's fee), and given a prime-time slot on BBC1, the film took its subject seriously and was intended to be 'frank and revealing' in its treatment. It achieved a 20-per-cent TV audience share (compared with 23.9 per cent on ITV) and BBC Research recorded a 'Reaction Index' rating of sixty-five.[32] An earlier profile of Jimmy Greaves received a rating of sixty-two, so the Best film was watched by a fifth of the TV audience with a strong response, but this in itself was divided, as qualitative audience-research material shows. Summarised questionnaire responses were ambivalent since some felt the film showed

> 'an altogether "glossy" picture of a man' and that 'no mention was made, even obliquely, to his many misdemeanours on the soccer field'...[Other groups] were 'grateful for the programme which had, for them, revealed in extremely convincing terms, both the man and the soccer "idol"'...and several viewers remarked that this had made them change their opinion of a football star they had hitherto considered grossly over-rated and distastefully big-headed into the bargain.[33]

McIlvanney's voice-over anchors a kaleidoscopic, fluid (some termed it 'chaotic') impression of Best's current life on and off the field. His 'world' was filmed at the Manchester United training ground, his 'digs' with his landlady, out socialising, and back in Belfast, and included some film of him in a league match. While observational, much of the footage was derived from highly orchestrated profilmic activity, of scenes set up (Best training, Best arriving at a nightclub) so that the subject is seen 'acting himself'. It is artfully composed material and edited in a hectic style, capturing the sense of Best's frenetic lifestyle and varied activities. The substance of this film essay is that Best is a new version of a traditional working-class sports hero. There are, however, interludes where the composition of images on screen combines with poignant interview voice-over to create a strong undertow of melancholy, of family missed, and the ephemeral quality of fame in exile. Comparing the working classes of Belfast and Manchester, Best as a footballer is situated in a longer tradition of Irish emigrant labour despite the glitz: 'To go on earning like a film star, Best must be prepared to sweat like a navvy' (Best shown training hard).[34] Similarly, Best is shown as preoccupied with financial security and 'outward symbols of achievement' but striving to replace the 'home' that has been lost to him.[35]

The film's sophisticated use of interview, sound and music bridging over visuals, complementing and provoking questions, is one of its most striking features.[36] As Brodie had claimed in 'The Pink' four years earlier, McIlvanney argued that Best remained essentially the same person with 'a self confident coolness about him that unnerves some men and fascinating most women. He seems to have a slower psychological pulse than the rest of us'.[37] Best's testimony suggests otherwise. Given that the film was partly shot in Belfast in late 1969, his remarks about his Ulster Protestant identity are revealing: 'I think if I hadn't played football I would have stayed in Belfast. Maybe I'd have been throwing stones at the Catholics the same way as a great many other people have been doing.'[38] The insularity of his upbringing was intensified by his having left home at such a young age: 'Even now when I go home, if I go outside the estates where I lived, I'm lost. I hardly ever left the area where I was born.'[39] Best recalls leaving Belfast (by boat) in a poignant memory of loss:

> I think that the first time I left Belfast as the boat was pulling out, I could see my parents on the quayside, I didn't really think that I was leaving home. It was like a little adventure; I was going away for a couple of weeks...but then I came back and the second time the scene repeated itself. I knew as we pulled

out that this time I was leaving home for a long time, and it made me a little sad.[40]

This confession towards the end of the film is edited to follow two audio clips featuring his mother and father, the latter talking about the lack of contact with their son: 'So far as letter writing I don't think it's on. He doesn't even *need* our letters. We're quite contented. We know he is doing very well and we don't care if he never writes so long as we know that.'[41] Another version of the transcript shows 'need' crossed out and replaced with 'read'.

Best ends by saying:

> 'Playing football is a very sad sport… I've got the shops and other business interests. So financially I've got nothing to worry about. But I don't think my heart would really be in it all the way.' [Best is shown at his half-built new house in profile/silhouette. MUSIC: 'Echoes of the cheers'][42]

We know this was not exactly the way the director envisioned the ending. Ignoring the fact that Best's mode of transport (as part of the 'jet set') was invariably the plane, Gibson confides to the sound editor that he has failed to capture a certain sequence he had envisaged to provide a final visual to go with the audio of Best's voice:

> I know that there should be a little speech which we used over George looking out over the sea and the boat going away, but for some extraordinary reason I haven't got it, so we're just going to have to make it up.[43]

Gibson's notes to his sound editor also indicate that Best's testimony (and his parents', recorded in Belfast) is in part scripted. Indeed, Best's recordings in Manchester required multiple takes (for example, 'Take 1: n.g. G. went wrong'; 'Speech 12 G. "rustled script pages"') and what amounts to direction because, in delivering the lines above, he was asked 'to drop his voice at the end for "sadness"'.[44] If we perhaps accept the staging of visual evidence of Best's world, the degree of control over the oral testimony is also closely shaped to aesthetic/dramatic ends, as is here shown. Gibson's organisation of the musical soundscape of the film sought to accentuate the themes of exilic loss, dislocation and melancholy underlying his subject, as he explained to the film's composer before filming was completed: 'this whole sequence should have music much the same as the beginning, but slightly more nostalgic. Bravely nostalgic if you know what I mean.'[45] This sense of premature ending, of an awareness of something lost back *there*, even while caught up in the full flood of enjoying the present moment *here*, pervades 'The World of Georgie Best'.

An explicit, televised exploration of this passing did not really come on screen until *Parkinson* (1973) (discussed below). In a different register, that of popular entertainment, just a year later *This Is Your Life* (Thames TV, 1971), by its very format, suggested the transitional phase of celebrity. An early-evening prime-time show, it was based on the premise of surprising a famous person at a public venue, taking them back to the TV studio, and presenting a half-hour celebration of their life achievements. Typically, it combined film clips, old 'family' photographs, and anecdotes told by family, friends and associates who had all conspired with the host (and 'us') in keeping the show a secret. The show host/compère narrates the life from a large red book and introduces long-lost friends ['Come in, Bud!'] and people who knew them before they were famous. Such people's voices are heard 'off-stage' recalling a memory, with a camera close-up on the guest's face: 'You haven't heard that voice for x years but we've flown them all the way from Australia to be here tonight.' The unpredictability of the 'surprised' guest and its live broadcasting in front of a studio audience provided the key pleasurable frissons of hide/reveal and remembering/reconnecting. It was a successful light-entertainment hybrid whose narration of fame was invariably sympathetic and celebratory.

Much of the charm of the show was the sometimes-awkward mixture of famous/non-famous family and friends around the guest as their life is praised, necessarily glimpsing the ante-famous past as part of the rise to achievement/recognition. The brassy fanfare signature and lounge-sound strings theme tune worked to lend a 'glitzy' showbiz aura to the weekly event. Even though the studio set was cheap, the production of the show required considerable technical skills (pre-credit outside broadcast to 'surprise' the guest; pre-recorded film inserts) and expense in arranging the appearance of other celebrities/guests. Key to the show's mode of address was the avuncular presence of Irish broadcaster Eamonn Andrews as he cajoled the star guest, discretely manoeuvred a family member with a hand on their elbow to face the right camera, and filled gaps or prompted people who had forgotten their lines.

The edition of the show that featured Best (27 January 1971) typically worked hard to avoid controversy or journalistic probing. Indeed, *This Is Your Life*'s affirmative spirit of sporting achievement disseminated his celebrity to wider audiences. After 'ambushing' Best backstage at a fashion show, in the studio Andrews repeatedly links segments in the programme showing still images with remarks about Best's known-ness: 'Yes, a face that has become famous in all corners of the world.' Following this, a filmed insert comprising a street vox-pop montage of women interviewees is screened for us and the studio viewers, with cut-away reactions from Best watching a monitor:

> Young woman 1: He's not pushy like some men are.
> Middle-aged woman 1: I think he's a very handsome young man.
> Young woman 2: He's lovely. [studio audience laughter heard over]
> Young woman 2: He's just got a certain something.
> Middle-aged woman 2: He dresses well; he's rather nice looking; he's a very good footballer.
> Old woman/strong London accent: I think he's marvellous!
> [Studio audience laughter; Eamon Andrews laughing with Best]
> Andrews: George Best scores again! Rather unusual, but they were all women, did you notice that, George?
> Best [heard off-camera, deadpan]: Very unusual.
> Andrews: Very unusual, I *don't* think.[46]

The vox pop distils key elements of Best's media persona as it was then. His football skills are merely one aspect of his celebrity, which also includes good looks, enigmatic personality, manners, and his untypical masculine behaviour ('not pushy'). The (male) producer's idea to use all-female respondents, Andrews' use of 'scores', and the tone of his line to Best works to inscribe him within a knowing male humour, to which Best's response is resistant sarcasm, not unlike the deprecatory strategy used against Frost joking about 'ball control'. In the early 1970s, Best's celebrity embodied the contradictory nature of masculinity in British culture: the physical poise yet notable temper and aggression on the field; his Lothario image and activity off it. By contrast, his celebrity masculinity betrays a fascination with fame itself and a narcissistic, consumerist interest in looks/clothes/hair style and a non-macho manner that suggests, if not gender-bending, then gender-blurring. In these terms he may be viewed as a precursor figure for the 'metrosexual' footballer epitomised in the figure of David Beckham in the 1990s.[47] These contradictions in the culture were worked through the television genres of the 1970s and 1980s, the chat show epitomising the confessional, self-revelation mode that defined a generation before 'reality TV'. One of that era's pre-eminent chat shows is examined in the next section, with Best as one of the programme's most notable interviewees.

PARKINSON (1973): PAST THE BEST

Following the success of Eamonn Andrews as a chat-show host (1964–9), the BBC had established Michael Parkinson's eponymous late-Saturday-evening chat show in 1971 (running until 1982). A former *Sunday Times* sports journalist, Parkinson's interview with Best on the show in 1973 set a pattern of TV appearances on chat shows that evolved over the next thirty years.[48] During the 1972–3 season, Best had announced his retirement from professional football (he returned to playing shortly afterwards). His troubled health and personal life had become a reliable circulation-boosting story for the English and increasingly bemused Belfast press. From Parkinson's introduction to the first topical question, the host articulates a sceptical but sympathetic line of questioning, allowing his guest to publicly exteriorise his motivations:

> I'm going to talk to someone who, at the top of the tree, is regarded as the greatest footballer there has ever been and, until recently, when he ought to be cashing in on his genius...he gave up a gilt-edged career that could have made him a millionaire, and for what reason? Well, here to answer that question...will you please welcome, George Best!

In conjunction with a series of ghost-written autobiographies and a curious collaboration with Parkinson published two years later, Best used the chat show as an intimate TV confessional.[49] He explains the state of his finances, his dislike of the predictability of the game and its routines, strains ('it's more like a job'), and pressures on relationships. He refutes the idea that as an entertainer he has no loyalty to his audience, and is frank about the effect that drink has had on his behaviour:

> Parkinson: 'That's an astonishing thing – what you're really saying is, you can't guarantee your conduct?'
> Best: 'Exactly, yeah.'
> Parkinson: 'Really?'
> Best: 'Yeah, I tend to do things on the spur of the moment and then have to sort them out later – usually in a different country.'

Best then flakily outlines his plans for property development in Spain, opening a discotheque, offers of exhibition matches in the US, and a meeting in Toronto about a soccer league. Parkinson's incredulity at this waste of football talent is palpable, but the interaction is intimate and 'blokey':

> Parkinson: 'I tell you what, mate, you're putting weight on, look there.' [in two-shot, poking Best's midriff]
> Best: 'That's why I feel good.'

As it was, Best played for the LA Aztecs (1976–8), and was finally, after some controversy, honoured in Belfast in 1978 by an Irish Football Association-sanctioned testimonial. But his playing days petered out as his alcoholism became chronic.

CONCLUSION

Taking four illustrative examples, this essay has shown how Best, from his earliest visibility on popular TV, performed as a celebrity sports figure. His off-football-field media work began as he rose to fame, and intensified during his playing career. It was never secondary. He was emblematic of the materialism, fame and follies of his era, and his later life, illness and death would become television spectacles. While in some senses he exercised the agency and enterprise of the self-made man, my analysis of television's structures, genres and production processes shows how these exerted pressures that shaped his celebrity image. Best's career as a columnist-cum-celebrity-TV-pundit and quiz-show participant ebbed and flowed during the 1970s and 1980s. He devised an after-dinner circuit speech 'road-show' act with the Queens Park Rangers player Rodney Marsh, presenting a double-act of sports anecdotes and innuendo that became adapted for television as *The Perfect Match* (Granada Television, 1989). Off-screen, his personal circumstances veered from bad to worse (marriage break-ups, alcoholism, prison), and he figured in a sinning, apologia and redemptive cycle. It is perhaps poignant that Best was serially interviewed by successful Irish or Irish-emigrant TV presenters who had survived the public attention that attends media celebrity. Infamously appearing drunk on *Wogan* (BBC, 1990), Best appeared on the daytime TV circuit, and was interviewed by Derek Kelly in a *George Best Special* (BBC Northern Ireland, 2000) and by Ulster's own Gloria Hunniford (*Open House with Gloria Hunniford*, UTV, 2003).[50] Bizarrely, as part of the celebrity celestial firmament, Best would appear on TV commenting on and 'advising' up-and-coming footballers (*Trouble with Beckham*, Channel Four, 1998), and was a guest on a revived *Parkinson* (BBC, 2001) with Posh and Becks and Elton John. Indeed, as the chat-show format underwent revival, revision and parody in the 1990s, Best was interviewed by Caroline Aherne in *The Mrs Merton Show* (BBC, 1995). The running thread through this televisual Best is the capacity for him to be moulded into television's myriad formats. By the 2000s, the very anatomy of his body had become the forensic focus of TV documentaries (*George Best's Body*, Channel Four, 2001); *Me and My Liver*, Channel Four, 2002). And then, finally, in death, as his corpse was symbolically returned like a prodigal son to Belfast, Best became part of a significant televised act of public 'mourning' that extended over four hours of network time on national channels. Television really was the making and waking of George Best.

ACKNOWLEDGEMENTS

The original research for this chapter was funded by a British Academy Small Research Grant; the preliminary findings were published as an essay in *Vacuum* (2005) at the suggestion of Colin

Graham. My thanks go to Malcolm Brodie; Gary Whannel; the British Academy and staff at the BBC Written Archives Centre, Carversham, Berkshire; Stephen Douds, then of the BBC; the Northern Ireland Sound Archive in Cultra, County Down; UTV, Belfast; and the BFI Reuben Research Library in London. This updated and expanded essay was presented as a paper in Dublin City University at the Sport, Media and the Cultural Industries in Ireland symposium in May 2018. It is dedicated to the memory of Hugh McIlvanney (1928–2019).

CHAPTER FOUR

The Lansdowne Road Riot of 1995: Ireland, the English far right and the media

MIKE CRONIN

THE INTERNATIONAL FRIENDLY soccer match between the Republic of Ireland and England, staged on 15 February 1995, was abandoned due to crowd violence after twenty-seven minutes. England fans tore seats from an upper stand and threw them onto other supporters below. Those England fans would later be involved in running battles with the Garda Public Order Unit when the ground was cleared. By the end of the evening, one man had died, twenty people had been injured, and forty arrested. In the hours that followed the disturbances there was a view, particularly from English commentators, that this was simply the latest example of the hooliganism that had been long associated with the national team. By the next day, in the subsequent media coverage, that story had changed. This was not another example of the English disease of soccer-related hooliganism but, rather, a pre-planned riot that had been orchestrated by the far-right organisation Combat 18, with a specific anti-Irish agenda.

The idea that the evening's riot was arranged weeks before by a group of extremists has proved an enduring one. In 2015, the twentieth anniversary of the riot (and as Ireland and England prepared to play their first friendly in Dublin since 1995), press coverage was still adamant about who was responsible for the night's events. Raf Diallo, writing for *Newstalk* in 2015 stated:

the chief perpetrator of the events was a Neo-Nazi entity known as Combat 18. Long associated with the football hooligan scene in the UK which was used as a recruiting ground for prospective members, British intelligence warned the Gardaí that the group intended to cause mayhem in Dublin. And trouble they certainly did cause. While *Amhrán na bhFiann* was being played, Combat 18 chanted 'Seig Heil' and 'No Surrender to the IRA', all the while giving Nazi salutes.[1]

The aim of this chapter is to explore what happened on the night of the riot, and to consider how the notion that a well-organised group of extremists caused the match to be abandoned emerged as the major and long-standing media narrative. Both the Irish and British media (and in particular the tabloid press) appeared certain that extremists were to blame. The claims were based on little or no evidence. They say more, as the chapter will explain, about wider British–Irish relationships and, in particular, suggest that the emerging narrative was more informed by the early stages of the Northern Ireland peace process than by any understanding of the state of English soccer hooliganism in 1995. The result of the media coverage of the Lansdowne Road riot has been a long-standing myth – one that has been constantly restated – that Dublin came under some kind of coordinated neo-Nazi attack on the night of 15 February 1995.

THE MATCH

The friendly match between Ireland and England was planned for Lansdowne Road midway through the qualification process for the 1996 European Championships. England had qualified automatically as hosts, and Ireland had won the first three games in their qualifying campaign (although they would ultimately fail to make it to the finals). The teams had last faced each other in Dublin in a European Championship qualifier in November 1990, and the game, a 1-1 draw, had passed off without incident. The friendly game fixed for February 1995 set Jack Charlton's Ireland against Terry Venables' England. The two teams were familiar with each other from playing regularly as teammates and opponents in the top-flight English leagues. The game was a 40,000 sell-out, with kick-off set for 6.15 p.m. to enable Sky to cover the game live. The English Football Association (FA) had taken an allocation of 2,700 tickets for travelling supporters; in the event the FA returned 900 tickets it had failed to sell. These were sold by the FAI to home fans, which meant that the segregation of England and Ireland fans was not as it should have been.

There had been violent incidents in Dublin city centre the night before the game, but these had not altered the way in which law enforcement planned to police the match. Shortly before kick-off, both sets of national anthems were jeered by the opposing fans. Ireland scored after twenty-two minutes. Four minutes later, an England goal was disallowed by the referee, and this was the catalyst for England supporters to begin ripping up seats and throwing them onto the supporters below. Fighting broke out between a number of England and Ireland supporters, with police and stewards also entering the fray in an attempt to subdue the England fans. Shortly after the game had been halted, following the first signs of trouble, the match was abandoned. Once the Irish and neutral fans had left the ground, the Garda Public Order Unit was sent in to remove the England fans from Lansdowne Road and to escort them to Dún Laoghaire ferry terminal, from where they travelled home.

The disorder at the game was covered extensively in the media in Ireland, Britain and beyond. The context for the game – a friendly – was especially important given the strides being made towards peace in Northern Ireland and coming less than a year since the Irish Republican Army (IRA) had declared a ceasefire, in April 1994. The friendly offered the chance for two nations moving closer to resolving their shared problem of Northern Ireland to enjoy their shared passion for soccer. Soccer had entwined Ireland and Britain over the decades through the constant movement of players across the Irish Sea to English teams, and, more recently, with the Englishman Jack Charlton leading the Irish national team to major international tournaments with a team that included many English-born players. However, despite the two countries' shared passion for soccer and the positive steps being taken in Northern Ireland, the match was abandoned due to the outbreak of violence. Many media outlets chose to encapsulate the Irish shock at the level of violence with the image of seven-year-old James Eager, who was attending the match with his father. Sitting in the Lower West Stand, directly beneath the England supporters and fearing that they would be hit by missiles being thrown from above, James' father led the boy to safety on the pitch. It was on the pitch, and visibly upset, that James was photographed, and 'within minutes, the image of young James Eager in his green scarf, a face of bewildered innocence in a sea of trouble, was beamed around the world'.[2] James' 'bewildered innocence' was initially the perfect image for the media to use to illustrate the thuggery of the England supporters. A young boy at a match with his father, there to cheer on his heroes, did not expect to be, nor did any right-thinking commentator believe that he should be, forced to endure the worst excesses of English football hooliganism.

The simple question, which framed much of the response to the crowd trouble, was whether this was an example of the hooliganism that had blighted English football for years, or something more sinister – especially given the 'No Surrender to the IRA' chanting – that potentially spoke to extremist political involvement. In the hours after the abandonment of the match, television news programmes positioned the riot as a manifestation of hooliganism, as did the following morning's newspapers. Through the following day the blame shifted, and the idea that the far right was to blame came to dominate coverage, as evidenced by discussion on *Channel 4 News* on 16 February 1995 and in the British and Irish newspapers from the morning of 17 February.[3]

Two points were highlighted in both the British and the Irish print media the day after the match, in which it was argued that what had happened in Lansdowne Road had political overtones. First, the British police had warned their Irish counterparts, in the run-up to the game, that thirty or so 'right-wing extremists' would use the event to cause trouble and highlight their affiliation with Ulster loyalism. Second, and seemingly explaining the aggressive anti-Irish and anti-IRA chants by England fans, was that, in the wake of the game, 'calling cards' from the Cheltenham Volunteer Force (CVF) were found in the ground and elsewhere in Dublin. The CVF, engaged in what it termed the 'England Invasion of Dublin 1995', reminded anyone who read the cards that, in their view, 'Ulster is British, No Surrender, God Save the Queen'. The combination of the advance warning of the arrival of English extremists and the apparent presence of the CVF in Dublin produced a narrative that positioned the events at Lansdowne Road as having been planned and executed by the extreme-right-wing organisation Combat 18. That narrative became fixed within the media, and has, despite the lack of hard evidence, been repeated ever since.

COMBAT 18

Combat 18 emerged in 1992 as a stewarding force to protect British National Party events from attack by anti-fascist organisations. Led by Charlie Sargent, Combat 18 split from the British National Party in 1993 in opposition to the party's faith in electoral politics. Combat 18 has always been hostile to the idea of democratic politics, arguing instead that an organised campaign of intimidation and violence against its opponents best served its purposes. The opponents of Combat 18 are defined loosely, and include immigrants, ethnic minorities, homosexuals and the left (and, in particular, anti-fascist groups and anti-fascist publications such as *Searchlight*). Combat 18 views itself as part of a global movement, has links to the far right in Europe and the US, and has always vocalised its support for Ulster loyalism. The membership of Combat 18 has never amounted to more than a few hundred, and what support it did find was among the fellow travellers of the Blood and Honour music scene, best personified by the band Skrewdriver and the 'Oi!' bands of the 1990s.[4] These bands promoted the politicisation of the skinhead music scene into a whites-only, anti-immigrant movement that was often engaged in violent action against its opponents. From the music venues where such bands could play, claims were regularly made, both by Combat 18 and its opponents, that it also sought to recruit new members from the terraces of soccer clubs, with well-known and well-organised firms of hooligans (in particular Chelsea's Headhunters). Although never outlawed in Britain, Combat 18 is closely monitored, wherever it gathers, by MI5 and the police, and many of its members have been imprisoned for violent crimes.[5] Combat 18 has remained on the fringes of mainstream political life in Britain, and has, like most far-right movements before it, been targeted by the agencies of the state and continuously open to internal divisions and ideological differences that have precipitated splits within the movement. That said, as Nicholas Goodrick-Clarke argued, 'the noisy protests, inflammatory rhetoric and criminal acts of the original NSM [National-Socialist Movement], BM [British Movement] and C18 involving racial attacks, arson and sabotage have exercised an influence on the formation of anti-immigrant feeling and even government policy that is out of all proportion to their actual memberships'.[6] So what, if anything, ties together a fringe far-right movement obsessed with white supremacy and what they perceive as the evils of liberalism and multiculturalism with a soccer match in Dublin?

THE BLAME GAME

For the first twenty-four hours after the violence at Lansdowne Road, the initial narrative was a simple one of an all-too-familiar strand of English hooliganism having been played out for a night in Dublin. The England supporters, who had a long history of violence when following their national team, had taken advantage of a friendly game to start a riot. It was a match that was readily and cheaply accessible, poorly policed, and, or so it appeared, one that neither the FAI, Lansdowne Road officials nor the gardaí were capable of dealing with. Despite the familiarity of the 'English as hooligans' narrative, it was one which, by 1995, was out of step with the changes that had transformed soccer. The English performance at Italia 90, the transformation to all-seater grounds, and the riches that had begun pouring into the game with the arrival of satellite-broadcast revenue meant that the game had undergone a shift that had taken it away from a support base of hooligans to a new moneyed, middle-class audience. The decision of UEFA (Union of European Football Associations) to award England the 1996 European Championships was seen by many observers as a symbol of the new bourgeois, post-hooligan nature of English football.[7] But if the events in Dublin were not a throwback to the days of English hooliganism on tour, what, then, was the riot in Lansdowne Road about?

The media narrative quickly changed over the first forty-eight hours following the violence, and became fixed around the idea that the riot had been premeditated and organised by Combat 18. The *Irish Independent* stated that 'Far-Right members of Combat 18, which has its origins on British soccer terraces, had been planning the Dublin soccer riot for almost three months as a protest against the Northern Ireland peace process'.[8] In a similar vein, *The Irish Press* said that 'it is estimated that Combat 18 has a hard core membership of 100 in Britain, but it is so well trained in disruptive practices that a small cell or group could create havoc'. The paper went on to note that 'the fascist emblems and slogans used by sections of the rioters at Lansdowne Road, particularly the taunts about the IRA, tend to support the belief that Combat 18 members had previous links with the UDA and the UFF in the North'.[9] The *Evening Herald,* under the headline 'Nazis planned Dublin trouble', quoted *Searchlight* editor Gerry Gable, who said that 'the word has been out on the streets for ten days before that there would be trouble in Dublin'. Gable went on to state that many of the rioters were 'working to a political agenda: to smash the peace process'. And if the deviant politics of the rioters were not clear enough, the newspaper wrote that 'the sinister group worship Adolf Hitler and their magazine features Nazi emblems and skull and crossbones'.[10] The *Irish Examiner*'s Noel Spillane wrote: 'I understand that a hardcore of English supporters were from the notorious Combat 18 group in London, a Nazi modelled group of Chelsea headhunters that have wreaked havoc at football grounds up and down England in the past'.[11]

By the weekend following the game, the press uncritically accepted the idea of the shadowy Combat 18 having organised and executed the riot. Despite no known Combat 18 members having been arrested, many Irish journalists took their briefings from *Searchlight* staff in London. The *Irish Examiner* led with a story about 'English neo-Nazi militants', and, quoting directly from a *Searchlight* journalist, argued that the friendly match had been 'hijacked by English neo-Nazis', a 'hit-squad' whose aim was 'to cause maximum trouble and to damage the peace process'. The paper went on to report that Combat 18 'encompasses English Nazi and fascist groups, Ku Klux Klan members as well as alleged UDA and UVF supporters'. In case any reader was in any doubt about the nefarious intentions of Combat 18, the article ended by recording that the movement's 'sickest element' took part in a 1994 trip to the site of the Sachsenhausen concentration camp, where they had 'posed for photographs standing by the wall reserved for mass shootings'.

In the space of a day following the Lansdowne Road riot, the story of another night of English soccer hooliganism had been transformed into a political story with a specifically Irish dimension. The troublemakers were not hooligans at all but a small group of committed and well-trained political extremists who, in the name of destroying the Northern Ireland peace process, were the catalyst for a major riot. These extremists conformed to every far-right stereotype: they were skinheads who were not only vehement white supremacists obsessed with Hitler but also anti-Irish and bitterly opposed to the IRA and all that it represented. It was a narrative that transformed yet another night of soccer-focused English hooliganism into something exceptional, namely neo-Nazis organising themselves, weeks if not months in advance, to specifically take their ideology and their support for the loyalist cause onto the streets of Dublin. By causing a riot they believed (wrongly) that they could somehow derail the Northern Irish peace process by creating some sense of political crisis.

The British media, far more versed than their Irish counterparts in covering English hooligans, followed the same trajectory and moved swiftly from football violence to politically infused riot. On the day after the riot, the British media followed their usual path when responding to yet another outbreak of the English disease. One issue highlighted constantly was the fear that the violence would lead UEFA to rethink its decision on England hosting the 1996 European Championships. *The Sun* led with 'Madness: kick these sick thugs into jail'.[12] The *Daily Mirror*, in the context of England hosting Euro 96, declared 'Sabotage: they are scum who care nothing for anyone or anything other than their own horrible violence'.[13] And the *Daily Mail*, reflecting on the steady decline in hooliganism, offered 'Back in the gutter again. Soccer savagery draped in a flag'.[14] The only newspaper to focus on the Irish angle was *Today*, which offered the opinion that 'it is appalling that the pond life that purport to follow England should riot at all. But in Ireland of all places, at such a politically sensitive time, simply defies belief'.[15] By the morning of 17 February, the British press had switched direction and heaped blame on the extremists. *The Times* led with 'Far Right football thugs engineered riot over Ulster', and *The Independent* headlined 'Nazi group behind night of violence'.[16]

One wonders whether the British and Irish media found in Combat 18 and a pre-planned, ideologically informed riot a mutual cause that served their separate agendas? If the Lansdowne Road riot had been caused by political extremists rather than the usual soccer hooligans, then the English could argue that they could still host Euro 96. Rather than a manifestation of the English disease of hooliganism, a factor that had been a constant worry in the planning for Euro 96, the presence of the far right in Dublin allowed the media and the FA to deny the riot was a football problem. The football authorities had argued through the planning of Euro 96 that they had the hooligans on the back foot, but the far right running amok in Dublin to disrupt the peace process was something different and not their responsibility. For the Irish, an extremist riot meant that inadequate planning was not their fault. They had planned for a soccer friendly, not some form of skinhead putsch. Combat 18 was a convenient focus for blame that shifted the attention away from simple hooliganism and, in different ways, exonerated English and Irish authorities.

Despite the clear-cut media opinion that Combat 18 had planned and executed the riot, that view received no real attention in British political circles. On the day following the riot, when asked about events in Dublin, British Prime Minister John Major stated: 'I agree that the behaviour of a thuggish minority at the match last evening was a disgrace and a great embarrassment. I do not believe that the people involved are sports fans, nor do I believe that they represent the true face of this country or British sport.'[17] Major offered not a view of extremist violence on the streets of Dublin but a tired answer and condemnation that could have served as a response to any English hooliganism of the previous two decades. In the Oireachtas the extremist angle was mentioned in both the Seanad and the Dáil. Senator Dan Neville stated that 'the hooligans disgraced themselves. They are not interested in soccer. Some of them have been identified with and are known members of the National Front.' Senator Pat Magner asked 'why were the fans mixed? Some of the England fans were members of the National Front who do not play around. Dogs would not be put with some of them, never mind ordinary people, and yet the fans were mixed. That was idiocy for which there is no excuse.' Most pointedly in terms of connecting the riot to the forces of extremism, Senator John Dardis stated that

I agree with Senator [David] Norris that what we saw last night was political. I want to draw a connection which is not as tenuous as might appear. Last week when we marked the 50th anniversary of the liberation of Auschwitz I said that it could not happen again. It must not happen again, but what we saw last night is a manifestation of what brought about Auschwitz.[18]

In the Dáil Liz O'Donnell laid the blame firmly at the feet of the extremists, stating that 'the blame for last night's violence lies with the perpetrators, the small group of people who travelled here with a political and violent agenda who alleged they were fans… the National Front and other notorious right wing elements from England were the root cause of last night's trouble.'[19] In the various speeches in the Dáil, a myriad of far-right movements, including the National Front, the British Movement, the British National Party and Combat 18, were all name-checked by various TDs in their comments on what had happened at Lansdowne Road. This reflected a misunderstanding of the far right as a single cohesive block with interchangeable names, and an indication of how Irish journalists, politicians and commentators had embraced the idea of extremists causing a riot in Dublin with no credible intelligence or agreement as to which group had actually organised the violence.

WHY BLAME THE FAR RIGHT?

So why did the far right, in particular Combat 18, emerge as the commonly agreed instigator of the Lansdowne Road riot? There were two reasons, both tightly entwined, for the media and politicians having decided on the guilty party, this being necessary to position what happened at Lansdowne Road as something other than English soccer hooliganism. By positioning the riot as an event orchestrated by the far right, the English commentators were able to preserve the new image of soccer in the run-up to Euro 96. It also helped that Combat 18, a shadowy organisation around which stories could be built, had links with Northern Irish loyalists. Given the slow moves towards ending the conflict, the imagery of the English far right seeking to disrupt order in Dublin while chanting anti-republican slogans would allow the Irish media, particularly the tabloids, to position the riot as a nefarious act aimed at highlighting opposition to any peace deal with the IRA. The sources for the idea that the riot had been pre-planned by Combat 18 came from within the organisation itself and from a pressure group involved in monitoring the far right in Britain. Within two days of the riot, the *Sunday Express* had secured an interview with Charlie Sargent, the leader of Combat 18.[20] He told the interviewer that 'we didn't care if England won or not, the lads were only there for a good fight and to teach the IRA bastards a thing or two, and to try and screw up the so-called peace talks'. Sargent also claimed that in the fighting 'those [Irish] who didn't run away went down like sacks of shit. Didn't even put up a proper fight.'[21] Sargent – who was paid for his interview – was enthusiastic about Combat 18 taking credit for the violence, and even posed for a picture in which he supposedly identified himself while pointing at a photograph taken during the riot. The tabloid media and many politicians and commentators were happy to take Sargent at his word. Combat 18, through its leader, had claimed responsibility for the violence, so the group must have been responsible for the night's events. In Sargent, Combat 18 was given a public face. His position as leader of the organisation (and perpetrator of the Dublin violence) was further heightened (and the Lansdowne riot more tightly connected to Combat 18) in an ITV *World in Action* documentary screened on 27 March 1995. The programme uncovered Combat 18's links to loyalist paramilitaries, its involvement in racial and soccer violence, and Sargent's leading role. The connection between the far-right organisation and the violent events inside Lansdowne Road appeared unequivocal.

Added to the claim of responsibility from Combat 18 was the apportionment of blame to the organisation by its bitterest critic, the magazine *Searchlight*. Founded by long-time anti-fascist activist Gerry Gable, *Searchlight* commenced publication in 1975. The magazine had close links with Anti-Fascist Action, and in the main highlighted the activities and political linkages between the National Front, the British National Party, Combat 18 and others on the right. *Searchlight* owed its existence to its work in exposing the race politics and associated violence of the far right. Following the Football Intelligence Unit media briefing on 16 February 1995, in which it stated it had informed the gardaí of the intention of known far-right extremists to travel to the game, the media followed that angle to the exclusion of any other cause. And who could tell the eager reporters most about a largely unknown and very small far-right group called Combat 18? *Searchlight* could. Following the Football Intelligence Unit briefing, *Searchlight* staff provided copy to a host of British and Irish media outlets. The *Sunday World*, for example, readily quoted *Searchlight*'s Tony Robson, who stated that Combat 18 had been planning the riot – and had made reconnaissance visits to Dublin – since before Christmas 1994.[22] The complexity for both *Searchlight* and Combat 18 was that, although respectively hunter and hunted, they needed each other to validate their existence.

In the hours and days that followed the Lansdowne Road riot, Combat 18, a small, fringe, far-right group, and its most vehement critic, *Searchlight*, respectively took and apportioned blame for events in Dublin. With Sargent's claim of responsibility backed up by information provided by *Searchlight* on the extent of Combat 18's planning and its execution of terrace violence, the media – especially the tabloids, which have always been alert to Hitler-obsessed thugs – declared that the Lansdowne Road riot had been caused by extremists who had flooded into Dublin.

The Irish government, seeking to understand what had *actually* happened in Dublin on 15 February 1995, requested Mr Justice Finlay to investigate the events at Lansdowne Road and to write a report, with possible recommendations for future high-profile sporting fixtures. In his report, published in April 1995, Finlay acknowledged that, three weeks before the match, the Football Intelligence Unit in London had alerted the gardaí that hooligan (as opposed to political-extremist) elements were intending to travel to Dublin with the express intention of causing trouble. On the day of the match, information was relayed to Dublin by British police regarding trouble at a ferry port among travelling fans, and that twenty people on a flight to Dublin had been observed wearing badges with the insignia of either the BNP or Combat 18. Gardaí had turned down the offer made from London that a member of the Football Intelligence Unit travel to Dublin and work as a spotter to identify known troublemakers. Perhaps most damning was that, whatever intelligence gardaí possessed about what might unfold on the night, they failed to pass this on to the FAI until shortly before kick-off. Once the trouble started, the lack of segregation of fans, miscommunication between officials, the deployment of only a small number of gardaí, and the delay in getting riot police into the ground all added to the confusion and the slow response.[23] In his report, Finlay explained that the serious violence was caused solely by England fans. Many of the fans who indulged in violent behaviour would have obtained tickets for the match through the England Travel Club. Second, the violence was planned and targeted, not a spontaneous reaction, and was not due to overcrowding, provocation by shouting or otherwise from Irish fans, nor to the progress of the match, nor to the referee's decisions.[24] Despite the media's reaction in the days after the game, Finlay did not expressly blame members of the far right for orchestrating the violence at Lansdowne Road. Rather, his report is a standard assessment of the ways in which English soccer firms had operated at home and across Europe since the 1970s.

Despite Finlay's findings that this was an act of hooliganism conforming to a long-established pattern rather than a riot provoked by the far right, it is remarkable how the narrative that the riot was caused by Combat 18 has persisted. In 2015 the media, when marking the twentieth anniversary of the riot, stuck to the far-right narrative established in February 1995. For example, the sports website The 42 stated that the riot 'was caused by a section of the travelling support representing neo-Nazi organisation Combat 18'.[25] The football site Tifo recalled that the England fans had 'among their ranks members of far-right political groups such as the National Front, BNP and the neo-Nazi Combat 18 and it was they who encouraged the Nazi salutes and catcalls that disrupted the national anthems'.[26] RTÉ argued that trouble started when 'the travelling supporters – far-right group Combat 18 were later identified as the source – in the Upper West tier began ripping out seats and hurling them at people below'.[27] What is remarkable about the retelling of the Lansdowne Road-riot story in 2015 is how the Combat 18 narrative is foregrounded and Finlay's official report, which is more reticent regarding a far-right causation, is barely mentioned.

THE RIOT IN CONTEXT

So what does the Lansdowne Road riot, and the media's embrace of a shadowy far-right organisation as the agency of violence, tell us? It is clear that the riot was in keeping with a tradition of English hooliganism, and was no different to what English hooligans had already done across Europe. The main difference in Dublin, as one participant (Richard) recalled, was that 'we are the only team to have a match cancelled by hooliganism. There was such a buzz after the referee stopped the game. Everyone was cheering: it was as if we had just won the World Cup. It was just mental. I've never experienced anything like it.'[28] And that, for the various firms that had travelled to Dublin, was their reward. They had managed to have an international fixture cancelled because of the disturbance they had caused. And this is what Richard and his ilk talk about: their successful day of hooliganism. They make no references to Combat 18 or to far-right extremism. For the most part, those who took part in the violence refuted any Combat 18 involvement and, as one hooligan noted, the media obsession with the far right meant that the riot was seen as political rather than the supreme act of hooliganism, concluding that 'our big day had been taken away from us'.[29]

The media was much enamoured of the idea of an active far right, and all shades of the press embraced the idea of Combat 18 orchestrating the riot, with little assessment of the facts. England fans did in Dublin what they had been doing anywhere they could for over two decades. The flags, the level of drunkenness, the organisation (or lack thereof), the chanting and the songs were all standard for any England match. So why, after twenty years of proudly being the best hooligans in Europe, did the England travelling support suddenly need help and inspiration from Combat 18? Many commentators pointed to the overt sectarianism of the England fans in Lansdowne Road, particularly in their singing of 'No Surrender to the IRA'. While the chant may have had extra relevance given the context, it was not a place-specific chant rolled out for Dublin. It was a chant they had sang since the mid-1980s and sang wherever they went.[30] What is more important, in light of the media identifying Combat 18 as the instigators of the riot, is the lack of evidence from film and photographs of the night, and later testimony from the hooligans themselves, of any Combat 18 insignia, flags or chants. Most critically, the man who claimed that the riot had been the work of Combat 18, its leader, Charlie Sargent, was not, despite his claims, in Dublin on 15 February 1995.[31]

Sporting fixtures between nations, especially close neighbours, are often the source of intense media scrutiny. National stereotypes, history and myth-making are all brought to bear on such occasions. In the context of 1995, the discourse around the violence at the game allowed such stereotype and myth-making to be freely applied. The English were hooligans who ruined the friendly. The Irish were the naive victims who had gone to watch the game and have a good time. The English hooligans were skinhead neo-fascists who wrapped themselves in the British flag and embraced loyalism and unionism, and who used the friendly to give voice to xenophobic views that denounced Ireland and republicanism. The events at Lansdowne Road demonstrated, or so it seemed, that no matter how the Irish economy or English soccer were becoming gentrified and moneyed by the powers of neoliberal finance, and no matter how culturally close the two nations were, there existed a schism of misunderstanding between the two islands that was given voice by English supremacists and seized upon by the media.

In reality, the Dublin riot marked one of the last high-water marks of English hooliganism abroad. The Premier League had come into existence in 1993, and from that point on millions of pounds of television and sponsorship money poured into the top flight of the English game. The new wealth evident in soccer, coupled with the legislative and investment response to disasters such as Bradford, Heysel and Hillsborough, meant that the game, and its surroundings, were transformed. The years following the riot also saw the massive growth of the Irish economy in the form of the Celtic Tiger.[32] In sporting terms, the growth of the economy, and the need to maximise the profits available from corporate patronage, led to the old stands at Lansdowne Road being demolished and replaced by the shiny new Aviva Stadium, which opened in 2010. In similar new stadia across Britain – with the addition of new police powers, the ready availability of CCTV and the general cleaning-up of the atmosphere around soccer – organised, regular hooliganism began to fade away from the mid-1990s.

With the passing of the hooligan element from the mainstream of the English soccer experience, there has been a growth in hooligan nostalgia.[33] In memoirs, documentaries and stage plays, the age of the hooligan is recalled with great gusto by former participants: honestly intentioned men who only wanted to fight each other and who had no desire to involve actual supporters of the game in their violence. Whatever the merits of such nostalgia, one thing is clear: all those former hooligans who have written about being in Dublin in 1995 ridicule the idea that the violence had anything to do with far-right extremism. Colin Ward dismissed the idea, writing, 'the police stated it was planned political violence, but as is their way never produced any factual evidence. The media, who love a Far-Right conspiracy theory, printed the police version word for word.'[34] Jason Mariner,[35] Paul Dodd[36] and others reminisce about the fighting in Dublin but do not reference Combat 18 as having organised their evening of violence. Despite the rush of the media to find more sinister causes for the violence in Dublin, it appears that while there may have been members of the far right in attendance (there always were at England matches), these individuals did not organise or direct the violence. The truth seems far simpler and more historically contextual: Lansdowne Road in February 1995 witnessed another example, albeit a particularly out-of-control version, of English hooliganism at work.

What of the links between the English far right and the forces of Ulster loyalism, given the media's belief that the riot was an attempt to derail the peace process (as if one night of soccer-related violence could affect a finely balanced political process that had been choreographed over many years)? Given that both the far right and some extreme loyalists, in addition to upholding the indivisibility of the United Kingdom, are racist and sectarian and have a well-documented hatred of the IRA, it is easy to see them as fellow travellers. It is known that members of Combat 18 spent time with members of various loyalist paramilitary groups, and that figures such as Combat 18's Charlie Sargent and loyalist Johnny Adair have expressed their shared beliefs. In 1999 two serving British army soldiers were charged with activities relating to membership of Combat 18. They had both served in Northern Ireland, had attended Apprentice Boys' parades in Derry, and had also invited members of the UVF to attend a Combat 18 fundraiser in Wigan.[37] Later, leading Combat 18 member Mark Atkinson would travel to Belfast to visit imprisoned Ulster Defence Association (UDA) member Stephen Irwin, who was convicted for his involvement in the 1993 Greysteel killings, a UDA attack on a Halloween party that left eight people dead. Upon his release under the terms of the Good

Friday Agreement, Irwin moved to London and joined Combat 18.[38] However, whatever connections did exist between Combat 18 and loyalism appear fleeting. The two groups – as is the way of those on the extremes – were wary of each other as both feared infiltration by the state. What connectivity they did have fits more broadly into the category of 'interested fellow travellers' that also included racist and neo-Nazi groups elsewhere in Europe, the US and South Africa. Combat 18 and loyalism may have much in common in terms of broad ideology, but they were also both focused on their own geographical locations. Ulster loyalism and English far-right extremism, for all that they shared, also had very separate, localised agendas.

In essence, the idea that the Lansdowne Road riot was caused by any linkage between Combat 18, loyalism and a far-right antagonism toward the peace process does not hold water. There is no evidence that loyalists from Northern Ireland known to the security forces were in attendance, and nor had there been any formal connections between loyalist paramilitary organisations and Combat 18 with regard to disrupting the match. The anti-IRA chanting in Lansdowne Road was typical of English football hooligans and reflected the eclectic range of causes they appeared to espouse.

The media coverage of the Lansdowne Road riot, and its targeting of Combat 18 as the cause, was simply misdirected. The riot and the associated violence by travelling England supporters was part of a well-rehearsed pattern. The media – too keen to look for a new angle on the English disease and perhaps placing everyday soccer hooliganism in the context of Anglo-Irish history – chose to spin a story (supported by both Combat 18 and *Searchlight*). That story depicted the evening's events as a product of visiting violent neo-Nazis with loyalist sympathies and an agenda to derail the Northern Ireland peace process. The fact that the story ran across all branches of the media, given what they collectively knew about English soccer hooligans, is quite remarkable. It is clear that the official Irish government inquiry found the riot to have been a product of active hooliganism exacerbated by Irish naivety in terms of planning and response, thereby making a bad situation worse. In the history of English soccer hooliganism, the events of 15 February 1995 were more extreme than usual, but the fact of such violence was, sadly, a mundane reality. That a fringe organisation from the ranks of the

British far right had orchestrated a major riot in Dublin, driven by a vehement hatred of the Irish generally and the republican movement in particular, was a media invention. Few of the journalists who spun the story of Hitler-obsessed skinheads rampaging through Dublin could have imagined that their reports would still form the accepted narrative of the evening's events two decades on.

The Mediatisation of the GAA's Commemoration of the 1916 Rising: 'A New Ireland rises'?[1]

SEÁN CROSSON

IT IS IMPOSSIBLE TO appreciate fully the forces that led to the Easter Rising of 1916, the Rising itself, and, moreover, how it has been remembered and commemorated without a consideration of sport. The Rising began against the backdrop of one of the highlights of the Irish sporting calendar. On Monday 24 April 1916, when many Dublin citizens were attending the Irish Grand National, Irish republicans occupied major buildings across the city, and the rebels' chief spokesperson, Patrick Pearse, read the Proclamation of the Republic on the steps of the General Post Office. Furthermore, the early advances of republicans in taking strategic points in Dublin city were helped considerably by the absence from the city of the many British military officers attending the horse race, held at Fairyhouse Racecourse in County Meath, some 25km from the capital. The Irish Grand National at Fairyhouse in 2016 marked the centenary (in an event unlikely to have been well received in such august surroundings in 1916) with members of Fingal Old IRA Commemorative Society re-enacting the 1916 Grand National. As noted in *The Irish Times* the following day,

> The 1916 race was recreated here, in heavily edited form, and without any fences, less that tempt fate. In the event, a horse called 'All Sorts' won again, safely with 'Civil War' — the 1914 victor — once more trailing back in fourth...The other re-enactment of Grand National day saw members of the

Fingal Old IRA Commemorative Society performing armed
manoeuvres in period dress, as a tribute to those who fought
and won the Battle of Ashbourne on the Friday of Easter Week.[2]

This event was but one of a range of 1916 commemorative events held
in 2016 in association with major sporting organisations and venues.[3]
It reflects a recurring feature of these sporting commemorations: the
association of sport with violence and militarism. This chapter will
contend that these associations attempt to provide a disciplining
reassertion of masculinity in response to the contradictions (and the
anxieties they reveal) apparent within the events themselves. This
includes the principal focus of this chapter, one of the largest and
most viewed commemorative sporting events in 2016, the *Laochra*
pageant organised by the Gaelic Athletic Association (GAA),[4] and
broadcast live by the Irish-language broadcaster TG4 on Sunday 24
April, exactly 100 years to the day after the first shots were fired in
the Easter Rising. This analysis is engaged centrally with the overall
concern of this collection to examine how 'media sport' (new and
old) 'reflects the values, politics, and social processes at work in
contemporary Irish society'. In approaching this subject, this chapter
draws on my previous examination of sport in film,[5] and, as with
that text, adopts a primarily cultural-studies approach, informed in
particular (in its focus on gender) by the work of Judith Butler[6] but
also, more specifically, by scholarship concerned with the historical
depiction of Ireland as female, the continuing resonance of this motif,
and its implications for contemporary Irish culture and society.[7]

Commemoration is part of what defines nations and their
configurations; the considerable investment of the Irish state and
various sporting organisations during 2016 in 1916 commemorations
highlights the importance of commemoration in both defining and
affirming the state itself and the role these organisations play in it.
However, this process is neither straightforward nor uncomplicated;
it is rife with contradictions, unresolved tensions and paradoxes.
Commemoration involves a constant process of writing and
rewriting, an ongoing renegotiation of the past in response to
contemporary developments and future aspirations in a process
that is intrinsically political.[8] The decision of the Irish government
in 2012 to include the official commemoration of 1916 as part
of the Decade of Centenaries Programme (from the enactment of

the Home Rule Bill in 1912 to the founding of the Free State in 1922) reflected, at least partly, an awareness of the complexity, and the potential divisiveness, of the various moments during the years concerned, none more so perhaps than the 1916 Rising. While not an official state event, the GAA's commemoration was nonetheless linked to the official state commemoration of 1916 on the same day: a requiem Mass held in the Church of the Sacred Heart, Arbour Hill, followed by a procession to the adjoining graveside of fourteen leaders of the Easter Rising. Indeed, in a press release published by the Department of Arts, Heritage and the Gaeltacht prior to that weekend's events, Minister Heather Humphreys clearly connected the *Laochra* event to this official commemoration:

> One hundred years ago this weekend, the Irish Volunteers were preparing to stage the Easter Rising, setting in chain a series of events which ultimately led to Irish independence. On Sunday we will solemnly remember the 1916 leaders who gave up their lives, before moving to the historic surrounds of Croke Park for 'Laochra', which promises to be a spectacular celebration of our culture and the GAA movement over the last 100 years.[9]

The GAA was a key force in defining Irish identity in the late nineteenth and early twentieth centuries, and it was one of the most active organisations in 2016 in evoking that period and commemorating events surrounding the Rising. However, as suggested by the question mark in the title of this chapter – partly taken from the title of the penultimate scene in the *Laochra* pageant – it is debatable how 'new' the depiction of Ireland within *Laochra* actually was, despite its foregrounding of multiculturalism and women, given its gendered configuration of Irishness and glorification of militarism. Indeed, as examined below, the show's own contradictions and ambivalence are apparent in the scene 'A New Ireland Rises' in its combination of nondescript global cultural signifiers with iconography linked to Ireland and the island's past.

SPORT, NATIONAL CULTURE AND THE MEDIA

The relationship of sport with national culture and identity is complex yet crucial when considering the popularity and passions that sport evokes internationally. A key force in the promotion of nationalism is culture; as Ernest Gellner notes, 'culture is now the necessary shared medium',[10] and sport is one of the most popular of such cultural activities, contributing considerably to citizens' identification with their nations. Indeed, in emphasising the banality of nationalism as a 'natural' and often unnoticed part of everyday life, Michael Billig has argued that modern sport has a social and political significance that 'extend[s] through the media beyond the player and the spectator' by providing luminous moments of national engagement and national heroes whom citizens can emulate and adore.[11] As Billig's remarks suggest, the mass media has had a crucial role to play in the popularisation of sport and, indeed, in asserting its political significance. Cinema's potential, in particular, as a powerful vehicle for the articulation and affirmation of the nation has been recognised in critical studies.[12] Susan Hayward in her study on French cinema identified how film may function

> as a cultural articulation of a nation … [it] textualises the nation and subsequently constructs a series of relations around the concepts, first, of state and citizen, then of state, citizen and other … a 'national' cinema … is ineluctably 'reduced' to a series of enunciations that reverberate around two fundamental concepts: identity and difference.[13]

It is this process through which Irishness is 'textualised' through the *Laochra* pageant that is the key concern of this chapter.

Gaelic games have repeatedly provided the media with a resonant motif through which (perceived) aspects of Irish identity have been encapsulated and represented. In international productions in particular, Gaelic games have at times been employed as a shorthand for regressive stereotypes associated with Irish people, including their alleged propensity for violence.[14] For indigenous producers, however, Gaelic games have afforded distinctive Irish cultural practices and, as such, were employed to promote and affirm the Irish nation and Irish identity, particularly at points where established conceptions of both were being challenged or reconfigured.[15] This process extends to the contemporary context wherein Ireland has experienced huge changes, economically and socially, over the past twenty years. While Gaelic games are a less prominent feature of contemporary fiction film, this chapter contends that the cinematic has now been incorporated and integrated into major sporting events themselves, including *Laochra*. Furthermore, the mediatisation of *Laochra* reveals the continuing relevance of a range of themes in association with Gaelic games, including the employment of these sports as key markers of Irish identity and the association of hurling with violence.

SPORT AND COMMEMORATION

As Neil Jarman has contended, 'memories of past events are primarily maintained and structured within membership of a social group rather than by individuals'.[16] As a key facilitator of social gatherings and groups, sport is a crucial part of how events are remembered, particularly in Ireland where sport has such a prominent role. Moreover, as both Paul Rouse and Michael Cronin respectively have noted, sport has featured prominently in how the Irish state has projected itself nationally and internationally post-independence.[17] This process of national myth-making through sport has received increasing academic attention, including O'Boyle and Kearns' recent comparative analysis of sponsored national myth-making in Irish rugby and soccer, in which the authors identified how these 'modern sports contribute to the (re)definition of national identities in the context of increasing marketization and mediatization of sport at different levels'.[18] In another recent study, of the transnational football fan, David Rowe noted how, 'as sport becomes more global and transnational in nature, the national is constantly re-asserted as a locus of collective identification'.[19] The remembering and commemoration of 1916 in particular has throughout the twentieth century and into the twenty-first often been located and associated with sporting events, venues and organisations. On the fiftieth anniversary of the 1916 Rising in 1966, the key commemorative events (discussed below) were hosted in the GAA's principal stadium, Croke Park, reflecting the strong connection of the association at the time, as now, with the Rising.

William Murphy has established that some 302 GAA players from fifty-three clubs, almost one-fifth of the estimated 1,500 to 1,800 rebels of Easter Week, participated in the 1916 Rising.[20] Though the GAA's initial official response to the Rising in 1916 was to deny involvement, in subsequent years the association has

made considerable claims for a significant role in the event and its
aftermath.[21] Speaking on the eve of St Patrick's Day in 1966, then
GAA president Alf Murray highlighted the contribution of the GAA
to the Rising, and stressed that the association 'regards its national
attitude as an essential part of the obligation that history and
tradition impose upon us if we are to strengthen the Irish character
and provide at least a part of the spiritual background that ensures
the continuance of the struggle for the nation's soul.'[22] Fifty years
later, in 2016, the president of the association, Aogán Ó Fearghail,
reiterated these remarks in the programme for the *Laochra* event,
observing that 'The active patriotism that the Proclamation of the
Irish Republic of 1916 proclaims is alive and well in our GAA clubs
and counties. The vision of a Gaelic Ireland with a sense of duty and
loyalty to nation is what the GAA lives out on a daily basis.'[23]

THE PAGEANT FORMAT

Pageants have been a recurring feature of GAA commemorative
events, including for its fiftieth-anniversary commemoration of 1916
in 1966, when the association hosted not one but two pageants:
Seachtar Fear, Seacht Lá (Seven Men, Seven Days) and *Aiséirí: Glóir
Réim na Cásca* (Resurrection: The Easter Pageant). *Seachtar Fear,
Seacht Lá* was performed again in 2016 as part of the major annual
traditional-music festival Fleadh Cheoil na hÉireann. Written by
Bryan McMahon, it featured actors playing the seven signatories to
the Proclamation giving an account of themselves and their actions,
accompanied by a cast of nearly 400.[24] While McMahon's pageant
ran from 17–19 March (and was subsequently performed again in the
GAA's Casement Park, Belfast, during Easter Week), the GAA hosted
a second pageant in Croke Park from Monday to Friday of Easter
Week 1966. *Aiséirí: Glóir Réim na Cásca* presented a nationalist
and triumphalist portrayal of the Irish struggle from 1798 to the
establishment of the first Dáil in 1919, foregrounding in the process
the roles of Patrick Pearse, militarism and children with regard to
the Rising, as well as stressing the theme of the reunification of the
island – all prominent aspects of the 2016 *Laochra* event.

The choice of the pageant format to commemorate 1916 (whether
in 1966 or 2016) seems particularly appropriate: the Rising was itself

a peculiarly theatrical event, described by Declan Kiberd as one of the 'most theatrical insurrections in the history of western Europe', and the events of that week and some of the actions of leaders of the Rising would certainly lend credence to such an assertion.[25] Patrick Pearse famously wore an ancient sword during the entirety of the Rising, and eventually insisted on its formal handing over during his surrender to the leader of the British forces, General Lowe. Indeed, pageants had been popular at St Enda's, the secondary school for boys set up in 1908 in Ranelagh by Pearse, with the mythological warrior Cúchulainn often depicted as the leading figure.[26] As noted by Róisín Higgins,

> Pearse's ideal Irishman would have been 'Cúchulainn baptised' …while the St. Enda's boys looked to the vibrant youth of Cúchulainn before 1916, in the aftermath of the Rising it was the hero's sacrificial death that defined his legend in the popular imagination. This aspect of the Cúchulainn saga in turn became inextricably linked to the death of Pearse.[27]

Significantly, these two key events were re-enacted as the opening performance of *Laochra*: Cúchulainn's vibrant youth as the boy Setanta playing hurling, and his death as a warrior on the battlefield. Moreover, as elsewhere in the production, physical combat was highlighted and celebrated in this scene in a lengthy fight sequence as part of a recurring return to military elements throughout the pageant. Accompanied by a stirring orchestral accompaniment, this initial re-enactment elevates violent and militaristic elements from Cúchulainn's life. These aspects are combined with both Irish and English narration, with garments and iconography associated with pre-Christian Ireland, and with sophisticated cinematography, including the use of Steadicam to follow events on the pitch and pre-recorded inserts of a Cúchulainn-like figure (played by prominent former Cork hurler of Fiji extraction, Seán Óg Ó hAilpín) striking a *sliotar* aflame and attacking with a sword. The performance also comprised an inclusive cast featuring both women and people of colour. This integration of older motifs with a more multicultural and representative depiction of contemporary Ireland was a recurring if sometimes contradictory aspect of *Laochra*.

LAOCHRA

Writing in the *Freeman's Journal* in 1909 (in an article republished by Pearse in the Christmas edition of *An Macaomh*), the journalist and translator Stephen McKenna remarked on the revival of the pageant at that time, and praised it as a cultural form that could 'gather together the broken threads of our national history'.[28] An examination of the *Laochra* pageant reveals a similar process, whereby the 'broken threads' of Irish national history are gathered together in a seamless and energetic expression of contemporary Irish identity. *Laochra*, which can be translated as 'warriors' or 'heroes', followed the playing of the GAA's Allianz League divisional finals, and consisted of a specially commissioned half-hour stadium production featuring a cast of more than 3,500 performers. The pageant presented aspects of Irish mythology and history, and (unsurprisingly) highlighted the role of Gaelic games in that story.

There were two principal modes for experiencing the *Laochra* event; one, televisual (via broadcast on the Irish-language TV station TG4), the other theatrical, with significant cinematic elements for those present at the performance in Croke Park. The cinematic aspects were evident in the combination of different forms of live performance – including re-enactments of episodes in Irish mythology featuring hurling, Irish dancing and reading/singing performances – rendered for television broadcast through pitchside camera, dynamic Steadicam sequences, and pre-recorded archive footage screened on three of the largest high-definition outdoor screens in Europe. The use of Steadicam to capture the event added a peculiarly cinematic element to the rendering of *Laochra*: invented by the American cinematographer Garrett Brown, one of the first films in which Steadicam was used extensively was the seminal Oscar-winning sports drama *Rocky* (1976), a key text in defining and popularising the sport-cinema genre.[29] With regard to the screens in the stadium, while two screens are normally present in Croke Park, a third 90m^2 screen was installed in the Hill 16 part of the stadium, reducing the crowd capacity from 82,300 to 81,000. Nonetheless, even at 81,000 this was the largest crowd ever to attend a GAA league final, which preceded the *Laochra* event. In addition to those in attendance at the stadium, the *Laochra* event and the preceding league finals attracted the largest ever audience for a TG4 broadcast, 'earning TG4 a share

Figure 1. Opening shot of *Laochra* (Source: Tyrone Productions Ltd)

Figure 2. Ireland personified as woman in *Laochra*
(Source: Tyrone Productions Ltd)

of 38 per cent of all people viewing TV in Ireland...In total, almost three quarters of a million viewers (739,000)'.[30]

The cinematic/televisual aspects of the production reflect the background of the show's artistic director and producers. Artistic director Ruán Magan is an award-winning filmmaker who has worked primarily in the documentary format, including the three-part historical series *1916: The Irish Rebellion* (2016). *Laochra* was produced by the TV production company Tyrone Productions, one of the most successful producers of entertainment and documentary content on Irish television. The company was founded by John McColgan and Moya Doherty, the producers behind the phenomenally successful *Riverdance* theatrical show, and aspects of that dance phenomenon were also evident in the *Laochra* event.

Laochra opens by immediately connecting elemental and stereotypical images of Irishness with Gaelic games. The pre-recorded footage that begins the TV version (and was shown on the screens in the stadium) opens with a shot of the gold-coloured GAA crest set against an elemental background of water and fire (Figure 1). This dramatic initial image gives way to a shot of a red-haired woman (played by singer Sibéal Ní Chasaide) dressed in a green cape and looking out upon an Irish landscape, which is dominated by water in the foreground and features a dramatic mountain in the distance (Figure 2). This figure is returned to through pre-recorded inserts throughout the event, and it recalls a key trope in representations of Ireland – one that was also invoked in the GAA's 1966 pageant *Aiséirí*. As noted by Anthony Roche, 'the central, and virtually sole, female role [in *Aiséirí*] is the allegorical personification of Ireland as "Éire" or Cathleen Ni Houlihan'.[31] This figure also famously featured in W.B. Yeats' play of the same name. While women are featured more prominently within *Laochra* (including in the Cúchulainn sequence discussed above), their inclusion is problematically juxtaposed with the recurring employment within the event of more-traditional representations of woman as Ireland.

The initial opening shots were followed by a montage of images associated with Gaelic games, from crowd shots of supporters presumably on their way to a game, to shots of the pre-match parades of legendary teams from counties Cork, Kerry and Kilkenny (including prominent former Cork and Kerry players Christy Ring and Páidí Ó Sé), and to scenes of Irish Volunteers drilling, British soldiers marching, and a return to the female figure from the beginning. There is in these scenes an inevitable marching towards what would appear to be a shared goal, despite the fact that some of the marchers actually have little in common, particularly if we consider the footage of British soldiers and Irish Volunteers. That goal would appear to be bound up with the female image of Ireland. Notably, while the image itself is female, all the participants in the other images are male. This creates a clear divide between the active male participants in sport and revolution, and the passive female representative of Ireland. Such problematic gender stereotyping is also evident elsewhere in the production, though simultaneously

at odds with the inclusion of women in other aspects of the commemoration.

Subsequent to this prelude, *Laochra* is structured around nine
scenes titled respectively 'An Táin – Scéil Cú Chullainn' (discussed
above), 'The Darkening Light', 'The Brightening', 'For God and
Country', 'Uprising – 1916', 'Coming of Age', 'GAA Heroes', 'A New
Ireland Rises' and 'Is Laochra Muid Go Léir' (We Are All Heroes/
Warriors). As the titles suggest, the pageant is indebted to established
configurations of Ireland and Irishness within which the GAA is
centrally featured. A further key focus of *Laochra*'s narrative arc is
the Irish tricolour and the Irish national anthem – the show builds
up to a climactic rendition of 'Amhrán na bhFiann' (The Soldier's
Song), which is accompanied by the formation of the national flag
on the pitch and by spectators in the stands. Apart from sport,
Irish dance (particularly, though not exclusively, in its *Riverdance*-
influenced mode) is also a key aspect of this commemoration.

The pre-recorded opening sequence ends with a return to the
female figure in the landscape, before we enter the stadium to witness
the performed and theatrical elements of the commemorative event,
beginning with the re-enactment of aspects of the Cúchulainn saga
already discussed. The death of Cúchulainn is followed by the
singing of the well-known Irish language song 'Óró Sé do Bheatha
Abhaile' (Óró Welcome Home), the lyrics of which were written by
Patrick Pearse to a much older Irish tune. The song itself is quite
provocative, personifying Ireland in the figure of Gráinne Mhaol (or
the legendary pirate queen Grace O'Malley), who is 'coming over
the sea/ Armed warriors along with her as her guard/ They are Irish
themselves, not foreigners nor Spaniards/ and they will rout the
foreigners'.[32] The words of this song fit uneasily with the inclusion
of recent immigrants – the new Irish – in the commemorative event,
including the preceding re-enactment of the Cúchulainn saga. The
performance of this song leads into a lengthy sequence focused
on Irish music and *céilí* dancing, followed by readings of extracts
from speeches associated with leading political and cultural figures
in Irish history, including the GAA's founder, Michael Cusack. The
words chosen from Cusack, in particular, capture the juxtaposition
of militarism and sport evident throughout the commemorative
event: 'A warlike race is ever fond of games requiring skill, strength
and staying power.'

This sequence is followed by a further reflection on militarism, in particular the First World War, with readings from the writings of John Redmond, Edward Carson, Thomas Hardy and Stephen Gwynn accompanied by images from the war displayed on the stadium's screens and relayed to the television audience. This entire sequence lasts less than a minute before the much longer 'Uprising – 1916' (part 4) begins with an image of a burning Irish Republic flag followed by the singing of the nationalist ballad 'The Foggy Dew' (which chronicles the 1916 Easter Rising) by Lisa Burke.

There then follows the recitation of the 1916 Proclamation of the Republic by thirty-two children from thirty-two counties across the island. This sequence affirms a further key trope evident throughout the event: the island as a unified space, as reflected in the images featured in the commemoration, including the repeated use of the image of the island of Ireland. This sequence elides the partitioned nature of the island while again simultaneously affirming woman as the personification of Ireland. This is the case despite the inclusion of girls in the recitation; the scene ultimately concludes with a return to the iconic female image and the singing by Sibéal Ní Chasaide of 'Mise Éire' (I am Ireland), Pearse's iconic poem that imagines Ireland as an old woman who feels abandoned and betrayed by her children. As this song is sung, a map of Ireland is formed on the pitch and surrounded by volunteers waving the flags for each of the thirty-two counties of Ireland (Figure 3). This becomes the centrepiece for the remainder of the event, and highlights a recurring theme: a united Ireland. The combination of this image, the singing of 'Mise Éire', and the return of the female figure introduced at the opening of the event reaffirms this reading for the viewer.

The foregrounding of children in the reading of the Proclamation indicates a further key concern evident in the 1916 commemorations: the embedding and affirming of historical elements (including those associated with gender and militarism) within a contemporary Irish context while simultaneously eliding the ruptures and disjunctures within the nationalist narrative. This New Ireland, while modern, youthful and energetic, is problematically positioned in relation to iconography, configurations and sentiments of a much older Ireland, with sometimes contradictory or paradoxical results. These contradictions are managed through a robust fetishisation of military elements as part of an attempt to bring order to the evident

Figure 3. A map of Ireland is formed on the pitch during *Laochra*
(Source: Tyrone Productions Ltd)

inconsistencies. The recitations by children in this sequence, for example, were prefaced by the arrival into Croke Park of members of the Battle of Ashbourne Commemorative Committee re-enactment group dressed in replica uniforms of the Irish Volunteers who participated in the Rising; the Croke Park setting was also surrounded by military paraphernalia, including cannons from the period.

A NEW IRELAND RISES?

The tensions and contradictions evident throughout *Laochra* are all the more apparent in the penultimate scene, entitled 'A New Ireland Rises'. We have already discussed the resort to militarism as one response to these contradictions; a further consequence is the ambivalence that becomes apparent as *Laochra* develops towards established signifiers of Irishness, an ambivalence that shares parallels with changing discourses of Irishness identified by Diane Negra in association with late Celtic Tiger Ireland. In her 2010 essay 'Urban Space, Luxury Retailing and the New Irishness', Negra mapped a 'transformation in concepts and discourses of Irishness in the ambiguous phase in which Celtic Tiger affluence largely continued but its novelty and sense of contrast to a formerly quasi "Third World" Ireland at the European periphery had worn off'.[33]

In place of the previous nostalgic and traditional representations of Ireland, Negra identified instead

> a new discursive formulation that emphasizes the integration of Irishness and globalization (where once Irishness was positioned as a respite from it), a shift in the emotional palette of Irishness from warm to cool, an emphasis on Irish glamour and a focus on Ireland as the exemplary scene of capitalism.[34]

In this context, she contends, 'Irishness is often very lightly worn and can even operate in counterpoint to more anxious displays of national identity'.[35]

While Negra's comments have relevance to the *Laochra* event as a whole, this is particularly so when we turn to the 'A New Ireland Rises' scene, which, accompanied by fireworks and pyrotechnics, brings a modern and dynamic turn to proceedings. This 'New Ireland' is energetic, youthful, though ambivalent regarding established Irish iconography, combining nondescript global cultural signifiers with tropes linked to the island and Ireland's past. The scene begins with a return to a centrepiece image of the island of Ireland (with no indication of partition) surrounded by volunteers waving flags from each of the thirty-two counties (Figure 3). The music and performance, entitled 'Reel of Arrivals', in this sequence is taken from Doherty and McColgan's theatrical show *Heartbeat of Home*, a work clearly indebted to their earlier, more successful, show *Riverdance*. As a whole, *Heartbeat of Home* combines Latin and Afro-Cuban music and dance with Irish music and dance, and these influences are evident in the dance sequences featured in *Laochra*. The pre-recorded sequences – shown only briefly in the TV broadcast but continued at length on the screens in the stadium – emphasise a casual, contemporary and (in Negra's terms) 'cool' global youth culture (see Figure 4). The dancing itself (described in the pageant's script as 'fusion dance') has few features familiar from Irish dance; indeed, there is nothing that one could identify as distinctively or recognisably Irish. Even the locations are unfamiliar, and are certainly not typical of the locations usually associated with Ireland. This is an Irishness, in Negra's terms, 'very lightly worn', though it operates 'in counterpoint to more anxious displays of national identity' evident in the stadium performance.

Figure 4. Global youth culture as represented in *Laochra*
(Source: Tyrone Productions Ltd)

Figure 5. Dancers in *Laochra* wear black outfits styled with Celtic
ornamentation (Source: Tyrone Productions Ltd)

Figure 6. Gestures of dancers in *Laochra* with military connotations
(Source: Tyrone Productions Ltd)

Here, an updated version of the global phenomenon *Riverdance* is performed with a large troupe of dancers dressed predominantly in black outfits styled with Celtic ornamentation and reminiscent of monk costumes (Figure 5). Visually, the energy and dynamism of the performance is communicated through the employment of fast-moving Steadicam operators who race across the pitch to capture the many performers as they dance. However, a further progression is evident in these latter performances of Irish dancing. While ostensibly displaying a freer and less constrained style than that associated with *céilí* dancing (featured earlier in the event), this dancing also demonstrates a high degree of discipline reminiscent of military practice both in formation and expression. Indeed, the structuring of the performance as a robust encounter between the dancers and the drummers (many of whom are playing Lambeg drums, associated particularly with the unionist tradition in Ireland) affirms this connection. Furthermore, the formations created by the dancers as they gather on the pitch are reminiscent of military configurations, with gestures also of military origin (Figure 6). In these aspects, the 'New Ireland Rises' scene reveals a disciplining of Irishness itself – this is evident throughout the *Laochra* event with the integration of military elements and gestures into the performance of aspects of Irish culture – as a response to anxieties raised by the inherent contradictions evident throughout the show as a whole.

CONCLUSION

Sport and sporting venues were key parts of how 1916 was recalled and commemorated in Ireland in 2016. As the largest sporting organisation on the island, the GAA hosted one of the most significant of these events, the *Laochra* pageant held on the centenary of the first day of the 1916 Rising. The dynamic visual rendering of *Laochra* for broadcast on the Irish-language TV station TG4 reveals the incorporation of the cinematic into contemporary major sporting events, including the employment of Steadicam, pre-recorded footage and big screens to enhance the stadium experience. As evident in previous indigenous cinematic (and televisual) depictions of Gaelic games, the promotion and affirmation of the Irish nation and Irish identity were also key concerns. Indeed, the format of *Laochra* was structured to disguise and obscure the ruptures within Irish history and Irish politics. The show as a whole repeatedly worked to naturalise and normalise a narrative of Irish history and identity that placed the First World War and the 1916 Rising as parallel paths on this journey, largely ignoring the divided and contested nature of Irish history, identity and the island of Ireland itself. This is a version of Irishness that appeals to long-established, regressive and gendered configurations of Irishness while simultaneously seeming to promote a modern and multi-ethnic contemporary Ireland. Contradictions such as these contribute to the, at times, ambivalent construction of Irishness presented in *Laochra*, evident in the combination of nondescript global cultural signifiers with iconography linked to the island and to Ireland's past.

Laochra is ultimately an event that through its contradictions and paradoxes speaks to the uncertainties and anxieties concerning contemporary Irishness, particularly when placed in relation to established conceptions and configurations of Irish identity. While foregrounding aspects of the New Ireland – whether in terms of gender or ethnic composition – it ultimately does so within the frame of older Irish tropes that constrain the possibilities for a truly reimagined and reconfigured sense of Irishness in the twenty-first century. More problematically, it contributes to an exclusionary discourse that constructs a passive feminine and active and militaristic masculine space while obscuring the complex and ruptured nature of the Irish past and present.

From Team of Aliens to #TeamofUs: The evolution of Irish-rugby advertising, 2007–17

COLM KEARNS

IN 2018 THE IRELAND RUGBY union team achieved only the third Grand Slam in their history, defeating France, Wales, Scotland, Italy and England en route to winning the Six Nations Championship. The jubilant public reaction to this triumph prompted a media debate about whether rugby had displaced soccer and the codes of the Gaelic Athletic Association (GAA) as the 'people's game'. The substance (or lack thereof) behind this debate will be addressed later in this chapter, but that such a claim was made in the first place is particularly notable given that, only a decade or so earlier, rugby in Ireland was largely perceived as a niche sport played and followed by a small but significant coterie of the privately educated middle classes.

This chapter will attempt to trace this shift in the sport's cultural cachet through advertising. Taking on board John Fanning's assertion that 'iconic brands perform national identity myths that resolve cultural contradictions',[1] advertising is a useful lens through which to examine how and why sport can stand for shifting ideas of national identity. Specifically, it focuses on Irish-rugby advertising from 2007 to 2017, as this period was not only one of notable success and popularity for the Ireland rugby team but also one that saw realignment of Irish society following the disastrous end of the Celtic Tiger economic boom. Given that, as will be detailed later, many media commentators conflated the perceived values of the Celtic Tiger with those of the Ireland rugby team, this realignment is particularly significant with regard to public perception and media representation of the team. Gary Whannel's concept of vortextuality will be used to explore the debate over whether rugby had become the people's game in twenty-first-century Ireland and the significance of this with regard to the advertisements examined.

This chapter does not claim to be a comprehensive study of Irish-rugby advertising for the study period but, rather, attempts to examine ads that signal significant shifts in the manner in which brands attempt to celebrate Irish rugby through Irish identity (and, consequently, celebrate Irish identity through Irish rugby). In doing so, it will map out a rough chronological progression and attempt to illustrate how new paths have been opened for Irish rugby advertisers, in addition to expounding on the significance of such paths for the sport's role in wider Irish culture in the near future.

SPORT AND ADVERTISING

Sport has long occupied a prominent place in advertising and in advertisers' attempts to tap into sociocultural currents. David Rowe discusses the value of sport to advertisers in terms of its conceptual flexibility, arguing that it can 'connect the past, present and future, by turns trading on sepia-tinted nostalgia, the "nowness" of "live" action and the anticipation of things to come'.[2] For Rowe, this ability to evoke nostalgia, relatability and anticipation appeals to advertisers because of what he terms a 'values vacuum', a situation 'whereby many people feel alienated, no longer believing deeply in anything, identifying with anyone, or feeling committed to any cause outside the immediate interests of themselves and their significant others'. This situation affords advertisers the opportunity 'to help supply meaning and commitment that rapid social change under late modernity or postmodernity have evacuated from so many lives'.[3]

Rowe is far from alone in expounding on the broad motives and strategies of advertisers in shaping cultural values. Authors such as O'Barr, Toland Frith and Mueller, and Falcous have done likewise,[4] but his articulation of sport's distinctive potential to realise these strategies is particularly useful. Sport is one of the few activities that can generate a temporary sense of local, national and even international unity in a world characterised by 'rapid social change'.

Advertisers attempting to appeal to a sense of collective identity, to galvanise a wide audience without resorting to the most blandly accessible narratives and imagery, can use sport to elicit feelings of passion and loyalty that may reflect on the advertised brand. Furthermore, sport's status as a mediated spectacle and its use of shared symbols and language makes it relatively easy to depict effectively within the short duration or limited canvas of an ad.

Joseph Maguire sees sport's wider cultural significance as a local and national signifier as particularly important in an era of encroaching globalisation, writing that alongside 'a greater degree of interdependence' and 'an increased awareness of a sense of the world as a whole', there is a 'resurgence of the local/national. These elements are two sides of the same coin.'[5] Sport arguably provides the clearest manifestation of the 'imagined community' of the nation, grouping disparate athletes together on the basis of shared birthplace and heritage under the umbrella term of the nation and united by shared national symbols (team jerseys, colours, flags and so on). In addition, it provides a wider context for the nation and defines its place within that context by setting a national team against its international peers, thus legitimating both 'imagined communities' through their status as peers and opponents within the ordered field of sporting competition. With national identity seemingly under threat from the encroaching global, and with sentimental attachment to it resurgent as a reaction to this threat, it is therefore an ideal concept for advertisers trading upon the 'values vacuum'. Therefore, they turn to sport, as Falcous writes, 'capitaliz[ing] on the sport–nation nexus as a way of resonating with national markets in their promotional media'.[6] Sport allows advertisers to apparently resolve 'cultural contradictions' by presenting idealised versions of national identity that reconcile the nation's uncertain present and future with the supposed glories of its past.

RUGBY AND IRISH IDENTITY: A BRIEF HISTORY

As the only major international team sport to represent Ireland on an all-island basis,[7] rugby ostensibly possesses distinctly significant potential as a vehicle for realisations of Irish identity (commercial or otherwise), but for much of the history of the Irish state the sport was perceived as a niche interest, played and followed chiefly by the privately educated Anglo-Irish bourgeois (with the notable exception of Limerick, which will be discussed anon). In the early days of the emergent Irish state, rugby officials were acutely aware of this perception, and were often at pains to counter it. In 1925 an *Irish Times* columnist opined that 'rugby...is suited better perhaps than any other game to the temperament of the Irish race' since it is not separated by 'politics nor partition, class nor creed'.[8] Soccer, which even then was the sport with the greatest opportunity to represent the fledgling state on the international stage, was of course divided along partition lines (with separate teams for the Republic of Ireland and Northern Ireland) that early governments were apt to dismiss (most notably in Éamon de Valera's 1937 constitution, which laid claim to 'the whole island of Ireland, its islands and the territorial seas'). The GAA, the organisation embraced by governments and media of the early Irish state as most representative of the nation's identity, discriminated (in both official and unofficial ways) on grounds of religion and politics. Indeed, even de Valera – a figure singularly associated with a monocultural and premodern vision of Irish identity – advocated that rugby should occupy a more prominent position in Irish culture. Fondly recalling the game from his schooldays at Blackrock College, de Valera claimed that, alongside hurling, it was closer to the national spirit than any other sport.[9] The rugged physicality of rugby certainly chimed with the idealised visions of Irish manhood espoused by the Church and key political figures in the decades preceding and following independence. Maguire, among others, argues that national identity, masculinity and sport are often intertwined: 'For the practices of nationhood and national identity are also the expression of male identity. Little wonder then that sports play such an important role in representing these embodied identity-forming traditions.'[10] Rugby's potent potential to manifest notions of heroic Irish masculinity would prove significant in later years, but for much of the twentieth century its public prominence was limited.

The monocultural vision of Irish identity, built on an opposition to perceived tenets of 'Englishness' such as modernity, urbanism and Protestantism,[11] saw rugby largely excluded from national narratives. As O'Callaghan writes, 'The discursive line between Gael and West Brit was drawn, and for a significant and vocal body of opinion rugby was on the wrong side.'[12] For much of the twentieth century, rugby was viewed as too elitist and too heavily associated with the culture of the coloniser to be embraced widely by the media (news or advertising) as redolent of an Ireland still strongly tied to the Catholic Church and committed to celebrating an idealised imagining of rural life. Even as Irish identity liberalised – with Seán Lemass' economic reforms of the 1960s and the election of President John F. Kennedy in the US leading to the emerging idea that it was possible to 'be Irish and modern at the same time'[13] – rugby still lagged behind the GAA and, increasingly, soccer as a galvanising force in Irish culture and society. As Irish identity continued on this path of relative pluralisation, soccer emerged as representative of the new 'national spirit'. Soccer had long been dogged by many of the same problems as rugby, namely a relative lack of success for the international team and an abiding association with British culture. However, in the late 1980s and early 1990s, the team achieved notable success under the management of Englishman Jack Charlton, and came to be celebrated by the media and the wider public as embodying 'a different, more relevant form of "Irishness"…an Irish identity which can be celebrated, in Fintan O'Toole's words, "without being encumbered by the dark complications of the North"'.[14] Conversely, international media coverage of the Ireland rugby team, as late as the mid-1990s, continued to focus on Arnoldian tropes of wild but romantic Irish peasants.[15] Rugby, then, seemed unable to chime with the emerging ideas of Irish identity in the late twentieth century; according to Tuck, it was viewed as too alien and elitist within the country, and incongruously traditional by certain media elements outside of it.

Professionalisation of rugby union in 1995 saw a shift in the sport's fortunes. Despite opposing the international move towards paying players, the Irish Rugby Football Union (IRFU) coped well with the development. Irish rugby's provincial structure facilitated centralisation of authority and talent, and allowed for the nurturing of successive generations of skilled players from the beginning of the twenty-first century. Under the management of Eddie O'Sullivan, and later of Declan Kidney and Joe Schmidt, the Ireland rugby team enjoyed a period of unprecedented and consistent success in the early twenty-first century. This ascent in the team's fortunes roughly paralleled that of the Irish economy, as the Celtic Tiger economic boom gained steam in the late 1990s and early 2000s. Fuelled by a combination of European Union funding, a construction bubble, and international companies attracted by low corporation-tax rates, the Celtic Tiger wrought significant changes across Irish society: a country dominated by emigration for decades began to attract burgeoning immigrant communities, while the previous fetishisation of rural life was eclipsed by a triumphalist celebration of business acumen and entrepreneurial values. In this new cultural climate, the values of the Ireland rugby team were celebrated in the media as redolent of those of a newly confident Irish nation. Marcus Free cites the *Irish Independent*'s Justine McCarthy ('We want to win things…Being a Paddy no longer means being the loveable loser') and RTÉ's Tom McGurk ('This is a fully professional team. You could call it a Celtic Tiger rugby team') eulogising the team's transformation 'as a distinctly "native" exemplar of the "Celtic Tiger" economy'.[16] Even after the financial crash of 2008 brought an end to the economic boom and led to subsequent reticence about the values it had supposedly embodied, the rugby team continued to be championed as a standard bearer of enduring Celtic Tiger qualities.

Rugby therefore occupies a curious space in the contemporary media imagining of Irish identity. It remains dogged by associations with Anglo-Irish bourgeois society and privately educated elites, but the consistent success of the team offers a prominent platform for celebratory visions of Ireland within the legitimating field of international competition. Furthermore, the tendency to perceive and depict the team as redolent of Celtic Tiger Ireland (or, at least, the supposed best qualities of it) is complicated by an underlying discomfort concerning the shifts in Irish culture and society brought about by the economic boom and subsequent crash. There is an 'ambivalence about the implication of jettisoning one's past',[17] a feeling of cultural whiplash brought on by moving from tradition to postmodernity while hardly 'stopping at modernity along the way'.[18] Conversely, the potential of sport to act as a unifying force in 'a postmodern world, often characterised by "multiple commitments, weak affiliations, loose associations and tentative arrangements"', and of rugby, in particular, to serve as a rare channel 'to exemplify a particular brand of masculine heroism' in modern Ireland[19] may go some way to explaining the sport's appeal to advertisers despite such complicated cultural baggage.

RUGBY AND ADVERTISING IN POST-CELTIC TIGER IRELAND

With the Ireland rugby team achieving significant on-field success without entirely shaking off the sport's reputation as the pursuit solely of the privately educated, Irish advertisers are seemingly left with two options as to how to portray the team. They can opt to emphasise the players' prowess and play upon the physically demanding – and often violent – nature of rugby, depicting Ireland rugby players as superhuman figures engaged in titanic battles that transcend the class distinctions of contemporary Irish society. The alternative approach is to implicitly assuage any suspicions that the players are alienated from fans and consumers by grounding them with a sense of community and history. These two approaches can be termed 'the superhuman' and 'the human'. They are by no means mutually exclusive; they occasionally overlap, as the following examination will demonstrate, but the distinction between the two approaches serves as a useful lens through which to view attempts to present rugby as representative of idealised Irish identity.

These two approaches will be elaborated through textual readings of significant Irish-rugby advertising campaigns from 2007 to 2017. These readings will be further supported by interviews with rugby fans and an official from the IRFU in an effort to explore both the conscious effort of shaping the image of Irish rugby involved in the conception of such ads and the bedrock of public opinion on which such efforts must be based. This analysis is drawn from doctoral research into the relations between sport, advertising and Irish identity that drew on a variety of research methods, including the interviews and textual analysis cited here together with audience surveys, social-media analyses, and interviews with advertising and sponsor professionals. These methods were adopted with a view to conducting an in-depth study of sports sponsorship that pays equal attention to all of the financial and emotional stakeholders involved, and traces the fault lines in their relationships. Thus, there is no presumption of a linear process whereby the IRFU's desires for Irish rugby's identity are reflected unilaterally through the ads and transmitted to fans who unquestioningly internalise it but, rather, that the discourses circulated by these ads emerge from, and exist in, a fluid relationship with public perceptions and official narratives of the sport in which each shapes, and is shaped by, the others.

The former approach can be seen most clearly in the 'Born of Our Land' campaign (2009). Commissioned by Guinness to mark Ireland's Six Nations campaign, the televised ad of the campaign depicts a dark, mist-shrouded wilderness. Wood sprouts from the ground and forms into huge man-shaped figures. These figures roar and form themselves into the position of a rugby scrum before the camera zooms out and a voiceover utters the campaign slogan. Through its slogan and imagery, the campaign depicts Irish rugby players as mythical figures of superhuman strength while also emphasising their intrinsic Irishness (portraying them physically growing from Irish soil). It is notable, too, in echoing nineteenth-century nationalist rallying cries to make young Irishmen 'racy of the soil'. Popularised by Thomas Davis' Young Ireland movement and later revived by Arthur Griffith's *United Irishman* newspaper, the phrase weaves together Irish identity and masculinity into an apparent destiny conferred by nature and maintained by sport.[20]

Despite Guinness' status within Irish advertising and its continuing arrangements with Irish rugby, the campaign was not unilaterally well received by the IRFU. An official in the organisation's marketing department revealed that the campaign did not chime with the identity of Irish rugby that it wished to develop. The official said that the IRFU had consulted a branding agency to help them position

> the team as representative of the country; humble and hard-working, so it doesn't suit us if you bring out an advertising campaign that's kind of cocky and snide, or edgy and alien-type players. We see a lot of inconsistencies sometimes. Guinness brought out a campaign a couple of years back with men of this earth and it was kind of like aliens coming out of the ground.[21]

While the IRFU's firm ideas on the sport's brand identity do not preclude ads that take 'the superhuman' approach, they certainly point to a firm belief that such overt self-aggrandising mythologising should at least be tempered by a touch of 'the human'.

The 'humble and hardworking' identity the IRFU strives for is exemplified in one of 'Born of Our Land's' contemporaries, 'It's Who Stands Behind You That Counts', a September 2007 campaign commissioned by O2 in anticipation of the Rugby World Cup that month. The televised ad features ageing Irish rugby players running along a darkened rugby pitch. The ball is passed between successively younger players, beginning with Willie John McBride (who played for Ireland in the 1960s and 1970s) and ending in the hands of then Ireland captain Brian O'Driscoll, travelling via players who turned out for Ireland in the 1970s, 1980s and 1990s. The ad creates a sense of Ireland improving with time as the ball is passed to progressively younger and fitter players, but also fosters a sense of continuity between Irish rugby's past and present. Like Irish society, Irish rugby could also be perceived as experiencing a sense of cultural whiplash, as the move to professionalism had greatly impacted the expectations and organisation of the sport for both players and fans. Interviews with fans, advertising professionals and IRFU officials (conducted during the study on which this chapter is based) recorded various assertions that the fame and fortune of modern Irish internationals did not create any sense of alienation between them and their fans. However, it could be argued that the sense of continuity with the sport's humble amateur roots in media texts such as O2's ad campaign help foster such an optimistic view of the current relationship between players and fans (and, indeed, wider Irish society). John Fanning has expounded on the appeal of amateurism and local community for Irish advertisers, arguing that 'in twenty-first century Ireland there is a feeling that life is moving too fast, that we may be jettisoning too quickly tried and trusted ways of life that have served us in the past'. As a consequence of this feeling, he asserts, Irish advertisers can thrive by solving 'cultural contradictions' through presenting idealised depictions of Irish culture that give the impression that contemporary consumers can maintain a sense of authenticity and tradition while still striding boldly into modernity. Among these 'cultural contradictions' are the balance between 'affluence and affluenza' (reaping the benefits of wealth without succumbing to any erosion of traditional values) and the balance between global and local identity.[22] 'Who Stands Behind You' can certainly be viewed as an attempt to reconcile the former contradiction, while Guinness' 2014 campaign 'David and Goliath' attempted to reconcile both that and the latter concern about global and local identity.

Launched in November to mark the Guinness-sponsored Autumn Internationals, 'David and Goliath' adopted wholeheartedly the approach of emphasising the current Ireland rugby team 'as representative of the country; humble and hardworking' through drawing connections with the sport's amateur past. The ad was part of Guinness' 'Made of More' series which also featured concurrent ads produced for Scotland, Wales and England, the other 'home nations'. All four ads took the form of mini-documentaries, celebrating storied figures and events in each nation's rugby history. The Scotland ad focused on Bill McLaren, a player denied an international career by tuberculosis and who gained a second career as a legendary BBC commentator. The Wales ad celebrated Shane Williams, an enormously proficient winger who was initially derided as 'too small' to play rugby. The England ad features vox-pop interviews with the inhabitants of the French town of Toulon, who praise Englishman Johnny Wilkinson's performances and conduct while playing for their local club. The Irish ad, in contrast to these three, does not focus on an individual but on an event, the Munster rugby team's famous 1978 victory over the mighty All Blacks of New Zealand. The win has had significant resonance across Irish culture, inspiring a play (*Alone it Stands,* John Breen, 2004), a book (*Stand up and Fight*, Alan English, 2005) and numerous retrospective articles in the decades since it occurred. Until the national team defeated the All Blacks in Chicago in 2016, it marked the only time an Irish men's team had triumphed over New Zealand, a nation long regarded as the premier exponent of rugby union.

The ad is narrated by the well-known actor Colm Meaney, and mixes archival footage of the crowd and on-field action with a technique known as 2.5D parallax, which conveys the impression of photographs having been converted into moving images. Like the ads focusing on Williams and McLaren, 'David and Goliath' celebrates the heroism of the underdog, most directly through its title, but also through its narration, which positions the All Blacks as nigh-unbeatable giants of rugby:

> One team dominates the game of rugby: The All-Blacks. Rivals surrender before a ball has even been kicked. 'And that's your fate today', the Munster team was told. But none of them listened. Not even their smallest player. With a single tackle he stopped Goliath dead. And every Irishman grew twelve feet taller.

Where the Irish ad notably diverges from its Scottish and Welsh counterparts is in its focus on a regional triumph rather than on a national one. Williams' achievements for Wales, rather than his club, are highlighted, while McLaren's background as a player is contextualised by his missed opportunity to play for Scotland and his later career as a commentator with a national broadcaster. 'David and Goliath', on the other hand, attempts to transform a regional triumph into a national one. Meaney's narration describes how 'every Irishman grew twelve feet taller' with Munster's win, naturalising the notion that Munster's triumph should be read as Ireland's triumph. Indeed, Meaney's voice, with its pronounced Dublin accent, furthers the notion that the entire country should take pride in Munster's achievement.

Liam O'Callaghan describes how the traditional cross-class egalitarianism of Limerick rugby culture has been retrospectively mapped onto all of Munster through media mythologising of the province's supposed traditions (among which the 1978 win over the All Blacks occupies a much-vaunted place). The discursive expansion of Limerick's rugby culture across the whole province creates a valuable identity for Munster, giving the impression that they 'subvert the quintessential middle-class image associated with Irish rugby in general'.[23] With this in mind, 'David and Goliath' can be read as an attempt to further expand 'a humble image of the team complete with a marked sense of place' from beyond the borders of Munster to Irish rugby as a whole.[24] The ad aired during the November 2014 internationals, thereby positioning it in the mind of any viewer with even a casual knowledge of rugby as implicitly associated with the contemporary Ireland rugby team. Through drawing this connection between the nigh-forty-year-old triumph of regional amateurs and professional international stars of the modern era, the ad implicitly fends off any suspicions of alienation between players and fans, tacitly defending against any accusation that a team of highly paid athletes, largely drawn from fee-paying-school backgrounds, cannot appropriately represent Irish identity and galvanise nationwide support.

It must be noted that the ad was not breaking new ground in taking this approach. In a focus group with fans carried out as part of the study reported here, a long-time rugby fan argued that Munster acted as something of an accessible threshold into rugby fandom for those who had been sceptical about the sport in Ireland: 'Munster made rugby sexy in this country. Munster convinced large swathes of people outside Dublin that this was a game worth watching, and it was primarily because they weren't "the posh boys from Dublin".'[25] Drawing a thread from O'Callaghan's writing through this fan assertion and the 'David and Goliath' ad, it becomes evident that Munster rugby's value as a discursive tool emerges from its ability to tie the glamour of the professional era to its humble amateur roots. The fan described how Munster players were seen as 'the farmers, the lads from town', while O'Callaghan quotes media coverage that asserted that they were 'ordinary Joe Soaps, brought up in the local community', assertions that obscure the reality of modern Munster players as highly paid, elite athletes in favour of a portrayal of them as amateurs in spirit, rooted in the community through a commitment that, in some nebulous way, transcends financial imperatives and connects them to the fans through this shared passion.

The following year saw Three Ireland (the Irish branch of the international telecommunications brand) launch its first major advertising campaign for Irish rugby since becoming primary sponsor of the national team following its takeover of telecommunications rival O2 the previous year. The campaign, titled 'All it Takes Is Everything', featured three Ireland players (Johnny Sexton, Robbie Henshaw and Paul O'Connell) engaging in feats of superhuman mental and physical strength. Scenes of the players demonstrating their strength and resolve in fantastically heightened ways are intercut with one another, sound-tracked by a minimalist piano track, and underpinned by voice-over narration by Ireland head coach Joe Schmidt:

> These are…psychological battles, as much as they are physical ones. All it takes…is everything that you can dig out. Everything that you can process. Everything that you can physically deliver. All it takes is knowing that no matter who or what's coming at you, you'll be ready. All it takes is everything.

With its supernatural imagery and focus on the players' prowess, 'All it Takes' might be seen to be taking its lead from the 'alien' hero worship of 'Born of Our Land'. The former is undoubtedly more grounded than the latter, with Schmidt's narration emphasising the hard work involved in playing for Ireland and the players being depicted in recognisable (albeit dramatically heightened) surroundings, but the ad appears to be closer in tone to the super heroics of 'Born of Our Land' than the myth-making odes to the gritty past of 'It's Who Stands Behind You', leaning more towards 'the superhuman' with subtle underpinnings of 'the human'. However, the supplementary texts of the campaign point to a more nuanced approach that attempts to combine the thematic frameworks characterised by these two predecessors. In addition to the main televised ads and various promotional images (posters, billboards, Internet banner ads, and so on), the 'All it Takes' campaign featured various supplementary videos issued via Three Ireland's YouTube channel. Three of these are mini-documentaries detailing the roots and rise of each of the three players featured in the campaign. These mini-documentaries attracted considerable viewing figures,[26] and are evidently the products of considerable time and energy on the part of Three and Boys and Girls (the advertising agency that produced the campaign). As such, their significance to the narrative and themes of the overall campaign should not be overlooked despite their status as supplementary texts to the television commercial.

Each of the mini-documentaries traces the featured player's journey from childhood, through schooling, to their first forays into junior rugby, to their careers as professional rugby players and status as revered internationals. This transition is depicted as seamless, not only because of the short running time of these mini-documentaries (which compresses the narrative of each player's rise to fame over the course of three and a half minutes) but also through the manner in which interviewees related to the player's early life (relatives, teachers, and so on) reappear in sections detailing their current professional career, underlining the idea that the player's early life and community is crucial to his success in the international realm of top-level rugby. Indeed, the video focusing on Sexton ends with the player's godfather insisting that he is 'still that young boy' who practised by kicking the ball against the back wall of the family pub, while the video centred on Henshaw finishes with his grandfather asserting that fame has 'never made a bit of change to him'. Furthermore, the videos function to ground the players in a defined sense of place and community. Each video begins with a caption locating the viewer (and the player) in a distinct Irish town,[27] and soon afterwards emphasises the player's connections to elements of traditional Irish community. Henshaw's proficiency in Irish traditional music is lauded, O'Connell's ex-employer in the local supermarket is interviewed, and Sexton's connection to a rural Irish pub run by the family of a legendary Irish playwright is emphasised.

Free identifies this sense of rootedness as key to the public appeal of the Ireland rugby team in the Celtic Tiger and post-Celtic Tiger eras. He argues that the fact that the majority of the Irish rugby team – as opposed to their soccer counterparts – played for clubs based in Ireland contributed to them being portrayed in the media as sincere standard-bearers for their community rather than mercenaries working for foreign clubs. He also describes how Munster's 2006 and 2008 Heineken Cup victories were frequently ascribed to the passion the players summoned up in their efforts to do their community justice: 'notions of playing for "the parish" and "the jersey," representing family and community, were frequently invoked'.[28] The bio videos' seamless transition from local community to national stardom conveys a similar sense of rootedness, allowing playing for Ireland to mean simultaneously representing the whole country and each player's particular local community (and, indeed, achieving the former through the latter). It could be argued, too, that this approach further bolsters the masculinity of the players. The 'posh boys from Dublin' described by one of the fans interviewed were once derided as 'Leinster ladyboys' by elements of the media and rival supporters, an insult that implicitly conflated their failure at the top level of the sport with a perceived unmanliness caused by their apparently cosseted lives. The 'All it Takes' campaign frames the featured players – and, by inference, their Ireland teammates – as bastions of idealised masculine qualities: decisiveness, determination, toughness and humility.

This approach of grounding professional rugby superstars through affirmation of their connections to elements of traditional Irish community rather than explicitly connecting them to the sport's amateur past was deemed successful enough to be worthy of emulation by Vodafone, Three's successor as primary team sponsors. Its 2017 campaign 'Who We Are is How We Play' echoes 'All it Takes' in many ways, but seems to be specifically influenced by the earlier campaign's mini-documentaries rather than its televised commercial, distinctly emphasising 'the human' over 'the superhuman'. Vodafone's campaign focuses on four players (Rory Best, Conor Murray, Tadhg Furlong and Tiernan O'Halloran), who are individually showcased in four short televised commercials. These commercials depict each player's rise from his childhood infatuation with rugby to his ascent to the revered status of Ireland international, essentially presenting a compressed, dramatised version of the narrative depicted in the mini-documentaries of 'All it Takes'. The Three campaign's documentary approach is eschewed in favour of having actors play younger versions of the featured individuals before culminating in shots of the players themselves in the dressing room before a match. The similarities between the campaigns are illuminating; much like the bio videos of 'All it Takes', 'Who We Are' strives to ground the players within perceptions of traditional Irish community and culture. Vodafone head of brand and communications, Anne Mulcahy, stated as much:

> The focus of the 'Who We Are is How We Play' is the real, regular people behind the players' on pitch personas. While they may be capable of extraordinary feats when they put on an Irish rugby jersey, they have had upbringings and experiences that every Irish person can relate to – whether it's your mother telling you for the fifth time to come in for your tea or memories of going to your first match with your dad. It was important for us to share these moments with Irish rugby fans and connect them with the players on a more personal level, because ultimately you shout louder for someone you know.[29]

Like its predecessors, 'Who We Are' demonstrates an implicit awareness of its audience's predisposition to view rugby players as disconnected from what they regard as authentic Irish society and culture. It is interesting that the Vodafone campaign opts to connect past to present in a less tangible way than the direct evocations of Irish rugby's (and, by extension, Ireland's) history in 'It's Who Stands Behind You' and 'David and Goliath'. Instead, 'Who We Are' follows from the mini-documentaries of 'All it Takes' in evoking the players' pasts to convey a sense of rootedness that grounds their dizzying cosmopolitan present in the realm of relatable Irish culture. Nostalgia is implicit in the idealised evocations of the players' childhoods in the Vodafone and Three campaigns, but it is not foregrounded to the degree that it was in earlier campaigns. Again, there is a note of idealised masculinity as the ads trace the growth of boys into men – the players mature as people but maintain a continuity with their childhood dreams.

CONCLUDING REMARKS

Vodafone had the good fortune to be taking over as primary sponsor of the Irish rugby team at a time when the team was experiencing a period of significant success. In November 2016, mere months after Vodafone had taken the baton from Three, Ireland defeated the reigning world champions, the formidable New Zealand All Blacks, for the very first time. In early 2018, while the 'Who We Are' campaign was still being aired, Ireland won the Six Nations Championship, completing a Grand Slam in the process. As was alluded to at the beginning of this chapter, the success and the rapturous reception of it in the media and among the wider public triggered media discussions about rugby's popularity in the country and its significance to Irish society.

Claims at the time that rugby had become the 'people's game' were met with derision from soccer and GAA fans, but also from more ostensibly neutral observers in the media who were quick to point out that the relatively low attendance and participation figures for rugby (beneath the sport's elite level as represented by the Ireland team) undercut claims that it was the most culturally significant or socially prominent of sports in the country. In *The Irish Times*, journalist Mary Hannigan noted that the RTÉ panel discussion that sparked the debate was comprised entirely of rugby coaches and pundits with an implicit bias towards championing the sport above others.[30] Nevertheless, the substance (or lack thereof) behind the self-interested assertions that sparked this debate is of less significance to us here than the fact that such a debate was engaged in at all. The idea of the 'people's game' is a fundamentally intangible concept, but it is one that can be illuminated by Gary Whannel's idea of 'vortextuality'. Whannel differentiates between 'the majority of sport on television, watched by small audiences, [in] regular routinized slots, often well outside peak viewing times'

and vortextual sporting events that 'dominate the headlines' to
the extent that 'it is difficult for columnists and commentators to
discuss anything else, even if they have no abiding interest'. Central
to vortextual sporting events is the manner in which they compress
the media agenda so that 'other topics either disappear or have to
be connected to the vortextual event...cartoons, radio phone-ins,
celebrity columnists, news magazines, cultural commentators, and
letter pages are all drawn in'.[31] Whannel discusses this concept in
international terms, referring to the general vortextual impact of
events such as the FIFA World Cup and the Olympics. However, its
significance can be applied in a local–national context in which the
performance of a national athlete or team on an international stage
commands enormous attention in their home country's media space.

Essentially, the idea of the 'people's game' can be read as an
argument over which sport creates the most vortextually absorbing
moments. In this, of course, lies the crux of the contradiction
behind this oft-trumpeted phrase 'the people's game', which refers
more to media interest and attention than to any more-organic
form of communal engagement. This may be particularly relevant
to the case of Irish rugby, which some have argued benefits from
disproportionate media attention owing to the preponderance of
media management personnel drawn from rugby-school backgrounds.[32] Nonetheless, the fact that such a debate could be
entertained certainly has significant ramifications for sponsors and
advertisers seeking to leverage Irish rugby into fostering positive
feeling for their brands across the country. 'Who We Are' and the
media reaction surrounding Irish rugby at the time of the campaign's
release point to a future in which rugby advertisers may compete with
those focusing on the GAA for the discursive territory of conflating
sport with notions of traditional community and authentic culture
in Ireland.

Fanning points out that GAA players have long held a
mythologised status in Irish culture (not least in advertising) as
symbols of community spirit and selfless passion, drolly noting that
'the level of heroism has now become a little demented, but the
advertising industry was never one to hide its hyperbolic light under
a bushel'.[33] While 'Who We Are' may in many ways follow on from
the approach of the mini-documentaries of 'All it Takes', arguably its
most direct antecedent in terms of Irish televised advertising is 'Club

and County', an Allied Irish Bank-commissioned 2015 campaign that depicts the rise of individual GAA stars from infancy to All-Ireland success. Like 'Who We Are', each ad in the campaign focuses on an individual player, and depicts his rise to the top of his sport with rapid montage, conveying a sense of seamlessness that implicitly emphasises the importance of his upbringing and community (most prominently through celebrating his local club). The GAA's claims to this discursive territory may seem stronger owing to its players' amateurism and the organisation's prominence within official national narratives of independence and cultural revival. However, Free argues that Irish rugby has been able to successfully maintain a perception of balance between ruthless professionalism and rooted amateurism, claiming that elements of the former are all the more palatable 'because [they are] more easily anchored in an ideal of communal service, rootedness, amateur ethos, and professional training as education and "home grown" development through the provincial "academies"'.[34] Rugby advertisers are therefore well placed to pursue strategies that position Irish players and teams as simultaneously internationally renowned and nationally authentic, neatly assuaging one of the cultural contradictions outlined by Fanning with regard to wider Irish society.

Furthermore, while GAA players' amateurism has seen them celebrated as paragons of loyalty, passion and self-sacrifice by Irish advertisers, there are indications that rugby players may now be beginning to be perceived as champions of similar virtues, but from a professional parallel to GAA's vaunted amateurism. The private-school associations that had previously seen rugby regarded with suspicion as redolent of Anglo-Irish culture may now be portrayed and perceived as indicative of intellectual prowess and an admirably professional outlook. A long-time rugby fan interviewed for this project, unprompted, championed the academic achievements of rugby players, asserting that 'Somebody told me that St Gerard's school last year, the senior cup team, the average score in the Leaving Cert was 510 points. They're authentic sportsmen primarily, but they also stick with the academic side because they know the career is short.'[35] The idea of rugby players as distinctly academic sportsmen is not limited to fan anecdotes; Free has noted the preponderance of former rugby players on the after-dinner speaking circuit of the business realm.[36] The professional veneer conferred by academic achievement (or the perception of it) contributes to the idea that the qualities that made them successful in the field of sports are naturally transferrable to the world of business. This idea can also be seen in a range of business articles that centre on what business professionals can learn from the leadership and tactical qualities of top rugby players. These professional values are now being perceived as cause for admiration of rugby players as paragons of mental prowess, rather than as cause for suspicion of them as members of the privately educated bourgeois. If rugby players can, as McSharry discusses, 'embody the meaning of heroism in the modern Irish context' with regard to masculinity, then this ability to apparently combine rugged physicality with intellectual nous is key to furthering that perception. Setting this development alongside recent ads effectively celebrating the supposed quasi-amateur virtues of the sport (community spirit, self-sacrificing determination, and so on), it seems that rugby is well placed to 'solve' cultural contradictions of modern Ireland.

However, the cultural and commercial cachet of Irish rugby was dealt a significant blow in the latter half of 2017 and early 2018 over the course of what became known as the 'Belfast rugby rape trial'. The trial involved charges of rape and attempted cover-up. Irish rugby players Stuart Olding and Paddy Jackson, two of the four defendants, were specifically accused of the sexual assault of a nineteen-year-old Belfast student. Though they were found not guilty in March 2018, the verdict was contentious for significant numbers of the Irish public. Furthermore, the revelation of misogynistic WhatsApp messages exchanged between the four men stoked public anger and led to media debates about the influence of their professional rugby-playing lifestyle on their attitudes towards women. A month after the verdict, the IRFU cancelled Jackson's and Olding's contracts with Irish rugby, citing the organisation's commitment to maintaining 'the core values of the game; respect, inclusivity and integrity'. It is difficult not to discount the influence of sponsors in this decision, many of whom made their discomfort with the trial clear to the IRFU and the wider public.[37] It remains to be seen whether the decision to quickly wash their hands of the players in question will preserve the positive image of Irish rugby in the long term. Viewing figures for Ireland's opening 2019 Six Nations fixture against England would suggest the sport has lost little of its public appeal in the immediate aftermath of the trial controversy.[38]

Notably, too, 'Everyone In', the Vodafone-commissioned TV ad that aired throughout the competition, leaned further towards the idea of the Ireland rugby team attracting a national community of diverse supporters, suggesting that, in the short term at least, advertisers seem confident that the public perception of Irish rugby will ride the storm of the rape-trial controversy in the wake of Jackson's and Olding's contractual terminations. Nevertheless, the controversy raises interesting points with regard to McFarlane-Alvarez's arguments about the simultaneous appeal and unreliability of 'brand ambassadors'.[39] It could be argued that the abstract notion of the Ireland rugby team is of greater importance to Vodafone (or any other sponsor brand) than individual players, who appear in ad campaigns purely in the capacity of representatives of the team. In this manner there appears to be a distinct flexibility to the symbolic power of Irish rugby (or Irishness in general), allowing it to trade on the personal appeal of individuals without being tied as closely to them as traditional 'brand ambassador' arrangements.

Ultimately, the rough trajectory of Irish-rugby advertising over the last decade illuminates a growing confidence in the sport's resonance within Irish culture, but it is a confidence that is nonetheless underpinned by an awareness of the need to foster such a resonance. The methods of achieving this have shifted from more-overt appeals to a mythologised past characterised by idyllic amateurism to more-subtle efforts to ground present players within an Ireland that is at once modern and traditional. The idea of the sport becoming the 'people's game' in Ireland may be just fatuous headline fodder, but as the Irish rugby team increasingly becomes the focus of vortextual media attention, the manner in which its social and cultural significance is discussed alters significantly; so, too, do the strategies employed by advertisers to tap into this significance. The success of these strategies in managing to at once accentuate the positives of the sport's private-school, professional-class associations while also grounding it in more palatable and familiar tropes of Irish community and identity points to distinct flexibility in 'the human' approach to rugby advertising.

PART III

ॐ

Women, Media and Sport in Ireland

CHAPTER SEVEN

Media Sport, Women and Ireland: Seeing the wood for the trees

KATIE LISTON AND MARY O'CONNOR

THINK OF WHAT IT IS TO A young woman to grow up to adulthood today – in an era of burgeoning participatory social media especially – in the belief that without any merit or any fault of her own, though she may be the most committed, able and the most stalwart of sportspeople, by the mere fact of being born a female she is the inferior of her male sporting peers. That this woman does not conform to traditional sex roles often makes her the recipient of micro aggressions, including the assumption of inferiority and her objectification in media portrayals of her achievements. Consider, too, those women who, bolstered by the increasing support available to them, gain access to the boardrooms of professional and high-ranking amateur sports teams and franchises, and to the dressing rooms for players and officials that initially were not sex-segregated or designed for access by and to women, with varying degrees of success. They experience physical-body, oral-language and communication forms that accompany male exclusivity. Body shaming was/is a norm for women in sports, as was changing/locker-room 'banter', which reinforced implicit and explicit sexism and misogyny. Serena Williams, for instance, is treated differently because of her 'race, her physique and her talent', and her sister Venus has sought to reclaim her right to be physically strong. In 2015 Venus Williams spoke about her focus on being strong on court and enabling her body to perform well, rather than public perceptions of how she looks.[1]

In the context of sport the historical legacies of exclusion from modern competitive forms around the world, especially those associated with more traditional forms of masculinity, have meant that, today, girls and women are usually underrepresented at all levels of sports relative to boys and men: for instance, as participants (athletes and officials) on the playing fields and courts (Cooky, Messner and Hextrum highlight that females comprise 40 per cent of participants but less than 5 per cent of televised media coverage);[2] on the sidelines, whether as coaches, managers or trainers (for example, Reade, Rodgers and Norman highlight disproportionate gender ratios in high-level coaching positions in Canada);[3] behind the scenes in policy-making and decision-making roles, such as team owners, executives, leaders on boards, sports journalists, and so on. No real progress has been made with regard to the number of women on international sports boards, there being varied progress across countries and within individual sports.[4] In the mediated sports world, too, women are a minority in traditional and newer forms of media coverage of sport.

This chapter considers the social and cultural issues relevant to the relationship between mediated sport and women. In the complex interplay between mass communication and sport, continuities and some changes can be seen in media coverage of sportswomen, which have implications for women's sense of place and belonging in the field of sport. Drawing on the authors' cumulative extensive personal and professional roles in sport (as former high-performance athletes, as a senior academic and sports administrator respectively, and as professionals who are consulted by, and contribute to, traditional and new sports-media outlets), the chapter first examines the paradoxical marginality of Ireland from the growing research on sport and gender. This is followed by a brief discussion of why media sport matters, conceptually and in practice. Attention is then given to various sociocultural and media sport dynamics that are shown, through empirical research, to lead to the reproduction of (mediated) sport as a largely male preserve, internationally. Thereafter, the empirical focus shifts to the 20x20 campaign. Launched in October 2018 to generate a cultural shift in gendered perceptions of sportswomen, its founding premises and early reception are examined. The closing section focuses on the future challenges associated with such cultural change, and on the interplay between conformist and challenging voices, and offers commentary on the potential for mediated discourses to reframe our understanding of women and sport.

IRELAND, SPORT AND MEDIA

In the expanding research on media sport and women internationally, Ireland is noticeable by its relative absence. Yet it is home to one of the largest national women's sports organisations in Europe, the Ladies Gaelic Football Association (LGFA), formed in 1974. By 2018 the LGFA had approximately 188,000 youth and adult members, all amateurs, which represented an estimated increase of more than 80,000 since the mid-2000s. Attendance at the finals of the LGFA's premier competition – the All-Ireland Championship – reached a world-record figure for attendance at a national or international women's sports event of 50,141 people in 2018, and the match, broadcast live on TG4, the national Irish-language station, took a 26 per cent share of the television audience.[5]

Individual sportswomen from the island have also achieved considerable success nationally and on the world stage in their respective areas of expertise: individually, Michelle Smith, Bethany Firth and Mona McSharry (swimming); Olive Loughnane, Sonia O'Sullivan, Derval O'Rourke, Mary Peters, Ciara Mageean, Maeve Kyle and Catherina McKiernan (athletics); Natalya Coyle (pentathlon); Katie Taylor and Kellie Harrington (boxing); Kelly Gallagher (skiing); Rosemary Smith, Nicole Drought and Danielle Murphy (motorsport); Leona and Lisa Maguire (golf); Wendy Houvenhagel and Caroline Ryan (cycling); Rachel Blackmore, Nina Carberry and Katie Walsh (horse-racing); Annalise Murphy (sailing); and Sanita Puspure (rowing). In such team sports as rugby union, soccer, hockey, basketball and Gaelic games (football and camogie), some athletes have won honours in more than one; these include Cora Staunton, Katie McCabe, Sarah Rowe, Lynsey Peat, Claire Molloy, Nora Stapleton, Briege Corkery, Hannah Tyrell, Yvonne Bonner, Ailish Considine, Lucy Mulhall and the two authors. Prominence has also been achieved by female sports presenters on popular television channels: Marie Crowe, Rachel Wyse, Jacqui Hurley, Joanne Cantwell, Sinéad Kissane, Máire Treasa Ní Dhubhghaill and Grainne McElwain.[6]

Ireland is of considerable interest given the social changes that have taken place in gender relations more widely, especially in the roles fulfilled by women. Having transformed from a largely conservative society in the Republic, in which women's (especially mothers') bodies and minds were, to a large degree, controlled by the Catholic Church's teachings on sex, fertility control and motherhood, today Ireland is a multinational, cosmopolitan, globalised society. Regarded internationally as having introduced progressive social change – including same-sex marriage by referendum, a relaxation of restrictions on abortion (in the Republic), an Electoral (Political Funding) Act that incentivises political parties in the Republic of Ireland to select at least 30 per cent female candidates for general elections, an active female caucus in the Stormont Assembly in Belfast, two female presidents since the 1990s, and female leaders of political parties – a space has been opened up for women's experiences to a degree not seen previously. Research from a range of organisations, such as the Rape Crisis Centre, the National Women's Council of Ireland, Women's Aid (North and South), and various efforts, including business,[7] Women for Election, #WakingTheFeminists, and so on, has crystallised attention around this social space. There is now, more than ever before, a greater desire to hear from, and listen to, women about their experiences.

The media landscape, too, has changed quite significantly since the early twentieth century. But, as O'Connor has suggested, middle-class, white men have managed, through their dominance of this and other key social institutions – such as Churches, state and schools – 'to get a stranglehold on *meaning*. What it means to be a man, what it means to be a woman.'[8] Discussions abound regarding the nature, control and function of media on the island. The emergence of new newspaper titles, including tabloids, in the 1970s contributed to a sharpening of competition in the media landscape. This was the same decade in which the marriage bar was finally removed for women working in the Irish civil service (it was lifted in 1957 for primary teachers), when the 'Contraceptive Train' travelled from Dublin to Belfast,[9] and when the LGFA, the Women's Football Association of Ireland and the Northern Ireland Women's Football Association were formally established within years of each other.[10] In 1979 the Irish national public-service broadcaster RTÉ also set up an internal working group on the issue of a more balanced gender representation (its report was published in 1981). By the mid-1990s, electronic media were opened up to broader commercial interests, and print-media titles were rationalised at regional and local levels. An Irish-language television station, TG4, was established in 1996, the majority of staff then female, and that became critical to the subsequent success of the LGFA. In the Irish media landscape, the last two decades have been characterised by the emergence of new radio stations and a national commercial-television competitor for the established public-service broadcaster in the Republic of Ireland. Globalisation has begun to affect all Irish media, leading to a situation of 'extraordinary pluriformity'.[11] Today, the narrative of inclusion prevails in media production and coverage North and South (vis-à-vis women and other minority groups), but questions remain as to whether and how media sport organisations have sought, formally or otherwise, to interrogate the existence of gendered assumptions in their various policies and practices. In light of this, it is claimed, rather unreflexively, that a lack of media coverage of women in sport is an objective reflection of market forces and the public's lack of interest.[12] Here, the simplistic premise – that there is a lack of interest in women's sports – is as much in need of deconstruction, and requiring substantiation, as is the naive conclusion that a lack of media coverage is an unfettered reflection of the production–reception chain.

In this context, sports play a secondary but nonetheless important reinforcing role in sustaining forms of male dominance in Ireland. Twentieth-century sport in Ireland was largely a male preserve.[13] Noting a paucity of research into the sport–gender nexus on the island, Liston[14] illuminated the shifting boundaries between the sexes in sport and, in so doing, observed a slow but gradual accommodation in relations between them. This impacted on the ways in which sportswomen viewed themselves, but also on how men have responded to them. Whereas, in the past, the degree of contempt for women in sport was stronger and more explicit, today this ideological construction is undergoing change. Those sports regarded as traditionally appropriate for males – characterised typically by high levels of physical contact or confrontation, a culture of risk and a 'mock' battle – reveal the cutting edge of this shifting boundary. The organisational consciousness attached to sports played by males is that of a group of higher social value, as is the general view of the wider public toward them. Women's increasing participation in sport has generated various kinds of resistance, involving some formal organisational changes (around funding and the establishment of development roles and women's sports committees, for instance) as well as informal adaptations by sportspeople, positive and negative. Having been socialised into a position of privilege, any move towards equality can feel like oppression to some males who cling to sport especially as their primary source of masculine identity. Women, too, have responded in different ways. For example, numerous commentaries – radio, television, print and e-media – on women in sport highlight the 'good news' story: that greater resources are now being allocated, comparatively speaking, in line with a value commitment to equality and inclusion. After all, women have now arrived at the sports fields, play courts, sports clubs and commentary boxes on the island of Ireland. But far fewer argue for *more* resources to be given to sportswomen relative to men, in order to attain a measure of gender equity and to mitigate the historical legacy of underdevelopment. This raises the question of how sportswomen are framed: against what standard, and whether and why they might be perceived as having earned the right to some, more, or greater resources.

Dunne,[15] too, has acknowledged a dearth of research, particularly in relation to analyses of gender and media coverage of sport in Ireland. Despite a recommendation from a 2004 Oireachtas joint-committee report on women in sport, which was co-edited by the first author here, there has been no action to instigate longitudinal research into the scope and nature of media reporting of women's sports. Individual research studies are thus the starting point. Free, for instance, highlighted the antinomies of Irish female boxer Katie Taylor in print and broadcast-media representations.[16] He provides useful illustrations of the celebration of her combative physicality, speed of punch, and boxing skill/technique on one hand, but on the other hand her construction as a figure of cultural and gendered conservatism. Equally, the underrepresentation and marginalisation of Irish sportswomen in a major broadsheet newspaper, *The Irish Times*, is confirmed by Dunne elsewhere in this collection, who found that, during a four-month study period, less than 4 per cent of sports images were of women. He also notes a very heavy bias towards coverage of certain sports in this national newspaper.

The overall effect of this was, he argues, that women in sport in Ireland were continually undervalued. When it comes to media sport, then, of what we do know, Ireland is broadly similar to most other countries. This is because the challenges of sexism (overt or careless), stereotyping and gender bias are almost intractable 'across time, space and content delivery platforms'.[17]

MEDIA SPORT MATTERS

Media sport refers to the communication of sports themselves (events, results, and so on) and of various explicit and implicit sporting and non-sporting messages that accompany this. Competitions, events, games and matches are not experienced in the immediate space where they take place but, rather, through an increasing variety of media formats – for example, traditional formats such as radio, television and newspapers, as well as via new and participatory media such as online news, live streaming, videos, blogs, communication platforms (for example Facebook and Twitter), and so on. In the sport-media commercial complex,[18] which is increasingly a global economic nexus, media sport has become so popular that even Rupert Murdoch has used it as a 'battering ram' to generate more pay-television subscribers.[19] Academics generally agree that the overall effect of mediated discourses is to naturalise key identity markers such as gender. In this construction, *who* and *what* counts, as do the *ways* in which they appear to matter. As a result, Toni Bruce has argued that 'there are strong theoretical and empirical reasons why we should pay attention to how the mainstream and increasingly web-based and social media talk about, write about, and visually represent sport'.[20]

Media sport marks women's bodies and behaviours in various ways – some explicit by their absence – such as their under-representation and marginalisation in media reporting. Yet others are more implicit in terms of the quality and types of coverage, such as technical camera work and editing across various media forms or the sexual humour and careless sexism that can accompany such coverage. As a result, 'regardless of what is actually happening (live in the sports space), it is the media's interpretation of that event that shapes our attitudes, values and perceptions about the world and

about our culture'.[21] In other words, the ways in which the public
views and consumes sport is shaped, to a greater or lesser degree, by
the manner in which it is framed by various media. Noteworthy in
this regard are the most recent (2015) findings of the Global Media
Monitoring Project, which reveals that sport is least likely to be
reported by women globally and is among the top three topics in
which women are least likely to appear. Women comprise 13 per
cent of the news subjects in sports-related topics, while men make
up 87 per cent of the news subjects in sport, worldwide.[22] This led
to calls to increase media content about sportswomen, not only
quantitatively but also qualitatively, in ways that challenge gender
stereotypes and the idea that sportswomen are somehow 'out of
place', and to develop journalists' awareness of gender issues in
reporting.

SPORTING WOMEN: 'NOT IN THE RIGHT PLACE'?

As the assumption goes, the presence of more women in sport,
examples of which were noted above, leads to greater equality.
'Add women and stir' is a liberal-feminist-inspired approach that,
put simply, is based on the expectation that women's greater
participation and visibility in sport, on and off the field of play
and in media sport, will be a force for good, in and of itself. Ergo,
in media sport, more women in sports journalism and as topics
of sports reporting will bring about positive change. Not to deny
the desirability of more coverage of women's sports as a general
principle, this assumption takes credulity too far if the implication
is that gendered politics would be so easily transformed. Often
used as a proxy measure of equality, the increased presence of
women in sport is not quite the same as inclusion or equity. Such
an increase does not (necessarily) challenge the long-standing
historical production of sport: for men, by men, about men. Why?
Because, for female journalists in one study,[23] the 'macho' habitus
that prevailed in sports journalism meant that they felt 'they [were]
not in the right place'. They felt constrained to negotiate their sense
of place in sport. 'More' is not simply 'better' in the face of the
historical consolidation of hegemonic power and privilege of men,
which is generally reflected in media sport. As Dunne puts it in this

collection, 'a symbiotic relationship exists between the media and sport whereby sport represents a social institution that normalises the hegemonic power and privilege men have historically held over women, which is consolidated by the manner in which sports are reported by the media'.[24] The larger questions are whether and how the momentum gaining around women in sport will translate into meaningful changes in policy, in discriminatory practices, and in the social and cultural value systems that operate in the media-sport landscape. This is important because a number of practices have been identified internationally in research into the patterns of media coverage that, considered together, are 'insidious' in nature and effect.[25] These are: gender marking, which is almost ubiquitous (see also Kitching and Bowes' discussion in chapter 9); de-athleticisation, also involving sexualisation, infantilisation and idealised femininity; and ambivalence.

When only a women's sports event or competition is marked, the male equivalent is reconfirmed as the unquestioned norm. This media pattern is generally triggered by the respective organisation/ federation in its title or label for the event/championship/tournament. International and Irish examples alike include gender-marked titles such as Women's World Cup, Ladies All-Ireland Championship, Women's Open Golf Championship, Women's National League and Women's Super League (WSL). As Fink argues, similar events for men do not include this gender moniker.[26] Woodhouse, Fielding-Lloyd and Sequerra go further,[27] using the example of WSL in particular: drawing on critical-feminist literature and theories of organisational change, they demonstrate the English Football Association's shift from tolerance, through opposition, to defining and controlling elite club football for women as 'new' but, ultimately, still shaped by traditional gender conceptions.

When non-sporting aspects of sportswomen's lives (such as personality, appearance, family and personal life) are foregrounded, oftentimes justified by media professionals in search of originality and 'news' for consumers, women are positioned as less threatening and more appealing to dominant ideals. Recent studies of online coverage also confirm this pattern.[28] Related examples include the descriptors of 'girls' or 'young ladies' in sports commentaries, and the use of female athletes' first names far more frequently than those of their male peers.[29]

Sportswomen are also subjected to discourses of idealised (hetero) sexual attractiveness, in effect de-athleticising them. Mirroring disagreements in feminisms more generally, researchers continue to debate whether images and text that emphasise beauty, grace and heterosexuality position sportswomen within a narrow male gaze and/or also offer more opportunities and possibilities for women to challenge these discourses. This has also led to some disagreements between sportswomen themselves concerning idealised expectations of femininity and to whom responsibility falls to challenge such discourses, if/when the opportunity arises. Often those women who can meet, more easily, the expectation of ideal notions of femininity in their physical appearance see less contradiction in representing themselves 'as they are'. Rarely, however, do they control the images, ideals and discourses produced by the mainstream and new media. In this regard, coverage of their lives outside of sport – as mothers, girlfriends, sisters or wives, for instance – can downgrade their sporting achievements and athleticism.[30]

At the turn of the century, Bernstein noted that 'a certain ambivalence emerges every time a female athlete is framed as a sexual being or is in fact covered by the media not for her sport performance, but because she is attractive and conveys sex appeal'.[31] Ambivalent representations of women in sport can therefore portray a positive discourse at first glance, but may also continue to hide and maintain the mechanisms of male dominance in sport through a subtle belittling of sportswomen. Ambivalence was identified as an important media-sport practice more than twenty years ago,[32] before the inception of new media, and it is one of the dominant framing techniques today. This includes coverage that celebrates women's prowess in sport but can also simultaneously trivialise them with references to aesthetic and sexual appeal, personal backgrounds and 'ordinary' lives.[33] Intentional or otherwise, attempts by media professionals to manage these conflicting discourses can reinforce such ambivalence, especially in light of the limited availability of on-the-job training for young journalists and for those in the profession who wish to stay informed of social and research developments.

Consistently, research shows that female athletes receive far less coverage, quantitatively speaking, than their male peers in the written media, broadcast and new media.[34] Though female athletes are now participating more, media coverage and marketing internationally does not reflect this. In fact, longitudinal studies show that media coverage has declined, across a range of platforms, despite women's increased participation and sporting performances.[35] It also seems that, of the available research on new online media forms, many reproduce the same gender imbalance in coverage. In general, then, this more limited coverage of women's sport has been clearly identified, leading to the conclusion that media sport 'reproduces, legitimates, and occasionally challenges ideologies of gender'.[36] Some countries, such as Canada and the Nordic countries, have developed substantial experience in gender mainstreaming, which is also reflected in their policy work on gender inclusion in sport. The US, too, is often cited as a path maker for women in sport, through the introduction of Title IX legislation. Less the heralded success than most accounts might claim, Title IX has a number of crucial caveats. Not only does its enforcement exempt contact sports from its scope, but also these sports are defined so broadly as to allow some organisations to resist the entry of females into culturally significant sports. Paradoxically speaking, then, Title IX is (in effect) toothless.[37] Elsewhere, the International Working Group (IWG) on Women and Sport also showed that opportunities and access to sports and leisure retain a degree of symbolic closure to those women who are especially responsible for domestic work.[38] Put simply, women are becoming more visible and accepted as athletes in their own right, yet women's access to the corridors of sporting power and their public visibility remains comparatively restricted.

Women remain underrepresented in formal leadership roles in sport: female representation on the board of international sports federations, national Olympic committees, and sports-governing bodies remains low (18, 17 and below 30 per cent respectively in 2016).[39] Around the world, drop-off and drop-out rates for young females continue to exceed those of young males, and sporting youths today are still far more likely to be coached by men. Nationally, Sport Ireland and Sport Northern Ireland, too, recognise gender imbalances in the ratios of males to females: as coaches, officials, adult participants (though ratios of males to females are decreasing), as CEOs, chairs and board members of National Governing Bodies of Sports (NGBs), and in media coverage.[40] In the all-Ireland context, the international successes of women's teams (in sports such as rugby union and hockey) contributed to a widening of the scope of available content within the media-sport landscape. Key decision-makers in state-funded media sport (for example, Ryle Nugent, sports editor at RTÉ) were empowered by these successes to continue to push a 'gender agenda' that had already taken root in the early 2000s. Reflective of this twenty-first-century agenda, a bimonthly publication, *Fairplay*, was launched to promote women in sport. Other NGB-sponsored publications have also expanded, such as the LGFA's *Peil*, while more recent online platforms have also grown exponentially – for example, Sportswomen.ie (which was live for three years), and Off the Bench and Fair Game podcasts, the latter having won best webcast series in the 2016 Realex Web Awards. Women's involvement in sport on the island is now a more animated debate topic on traditional and new-media platforms, manifest in television series such as *Jump Girls* (RTÉ) and *Mná Spóirt: Croí is Anam* (TG4 and BBC). It was into this social milieu that, recently, a campaign was launched on the island of Ireland to create a measurable cultural shift in the presentation and perception of women's sport by 2020, one of three core objectives being a 20-per-cent increase in media coverage. The strapline for this campaign highlighted the importance of women's visibility – as sporting role models – but also the need for cultural exposure to sport in order to normalise women's sense of place and belonging in sport.

20X20: 'IF YOU CAN'T SEE IT, YOU CAN'T BE IT'

The 20x20 campaign was launched in October 2018, and championed by the Federation of Irish Sport (FIS), the representative organisation for over a hundred NGBs and Local Sports Partnerships (LSPs) on the island of Ireland. The idea originated with creative marketing agency Along Came A Spider (ACAS) and its female founders, Sarah Colgan and Heather Thornton, who approached the FIS chairperson, Mary O'Connor (second author here). Collectively, they shared a motivation to challenge the cultural barriers that they had faced and/or observed, notably the accepted undervaluing of women in sport. Colgan, for instance, highlighted that her own increasing awareness of her unconscious biases as a parent had motivated her: 'my own auto-pilot reaction with my daughter of basically being much more determined that my son would play sport'.[41] As an inter-county player, O'Connor had direct experience of low media coverage and paltry attendances at games. She was motivated by a cocktail of past frustrations, but also by the strategic opportunity generated by her role to bring about positive change for future generations. Having observed the ways in which previous efforts around the gender agenda had fluctuated, mainly because they were spearheaded by individual organisations and/or did not have mainstream or widespread support, the campaign organisers focused on securing the commitment of NGBs and LSPs over a two-year period. These groups, including the Female Sports Forum in Northern Ireland, were identified as critical to the potential success of the campaign. Lacking a weighty financial incentive that could be offered to secure buy-in from these groups – by way of comparison, phase one of This Girl Can had a fund of £10 million from Sport England – a powerful social and moral message was instead required to garner their commitment and future support. This was identified as the potential societal value that could be generated from the promotion of women in sport and, in particular, the ways in which NGBs and LSPs could become cultural architects of this, staking out their contribution to transformational change.

The campaign is organised around five phases/chapters, the first aimed at raising awareness of the subliminal bias held towards women in sport. Sixty-five NGBs and LSPs signed the 20x20 charter at its launch on 15 October 2018, committing themselves to a 20-per-cent targeted increase in one or more of the three action areas – media coverage of women's sport, participation levels and live attendance figures – each organisation having autonomy in terms of the area(s) most appropriate to their programmes of work. Each NGB/LSP was also given access to campaign assets and content, as well as time to create an action plan under the respective pillar commitment (media coverage, participation, attendance). Phase two of the campaign was launched on International Women's Day 2019. It called on NGBs, LSPs, clubs and individuals to publicly announce their pledge as part of the campaign ShowYourStripes (Twitter: #Showyourstripes), and an invitation was extended to all schools (primary and post-primary) to engage in physical activity at twenty minutes to or after any hour on that day. Phase three was launched at the time of writing, and focused on the importance of role models.

Despite the absence of a formal budget, the launch of 20x20 was heralded a success. The females who spearheaded the campaign maximised their soft-power opportunities for influence, and drew on their positions of status in sport, PR and media. They designed and communicated a clear set of authentic goals that was successful in attracting endorsement and sponsorship. Media partners were secured, in RTÉ Sport, TG4, *Off the Ball* (Newstalk), SportsJOE and Her.ie, each of which has also committed to increasing its coverage of women in sport by 20 per cent over the course of the two-year campaign. The involvement of five sponsors – Lidl, AIG, Three, Investec and KPMG, supported to a lesser degree by Healthy Ireland – has been central to the successful launch of the campaign, each of the five sharing associated costs equally. Three of these were already committed to supporting women in sport through their sponsorships of Dublin GAA (Gaelic Athletic Association), women's professional golf, the LGFA, the National Football League and the national senior women's soccer team. Five ambassadors were also identified, each associated with the five sponsors: Louise Quinn (soccer), Sarah Rowe (Gaelic football), Laura Twomey (camogie), Leona Maguire and Stephanie Meadow (golf).

The absence of a designated campaign fund has, by necessity, shaped and constrained the focus: raising public consciousness and agreeing a set of attainable and measurable targets in the three action areas. Outcomes for 20x20 will be evaluated against the benchmark figures generated by Nielsen Research (during the monitoring period 8 August–7 September 2018) and by the NGBs and LSPs; the former carried out an audit of Irish media before the campaign launch, while each sports organisation also provided prior benchmarking data on participation and attendance. Nielsen's pre-campaign audit included broadcast-television listings across thirteen channels in Ireland, twenty sports-media websites and seven print-media publications (including the Sunday newspapers). Analysis indicated that 3 per cent of print coverage of sport and 4 per cent of online coverage was dedicated to women's sports, while less than 20 per cent of all televised sports features related to either women only or to mixed-sex sports. Nielsen's benchmarking data also highlighted the decreasing participation gap between the sexes in sport and the need for more female role models.

Acknowledging that, at the time of writing, 20x20 has been running for approximately seven months, prominent campaigners have been surprised, thus far, by its positive reception. More scepticism and cynicism were anticipated than has been shown to date, publicly at least. There have been some (anecdotal) accounts of negative responses: from those who were obviously threatened by change involving either the (further) opening up of sport to women and/or the associated challenge to preconceived ideals around femininity. Since the launch of 20x20, Sport Ireland, too, has formalised its 'Women in Sport' policy (announced on International Women's Day 2019), and confirmed Lynne Cantwell and Nora Stapleton (former Irish international rugby players) as chair of the new committee and Women in Sport lead respectively. This initiative built on an extensive review carried out in 2018, and has established four key target areas (supported by an annual fund of €2 million): coaching and officiating, active participation, leadership/governance and visibility. Given the overlap between the deliveries of these two major initiatives by Sport Ireland and the FIS, there may be some challenges in measuring outcomes for both separately; after all, correlation is not causation, and multiple variables are at play in a complex policy field like sport.

It also remains to be seen whether the positive energy that has been harnessed by the 20x20 campaign can overcome any politics or power struggles associated with ownership of the gender agenda in sport, not least the organisational and political capital to be gained from being the real or perceived leader for women in sport. As one of the 20x20 campaign organisers made clear to the first author, 'women in sport belongs to no one individual or organisation'. More broadly, further work will be required to understand the success factors that bring some women, but not all, to respond positively to such campaigns. Indeed, as Sport England noted of This Girl Can, despite inspiring almost three million women to take up physical activity since its 2015 launch, it did not reach some women to the same level – for example, those women who bore the greatest responsibility for lower-paid, routine work, and those who fulfil the bulk of domestic duties. Some ethnic groups in England were also identified as being 'harder to reach'. The new strapline for This Girl Can, 'Fit Got Real', seeks to become more diverse by greater encouragement of women of varying ages, ethnicities and socio-economic backgrounds with regard to exercise in their daily lives. It also remains to be seen whether campaigns such as 20x20 can create the cultural space needed for a more cohesive and concerted challenge to male-dominated organisational cultures. The chapter concludes by reflecting on these and future challenges associated with such cultural change.

ALTERNATIVE FUTURES AND FUTURE CHALLENGES

On the island of Ireland (as elsewhere), the marginalisation of women in sport has partly contributed to the absence of critically informed debates about the various initiatives, planned or underway, to address underrepresentation. The relative exclusion of sport from wider feminist initiatives is also a contributory factor in this. There is often a fear of potential negative repercussions when speaking out about women in sport, of being perceived as 'yet another complainer' voicing anger and disillusionment, especially in the burgeoning media-sport opportunities for female contributors. This has led to a situation overall in which conformism and containment have largely prevailed in relation to the gender agenda in sport. Absent, then, are more radical voices concerning the pace, volume and impact of such change in the context of gender equality in sport. Lacking this diversity, the potential danger is that the better sportswomen get, the more they might be restricted, symbolically, if the organisational cultures that provide the basis of gender inequity remain unproblematised. Why, for instance, has the question of gender quotas in sport been sidelined since it was raised by the then minister of state for sport, Patrick O'Donovan, a number of years ago?[42] What were the sportive diplomatic channels that were clearly activated and which led to the relative silencing of a minister who sought to apply a 'kick under the table' to NGBs regarding quotas? Furthermore, in light of international developments around gender mainstreaming, why has neither government in Belfast or Dublin, nor the two state-funded sports bodies (Sport Ireland and Sport Northern Ireland), formalised a policy position regarding gender equality or equity? And what of the composition and views of the growing fan-and-spectator base for women in sport? These may be consumers of sports media more generally, they may comprise both sexes, and it will be important to assess whether sport remains sexist for fans – for example, through the ways that female athletes might be portrayed, ongoing sexism in the media, or any heteronormative assumptions that female or male fans watch sports solely to gaze at males or females respectively. If 'sex sells', this has important implications for journalistic practice in media-sport coverage.

While current approaches aim to open up the cultural space into which women might reach the *same* level as their male counterparts, in doing so there are wider structural challenges to overcome that might allow women to *start* at the same level as men. In this regard, networking between women and the development of leadership and media competencies will be critical to their embodying the media-sport landscape and the sporting corridors of power. Much of the existing research, too, on media sport, has focused on gender differences. More sensitivity to gender similarities is required going forward, including the ways in which media sport might also constrict the frame of reference for masculinities. Wider changes to the composition of the population on the island of Ireland will also require greater research attention in media-sport work: to intersectionality and to identities – ethno-religious and national – given the naturalisation of many migrants and those with refugee status (including female sports stars Sanita Purspure, Gina Akpe-Moses and Patience Jumbo-Gula).

As an important cultural artefact and agent, media sport reflects and reinforces deeply embedded norms about gender. There is the potential, too, for the inclusion of media-sport content that might challenge the ways in which people think about women in sport. As the early reception of the 20x20 campaign has highlighted, there is an appetite among the general public, who do take an interest in women in sport. Of course, there are dangers in making generalised statements about any social grouping. This is especially relevant given the contentious debates around women (for example, #MeToo) and currently in athletics – for instance, where women are a 'protected category' for the purposes of single-sex competition. It is hoped, then, that the spirit of this chapter is taken as observations on tendencies, where individual exceptions to any widespread pattern will exist. For, one day, a boy might grow to manhood in the belief that, by the mere fact of acknowledging and celebrating his sister's involvement in sports, through the vehicle of media sport she is by right his sporting equal, if not, in some cases, his superior.

Undervalued and Underreported: The coverage of sportswomen in the Irish print media

CIARÁN DUNNE

As highlighted in the introduction to this collection, a significant amount of attention has been given internationally to the coverage of sportswomen in the media. Such studies have consistently found that sportswomen are underrepresented and marginalised in media reporting.[1] Although, in Ireland, the topic of sportswomen in the media has been increasingly debated across various media in recent years, there has nonetheless been a dearth of empirical research on the topic. With few exceptions, such as Katie Liston, whose chapter (with Mary O'Connor) precedes this one, analyses of the coverage of sportswomen in the Irish media have been conspicuous by their absence. With this in mind, a content analysis, informed by Gramsci's hegemonic theory,[2] was conducted to examine the photographic coverage of sportswomen in a major Irish broadsheet print newspaper, *The Irish Times*. Based upon a data set of 471 pages and over 1,600 images collected over a 4-month period, the findings reveal that less than 4 per cent of photographs were of sportswomen, indicating that the Irish situation mirrors international research, and reflects a continuation of the status quo in terms of how sportswomen and women's sports are undervalued and underreported in the media.

SPORTSWOMEN AND THE MEDIA

While women have historically been marginalised in the field of sport, literally and metaphorically left on the sideline, female participation in sport has actually increased significantly in recent decades.[3] However, despite greater participation rates, the coverage sportswomen have received in the media remains significantly imbalanced.[4] When exploring this phenomenon, studies typically focus on the frequency (quantity) and/or nature (quality) of coverage of sportswomen across traditional media as well as on more recent online-media platforms. Such studies have been conducted in a wide variety of countries, including Australia,[5] the US,[6] Hungary,[7] the UK,[8] New Zealand,[9] France[10] and Poland,[11] yet the findings are compelling in their consistency, revealing that sportswomen receive extremely low levels of coverage compared with their male counterparts, with relatively little attention being given to sports that are typically dominated by women. While figures vary across region and time periods – for example, reporting of sportswomen may spike in the context of major sporting events such as the Olympics Games – there is a recurring pattern whereby, on average, sportswomen receive 10 per cent or less of total sports coverage,[12] with some studies indicating levels as low as 2 per cent.[13]

Despite the underrepresentation of sportswomen having been highlighted for several decades, the deficit has not been addressed to any meaningful extent. With the advent of Web 2.0 and the increasingly democratised nature of content creation and dissemination, there may be hope, if not expectation, that coverage of sportswomen on online-media platforms would be more equitable and bridge the gap so evident in traditional media. However, multiple studies indicate that this is not the case.[14] Furthermore, where attention is given to sportswomen, they are often sexualised, trivialised or infantilised.[15] This lack of coverage in turn may have important implications for women's participation in sport and, consequently, for their health, and raises important questions about the role the media may play in reflecting or reinforcing gender inequality.

MEDIA AND SOCIETY

The rationale for examining the coverage and representation of sportswomen in the media stems from a recognition of the highly influential role media play in society. By presenting certain kinds of information in certain kinds of ways, the media influence the public's awareness of, and concern for, specific issues. Cortés[16] argues that the media, be it explicitly or implicitly, play five important roles in teaching those who consume content: they (i) present and (ii) organise information about individuals and groups, they (iii) disseminate values, (iv) create expectations and (v) provide models, including role models, for individual and group behaviour. Equally, it may be argued that when the media do not cover a certain issue, it can become marginalised in the public's collective mind. Indeed, by deciding what merits coverage, traditional print and broadcast-media organisations have historically acted as gatekeepers through which 'they provide what is seen, heard, and read, along with the type and amount of coverage given'.[17] It is important, therefore, to recognise that the media do not adopt a passive and unbiased stance in relation to the content they (fail to) disseminate, nor do they constitute an unfiltered reflection of social reality. Instead, they exert huge influence over what information enters the public domain for mass consumption, and how the public perceives such information. By presenting ideas, events and people in a particular light, the media inform the public's perception of 'reality' while simultaneously moulding this reality. They provide us on an ongoing basis, across a variety of fields, including sports, with a diversity of 'attractor images' that can be understood as 'images (in the broad sense of the word, not restricted to the visual sense) that orient a culture's thinking and feeling about a topic'.[18] Attractor images can, in turn, influence our attitudes and behaviour. Indeed, Croteau and Hoynes[19] contend that the media constitute a potent socialising agent, disseminating values, beliefs and norms that are internalised by audiences. This is echoed by Bernstein and Kian, who comment that 'the more the viewer watches, the more the viewer will form expectations about reality based on the represented world, rather than the experienced one'.[20] With this in mind, to the extent that they influence values, beliefs and behaviours, the media wield tremendous power within society.

Intimately related to power is the concept of hegemony, 'the occupation of a dominant position in any system',[21] whereby the occupation of this position is based on socialised consent and coercion. Importantly, the media can play an integral role in either reinforcing hegemonic structures within society or challenging them. Gramsci's hegemonic theory, which posits that the dominant group in society has the ability to inform and manipulate the cultural values, norms and behaviours to the extent that this dominance is seen as inevitable and desirable, offers a useful lens through which to study the coverage of sportswomen in the media, particularly given that sport has traditionally constituted 'a key social activity for males in the preservation of stereotypical masculine behaviour, attributes and ideologies'.[22] As such, the underrepresentation of sportswomen in media coverage, as well as in the field of sports journalism, serves to reinforce the status quo. In the case of newspapers, for example, which represent a record of the day, this underrepresentation of women underpins their exclusion from a domain that culturally constitutes a significant symbol of power.[23] Furthermore, a symbiotic relationship exists between the media and sport whereby sport represents a social institution that normalises the hegemonic power and privilege men have historically held over women, which is consolidated by the manner in which sports are reported by the media.[24] As such, it can be argued that the lack of attention afforded to sportswomen in the media, be it a deliberate strategy or the result of unconscious bias, serves to maintain the historical male dominance over women in society, and protect the sporting arena as a male-dominated space.

The aforementioned marginalisation and, where presented, trivialisation and sexualisation of sportswomen is a manifestation of masculine cultural hegemony, and serves not only to devalue women's sports but also to reinforce the stereotypical view that women are outsiders to sport, as well as to undermine opportunities to make women's sport more popular. As O'Neill and Mulready contend:

> If women's sports are not even on the radar of most people, then there is indeed little hope of creating readers' interest and popularising female sports, or encouraging women to change their role models and take up sport. Omission from the news agenda (systematic absences) can be as powerful an influence as that which is included.[25]

This point raises the issue of the consequences of the relative lack of media coverage, beyond the aforementioned reinforcement of masculine cultural hegemony. Media coverage of women's sport, for example, provides girls and women with strong role models, someone to look up to and emulate.[26] This can stimulate the level of participation in sport among females, which in turn has implications for a wide variety of physical and psychological health outcomes, including educational attainment.[27] Indeed, the importance of strong female role models for young girls is very significant given the very high drop-out rate from sports among girls during early adolescence,[28] as well as findings from a study of over 22,000 teenagers in Ireland, which concluded that boys in their mid-teens were 34-per-cent fitter than their female counterparts.[29] This issue forms part of the rationale for the 20x20 movement, which was discussed in detail by Katie Liston and Mary O'Connor in the previous chapter. Furthermore, in terms of the sportswomen themselves, coverage in the media raises their profile, increases their marketability, underpins sponsorship deals and, consequently, their ability to generate revenue for themselves. This in turn has an impact with regard to women's personal agency, independence and autonomy in society, thereby highlighting the need to examine the media coverage of sportswomen.

THE IRISH CONTEXT

Despite the established body of empirical research relating to the coverage and representation of sportswomen internationally, very little research has been conducted in the Irish context. In 2004 one of the recommendations of a report from the Oireachtas was for an increase in longitudinal research into the scope and nature of media reporting of female sports in Ireland. This stemmed from an acknowledgement within the report that media coverage constituted one of the principal obstacles to female involvement in sports.[30] However, very little formal research was actually conducted, despite this recommendation.

One of the few exceptions was the research conducted by the Dublin Sports and Recreation Council, which in 2002 conducted its first annual empirical study of the coverage of sportswomen across six major Irish newspapers. While drawn from a relatively small data set, the results largely mirrored those of similar studies in other countries, revealing that only 2.78 per cent of photographs in the six newspapers were of women. While this had increased to 3.3 per cent in 2005, by 2007 the figure had dropped to its lowest ever, at just 1.2 per cent, reflective of 'the absolute predominance of male imagery and male activities in the presentation, and therefore perception, of sport in our national newspapers'.[31] These results perhaps reflected a long-established attitude within Ireland that sport represents a fundamentally male domain, with little attention assigned to sportswomen.[32] This attitude was exemplified by the journalist Kevin Myers in 2004 in *The Irish Times*. In an article discussing the coverage of women's sport in Ireland, Myers remarked,

> What our sports reports cover are sporting events which people really want to watch ... We don't want to watch women playing sports because, generally speaking, they're not very good. They're small and they're weak and they're slow, and watching an average woman throw an object is a deeply moving tragedy.[33]

In more recent times, in 2014, in an article in the same newspaper entitled 'If Women's Sport Struggles for Coverage It's Not Because of Sexism – It's Because You Can't Make People Care', Malachy Clerkin, a leading sports journalist in Ireland, argued that

> Women's sport's most basic problem when it comes to media coverage is that you can't force people to care. It's the same problem with all areas of sport that don't get as much attention as they would like ... People will engage or they won't and all the marketing and media backing in the world will lead only so many horses to water.[34]

This stance echoes an argument articulated in the *Irish Examiner* in 2011 on the question as to whether women's sport receives appropriate media coverage: 'On the basis that everyone milks their own cows, we can only speak for this corner of the media world, and here the key word is appropriate: as in, coverage which is appropriate to the level of interest.'[35] As such, there is an implication that the media simply report on, and in no way shape, attitudes towards women's sport in Ireland, and that the lack of coverage is an objective reflection of public interest in specific sports and the practitioners of these sports.

This position was, however, openly challenged by the chairperson of the Dublin Sports and Recreation Council in its 2007 report: 'The imagery in our national newspapers is not a passive reflection of reality – it is a powerful subconscious influence on the shaping of the reader's perception of reality and, in turn, on the shaping of reality itself.'[36] Furthermore, in 2015 the president of Ireland, Michael D. Higgins, himself spoke about the underrepresentation of sportswomen and highlighted that women's sport is often regarded as of secondary importance, with success leading to momentary recognition but insufficient ongoing support. Indeed, within *The Irish Times* itself there has been an ongoing discussion of the issue in recent years, with one of the paper's few female sports journalists, Mary Hannigan, in 2015 acknowledging that 'there's a fair old distance to be travelled yet before we see our top-achieving sportswomen given the column inches they merit'.[37] Indeed, in both print and online media there is broad recognition of the lack of attention paid to women's sport, yet there is a notable dearth of formal empirical research into the topic in an Irish context. The study presented in this chapter therefore constitutes an attempt to both highlight and partially address this lacuna.

Juxtaposed with the lack of coverage of women's sports in the media is the increasing level of participation in sport among females. While this increase may bring into question the thesis that low media coverage undermines participation, it is important to recognise numerous other factors driving the increase in female participation in sport. In the Irish context, recent years have seen concerted efforts undertaken by the respective representative bodies to offer females more-structured, better-quality and more-affordable opportunities to engage in sports such as soccer, Gaelic football,[38] camogie and rugby. This has been further boosted by a growth in sponsorship of female sports, such as a major investment by the supermarket chain Lidl in the Ladies Gaelic Football Association. Furthermore, initiatives such as Support Her Sport, which aims to promote sport among girls in Ireland, coupled with the highly successful This Girl Can campaign in the UK, may also constitute influential factors. As such, in spite of the low coverage afforded by the traditional media, there are other external variables to be considered when reflecting on the increase in sports participation among females. Indeed, the rise of social-media platforms with huge numbers of subscribers, coupled with the increasingly democratised nature of content creation, means that media institutions such as print newspapers, which traditionally played the role of content 'gatekeepers', have been challenged in a fundamental way.

According to the Sport Ireland *Irish Sports Monitor 2017* report,[39] the gender gap in sports participation reduced from 15.7 per cent in 2007 to 4.5 per cent in 2017, with females aged forty-five or over more likely to participate in sport than males of the same age. Indeed, it is also worth noting that several of Ireland's most successful sportspeople on an international stage are women. In particular, boxer Katie Taylor is arguably Ireland's most successful ever sportsperson and 'a major national twenty-first century sporting celebrity in Ireland',[40] having won eighteen gold medals at international level between 2005 and 2015, including five consecutive world-championship victories and Ireland's only gold medal at the 2012 London Olympics, before turning professional in 2017 and going on to become the reigning World Boxing Association, International Boxing Federation and World Boxing Organization world lightweight female champion in 2018 and 2019. Indeed, in the 2018 Teneo Sport and Sponsorship Index, Katie Taylor ranked as the most admired athlete among the Irish public. In 2018 the Irish senior women's hockey team enjoyed unprecedented success by reaching the final of the World Cup in London, while in 2014 the Irish women's senior rugby team reached the semi-final of the Rugby World Cup. In 2014 Stephanie Roche, the only Irish footballer, male or female, ever to be nominated for the award, was placed second in the FIFA (Fédération Internationale de Football Association) Puskás Goal of the Year Award. Furthermore, the 2018 women's All-Ireland Gaelic football final, with an attendance of 50,141 people, was the biggest women's sporting event of the year in Europe.

While these successes did receive significant media coverage, the general attention paid to women's sports in the Irish media has been extremely sparse for many years. In a bid to address this imbalance, a bimonthly publication titled *Fairplay* was launched in 2002 to promote women in sport in Ireland, but later ceased circulation. In January 2015 an online platform, Sportswomen.ie, was launched by former international hockey player Sharon Hutchinson with the aim of counterbalancing the lack of coverage of women's sport in Irish media, to encourage female participation in sport, and to present female role models. In addition to this, in 2016 a podcast entitled *Fair Game* was established with the aim of addressing the lack of media attention afforded to sportswomen in Ireland. More recently, in 2018 the 20x20 campaign was launched, supported by the Federation of Irish Sport, with the aim of increasing the coverage of, participation in, and attendance at women's sport by 20 per cent by the year 2020. It is evident, therefore, that the discussion in relation to the coverage and treatment of sportswomen in Ireland is a very current topic of ongoing debate, and one which can be enhanced by the addition of further empirical data. With this in mind, a study was conducted to examine the coverage of sportswomen in a major Irish broadsheet.

STUDY OVERVIEW

The study consisted of a gender-based content analysis of photographic coverage of sports in a major Irish print broadsheet newspaper, *The Irish Times*. This is Ireland's oldest newspaper and, according to the Audit Bureau of Circulations, had a combined daily print and epaper circulation of 79,406 in the second half of 2018. The paper is commonly accepted as Ireland's authoritative paper of the day, with readership evenly split between 51-per-cent male and 49-per-cent female. Content analysis was employed given that it permits transparency and is the most commonly used method of analysis in investigations of sports media.[41] Photographic coverage was chosen given the powerful impact that photographs have in framing a topic, particularly sports, coupled with the cultural meanings they carry.[42] Indeed, it has been argued that in the field of sports media, photographic coverage exerts greater influence on consumers than textual.[43] One aim of the study was to explore the idea that the print media reinforce the traditional hegemony of masculinity in sports through the disproportionate photographic coverage afforded to sportsmen rather than sportswomen. The data set consisted of three sports supplements, 'Weekend Sports', 'Sports Monday' and 'Sports Wednesday', which the newspaper publishes on a weekly basis. While there is some degree of sports coverage in the newspaper on a daily basis, these three are more substantial, pull-out supplements provided with the main paper.

The sampling frame for the study was a four-month period in autumn/winter of 2015. This equated to forty-nine supplements totalling 471 pages. A database was created and the number of photographs in each supplement was counted and categorised under three discrete headings; (i) male(s) only, (ii) female(s) only, and (iii) both (that is, male and female). Photographs of males or females that appeared in product advertisements in any of the supplements were not included, nor were photographs of the journalists who wrote stories in the supplements. Photographs depicting more than one male were counted as a single unit of data, and likewise with females. Data were also gathered regarding the specific sports the photographs related to. This would reveal which sports received greatest photographic attention, irrespective of whether males or females are represented in the images. The study was limited insofar as it focused exclusively on photographic content from one major hardcopy newspaper rather than collecting data from other newspapers, and data were not collected from the newspaper's online platform. It should also be noted that photographs of sportspeople that appeared in other sections of the newspaper (for example, a photograph of a captain lifting the trophy after winning an All-Ireland championship commonly appears on the front cover of the newspaper on the following Monday morning) were not included in the data set.

FINDINGS

Frequency and categorisation of photographs

As mentioned above, the total data set for this study comprised forty-nine sports supplements amounting to a total of 471 pages. The total number of photographs in this data set was 1,618. A breakdown of these according to the three categories is shown in Table 1. These results highlight a very substantial dominance of photographs of sportsmen compared with sportswomen, with the former comprising 95.3 per cent of all photographs. Females accounted for 3.83 per cent of the total number of photographs,

while photographs comprising males and females accounted for
0.87 per cent.

Table 1. Photographs based on categorisation

	Male	Female	Both	Total
Number of photographs	1542	62	14	1618
% of total	95.3	3.83	0.87	100

Sports receiving photographic coverage

A total of twenty-three different sports received photographic
coverage in the data set. These sports are listed in Table 2, along with
a breakdown of 'male', female' and 'both' in each case. As mentioned
previously, Gaelic football, hurling and camogie are indigenous,
amateur Irish sports organised under the aegis of the Gaelic Athletic
Association (GAA). Gaelic football (ranked 3) is played by men
and women (although not in mixed teams), hurling (ranked 5) is
played exclusively by males, while camogie (ranked 16), which is
very similar to hurling, is played exclusively by females. All three are
competitive, physical-contact sports played on grass with teams of
fifteen players. It should be noted that in the category of hurling, a
male-only sport, there was one photograph of a female, and this is a
government minister who was pictured in relation to an attempt to
get hurling and camogie added to the UNESCO list of the world's
intangible cultural heritage, which was achieved in November
2018. In the category of 'other', photographs were included that
related to awards ceremonies with sportspeople from a variety of
different sports, and to administrative figures in bodies such as the
GAA, which represent multiple sports and therefore could not be
categorised under one particular sport. As can be seen, the top five
sports in terms of frequency of photographs were rugby, soccer,
Gaelic football, horse-racing and hurling. These accounted for 87
per cent of all the photographs in the data set. Within these top five
sports, photographs of females accounted for just 1.84 per cent of
the total number of photographs (that is, twenty-six out of 1,410).

Table 2. Number of photographs based on sex and sport

	Male	Female	Both	Total
Rugby	571	5	3	579
Soccer	491	5	3	499
Gaelic football	187	13	1	201
Horse-racing	65	2	2	69
Hurling	63	1	0	64
Golf	56	4	1	61
Boxing	25	3	1	29
Athletics	7	8	2	17
Tennis	14	3	0	17
Mixed martial arts	8	3	0	11
Cricket	9	1	0	10
Hockey	8	1	0	9
Motor-racing	9	0	0	9
Cycling	7	0	0	7
American football	6	0	0	6
Camogie	0	6	0	6
Basketball	3	1	0	4
Rowing	1	3	0	4
Equestrian	3	0	0	3
Australian Rules football	2	0	0	2
Sailing	1	0	0	1
Snooker	1	0	0	1
Swimming	0	1	0	1
Other	5	2	1	8
Total	1542	62	14	1618

Out of the twenty-three sports that received photographic coverage, in nineteen of these there were more photographs of males than females, the four exceptions being athletics (ranked 8), camogie (ranked 16), rowing (ranked 18) and swimming (ranked 23). There was also a notable absence of photographic coverage of sports typically dominated by women, such as gymnastics.

Table 3. Females as percentage of total photographs based on sport

	Total number of photos	Photos of females	Females as percentage of total photos
Camogie	6	6	100
Swimming	1	1	100
Rowing	4	3	75
Athletics	17	8	47.06
Mixed martial arts	11	3	27.27
Basketball	4	1	25
Tennis	17	3	17.65
Hockey	9	1	11.11
Boxing	29	3	10.34
Cricket	10	1	10
Golf	61	4	6.56
Gaelic football	201	13	6.47
Horse-racing	69	2	2.90
Hurling	64	1	1.56
Soccer	499	5	1.00
Rugby	579	5	0.86
American football	6	0	0
Australian Rules football	2	0	0
Cycling	7	0	0
Equestrian	3	0	0
Motor-racing	9	0	0
Sailing	1	0	0
Snooker	1	0	0
Total	**1,618**	**62**	**3.83**

Table 3 lists the sports in the data set that had the highest percentage of photographs of sportswomen. Unsurprisingly, given that it is a female-only sport, camogie ranked joint first (with swimming) in this list. What is notable, however, is that adding together the total number of photographs from the top ten sports that had the highest-percentage photographic coverage of sportswomen (that is, the first ten listed in Table 3), these sports account for a total of just 6.7 per cent of all photographs in the data set. This indicates that, although there are instances when sportswomen do receive more, or at least comparable, photographic coverage with their male counterparts, this typically occurs in relation to sports that receive very little coverage overall, and which are located at the periphery of the media's interest.

DISCUSSION

The results of the study closely reflect the findings from existing international research, indicating a gross imbalance in the photographic coverage of sportswomen in comparison to sportsmen. This imbalance is particularly evident in the five sports that received the greatest level of photographic coverage: rugby, soccer, Gaelic football, horse-racing and hurling. In each of these, with the exception of Gaelic football (registering 6.7 per cent), less than 3 per cent of the photographs were of sportswomen. In the case of hurling, given that it is a male-only sport, this finding is to be expected.

As mentioned, the coverage and representation of sportswomen in Ireland is a topic that has received greater attention in recent times, and one that is discussed in great detail in the previous and following chapters. Indeed, it should be pointed out that, despite the findings of the study, *The Irish Times* itself constitutes an active forum for this discussion, and the newspaper sponsors the annual Sportswoman of the Year awards in Ireland. Furthermore, in early 2016 *The Irish Times*, in recognition of the underrepresentation of sportswomen in the newspaper, introduced a new section entitled 'Women in Sport', which is published every Thursday as part of the main newspaper and is dedicated to reporting about women in sport. The decision to introduce a section devoted exclusively to women in sport once a week is an interesting development. On one hand, it can be argued that this helps to raise the profile of women's sports and promotes female participation in sport in Ireland, thereby complementing the 20x20 movement. On the other hand, it can also be suggested that by dedicating a special section on Thursdays to women in sport, it further reinforces the idea that women's sports are on the periphery of media coverage and an afterthought compared to men's sport. Furthermore, it may draw attention away from the underrepresentation of sportswomen in the paper as a whole, and normalise the segregation of coverage of sportswomen and sportsmen.

In the Irish context, we find ourselves at an important juncture in terms of the coverage and valuing of women's sport. The findings of this particular study suggest that the traditional mainstream media, as exemplified by *The Irish Times*, appear to be largely maintaining rather than challenging the status quo in relation to the coverage of women's sport. As such, the traditional male hegemony in sport appears to be supported by the coverage afforded to sportsmen and sportswomen respectively. Instead of being visible and central to the field of sports reporting, sportswomen remain largely invisible and peripheral. Indeed, this is a form of inequality that has important implications for power relations in society. Conversely, the increase in debate on the topic in recent times, coupled with the introduction of new fora through which the profile of women's sport is being raised – such as the 20x20 campaign, *Fair Game* podcast and Sportswomen.ie – highlights a more proactive position being adopted by women themselves. This constitutes a grass-roots effort to highlight the issue, empower females, challenge the traditional beliefs relating to females and sport, and ultimately create a 'rupture in the articulation of sport and masculinity'.[44] Furthermore, the sparse attention afforded to sportswomen in the Irish media fails to reflect the reality of female participation in sport and the aforementioned rapidly narrowing gender gap between males and females, and also limits Irish females' exposure to sporting role models who they may seek to emulate. This perpetuates a vicious circle, whereby a lack of media coverage undermines the growth in popularity of women's sport, thereby hindering sponsorship opportunities, which means less money available to invest in promoting women's sport, which again leads to less media coverage.

CONCLUSION

This chapter has examined the photographic representation of sportswomen in the Irish print media by conducting a content analysis of the photographic coverage in a major Irish broadsheet.

An analysis of such images is relevant given that 'images contribute to the perpetuation of attitudes towards and perceptions of women's sport'.[45] The study itself constitutes one of the few empirical studies on this topic in the Irish context. While discussion on the disproportionately low level of coverage afforded to sportswomen in Ireland, both historically and in contemporary society, has certainly increased in recent times, the dearth of concrete empirical data to objectively highlight the issue and act as a reference point for future research has been notable. It is therefore hoped that this study will serve as such a reference point and further stimulate constructive debate and action on the topic, as, indeed, will the next chapter.

Given the influential role of the media in directing attention, creating and perpetuating values, shaping attitudes and informing behaviours, the question of how sportswomen are treated by the media is of huge importance. As Croteau and Hoynes remark, 'talking about social life without including a discussion of the role of mass media risks missing an important element of contemporary society'.[46] The results of the current study highlight the ongoing issue of gender inequality in media coverage and the marginalisation of women's sport, providing further support to the argument 'that sport and media function hegemonically to reproduce a problematic gender order that affirms male dominance over females'.[47] The highly gendered sports coverage demonstrated by the findings of the current study mirrors the results of existing international studies, and resonates with the point made in the introduction to this book, that sport has traditionally constituted a forum for gender displays. The study also reveals a very heavy bias towards the coverage of a small number of sports in the newspaper in question. While this finding is not necessarily related to gender inequality, it does raise questions about the degree to which media outputs actually represent the genuine interests of the public.

The findings are arguably of greater concern when considered within the context of increasing levels of female participation in sport. From a social reality at the end of the nineteenth century in which women were excluded or discouraged from engaging in sport – exemplified by the argument of Pierre de Coubertin, founder of the modern Olympic Games, that women should only be spectators – to one in which both males and females represented all 204 participating nations for the first time in the 2012 London Olympics, females have over the last century progressively challenged the hegemony of masculinity in sport. As increasing numbers of females engage in an increasing variety of sporting activities, the field of sport has, as stated by Liston, 'emerged as a "battleground" over gender identities'.[48] Despite the fact that females have been claiming their place in sporting domains traditionally monopolised by men, the media coverage afforded to them appears to be firmly rooted in a past that situates sportswomen as marginalised and inferior to their male counterparts. However, as O'Neill and Mulready remark, 'It is no longer acceptable for the world of newspaper sports reporting to be one where women are routinely invisible'.[49]

Given the power of the media and its ability to influence the beliefs, attitudes and behaviours of society, there is much scope for further examination of the coverage afforded to sportswomen in both traditional and new, online media platforms. Additional research that focuses on other publications, or that longitudinally compares coverage within a single publication, would be welcome. In addition, while this study has examined only the quantity of coverage, there is much potential for further studies to examine the quality of such coverage, be it through analysing how sportswomen are depicted in images or analysing the written texts relating to them. Furthermore, given the shift towards accessing content online, analysis of how sportswomen are represented in online content – including media websites, blogs and social media such as Twitter – would also be useful, as would studies that examine the role of gender as it relates to sports reporting (for example, editors, journalists and photographers). Overall, ongoing research on this topic will facilitate comparisons over time so as to gauge how the coverage of, and attitudes towards, sportswomen in the Irish media are or are not changing.

'Top of the tree': Examining the Irish print-news portrayal of the world's best female amateur golfer

NIAMH KITCHING AND ALI BOWES

THIS CHAPTER EXAMINES Irish print-news coverage of Leona Maguire, a professional golfer from County Cavan. From 2005, aged eleven, Maguire and her twin sister Lisa became visible in the sports media in Ireland for their early-age golf talents. Since then, there have been over 1,500 articles written about Leona Maguire in the national papers in the North and South of Ireland. Given this level of attention, there is a need to critically consider the media coverage of Maguire, particularly when set against an ever-increasing discussion around representations of female athletes in both academic and media discourses.[1] The aim of this chapter, then, is to investigate print-media representations of Maguire as a young female athlete in 2018, the year she transitioned from the top of the world of amateur golf to the professional ranks. The year 2018 was also a significant year for women's sport, following debates on pay parity and sponsorship, increased visibility of female analysts and commentators, and the growing presence of female athletes in online media.[2] Traditionally, female athletes in the sports media were either ignored or sexualised and trivialised in 'pretty or powerful' discourses that situated femininity in opposition to athleticism.[3] Here, the authors assess the extent to which such tendencies have been reproduced or deviated from, and the part that constructions of national identity play in Maguire's representation. The ensuing sections outline some background on Maguire, along with existing literature on professional women's golf, media representations of female athletes and golfers, and the critical-feminist outlook used in this chapter, before presenting the analysis of the Irish print-media coverage of Maguire. This chapter highlights a largely positive shift away from traditional ways in which female athletes have been represented in the print sports media. In the case of Maguire, this shift is framed by national discourses that serve to somewhat legitimise her place in the Irish sports media. However, questions remain around the quality and quantity of female sports coverage, particularly when juxtaposed with coverage of men's golf.

MAGUIRE AND WOMEN'S PROFESSIONAL GOLF

Leona Maguire and her twin sister Lisa have achieved significant feats in amateur golf, winning numerous international tournaments in Ireland, Britain, Europe and the US at both individual and team level. Having represented both the Junior Ryder Cup and Solheim Cup teams, the Maguire twins became the youngest players ever to play in the Vagliano Trophy (2009) and Curtis Cup (2010) tournaments. Representing Ireland, they also won the European Girls' Team Championship in 2009, a first for an Ireland girls' team. Having completed primary and secondary school in Ireland, and achieving highly commendable Leaving Certificate results, in 2014 the Maguires left Ireland to join the golf programme at Duke University in North Carolina. While there, Leona excelled: in three of her four years at the university she won the Mark H. McCormack medal for the number-one female amateur golfer in the world (2015, 2016 and 2017). In 2015 she was invited to partake in a professional event, the Ladies European Masters on the Ladies European Tour (LET), and finished runner-up (she was ineligible for the €50,000 prize money). In 2016 she represented Ireland at the Olympic Games and, as one of just three amateurs in the field of sixty players, finished twenty-first, with her sister Lisa caddying. In the same year she won the Smyth Salver as the leading amateur at the Ricoh Women's British Open. In 2018 Maguire broke Lydia Ko's record for the number of weeks as number one in the world amateur golf rankings (134 weeks), and finished her college career that year with the lowest career scoring-average record. Later in 2018 both Leona and Lisa Maguire turned professional, signing to Niall Horan's golf-management company Modest! Golf, and making their professional debuts on the Ladies Professional Golf Association (LPGA) Tour. At the end of 2018 Leona Maguire missed out on the final stage of qualifying for the LPGA Tour by one shot, and subsequently received a card on the secondary Symetra Tour. In December 2018 she earned her LET tour card. In April 2019 she won her first event as a professional on the Symetra Tour, the Windsor Golf Classic, earning $22,500 in prize money.

The life of a professional athlete, and particularly that of a professional golfer, is often presented as a highly sought-after, idyllic existence with a generous rewards system. However, while the financial rewards for the top male golfers are substantial, the majority of professional golfers fare poorly; some players 'gamble' on pursuing golf, while others have made conflicting choices to sign restrictive contracts for regular pay as opposed to monetary uncertainty.[4] Disparities exist between male and female professional golf in terms of visibility, endorsements and prize money. Although golf provides an avenue through which women can play professionally, more men have the opportunity to do so, and when they do they make more money than women. Approximately one third of LPGA players will break even or make a profit in an average tournament, once they have accounted for expenses, caddy fees and entry fees.[5] In 2018 the prize money available at the men's British Open was $10.5 million, compared to $3.25 million for the women's British Open. In 2018, when Francesco Molinari earned £3,652,504 on the European Tour, the top earner on the LET (Georgia Hall) accumulated £456,110. This was only marginally more than the earnings of the seventy-fifth-ranked European Tour player, Ashley Chesters (£450,231), whereas finishing seventy-fifth on the LET earned Kelsey MacDonald £14,508.[6] Along with financial pressure, Douglas and Carless revealed situations of considerable psychological distress among women professional golfers, with examples of self-harm, bullying, loneliness, family difficulties and inability to cope with the demands of professional sport.[7] In terms of visibility, while there are over thirty male professional golfers from Ireland on worldwide golf tours, the Maguire sisters and Stephanie Meadow are, at the time of writing, the only female professional golfers from Ireland on international golf tours (Leona Maguire and Stephanie Meadow have secured their full LPGA Tour cards for the 2020 season).

PRINT-MEDIA REPRESENTATIONS OF FEMALE ATHLETES AND GOLFERS

Sport, including golf, is often constructed as a male domain, and the sports media and hegemonic masculinity are often inextricably linked.[8] Women's inclusion within the sports media is thus problematic: when women do find themselves on the sports pages of the popular press, they are often represented in ways that restrict our imagination about women's sport and reinforce the hegemonic position of men in sport.[9] While the sports media can be used as a source of empowerment, it often still adopts traditional approaches in the presentation of women, where they are trivialised, sexualised and underrepresented, while men's sport is privileged.[10] Ciarán Dunne's study of photographic representations in *The Irish Times* (see his chapter in this volume) found that sportswomen and women's sports are undervalued and underreported.[11] There is evidence of change, however, with some movements towards a greater awareness and coverage of female athletes in the sports media. Petty and Pope's study of media coverage of the 2015 Women's World Cup found a removal of gender marking, where women's sport was reported *as sport*.[12]

While the global game of professional golf can result in touring professional golfers being defined as 'borderless athletes', through media depictions internationally recognised professional golfers such as Maguire can take on cultural significance and become viewed as embodiments of the nation and national character.[13] In terms of female athletes, media coverage of international sporting events, or events where athletes are marked by their nationality, may be less likely to be gender-marked. These 'media rules' are 'bent' when presenting international sportswomen who are representing and, more importantly, winning for the nation.[14] Similarly, in contrast to gender ideologies of female weakness, Toni Bruce highlights how female athletes, when representing the nation, can be 'represented in ways that emphasised physical power, strength and domination', and a later study describes how women are valued as athletes rather than 'women' or 'female athletes' when representing the nation.[15] Significantly, in Ireland, following Katie Taylor's 2012 London Olympic win, the Irish media emphasised her transgressive power, her gender, her national identity and even the potential for her to challenge sexism and traditional gender binaries.[16] Free suggests that the Irish media presented her as a figure of cultural and gendered conservativism, where, 'she is both contained by her media representation, and contains herself within the strictest hegemonic discourse of chaste, dutiful, "Irish", femininity.' Although Bairner notes that middle-class individual sports such as golf often do not associate with national identity, given that moments of national identity *are* associated with sportswomen's success, this study may make a useful contribution to understanding the mediatised individual female athlete in Ireland.[17]

Female golfers in the sports media have an ambivalent history, where golf media has been shown to replicate the same exclusionary practices that are evidenced within the game. Although it has been highlighted that rising audience interest in women's golf brought about challenges to golf's 'masculine hegemonic entrenchment', both televised and print-media coverage of golf have continued to offer representations that reinforce divisions of gender, class, disability and race.[18] Two studies of golf magazines revealed how women were underrepresented and deemed inferior athletes who lived conventionally feminine, heteronormative lifestyles.[19] In Billings, Angelini and Eastman's examination of over 200 hours of nationally televised PGA (Professional Golfers' Association) and LPGA (Ladies Professional Golf Association) golf across eight US television networks, a multitude of gender differences in on-air golf announcing was found.[20] They described how women golfers were more likely to be described in terms of why they succeeded or failed (with luck as a major factor), whereas men were more likely to be described in terms of their physicality or personality. Research on the media coverage of Annika Sorenstam's involvement in the 2003 PGA Colonial Tournament offered a degree of challenge to the traditional depictions of women in the golf media: on one hand, commentators were likely to highlight Sorenstam's emotions and outside pressures, but on the other, there were also examples of non-gendered explanations of her successes, too.[21] More recent research by the authors describes the print-media representation of professional female golfers as a double-edged sword, with positive, informed coverage littered with gendered language.[22]

THEORETICAL FRAMEWORK AND METHODOLOGY

The latest golf-participation figures indicate the low involvement of females in the game worldwide, with females typically comprising less than a fifth of all participants in Great Britain and Ireland.[23] Historically, golf-club settings have been unequal and exclusionary institutions, where females have struggled to gain a presence, and gender discrimination has been experienced by female golfers of all ability levels.[24] Exclusionary practices continue to impact the modern game, where women still struggle for equality of access, participation, employment and decision-making.[25] Historical golf traditions and institutionalised gendered practices contribute to a culture that inhibits involvement and legitimises inequality, and women have been regarded as outsiders in the world of professional golf, even on the LPGA tour.[26] Taking this into account, this chapter is theoretically framed by critical feminism, a perspective that acknowledges underlying gendered relations. While feminist perspectives that focus on equality and discrimination are criticised for oversimplifying females' diversified dispositions, critical feminists write in relation to power, where gender relations are often defined by hegemonic masculinity and supported by cultural norms of male domination and female subordination. Feminist analyses of the sports media 'have been at the forefront of interrogating gendered hierarchies and gendered expressions of power'.[27] Thus, critical feminism as used in this chapter acknowledges the normalisation of patriarchal power relations.[28]

A large body of research exists that centres on print-media analyses of female athletes, with this methodology featuring significantly in qualitative research into women's golf and in examinations of female athletes in Ireland.[29] This research extends this work by investigating the print-media coverage of Maguire as a professional female golfer within newspapers in Ireland. News articles written about Leona Maguire in 2018 were collected via the online news database Nexis UK, through which the authors searched for newspaper articles in publications on the island of Ireland using the keywords 'Leona' and 'Maguire' (both anywhere in the text). From her first appearance in August 2005 up until December 2018, there were 1,686 articles written about Maguire in Irish print publications. Following an initial examination for duplicates and other anomalies, and filtering for national news, this resulted in 134 articles from the following print-media outlets: *The Irish News, Belfast Telegraph, The Irish Times, Irish Independent, Sunday Independent, Irish Daily Mail* and *Irish Examiner*.

Following an initial reading of the data set, the number of articles for analysis was reduced to 116, to account for 18 irrelevant articles or those where Maguire's name was mentioned without elaboration. Of these 116 articles, 44 had Maguire as headline news, 33 focused on men's golf (professional and amateur), 29 centred on women's golf, and 13 were on wider golf topics. As part of the data collection, the researchers recorded a number of particulars about the data, including the date, newspaper, journalist, headlines, page number/ section, associated image and word count. Of the 116 articles, 32 had an associated image (28 per cent). Five of these photos were of Maguire alone, with four of Maguire alongside her twin sister Lisa. The other images were of male professional golfers (10), female amateur golfers (7) and others (6).

All 116 articles were subject to a process of thematic data analysis. Braun and Clarke identify six phases of thematic analysis, including immersion, searching for and identifying themes, reviewing themes, defining and naming themes, and writing the report.[30] The analysis of each text was carefully managed by both researchers through a process of open and axial coding over multiple stages. Initially, both researchers were involved in open coding the dataset in isolation, where the researchers immersed themselves in the data and read the newspaper articles. In this stage, early patterns and themes were identified through open coding, and all themes were reviewed independently by the authors. The next stage of the analysis involved a form of axial coding, where the researchers combined to jointly analyse the identified open codes and early themes, again searching for significant patterns in the data set across the researchers' initial analyses. The final stage of the analysis involved the two researchers jointly analysing the key themes identified from the data set and initial analysis process. The major themes were identified as: (1) Maguire as a legitimate or serious athlete, (2) Maguire as a model Irish citizen, and (3) coverage of Maguire dovetailing with coverage of men's golf. The ensuing sections detail these themes.

'TOP OF THE TREE': MAGUIRE AS A LEGITIMATE OR SERIOUS ATHLETE

One of the striking features of the print coverage of Maguire was an appreciation of her as a legitimate athlete who has experienced vast success. Maguire's high profile of achievements and records were frequently documented; for example, in February 2018 *The Irish Times* reported:

> Last year the Cavan native claimed five wins on the US collegiate circuit and topped it off by taking the Annika Award for the best player of the year in American college women's golf and in doing so became the only one ever to win the award twice. However, her biggest win came at the British Amateur Championship at Pyle & Kenfig which helped her to extend her lead at the summit of the rankings.[31]

Maguire's position at the 'top of the tree' either as world number one or world number two was mentioned in thirty-one of the 116 articles, in both headlines and as descriptors in the main body of text.[32] For example, this headline in February 2018 featured in *The Irish Times*: 'Leona notches up another milestone; Cavan native has broken the record for number of weeks ranked amateur world number one'.[33] Later in the year, in an in-depth piece, Brian Keogh wrote about, 'her college record – two National Player of the Year awards and 10 career wins en route to breaking Lydia Ko's record for the most weeks at the top of the World Amateur rankings with 135...'.[34] Following the end of her 135-week reign as the female world amateur number one, Maguire's world ranking of second (and often her former success as the best amateur in the world), was still drawn upon extensively by journalists: 'Currently second in the World Amateur Golf Ranking, Maguire has achieved almost all her amateur goals';[35] 'The former amateur world No 1 will tee it up at the LET's new Andalucia Open de Espana'.[36]

Alongside Maguire's prominent position as one of the most successful female amateur golfers of all time, much of the reporting focused on her impressive feats and golf ability. For example: '...it was Maguire's...sixth consecutive round in the 60s as a pro';[37] 'Leona Maguire opened with a five-under 65 to share the lead';[38] 'Maguire posted five birdies – at the sixth, eighth, 10th, 12th and 16th – in a bogey-free 67 final round before adding the critical extra birdie at the first playoff hole to guarantee her full tour card.'[39] Maguire was frequently termed a 'star' (nineteen articles), while other affirmative descriptors such as prodigy, talent and professional were used interchangeably.

Related to performance was Maguire's presentation as focused and nerveless, particularly in gaining her professional LET tour card at the end of the year. During LET qualifying in December, Brian Keogh used the headline 'Maguire full of confidence', while she was also described as making sure 'each stride has been solid and surefooted so far'.[40] An *Irish Independent* headline post-tournament read 'Maguire holds nerve to claim Tour card in tense play-off'.[41] Presenting Maguire in this way is in contrast to the ways in which the media presented female professional golfers in the past, as led by emotions and succeeding because of luck.[42] Unlike historical representations of female athletes, and similar to the authors' recent study, the print-media reports here afford Maguire the credibility and legitimacy of a serious professional golfer.[43]

MAGUIRE AS A MODEL IRISH CITIZEN

Less conspicuous but ever present in the print-media coverage was the multifaceted presentation of Maguire's Irishness. Given that Maguire was in college in the US in the four years up to 2018, and the fact that she remained in the US through her transition from amateur to professional golfer, she could be considered a global or at least international athlete. In spite of this, tags of locality and place were regularly used to describe her. Maguire was described as 'Ireland's Leona Maguire' (four times), as Irish (four times), and as a 'leading Irish professional golfer' 'representing Ireland at the Olympics' and a member of the Britain and Ireland Curtis Cup team.[44] The *Irish Examiner* reported 'she represented Ireland at the

2016 Olympics, led the Britain and Ireland team to victory in the 2016 Curtis Cup, and won the 2017 Ladies British Open Amateur Championship'.[45] Much more prominent than the national tags in the print coverage was the description of Maguire as a golfer from Cavan/County Cavan or as a Cavan native (twenty-six times), and as being from Slieve Russell (seventeen times), though the Slieve Russell tag only appeared in articles following her announcement that she was turning professional. All of this evidence combined illustrates the regularity with which local and national citizenship was attributed to Maguire. Similar to the first theme above, the use of national/local identity here supports the construction of Maguire as a valued athlete and legitimises her as a national sporting representative. Similar to Harris et al.'s research on the presentations of the US Ryder Cup team in American print media, the use of local and national tags to describe her might reflect a sense of attachment by the print media in Ireland, and reframes Maguire from being simply an individual professional golfer to a symbol of Cavan and Ireland.[46]

Further to Maguire's depiction as a local and national representative, there is evidence of the media referencing personality traits in descriptions of her that could be understood as valued national characteristics. Maguire was presented as a 'genuine female role model', a sentiment cited in interviews with Irish amateurs Sara Byrne and Molly Dowling.[47] It was expected that her success 'will also attract new players to the game'.[48] An *Irish Times* article written by Philip Reid described Maguire as hard-working, modest, humble, a prodigy, a disciple and the hottest player in the amateur ranks.[49] Free wrote about this in relation to boxer Katie Taylor, where she was repeatedly framed as focused, disciplined and modest, all of which fitted within the cultural ideal in Irish sport of 'not getting above yourself'.[50] Maguire's education and academic achievements were regularly mentioned; she was described as 'the teacher's [*sic*] daughter', referring to her parents, both of whom are primary-school teachers.[51] Maguire's 'impressive academic and sporting achievements' were alluded to, and she was also described as 'hugely gifted academically'.[52] There was some discussion around academic and career choice, where 'Maguire will combine finishing her academic studies with more collegiate golf events.'[53] There was mention of both Lisa and Leona refusing the opportunity to turn professional 'until completing their degrees', while Leona's pursuit of a degree in psychology was mentioned a further four times.[54] Leona was quoted as saying:

> The number-one thing Padraig (Harrington) said to us a few years ago at an awards ceremony was that the hard work it would take to complete our studies and get a degree would be the same hard work it takes to succeed on tour.[55]

The depiction of education is indicative of the class-based nature of golf, and particularly the cultural capital that revolves around the game in Ireland; it may also be illustrative of the class profile of newspaper readership.[56] Further, some of the media discourse around Maguire's personal characteristics could be aligned with the systematic focus on academic excellence and achievement related to middle-class girls and schooling in Ireland.[57] This multifaceted presentation of Maguire as a role model, humble, hard-working and highly educated, demonstrates what has been termed the 'model citizen'.[58] Here, Maguire's national and local identities have superseded the other constructs, but the centrality of gender and social-class ideals are significant – something that will be further alluded to in the conclusion.

COVERAGE OF MAGUIRE DOVETAILING WITH COVERAGE OF MEN'S GOLF

This theme deals with the positioning and quantity of coverage of Maguire within and between articles on men's amateur and professional golf. The peak time in the calendar for golf media coverage is the summer months. As outlined in Table 1, over half of the 116 articles on Maguire were written in the months excluding April through August; this is surprising considering that the peak season for women's golf is also in the summer months.

Table 1. Number of articles written on Maguire in 2018

Jan	Feb	March	April	May	June	July	Aug	Sept	Oct	Nov	Dec
7	6	6	13	9	16	3	7	10	9	12	18

Of the 44 articles with headlines mentioning Maguire, just 16 are between June and October, while there are fourteen alone in December, a month that is often considered as off-season. Of these 14 articles, 11 were about Maguire's performance at qualifying school, 2 featured Stephanie Meadow, and one was an end-of-year review.[59] While Table 1 demonstrates the significance of increased coverage around Maguire's move to turn professional towards the end of the calendar year, it also highlights the marked drop in coverage in the summer months, particularly in July and August. While the total quantity of print coverage dedicated to golf in the sports pages by calendar month is unknown, three of the four men's major golf championships took place in these two months in 2018, and it is possible that this negatively affected the coverage dedicated to Maguire. It seems that even if Maguire were to pull off a high-profile-tournament win in the summer months, the print coverage of such a feat might be undermined by coverage of men's golf at that time.

Of the 116 articles included in the analysis, thirty-three of the articles on Maguire were shared with men's amateur or professional golf; the authors deemed these 'shared' articles. While the spread of articles on Maguire across the calendar year is significant, also of interest to the authors is the quantity of coverage within these shared articles. Of these thirty-three articles, fifteen (47 per cent) had associated images. In the overall dataset of 116 articles, just 28 per cent of these had an associated photo, perhaps confirming the prominence of the shared articles. In some instances in the thirty-three shared articles, Maguire was presented almost as an afterthought, usually at the end of the article. For example, in a piece on Rory McIlroy, Maguire was named alongside other players from Ireland in the last line: 'Michael Hoey and Cormac Shervin are in action in the SSE Scottish Hydro Challenge, with Leona Maguire and Stephanie Meadow set to tee it up tomorrow in the Symetra Tour's Island Resort Championship.'[60] In an article on the PGA Tour's BMW Championship, the final paragraph was dedicated to Maguire: 'on the Symetra Tour, Leona Maguire closed with a four-under 68 to finish tied for 11th on 10-under par in the Garden City Charity Classic in Kansas'.[61] Eight of the thirty-three articles had Maguire as the headline story, and in some of these her achievements dominated the piece.[62] However, other articles where Maguire was the subject of the headline were accompanied by minor reporting. For example, in September 2018 in the first round of a Symetra Tour event, Maguire shot a five-under-par sixty-five to share the lead, and the only newspaper article to cover her performance gave it very little space.[63]

In relation to the thirty-three articles shared with men's golf, the authors calculated the percentage of coverage (word count) dedicated to Maguire, which ranged from 2 per cent of the article to 85 per cent, with an average of 24 per cent. In only two instances was more than half of the word count dedicated to her. On one hand, the strategy by the media to include brief coverage of Maguire's performance within the reporting of the men's game draws attention to the women's tours. As explained in Crosset's ethnographic research on the LPGA tour, 'any press coverage (even hurtful) is better than no press'.[64] However, it can also serve to maintain men's golf in its hegemonic position, as Olympian Sara Treacy outlined in an interview: '…it's pages and pages about the same sports, same players. You very rarely read about Leona Maguire, for example, but if she was a male golfer, she would be all over the papers'.[65] Even though some of this coverage is bitesize, it is worth considering that Maguire appeared as the headline in eight of these thirty-three articles. When compared with the photographic coverage of Maguire within these shared articles, it appears that the newspapers were much more likely to use Maguire for headline attention than for image purposes.

The evidence here suggests that men's-golf coverage may dictate the timing and extent of coverage of women's professional golf, where articles on Maguire dovetailed within and between, and sometimes at the end of, coverage of men's golf. Unsurprisingly, a hierarchy of coverage exists between male and female golfers, where, perhaps, the exploits of Maguire were used to fill the column inches within quieter periods of men's golf. Along with this, men's golf dominated the articles that were shared with Maguire in terms of headlines, word count and associated images. In these instances, Maguire was more likely to be used for headline than image purposes. Overall, in the quest for greater media coverage for female athletes, it appears perhaps that it is not better performances that will earn female professional golfers more acclaim but, rather, performing at the right time in the season.

CONCLUDING REMARKS

Contrasting with the 'rules' Bruce identifies in traditionally oriented media coverage of female athletes, the print representation of Maguire positions her within the 'current rules' where, rather than typical examples of sexualisation and gender marking of female athletes in the media, she is portrayed as a serious athlete and a model citizen.[66] Aside from Maguire's depiction as 'the teacher's [*sic*] daughter', 'a genuine female role model', 'the Cavan woman' and a handful of descriptors linking her to Irish women's golf, the language used in the media representations of Maguire is gender-neutral.[67] Gender was, in fact, conspicuous by its absence and, in contrast to Koivula's findings, Maguire was often referred to by her last name, thereby mirroring the presentation of male athletes.[68] Negating the positioning and quantity of the print coverage, descriptions of Maguire appear to be purely based on a factual discussion of either her upcoming tournaments, her mid-tournament performances, or her final tournament score and ranking. These gender-neutral representations of Maguire mark a shift away from how female athletes have been traditionally presented, and represent some progress in the print-media's coverage of a sport that historically has been gender-segregated. On the surface, the absence of conventional media depictions of a female athlete here is positive. However, the quantity and positioning of the coverage were questionable, and there were few in-depth pieces that might convey an athlete's personality, performances and career trajectory. Just nine of the 116 articles on Maguire were over 500 words, with three of these shared with her sister Lisa, and another three published in early January as 'season preview' pieces.

More significant than gender in the representation of Maguire was the centrality of place and, more specifically, her association with Cavan, Slieve Russell and Ireland. These local and national identities became central to the presentation of Maguire in the newspaper articles. This strategy has been observed by others, including Bowes and Bairner, who describe how women in international sport have a role to play in embodying the nation.[69] Though it has been reported that professional golf is 'relatively inured from displays of nationalism', there are always indicators of nationhood, none more obvious than the national flags placed next to the names of each competitor on tournament scoreboards.[70] Depicted as the 'model citizen', Maguire became a representative of her locality and nation, quite apart from female professional golfers in the authors' recent study, who represented both nation and gender.[71] However, while the focus on Maguire's academic achievements in the articles is positive in and of itself, it also harks back to dated and traditional depictions of female athletes, particularly (though small in number) in descriptions of non-sport-related aspects of Maguire's life. The positioning of education in the articles is also potentially gender-related, where schooling is highly regarded among middle-class girls in Ireland. Perhaps this is unsurprising when considering her position within the conservative, male-dominated, middle-class institution of golf. As such, the print articles convey important messages about gender, social class, golf and national identity to their readership.

In April 2019 Maguire won her first tournament as a professional, the Windsor Golf Classic Trophy. The following day her image appeared on the front page of the *Irish Independent*, the most prominent newspaper in the coverage of Maguire presented here. Maguire is one of the five female-athlete ambassadors in Ireland for the 20x20 media campaign that, among other goals, aims to increase media coverage of women's sport by 20 per cent by 2020 (see Chapter 7: 'Media Sport, Women and Ireland: Seeing the wood for the trees' by Katie Liston and Mary O'Connor). She also has active Twitter (5,865 followers) and Instagram (2,584 followers) profiles through which she promotes her achievements, experiences and sponsors. While traditional media are important in the promotion of female athletes, new and online media may also give opportunities to athletes like Maguire to frame their own coverage and to self-represent.[72] Future research by these authors aims to further investigate the world of female professional golf, with a focus on athlete advocacy and new-media representations of these athletes.

CHAPTER TEN

Women, Media and Sport in Ireland: A round-table discussion

KATIE LISTON

THIS CHAPTER PRESENTS AN edited transcript from a round-table discussion, held at Boston College, Dublin, on 18 May 2019. Present were the editors of this collection (O'Boyle and Free), historian Mike Cronin, who has also contributed elsewhere (chapter 4), and six female round-table participants drawn from the worlds of sport and media: Dr Katie Liston (chair; Ulster University), Cliona Foley (freelance sports journalist), Mary O'Connor (Federation of Irish Sport), Sinéad Kissane (Virgin Media rugby correspondent), Dr Niamh Kitching (Mary Immaculate College, University of Limerick) and Jacqui Hurley (RTÉ Radio Sport). Cumulatively, their multiple roles have involved high-performance sports competition (national and international), sports governance and administration, academic research and media coverage (print, radio, television and newer forms).

The purpose of the round-table discussion was twofold. First, to generate insights into the sports–media nexus, and women's sports in particular, from those at the coalface. The experiences of such a group are not easily summarised or consistent given the demands made on professional working women in multiple roles. Nor are these always captured adequately or in a formal and structured manner such as this. For this reason, the chapter offers a number of important practical and policy insights that will be of interest to students, academics, sportspeople and media professionals alike. The second purpose was to grasp a unique opportunity for enabling advocates of, and for, women's sports, but also highly regarded specialists in their own right, to engage with each other, in effect bringing theory and practice into greater congruence with each other.

The round-table was structured around a framing chapter (Chapter 7: Media Sport, Women and Ireland: Seeing the wood for the trees, by Katie Liston and Mary O'Connor) and a series of semi-structured themes that were circulated to participants in advance. Through engagement with each other, and the natural ebb-and-flow of the discussion (which lasted over two hours), a number of interesting insights emerged. The key themes in this edited transcript encompass the views of participants on the current state of play as regards media sport and gender, changes in the organisational cultures of media and sport that have favoured women, the content of media coverage of women's sport and the tensions associated with gender marking, varying views on gender quotas, new-media forms and their importance for women's sports, future challenges, and markers of success.

Given the length of the discussion, it has not been possible to include a full transcript here. It is anticipated that other versions (incorporating additional themes, such as diversity and challenging gender essentialism) will be made available in podcasts. At the time of writing, two new-media outlets are considering the audio for subsequent release.

Dr Katie Liston (KL): I see this as an opportunity to get a group of different professionals around the table, who are interested in sport and media, whether from a research perspective, a practical perspective or a professional journalistic perspective, with a sensitivity regarding the underrepresentation of women in sports media. To start with, could you explain who you are, your current role, and a short version of how you've come to be in that role?

Dr Niamh Kitching (NK): I'm a PE graduate and also a former international golfer. I played with Ireland from the age of eighteen until mid-twenties. I did a PhD examining golf and golf culture in Ireland, and from there I worked in Junior Golf Ireland, the PGA [Professional Golfers' Association] in England and the PGA in Ireland. I lectured in Limerick Institute of Technology and I'm currently a PE lecturer in Mary Immaculate College. I'm researching women's professional golf with Ali Bowes of Nottingham Trent

University, focusing on opportunities, pay disparity and how golfers are treated in the game and represented in the media.

Mary O'Connor (MO'C): I'm currently the CEO of the Federation of Irish Sport, an advocacy body that speaks to and advocates to government about the value of sport in Ireland, not just physical and emotional well-being, but also the value to society, economically and in terms of community. Economically, it's probably one of the only government departments where you put money in and you get money back out through return on investment, so we're trying to work with the government National Sports Policy that was launched in July 2018. I sit in the steering group. We are seeking to implement that policy over ten years. In the first three years we've had a high number of actions. I am very lucky to be in that position because I love all sports. I used to play for Cork for seventeen years as a dual football and camogie player. Those experiences instilled a kind of passion in me and I wanted other girls to be given the opportunity in a meaningful way to participate in sport. We have over 106 members, seventy-five national governing bodies, and twenty-six local sport partnerships that I had an opportunity to actually engage on the 20x20 campaign [see chapter 7]. It's taken off totally organically as a not-for-profit campaign.

Cliona Foley (CF): I'm a freelance sports journalist. I was a PE teacher. When I was doing PE as a student in the late Seventies/early Eighties I used to spend my summers in America. I wanted to be a sports journalist, so I was following a lot of American media, which I felt was the barometer for good sports writing. When I was working as a PE teacher, and even in college, the men's teams were really celebrated when they won anything, the women's teams weren't. That never sat well with me because our gender balance in PE college was about 50/50. And then when I went teaching, I taught in an all-girls' schools for about seven years. I had conversations with school principals and nuns – 'Why are the girls' successes not even in the local papers?' So I used to send in the results. We never saw women athletes on TV unless it was the Olympics. And similarly with the papers, you saw very little coverage of women's sport. So I saw first of all, we're not seeing it. And secondly, why are there no female sports journalists? And if there was a female sports journalist, would you see more of that? I did a one-year journalism postgrad in Dublin City University and I got a placement in the *Irish Independent*, doing some work in the sports department, then freelance stuff. I worked in the '*Indo*' as staff for about twenty-five years, then three and a half years ago went freelance because the landscape of newspapers and how they're working, with digital and everything else, is changing. I thought it might be time to diversify. So now I write freelance, I do a bit of broadcasting and advocacy for women in sport because there's no constraints, I work for myself. I went to Newstalk. At the time the *Off the Ball* programme hadn't been concentrated as a model. I said we have a lot of sport but we rarely hear female voices, it sounds like six boys chatting down the pub. I suggested that they should do a women's programme. And they were like, 'We're happy with what we do at the moment.' The problem for women athletes, particularly team sports, is you have to do really well before you get covered. I said, 'Can I come in and do a few pilots? I'll do it for nothing.' They said, 'Fire away.' So I got a few allies in there. A few people in there were brilliant to me and said 'Here, I'll produce for you', 'I'll do it on my spare time' or whatever. So the two pilots ended up being two years. Then a year ago they said they'd like me to do it twice a month and we'll pay you a retainer to do that but also a few other things.

Jacqui Hurley (JH): I work in RTÉ as a sports presenter. I do *Sunday Sport* on Radio One and work across a lot of the news bulletins as well. I always had a deep interest in sports. I played basketball for Ireland, camogie for Cork. The media communications and English degree I took at Mary Immaculate College sat well with my interests. It offered me an internship in America. I worked for a CBS affiliate in Mississippi. It was a great chance to learn the nuts and bolts, everything from running cameras, autocue, filing scripts for stories, and eventually they put me on air. When I came back to fourth year in college, I was already employable as a journalist. RTÉ were looking for contributors for a kids' programme, and they asked me up for an audition. I did the sport slot, and they offered me a five-minute slot talking about sports or a five-minute slot talking about celebrity gossip. I loved the media, but sports was the passion behind it. It wasn't getting on TV. It still isn't now, actually. And it's funny, because if you look across the demographic of the room, I would class of lot of people in the same boat, that it's not about you, it's about the story. And I think a lot of sportswomen tend to be like that. I've been in it now since 2006. We don't have the suite of rights that we had [see chapter 12], but I definitely think there's an opportunity in that because there is more of an open mind to outside opportunities. This year for the very first time we're doing the women's soccer World Cup. We would never have even dreamed of going at that. If we had all of the men's rights, we wouldn't have had the money, so with the challenges there are definitely opportunities.

Sinéad Kissane (SK): I work with Virgin Media TV, one of Jacqui's rivals. I started there full-time in 2005. I was always interested in sports. My dad used to coach Katie when she was in school. I was thinking this morning of her relay team, they definitely were our first idols. I suppose you don't realise at the time but they are people you look up to, so I'm delighted to be here today. Athletics was our thing. We were always treated the same, especially because community games was a big thing for us growing up. If there was an under-ten 200 metres for boys, there was an under-ten 200 metres for girls, everybody's success was always celebrated the exact same. When I came into journalism I didn't have that kind of sense of disparity between the way girls and boys are treated because of that background. So I did Arts in UCD [University College, Dublin], specialised in English for two years after that, did a master's in journalism in DCU [Dublin City University], two months' placement in TV3 and stayed there freelancing for a few years – Radio Kerry, too. Last year I became rugby correspondent. It was a position I had to fight for. I'd to literally walk to the chief executive and say I want to be made this position. I also have a column for the *Irish Independent* every Saturday, and it was really only through that I began to see or even write about women in sport. So I think that the space in the *Irish Independent* gave me a chance to kind of understand that and ask questions as to why this is happening.

KL: I have a background in sport, thanks to Sinéad's dad as my coach in school in Kerry. I moved to study social science at UCD, where I was then exposed to soccer and rugby, primarily. So I was fortunate enough, growing up in an era where it was becoming more acceptable for women to participate in sports. I was able to avail of opportunities to play sport to quite a high level that women that are older than us might not say quite so much. I started to study sport, and more seriously at postgraduate level from the background of sociology – understanding the place of sport in society, and because I had an interest in gender that carried through to my doctoral research. And it has broadened into other things now in relation to identity. As I become a little bit older I've had to engage with media much more, and I've had different experiences, some very positive, some very negative. Maybe the newer forms of media are perhaps more flexible and have created a lot of opportunities?

So bringing us up to date a bit more, what would you say now is the current state of play regarding media sport, and its portrayal of gender, or specifically women?

MEDIA SPORT AND GENDER: THE STATE OF PLAY

CF: I'd give you a good example. I would stress I'm a sports journalist, I don't regard myself as a female sports journalist. And that was really important to me. I take gender out of me. When I started in '89–'90, you couldn't specialise in any particular area. You had to cover all sport and I wanted to cover all sport. Even as a journalist I would have subsumed that female side of me in order that I would not be seen as different. I made myself be as anonymous and as generalist as possible in order to get the work done. Because, like Jacqui says, it's about the story. Back then we used to get into the men's dressing rooms in the GAA [Gaelic Athletic Association] and it was sensational because you got extraordinary copy and extraordinary reactions. I would have had problems sometimes getting into dressing rooms. My thing was always 'Hold on, are the physios in there?' and they go, 'Yeah'. I go, 'Male or female?' 'Female.' I go, 'Right, I'm doing the job.' I had to develop a technique for grabbing a towel and handing it to them and looking only there [indicating face level]. In fairness, the guys are brilliant. I do remember a player shouting one time, 'Who's the bird?' Some of us would have got the letters going, 'Who the hell are you, do you get the men to write the match reports for you?', blah blah blah, you'd get particular hate mail from one guy in Dún Laoghaire and my favourite bit about it was he used to actually send the paper and any articles I had were scrubbed out in red and crossed out. One time he said, '… and my wife and my daughters agree with me', which I thought was a classic. But also I went in there thinking I could possibly change this a little. When you work for a commercial entity, what were the reasons for them not covering women's sport? The constant answer you got was, 'Nobody's interested. Look how few people go to the women's game. So we're not going to put staff on these jobs. Spaces are at a premium so we're just going to cover the things that most people are interested in.' My argument would be, 'How can they be interested if they don't know about it?' A good sports story is a good sports story, irrespective of gender. But you struggled with editors in the newspaper business. I come back to this thing of team sport. It doesn't happen in athletics, it doesn't happen in swimming. When the women's 100 metres comes out, or the women's butterfly races come on, it's all viewed equally. I went in initially asking questions and pioneering. After a while – for your career – you think they're just going to see me as constantly nagging them and there is a point at which that flips. We're in a position where other people who were there for a while maybe wanted to be anonymous, but I remember Claire Balding being interviewed a few years ago, she was saying she had a choice between doing the Women's Boat Race and a huge sporting event, the Derby. She said, 'I'm doing the Women's Boat Race.' And I remember thinking 'Thank God she did this' because she now has the profile to do it, whereas I would have at the start not really wanted to rock the boat, considered myself as just a journalist, not a female sports journalist. I cover more men's sports in my job than women's sport, because that's just how the game works. But there is a point at which you go, 'Lads, that's not right. We do need to carry the women's results on the six-o'clock news in the same way that we carry the men's.'

SK: It's something as small as telling your colleagues, 'We actually need to put that in.' And your colleagues are only now kind of listening to you and realising.

JH: I was in a meeting where one of my colleagues said, 'What's on tomorrow?' I said, 'The Champions League Final is on.' And he was like, 'Who's in it?' 'Lyon and Barcelona, it's gonna be a huge match.' Imagine not knowing that Liverpool and Spurs were in the men's! He didn't even know it was on. I said, 'Lads, you need to carry an RVO [i.e. reader voice-over for edited highlights] on that.' 'Okay, grand, we will.' But if I didn't remind them, they wouldn't have even known it was on, so I think we're all at a point now where we can say things and not feel like you're nagging people. I think that's the difference.

SK: The thought that what we're doing is nagging in itself is wrong, that we even think that or people should think that that's what we mean by trying to create more interest. But it's those little things, even to get something in, that's a mini success. There's all these little mini things you're doing that make up the bigger picture.

CF: I was lucky... the [male] group sports editor at the *Indo* at the time... had a policy of sending a male reporter to do the All-Ireland women's finals, football or camogie, which I thought was fantastic. 'I don't want a woman covering it. I want a man's view. I want to be really objective and analytical.' But over the years when I was there, when he went, there was an assumption that you would do it. The GAA correspondents and editors would never cover the women's games. The men's season had just finished and they were tired. There was always a presumption that I would do it because I was a woman and I was interested – in inverted commas. But even last year at the women's football finals, I noticed senior GAA correspondents from newspapers doing the women's game. I had never seen that before. Normally, it's second-tier reporters, juniors or freelancers. To be more balanced and getting more space they have to be the people who are interested. It must be people in the sports department recognising and covering things.

KL: The three of you have said that at some point you begin to gain more confidence in your role, you become more willing to say something, whether it's the micro conversation or drawing more formal attention to women's sports. Is that just your own sense of growing confidence or is there also something that's changing in the organisational cultures of media and sports?

JH: I think it's both, because now there is a broadly accepted norm that we need to do more. I think 20x20 has made people have the conversations. I don't believe in quotas, but 20x20 has actually given people realistic targets. In the office people are going, 'Oh yeah, okay, we better improve those statistics.' One of my bosses would always say, 'If you have an opportunity, take it, don't shove something in there and be tokenistic.' That's what I would like to say, that you'd go, 'Look, do it.' To your other point about confidence, I started presenting *Sunday Sport* when I was twenty-five. Whatever about being the first woman on the programme, I was also the youngest, and there was no way I was going to put a foot out of line. I went from doing four-minute sports bulletins to presenting a four-hour programme, and I hadn't a clue what I was doing. I genuinely was looking at Con Murphy, saying, 'Pull me through this thing, because I don't know.' So it would have taken me a long time to open up my mouth, whereas now I would regard myself as one of the senior radio presenters there. I'm not saying they wouldn't have cared ten years ago, but certainly now I can walk into my boss' office and make a suggestion and he will absolutely listen to it, so I think it's a growth thing, both personally and culturally.

SK: It's awareness and confidence. I remember, after the relay silver in the World Juniors,[1] getting on to an editor of a Sunday newspaper and not seeing the picture on the front page of the sports section. So I just sent him a message saying, 'How come there is not, at the very least, a picture of this team on the front of your sports section?' Now, that is awareness and confidence. I was just so goddamn mad that it was not being recognised. A few years ago I would not have done this, but I had to get on to them and say this is not good enough.

MO'C: As a society, Ireland is evolving. A lot of the NGBs [National Governing Bodies of Sport] have got their act together, Sport Ireland has allocated €18 million to women's sports since 2004. That has led to a whole plethora of different sports finding their voice, bringing athletes through. And I think modern media forums help. You have the radio stations and online media, and so on, but you also have people being their own journalists. That's the one thing that we're trying to get across to the athletes, not just the elite athletes. I'm talking about the girl or the young woman who's just doing her 5k. They can tell their story via their own online platforms. That's really important because we need people to empathise and be inspired by different people with different abilities out there. And it's really important to remember that sport in Ireland for women is in its infancy. If you look at Ladies Gaelic football, it is the most progressive sport in the country, with over 188,000 members. That didn't exist fifty years ago. So you have to recognise that in a lot of sports in Ireland there is a need for a mechanism to have visibility, not just in terms of participation, but in boardrooms, and as administrators, as officials, players, coaches, and so on. I want to give the opportunity for girls to have a meaningful involvement in sports. We've still got a long way to go. There are a lot of niche and emerging sports in Ireland that give such fantastic opportunities. When I was growing up, there were three main field sports and they're great, but some girls don't want to get involved in contact sport. And it's about saying, 'What are the other sports you can try?' There's indoors, outdoors, sea, land, team, individual. It's about making them and their parents aware of those opportunities to participate. That's where the media comes in.

SK: When you say 'meaningful involvement', what do you mean by that?

MO'C: For instance, if you go to primary school, you might get an opportunity to try badminton over a two-week period and then it's gone. It's about having somebody coming in to try badminton, they'll try it for six Wednesdays in a row after school, there's an opportunity, a sustainable structure, where a coach or a club will come to the badminton hall and work on sustainability. NGBs are looking at how we can grow our coaching base and help our clubs, help our volunteers instil confidence in them that there's actually something that they're going to have a meaningful opportunity to participate in afterwards. Sport, when I was growing up, was rigid, the best fifteen played or the best one won. It's becoming a little bit more holistic now. We need to look at the bigger picture. There's an obesity epidemic, there's a sedentary epidemic in Ireland. So it's about saying that sports is positive, it's about having friends, being social, and looking beyond the elitist side.

KL: One of the things we draw attention to in the framing chapter [chapter 7] is the importance of media profile, not only the amount of coverage, whether it's print, or digital or whatever, but the quality of that coverage. America is sometimes ahead a little because the profession occurred earlier. Niamh, you picked up on that in your work on Leona Maguire [chapter 9].

CONTENT OF MEDIA COVERAGE OF WOMEN'S SPORT

NK: Toni Bruce, based in New Zealand, has identified about thirteen rules on the way sports women are presented in the media. In the past they were compared with men's sports and presented in an ambivalent fashion. They were sexualised, they were objectified, and their femininity was emphasised. There was a heteronormative element as well. And so that's the previous or traditional presentation. Currently, they're presented as model citizens or emblems of national identity, or as serious, legitimate athletes. Going forward, there's the use of new media to present themselves. We found a parallel with Toni Bruce's current rules in relation to the way Leona Maguire was presented. Leona Maguire was presented in three different ways in national newspapers in 2018, when she just came off the back of three years in a row being ranked as the world's number-one amateur female golfer and was making the transition to professional golf. Firstly, she was presented as serious, legitimate, as world number one. Secondly, she was presented as the model Irish citizen. National identity was referred to a lot, her being from Ireland, from Cavan, from Slieve Russell. The model-citizen bit was the reference to her education, her psychology degree and when she was going to graduate, her being the teachers' daughter, because both her parents are teachers – a typical middle-class girl. It was appealing to the golf readership, possibly. The third thing was the quality and quantity of coverage. Eighteen of the 116 articles were in December, the off season for golf. Three were in July, peak golf season. So it's not only women athletes performing to a high level and winning that will get them into the newspapers. If somebody like Leona Maguire achieves something really big in the peak season, where would she be positioned in relation to Rory McIlroy finishing in the top five in the US Open or something?

CF: On golf, that role model, that perfect-citizen thing, that's not gender. Competitive elite sport is primarily middle class, very non-inclusive, actually. Also, collegiate sport in America, they sell that academic thing. It was her college that was selling her a lot of the time. I do think the game has radically changed since 2015. And it was by pure accident that I happened to fall into that, to see that there were opportunities there. Some women's sporting organisations have livestreaming. UEFA [Union of European Football Associations] will livestream the Champions League final today. I don't think it's on mainstream. But the worry, particularly with social media, is how do you create new interest outside of that vacuum? So we can all talk to each other saying we're interested in female aspects of sports. But how do we reach the people who – Malachy Clerkin wrote an article a few years ago, 'Why Don't People Care About Women's Sport?' – how do we make people care about them?

KL: Listening to you all, it seems that there's a tension we're constantly managing. In the ideal world we want sport to be gender-neutral, whether as a working professional, writer, academics, former athletes, but at the same time, there's gender marking. Do you gender mark because it is a competitive advantage, if we want to be consumerist about this, but also because almost half the population participating in sport are women? Or do you not?

SK: There's a big contradiction there that sometimes we don't know how to manage. Years ago, people said there's not enough interest in women's sports, but I always thought that there is absolute responsibility on media organisations to give it the coverage it needs, because it's coming from a different historical context.

KL: A legacy of underdevelopment compared to male sport.

QUOTAS VERSUS MERITOCRACY

SK: And Jacqui, what you said earlier about quotas, I would have been absolutely anti-quotas for women, but because women are coming from a different starting point to men, I do believe it's a way of accelerating women's sports to a point where they can try and compete with men's sports. The biggest argument against quotas is meritocracy. Show me ten jobs where you are 100-per-cent sure meritocracy worked. We all know a lot of times that it doesn't exist. So, I definitely think there is a contradiction in some ways, but it is coming from a different historical setting to men so it should be given more of an emphasis irrespective of its wider popularity.

KL: Yes, quotas are a principle that obviously don't just apply to women in sport, they apply to any minority. They have been very successful. I can think, for example, of NFL [National Football League], the disparity between what were called black athletes and Caucasians. You very rarely saw black athletes in some of the key decision-making roles. And the Rooney Rule was another feature in trying to promote the numbers. Sometimes, women themselves have different views on this, as did, indeed, the former junior minister for sport of the time, Patrick O'Donovan, when he raised the possibility. I think quotas have been misunderstood. The research on quotas would indicate that, irrespective of gender or ethnicity, where people are appointed through a process where it's quota-sensitive, everybody gets a lift because the best candidates are in place. So meritocracy is an ideal, absolutely. But actually what quotas do is they force those who are already at an advantage to up their game. They only open up the opportunity for others who were previously excluded, in this scenario women, and then let the best man or woman win because it's not as if a quota is going to put a poor woman above a better-placed man, it's that there is an opportunity to get those minority groups in to be competitive, and then after that let's see what happens. So the idea of setting a quota is actually that it is time-limited and is therefore needed to redress an imbalance, and then when it's reviewed, see what's been the success and move forward.

MO'C: Currently looking at quotas in NGBs, it's fair to say that some of them, because of their history and tradition, probably feel threatened. But I read something last week, I think it was from Bríd Horan in the 30% Club, that quotas aren't about gender balance, they're about better performance. That's exactly what quotas are. Sport Ireland did a survey in 2018. Sport Ireland surveyed the sixty-six national governing bodies of sports. There are 687 board members. One hundred and sixty-one of them are women. That's 23 per cent. And there's twenty-four NGBs in Ireland who have CEOs and six of them have female CEOs. That's rowing, swim, golf, camogie, ladies [football] and now canoe as well. That gives you a baseline where we're at, but there's the mechanism within our organisations then as to how that change can happen. Sport Ireland are working really hard with national governing bodies around governance, but some NGBs are hiding behind their constitution, arguing that the constitution would need to be changed. The recent appointments of the two director generals or CEOs of ladies football and camogie on the GAA central management is a step in the right direction.[2] And more needs to happen. If you look at the newer organisations in Ireland, the niche and emerging ones in particular, especially those with worldwide membership, are a lot further down the line in terms of board members being female, up around 45 to 50 per cent. Maybe that's because of the world societal influence. So I'm hoping that that'll have a contagion effect.

KL: What do the rest of you think about the topic of quotas?

SK: When I said earlier that I don't agree with them, it's in the sense that, as you say, they have been misunderstood. As Mary says, not gender balance but better performance, I'd be all for that. In a government sense, in the elections Patrick O'Donovan was talking about an equal balance of candidates and then let the people decide. That's where we need to be as opposed to saying, 'Look, let's put this person in.' If you look at the FAI [Football Association of Ireland] situation, Niamh O'Donoghue, who was only appointed to that board in 2017, she was the first-ever woman.[3] When you look at the age of the FAI, to have a first female appointed to a board that recently will tell you that there's a long road to be travelled. In a lot of sports in Ireland now, you have some very powerful women in CEO positions. Mary has outlined six of them. There are people like Sarah Keane,[4] who have been part of big movements going forward. But there isn't enough of them. The more key decision-makers we have at the board table, the more it trickles down, it's not just about media and representation. It's actually in all of the rooms, not just the rooms with the microphones.

CF: I struggled with the gender-quota thing because I want to be there on merit and I don't ever want to have anybody say to me, 'You only got this because they were trying to balance the percentages.' So I'm conflicted on the quota thing, but I absolutely see where you're coming from. For years I've been saying, 'Why are we not watching top female athletes analysing men's games?', for example as I saw Liz Howard doing in the Seventies in Ireland, and nobody said anything. And then it stopped. And now it's started again and it's brilliant to see it in rugby and in GAA. I would love to see the equivalent, more men analysing women's games as well just to balance it. But if you look at social media, last week when Joanne Cantwell was the first female presenter of *The Sunday Game*, and Ursula Jacob was on, both of them brilliant at their jobs, you still saw online people going, 'What are they doing with two women there? I can't listen to that.' So the knuckle-draggers are still there.

GAME-CHANGERS AND NEW MEDIA

NK: I don't know if any of you saw the article from Sally Jones in *The Telegraph* on Thursday. She's a BBC correspondent, one of the first live BBC sports broadcasters in the Eighties. The support is there now online for people like her and maybe some of your stories to be told in relation to previous experiences. To take one quote from what she said, 'When I presented daytime coverage of the Seoul Olympics in 1988, one high-profile presenter charmingly put it about that I had only been offered the gig because I had slept with a BBC editor: infuriating, particularly as I was famously prudish and the editor, a portly chain-smoker, provided little temptation.'[5] So the article is really worth looking at. It's really exciting to see the transformation in terms of how female athletes now can be presented and represented online. To turn all Sally's experience on its head, if you look at the example of Tayla Harris, from the AFL [Australian Football League], and that photo that emerged in March, the media are still not sure how to deal with something like that.[6] Should we put it up? Should we take it down? And what's the reaction to it? The Twitterati were at it to try and make a negative thing out of it, but I just think we're still trying to come to terms with new media and certainly, from a research perspective, we cannot keep up with what's happening and how things are going to change.

CF: It has helped the growth of appreciation of female athletes so much. Now there's an opportunity for women to go, 'Hold on, that's not right.' It's changing how media outlets are doing things, including newspapers, who before could always say nobody's interested. But somebody was saying earlier that it's media's duty to cover women's sports. I worked for a newspaper, their entire *raison d'être* is to sell papers and make a profit.

SK: I think they should, absolutely. What is again really important as a game changer is having female analysts on. We've always had female presenters, female reporters, but just even seeing Ursula Jacob – and I think RTÉ have been a leader with this – her giving her opinions, not being afraid to say her opinion, her opinion being just as valid as the two other lads', I think that is massive. And even with the women's coverage as well, some of the best debate I saw all year was after Ireland finished their Six Nations campaign, and they were talking about where the state of women's rugby will be now in Ireland – seeing women involved, not just asking questions, giving their opinions, disagreeing with one another, and not being afraid to do so, having an opinion and being passionate about this, and not being afraid of the consequences through social media or whatever.

MO'C: What's really important as well is the consistency of it. And as a past camogie player, I used to always say, 'Well, if the camogie All-Ireland final is bad, camogie's in trouble', because people's perception of camogie was based on that one game because it was the only televised one. Also it was possibly the only time you'd see a female analyst on *The Sunday Game* and as a player every season. *The Sunday Game* would start and I would hope that in the images there would be a camogie player or footballer, and it was never there in my time playing. Now going back to the point around Twitter, athletes go on Twitter to try and tell their story through social media. Men sports stars will go on Twitter because they know straightaway they have a profile. For example, the night Johnny Sexton came on Twitter he ended up having 200 followers and the following morning he was at four and a half thousand simply because he was Johnny Sexton. I don't think that happens for female athletes. You have to build up and tell their story and actually become successful. That's where the hockey last year was brilliant. Each one of those hockey players on that team were able to tell their story so eloquently as individuals and as a team in terms of what they were trying to do, and I think that really endeared them to our society, it generated conversation in pubs, among men and women.

The one thing about 20x20 that I was adamant about when I was helping develop it was I don't want it to be a comparative. I said, 'Let 20x20 be about action', about people. I think that's what has really been the success of it, people just showing their stripes, demonstrating what they're doing. It could be a tiny, minimum piece or it could be an elite athlete. And that's really the key of the campaign, along with securing five blue-chip sponsors who have shown support of women in sport previously. Also, you had media partners who really bought into this and were saying, 'How can we do more?' Anybody involved in this type of campaign will tell you you normally don't get that many media partners or sponsors totally cooperating, so that is the real success of the campaign.

SK: Where are we at in terms of how we report on women? I think we can all remember when Ireland made the Rugby World Cup semi-final and Fiona Coughlan said afterwards that she was taken aback with the lack of criticism of the way the team performed in the final. Maybe we are overly positive because we feel we need to push them a certain way and if anybody male or female are critical of female athletes, are we afraid that we might be just being sexist?

CF: Because the majority of sports journalists are male they worry about that. And I know even men coaching women will say to you privately that they worried that they're being too hard on them. They're worried they're being too demanding. They're saying, 'Do I have different standards?' First of all, female athletes want to be analysed objectively, they all tell you that: 'Bring it on, tell us. Tell us what you think.' I find they're not worried about the criticism. And I find that female analysts are probably the bravest, men are more wary. And they probably need to be educated that gender doesn't matter, so just analyse them as athletes.

JH: They don't have the information, that's the problem. If you said, 'Here's a profile of Rena Buckley, she has eighteen All-Ireland medals,' what you probably get from the male analyst is, 'Oh, I've heard of her, she's brilliant. Where does she play? Maybe midfield? I'm not sure', whatever. Whereas if you actually gave them the information and said, 'Go up and read about this', or for instance, for the Women's World Cup this year, we're doing it on RTÉ, both Richie Sadlier and Kevin Doyle are working on it, both of them said, 'I know we have the rights to that. I'd love to work on that.' Both of them are brilliant analysts of the men's game, but they've shown an interest in the women's game, they will go and be diligent, and will go and watch women's football, and they will inform themselves because I think if you're a male analyst in a women's game, or a women's analyst in a male's game, it's the information. Bríd Stack is going to be on our team again in two weeks' time, and I'm mentoring her in this other programme through ladies Gaelic football.[7] She was saying to me the biggest thing she had done was the Kerry–Dublin game with Tomás Ó Sé and Ciarán Whelan. RTÉ had positioned her in between the two men. Inevitably, there came to a discussion about the rivalry between Kerry and Dublin, which is exclusive to them. The two boys ended up getting into a debate across her and she was in the middle of it on TV and all she could literally do was turn her head from side to side, and then it came to a point when she contributed her opinion, but it wasn't actually needed because it was about a rivalry. And she was talking to me about the right way to go about that. Because she had never been in a position where she had played against them, she actually didn't have the relevant information to say, 'I marked that lad in a match once and he was a tidy little corner forward', or whatever, whereas the lads are in the same position when it comes to the women's game. So what I think that they both need is to find a way to get the information to be able to manipulate it to the situation. You can get the highlight reels of men's games, but if you're trying to educate yourself on women's team sport, the media organisations have to supply the resources.

MO'C: At the 2012 Olympics we all knew about Katie Taylor and her ability, but for me what gave her even more credibility was that you had Mick Dowling and Bernard Dunne knowing everything about her techniques, and so on. A lot of the guys, they'd be admirers but they don't have the detail. There are very few stats used in women's games in terms of covering them prior to the match. In newspapers they don't even print the full fifteen in a team. Rena Buckley said at *The Irish Times* Women in Sport awards that women want to be criticised more in the media. And that's the thing with the rugby coverage, those three women had their research done and that's important to any athletes, male or female.

CF: Women in media organisations will probably lead that because they may be more familiar with women's games. The *Indo* had a particular way of covering the All-Ireland finals, where they would rate all the players. So when it came to the women's finals, they agreed to do it for them, too. Sometimes, it takes somebody within the organisation to say we must do this the same way as for the men and then the template is there.

JH: On *Sunday Sport* in the afternoons, it got to the point where Derek Kinnevey, who used to be the PRO for ladies football, started texting me with updates during the games after I asked him for a better way to get information to us, and then you would put all that information on air. It's ridiculous but otherwise I'd have had to wait till half past six to get anything back from a match, and we're on air for four hours from two o'clock to six o'clock. In that same time I could go on Longford's Twitter account, Louth, I could get their hurlers' information before I could get Division 1 ladies-football results. In fairness to Derek, he was progressive enough to do it, and Jackie Cahill is doing a great job with ladies football as well. But I do think the other organisations could learn a huge amount from it. Mary McGuire in Basketball Ireland has effectively created her own TV channel. She did a post-match interview with Kieran Donaghy after Tralee won the league this year. That was probably viewed 5,000 times within the space of an hour because it was hilarious. He was cursing, but it was total gold. You couldn't put it on TV, but it was dynamite on social media. She created a vehicle to get that information out there. And it is by the minute. If I wanted to know the score in the basketball cup finals, I could have got it within a minute. Other organisations need to follow that.

MO'C: From a Federation of Irish Sport point of view, for the 20x20 campaign we asked all the national governing bodies to send us their high-level events for a first ever 'Women in Sport Calendar'. Next year, national governing bodies have to get better at saying this was the halftime score, the final score, and so on. It's one thing saying that the event is on, but if you don't report on what happened afterwards, you're going to lose any audience or any traction you had built up.

FUTURE CHALLENGES IN SPORTS REPORTING

KL: Looking to the future in the context of sports reporting, and for women's sports more generally, what do you think are the challenges for you working in those professions? You've mentioned negotiating office politics a lot of time. Do you see that continuing? Do you see other challenges, moving forward?

SK: One of the biggest things that struck me a few years ago was that I realised that sport and the way it was reported was created by men for men. There was a while where I struggled with questions. We ask men a certain type of question, does that mean we can only ask women that kind of a question. I wrote years ago about the effects of menstruation on women, and why this is not spoken about in general. And always the comeback was we don't ask men about that. We don't ask men about pregnancy or the effects on their bodies. Of course we don't because they don't deal with it. But why can't we just take ownership of the fact that women are different, and that's okay. I wrote a piece about how female athletes have been pregnant and how that affects them and how they deal with it. Before it would have been all 'No, it has to be the same as male.'

CF: I find young male sports journalists very open to that. Some particular guys at Newstalk would say things like, 'That's amazing that woman could do that after coming back from pregnancy. Tell me, how does a woman's body change?' I used to get this same argument in my head about why do I mention that somebody is a mother? But that's a massive thing because her body has undergone an unbelievable physiological change. I also still believe that women do most of the parenting. In sports writing a lot of the women writers are not parents, because I think sports writing as a career has particular demands. It's 24/7, you don't do shifts, it's amorphous, every weekend. This might be one of the reasons why there aren't as many women sports writers, whereas there's far more women [in sport] now. If a female athlete is combining that, then we should talk about it. It's just part of their overall being.

JH: I was listening to Ronan O'Gara being interviewed on *Off the Ball* the other night. He's obviously got a big decision to make about his future [as a rugby coach]. And Joe Molloy asked him a couple of times, 'What are you thinking?' He said, 'Well, look, it's not just my decision. Now, you know, there's Jess and the kids.' And I said, 'Thank God he said that because that woman has given up her life with him.' He said he has five children, and he moved to France and then down to New Zealand after playing for twenty years for Munster and they were childhood sweethearts. So she has been with him through the whole thing. But I just thought, this is good now because it hasn't been introduced in the interview, but organically he has brought it up three separate times now, so that people understand that he has more responsibilities than just what he does on the coaching field. You're starting to see more of those stories.

MO'C: What is your view on some clubs taking gender out of their names, for instance Dundee Football Club in Scotland, Derry City?

CF: Well, if you say the Irish team, everyone automatically assumes it's the Irish men's team, but when you said the Irish hockey team last summer, you didn't have to say women's and I deliberately didn't write women's because the prime team at that moment that the country was interested in, the Irish hockey team happened to be women, but historically things are gendered. I put my hand up, I think I invented the Rebelettes! I think Niall Scully invented the Jackies[8] – a really male sports reporter who works with *The Herald*. I'm almost certain, and people said, 'Oh, that's really reductive.' Actually, those gender-neutral identity identifications, I think, are better. The Red Roses[9] is a classic example. Others are the Silver Ferns or whatever it is.[10]

SK: It's something I would have railed against before, but let's reclaim it. Why are we seeing this as a negative thing?

CF: I felt to give them an identity with one word meant I wasn't going to have to write the Cork ladies football team. I don't like the word 'lady'. And it was immediately identifiable, same with the Jackies. I don't think that they're diminishing, it gives them a strong identity. It's a brand and Red Roses is a classic example of it on our podcast, we've actually said, 'Give us ideas', we'd love a name for the Irish women's rugby team. You give them a separate brand to give them an identity that everybody respects. The Green Army was an interesting one, the hockey one.

SK: I would have disagreed with the Rebelettes thing before, but I think it's okay to change your mind on things as you grow up and develop. If we approach this positively, then we might help everybody else as well.

NK: Returning to golf, Ali Bowes and I are looking at a story now in relation to how the European Tour and the Ladies European Tour have represented female athletes on Twitter in relation to an event that was held last year, a mixed-gender event. I wonder, are they moving beyond that kind of pretty and powerful picture? Golf has been open about trying to present itself as more inclusive, as family-oriented, as fun and entertaining, and they're trying to do these short forms of golf. I wonder how much of it is related to profit and how these women athletes are being used as commodities.

CF: When the England women's World Cup team were announced they used celebrities to announce the players, and that's okay. But it would have been much more valuable if you had the top Premiership players saying this is why she's been picked instead of some fabulous celebrities going, 'Oh, she's a fantastic player', and they didn't tell you anything about her. You've got NGBs like the FA [Football Association] trying to expand their audience. So they have to go down the social route, by doing that sometimes trivialising the athlete. Wimbledon historically put the good-looking female players on Centre Court – doesn't happen anymore, but it did happen there. A huge problem women have is how do you get equality if there isn't a financial base first. I think sponsors are changing. There was the Helena Morrissey case [i.e. CEO of sponsor Newton Investment Management] where she said, 'We're not sponsoring the [Oxford-Cambridge] women's Boat Race unless you put it on at the same time and the same venue with the men.' And then Claire Balding also said she's covering it if it's on. I think commercial partners are going to influence this. But let's not pretend things are changing. How many people went to watch a women's hockey club match in Ireland in the last year? That hasn't changed. They have got sponsors on the basis of the World Cup performance, but if people don't go to their games, if money doesn't come in, private media companies who are only in it for the profit will go.

JH: Golf, tennis, basketball have found a way to get into the men's market [i.e. secured a share in a sector dominated by commercialised sports played by and predominantly consumed by men] through the LPGA [Ladies Professional Golf Association], mixed tennis tournaments, WMBA [Women's National Basketball Association]. The sports that have been most successful have aligned themselves to the male tour. What's happening here, particularly with camogie, ladies football, the double-headers are definitely going that direction. That's the way to commercially bring sponsors on board. Then you have the likes of Littlewoods doubling up and doing hurling and camogie. When you look at the pay, though, Louise Quinn, Katie McCabe, all of these people playing football in England, this is not paying them a salary that's life-changing money. Louise Galvin gave up a full-time job in Limerick working as a physiotherapist in a hospital to go to Dublin. It's a dream of hers to play rugby for Ireland. But she has taken a significant pay cut to do so, and had to move her whole life to Dublin. We are asking a lot of our female athletes to do what we call professional when in reality it's really only semi-pro.

MO'C: It's the same with the AFL [Australian Football League] in Australia with the girls who've gone over there recently. It can't be life changing-money either.

SK: I recently did a piece with Leah Lyons who plays in the Tyrells Premiership [the elite women's rugby competition in England]. She plays 15s rugby for Ireland and she said she doesn't get paid for playing in the Premiership. They don't even get expenses, so the club found her a job that she does a couple of days a week. It just pays her rent. This is the extent that female sports people are still going to try, and she's only really doing that so she can be a better player for Ireland.

CF: The narrative in English rugby is that they're all professionals, they're professionals if they're playing for the English team, but at club level they're not professionals. I don't think equality of pay is ever going to happen unless you get the audience sizes. Sponsors can help to put pressure on organisations to improve how they treat their athletes.

JH: I noticed when I was doing research for the World Cup, Ada Hegerberg, who plays for Norway, is not playing. She said, 'I'm not playing for you until we get equal pay.' Why didn't the rest of the team say they're not playing?

SK: The Irish women's [soccer] team all stood together. It was probably the first time that we've seen a group of women come together, sick to death of the conditions that they had to put up with under the FAI.[11]

CF: It does take brave athletes to do that. It took brave athletes at the LTA [Lawn Tennis Association] back all those years ago.

SK: After the [2018] Women's Rugby World Cup, where there was the part-time coach that the IRFU [Irish Rugby Football Union] had put in, I was speaking to a few of the players. There was a genuine fear of speaking out, their development in the game is at a certain point. They didn't want to come up against a massive power like the IRFU. What makes the women's soccer team really impressive is that they went against that fear.

KL: Why RTÉ's coverage of the Women's World Cup will be so important, Jacqui, is that you will be placing front and centre not only who they are on the field of play but what they're doing off the field of play to try to achieve equal pay.

JH: If Title IX in the US was, of the last decade, what has changed women's sport, then an equal-pay lawsuit is going to be what is going to change it for future generations.

MARKERS OF SUCCESS

KL: And that's why role-modelling has been at the heart of 20x20. So I'm going to ask you just to finish with one idea each. On role-modelling, my nephew plays out the back once a week with my partner Róisín. Róisín is Auntie Róisín and he's never seen her play football. She played for Northern Ireland. He was asked at school two weeks ago to write a story about his favourite role model, so he wrote about Auntie Róisín, 'because she's really good at football, she works really hard, she always focuses on skill, she's really encouraging, she teaches me about my left foot and my right foot', for this wonderful story. And he doesn't know that she's a former Northern Ireland international, a former youth hockey player, all of the things that we instinctively think about when we talk about sportswomen, so that for me would be a marker of success for me. It's already happening, but of course it needs to be more systematic and coherent. The role-modelling discussion we're having hits the kernel, and reducing that cognitive dissonance is critical because that's when it has its greatest impact. So that for me will be one to finish with. For the rest of you, what will be a marker of success for you?

NK: I just think more collaboration between the men's and the women's versions, so like we have seen with golf merging, and hopefully that will have an impact in that game. Even just in relation to the events, more mixed-gender events. And then equal coverage, to some degree, of both.

CF: I always come back to the audience size and people caring. If you get more people through the gates, then they will bring money into the sport. It comes back to development of the sport and people getting better at the sport, which brings sponsors and that brings media. It's fantastic to have 50,000 at a women's sport event, but I don't see the consistent interest. I look online and I see some brilliant work being done – The42.ie – and then you go down to the comments section and there's no comments because people literally don't care. Most of the people who consume sport are men, and they seem to be most interested in men's sport. Finally, the French women's rugby team are really interesting. You watch the home games, the Six Nations, they always have huge crowds and they're really mixed gender, both men and women and loads of young boys. Whatever they're doing right in French rugby is really interesting. I'd love to see more mixed audiences, but bigger audiences. That will lead to so much.

JH: The reason why men's sport is so successful in this country is because of the event. When I went to college in America for a year I got a glimpse of what tailgating is, where people just go and support American football. It's like what we have with the GAA here, people going and supporting their home town. If we could find a way to create an event around women's sports that brought people to the day, not necessarily just the match…this year, Mary, is the ten-year anniversary of your first five-in-a-row with Cork ladies footballers. Why could we not create an event around the ladies football this year that says, 'What an amazing team'? It's all about finding a way to bring people with you to share the stories. Lots of people that I met when I was in America didn't give a hoot about the match. But what they loved was that they were barbecuing with their neighbours. Then they went into the match. They enjoyed the hour of the game, but they were gone from their houses for about seven hours. So if I had one wish for the future, it would be to start creating an event, not just a sports match.

SK: I would like to see more females at decision-making. I do think it is changing. I remember the time when we spoke about O'Donovan's recommendation about a sports quota, he was basically laughed off. But I remember those Oireachtas meetings soon after that. Philip Browne [CEO of the Irish Rugby Football Union – IRFU] was asked, and he disagreed strongly, he didn't feel there were enough females around who would have the knowledge to go into those positions. That's all changed now. There are new women in rugby now. It's completely different from everything Philip Browne said before. So I would like to see more female representation because women do bring a different view, they will be unbelievably qualified. Sometimes even with the quota, you almost need to be pushed into a position because you just don't see yourself in it. Sometimes, men are the best people to do this. I'm the vice-chairperson of the Rugby Writers of Ireland and I'm becoming the chairperson. It's only a small thing, but I never would have even thought about something like that.

PART IV

෨

Broadcasting and the Political Economy of Sport

CHAPTER ELEVEN

The GAA and Sky Sports, 2014–17[1]

PAUL ROUSE

> With our TV rights we're constrained, rightly, because we wouldn't get away with selling the rights to the championship to Sky Sports or somebody like that, even though those organisations have expressed an interest. With us, we start from this point – how can we best promote the games and make them available to the maximum number of people.
>
> Páraic Duffy, Gaelic Athletic Association
> director general, 2013[2]

> The GAA have confirmed details of their deal with Sky Sports, with the satellite broadcaster securing rights to 20 games in this year's All-Ireland football and hurling championships... Sky Sports will broadcast 14 matches exclusively on the pay-per-view channel.
>
> *Irish Times*, 1 April 2014[3]

ON 1 APRIL 2014 the Gaelic Athletic Association (GAA) announced a new three-year broadcasting-rights deal, which involved the sale of exclusive rights to certain GAA championship matches for the first time to Sky Sports. This chapter will, firstly, examine the reasons the GAA advanced for doing a deal with Sky Sports; secondly, place the deal within the context of the GAA's history, its rules and its apparent evolution; and, thirdly, make observations about the immediate impact of the deal, notably by examining viewing figures.

The decision to sell exclusive rights of games to Sky Sports revealed, in vivid detail, the tension between the GAA's nationalist rhetoric of representation and inclusivity as a uniquely Irish organisation and the neoliberal logic of its actions in selling its broadcasting rights in order to maximise profit. Doing a deal with Sky Sports also underlined the extent to which the GAA had been transformed in the new millennium. For all the imagery of the advertising rooted in its popular base in communities across Ireland, and its avowed commitment to the 'amateur status' of its players, there was no denying that rapid, all-pervasive commercialisation was revealing how the GAA's actions stood increasingly at odds with its oratory. Ultimately, the deal with Sky Sports underlined the extent to which the GAA's *Official Guide* was now framed by a mission statement and included rules that were entirely at odds with the way its officials were acting.

For the week that followed the announcement, a media storm raged around the decision. On 2 April 2014, for example, the *Irish Independent* headed a report, 'GAA Faces Backlash Over Sky Sports Deal', while *The Guardian* headlined 'Gaelic Football and Hurling's Ruling Body Accused of Selling its Soul to Sky'.[4] However, the reaction to the GAA's deal was more than a mere media storm. The association faced widespread criticism from its own membership about the decision. Motions calling for the ending of all deals with Sky Sports were passed by clubs and by county boards (including Dublin, Leitrim, Clare and Roscommon), and various members were trenchant in their opposition. For example, letters to newspapers included one to the *Limerick Leader* that described the deal as 'a thundering disgrace', and referred to 'dismay', 'anger', 'disgust'.[5] Members in Connacht eventually launched a 'Keep Gaelic Games Free to Air' campaign.[6] The arguments pressed into the political sphere with every county council in Connacht, and several other county councils in other provinces, passing motions in opposition to the GAA's selling its screening rights to Sky Sports.[7] GAA President Liam O'Neill and Director General Páraic Duffy were called before the Oireachtas Joint Committee on Transport and Communications to outline the rationale for the association's new broadcasting contract with Sky Sports.[8]

Against that, there were other elements within the GAA who were entirely happy with the decision. A spokesperson for the Gaelic

Players' Association, the body representing inter-county Gaelic footballers and hurlers, who constitute around one per cent of the playing base of the GAA, said,

> We'd welcome it and the reason why we would welcome it is quite clear. We believe that any move by the GAA that increases exposure for our games and our players is welcome by the Players' Association…I think the GAA is safeguarding its own commercial future. It is a commercial move. It needs to be commercially viable and it needs to compete with other sports.[9]

Other commentators, such as the *Irish Independent*'s GAA columnist Martin Breheny, viewed the supposed 'backlash' as the product of a hysterical overreaction, notably driven by the self-interest of the national public-service broadcaster RTÉ, which generated a controversy around a run-of-the-mill decision to maximise revenue of the sort that sporting organisations make all the time.[10]

Opposition to the Sky Sports deal was fuelled by the failure of the GAA to set out a coherent, sustainable logic to its decision. This was particularly important because, for many years, the GAA had stressed time and again that it would never put its championship matches onto Sky Sports. This was repeated by a succession of GAA presidents since the 1990s, and found eloquent expression at GAA Central Council meetings and at annual congresses, where delegates proclaimed, 'It is very important to hold what we have and we want our games without having to pay an extra charge' and 'I say we've been served well by our national networks and by TG4. Let us not be blinded…Is that the way we're going to treat the people who built up the association? Let us not sell our soul.'[11] As if to emphasise its rhetorical commitment never to sell its games to Sky Sports, in 2011 'the GAA hierarchy told the Department of Communications, Energy and Natural Resources that it would not sell rights to a foreign channel as it was "contrary to the culture and national ethos of the association"'.[12]

THE GAA'S 2014 MEDIA DEAL AND IRISH EMIGRANTS

The central part of the GAA's media deal in 2014 – designed to run for three years – was the allocation of live TV broadcast rights in

Ireland for the All-Ireland senior football and hurling championships. Here, the GAA gave RTÉ the rights to broadcast thirty-one matches and Sky Sports the rights to broadcast twenty matches. Excluding the shared matches, RTÉ was left with the exclusive rights to twenty-five matches and Sky Sports with the exclusive rights to fourteen, with six matches shared. On top of this, a further suite of deals involved the creation of a new online digital-TV service for emigrants called GAAGO.[13] Games shown on Sky Sports were not part of this service for emigrants living in Britain.[14]

In the aftermath of the deal it was repeated time and again by the GAA hierarchy that this was not a deal made for money. What *is* accepted is that the money paid by Sky Sports was not transformative. The exact sum paid by Sky Sports has never been released, but the increase in media income earned by the GAA amounted to just €356,000 above what the GAA had previously been making.[15]

If not for money, then, why was the deal made? In its press release about the deal, in a series of interviews with media outlets, and, later, in testimony to the Dáil Committee on Transport and Communications, the GAA advanced two primary reasons: providing coverage to Irish emigrants, and raising awareness of the game internationally.

Turning first to the issue of providing a service to emigrants, the Dáil Committee on Transport and Communications was told on 15 April 2014 by the GAA hierarchy – represented by its president, Liam O'Neill, and its director general, Páraic Duffy – that 'this was the priority issue in our approach to the rights negotiations'.[16] In this context it is easy to see how developing GAAGO was a logical and laudable initiative, as was the transmission of forty-five live games on free-to-air TV in Australia. As it turned out, almost none of these forty-five games were shown live on Channel Seven; rather, they were shown as deferred broadcasts, once the late-night film was over. The transmission of games on Channel 7, whether live or deferred, was abandoned after the 2014 season was completed, and was not replaced by any new element.[17]

The central point in the argument presented by the GAA was that the deal with Sky Sports was designed to serve Irish emigrants living in Britain. The GAA told the Dáil Committee on Transport and Communications that '11 million households in Britain' would now be able to see live GAA matches. Páraic Duffy, the GAA *ard stiúrthóir* (director general), also announced on radio, 'If we hadn't made this deal with Sky, there is a huge Irish population in Britain that would see no games live. They will now see 20 games live.'[18] However, eleven million households in Britain did not have Sky Sports in 2014 – the figure may have been somewhere around four or possibly five million (Sky Sports does not release these figures); what the '11 million' households had in 2014 was Sky TV, a platform like Sky TV or UPC in Ireland.[19] And every one of those '11 million' households already had the opportunity to watch live GAA matches weekend after weekend. Premier Sports, part of the Setanta Sports organisation, had since 2009 broadcast every championship match shown live in Ireland all across Britain; it did so for a subscription of £10 a month. The advertising campaign mounted by Premier Sports, including advertisements in the newspapers and online, makes it difficult to imagine that many Irish emigrants could not have known that Premier showed live GAA matches. More than that, Premier Sports also sponsored Warwickshire GAA and the London junior football team, and actually broadcast *every* live GAA match shown in Ireland, including club games and league games shown on TG4, Setanta, TV3 and RTÉ. This amounted to some 100 games in a year.[20]

Now, under the new Sky Sports deal, Premier Sports lost the twenty inter-county matches that were shown on Sky Sports, including the All-Ireland semi-finals and finals in both hurling and football, though they retained the remaining games as previously. The upshot was that, instead of just paying the £10 per month for Premier Sports, Irish emigrants who wished to see all televised GAA championship matches were now required to pay at least £30 per month for Sky Sports.[21]

Ultimately, when the rhetoric of serving emigrants is stripped away, what is left is the provision of a service that was already available but was now fragmented and cost at least three times the earlier price.

RAISING AWARENESS OF GAELIC GAMES OUTSIDE IRELAND

The second aspect of the deal with Sky Sports relates to the expressed desire of the GAA to raise awareness of Gaelic games abroad among people who had never – or as good as never – heard of the GAA or seen its games. This is something that no lover of hurling or Gaelic football could criticise in principle. But what exactly was the purpose here? What was the GAA's plan? What was the virtue of raising awareness, or was that awareness supposed to be virtue in itself? Ultimately, it seems reasonable to ask the basic question: To what end?

What *is* apparent is that the spread of particular sports into countries where they have not previously enjoyed a substantial presence in the modern era is a complex phenomenon.[22] There is clearly a global television market that can facilitate the spread of sport. Almost always, however, this involves 'a few privileged sports' outmuscling others. As Wladimir Andreff argues, 'In fact, television exacerbates all other factors of uneven economic development across different sports.'[23] It is possible for sports to attract new players and new audiences across the globe, but it requires clarity of purpose and the significant commitment of time and resources. Even then, there are no guarantees. A local guide in Ireland on the challenges involved in spreading a sport can be found in the GAA's continued attempts to spread hurling across Ireland; these attempts have enjoyed sporadic success, at best. For example, despite intensive television coverage for more than two decades, there remains only one hurling team from Connacht and one from Ulster in the top two tiers of inter-county hurling. There is no convincing evidence that this will change in the foreseeable future.

The essential point here is that there is no evidence that the GAA chose to sell its games to Sky Sports as part of a coherent plan – or any plan – to internationalise its games in any meaningful way. The claims around raising awareness of the GAA internationally are something that have been repeated at a series of GAA meetings from its very earliest years.[24] Ultimately, in respect of the sale of games to Sky Sports, the ambition to raise awareness of Gaelic games internationally offered an obvious rhetorical justification for the decision, but such rhetoric was untethered from any other initiative.

DEBATING THE DEAL

It is clear that some within the GAA hierarchy were wounded by the manner in which they were questioned (particularly on RTÉ) after the Sky Sports deal was announced in April 2014, and by the criticism of their decision. The GAA president, Liam O'Neill, said,

> Last night's (Tuesday's) performance by RTÉ was shocking and you must recognise that yourselves. You know about balance and fair play and you know that what happened last night was not fair. The tenor of the whole coverage…I felt disappointed. There was no part of the RTÉ coverage across their entire platform that was balanced. I haven't expressed it to them yet but I will…I don't think in fairness to them that there was anything negative they could throw at us that they didn't.'[25]

Particular exception was taken to the 'claim which would have it that the GAA went to Sky for the money'.[26] A Dáil Committee on Transport and Communications was told by the GAA's director general, Páraic Duffy, that any suggestion that the GAA was driven by financial ambitions in its deal was 'cynical' and 'cynicism has always been the easy refuge of those who are afraid to engage in analysis and reasonable debate'.[27]

There are many basic questions that would be central to any such debate. First, about how an organisation that makes so much of its commitment to being community-based, to being open to all, to being inclusive, chose a broadcasting policy that is, in significant part, inimical to those aims. How could one profess the values that the GAA professes and at the same time sell exclusive rights to a broadcaster that was subscribed to by just one-in-six of the population of Ireland in 2014?

On a practical level, the GAA had an avowed policy of combatting alcohol abuse. It set up a task force to examine the issue and then set out a clear series of protocols, including the refusal of sponsorship from alcohol companies. But research shows that sport shown exclusively on pay-TV doubles and even trebles the proportion of the audience who go to licensed premises to watch it. More than that, research also shows that a significant proportion of parents who go to licensed premises to watch pay-TV sports events also bring their children with them. Indeed, that figure reached one in five. The internal contradiction in policy in respect of alcohol is obvious.[28]

Why also was the Irish broadcaster TV3 excluded from the deal, given the manner in which it had successfully provided the previously long-cherished alternative to RTÉ? It should be remembered that the great loser in the 2014 media-rights round was TV3, not RTÉ. This was the case because TV3 had lost the rights to the live broadcast of *any* GAA match, while RTÉ retained the rights it previously held.

Finally, why were the rights to broadcast GAA matches to Africa, Asia and America taken from Premier Sports? Presumably, the answer to that question – although one was never provided – lies in the ambition to spread the association's GAAGO service. But, even if that is accepted, how does it fit with the supposed ambition to internationalise the audience for games?

THE GAA AND SKY SPORTS: RHETORIC AND RULES

It was more than a little surprising that the GAA hierarchy was taken aback by adverse reaction to its Sky Sports deal. For twenty years the organisation's leadership had repeated time and again that it would never do a deal with Sky Sports. These statements were unequivocal and continued right up to the time the deal was made. Sometimes, they were made at the GAA's annual congress, as when the then president of the GAA, Jack Boothman, said: 'The GAA can never in conscience decide to sell television rights to any media provider who will not be widely available throughout the country and which will not be national in character. We are not going to sell our people down the river for money.'[29] GAA presidents from the 1990s up to Christy Cooney (2009–12) repeated this commitment not to sell the exclusive rights to GAA matches to Sky Sports.

Then, in a book published in 2013, *Irish Examiner* journalist Michael Moynihan quoted GAA Director General Páraic Duffy saying the GAA would not sell TV rights to Sky Sports and that the reason for this was that it could not do so even if only 10 per cent of the population didn't have Sky Sports. The logic was straightforward: 'There's a sense that the GAA belongs to everybody in Ireland, that it's in every parish and village, and that there'd be enormous resistance if we were to take the games off free-to-air, even though the majority of the population probably has access to Sky.'[30] Six months after the publication of the book, the GAA announced its deal with Sky Sports.

As well as the rhetoric of its officials, the context of the GAA's *Official Guide* also merits consideration. The *Official Guide* is absolutely clear that the GAA's relationship with Irish nationalism is fundamental to its operation. On the first page of that guide – in what amounts to a three-paragraph 'mission statement' – it is claimed that those who play its games and who run the organisation see the GAA as 'a means of consolidating our Irish identity'. More than that, it sees the 'primary purpose of the GAA' as being 'a means to create a disciplined, self-reliant, national-minded manhood'. And more than that again, all of this amounts to 'the expression of a people's preference for native ways as opposed to imported ones'. The *Official Guide* moves on to note that, because of partition, 'Ireland's claim to nationhood is impaired', and concludes: 'Today, the native games take on a new significance when it is realised that they have been a part, and still are a part, of the Nation's desire to live her own life, to govern her own affairs.' Further, there are short portraits of the men who founded the GAA, in which they are lauded for the commitment to the creation of a 'Free and Gaelic Ireland'. There is also a reprint of Archbishop Thomas Croke's letter, written in support of the GAA in December 1884, in which he pledges his support for the GAA against the 'degenerate dandies' of the Empire and their games, which were mere 'effeminate follies'.[31]

It is one thing, of course, to have a mission statement and altogether another to have actual rules that give meaning – or attempt to give meaning – to broader ambitions. And the GAA has a slew of rules in its *Official Guide* that are framed around these ideas of Irish nationhood. For example, the GAA commits itself to 'actively support the Irish language, traditional Irish dancing, music, song, and other aspects of national culture'. It also commits to 'use all practical endeavours to support Irish industry, especially in relation to the provision of trophies and playing gear and equipment'. Indeed, the GAA's rule 1.4 states that 'The Association shall use all practical endeavours to support Irish industry…'.[32] The contradiction between the GAA's rules and its sale of its games to Sky Sports is obvious. In this respect it is worth noting the comments of TV3's director of broadcasting, Niall Cogley, who expressed his disappointment that his company had been cast aside in favour of Sky Sports:

TV3 has been proud to broadcast the GAA championship free to viewers throughout the country over the past six years. TV3 made a very commercial bid for the next three years but this appears to have been superseded by the GAA's preference for a pay television strategy.[33]

THE GAA'S SKY SPORTS DEAL: SUCCESS OR FAILURE?

The controversial nature of the deal with Sky Sports appears to have induced in the GAA leadership a desire to pronounce the success of its decision at the earliest possible juncture.[34] Viewing figures were claimed by Director General Páraic Duffy to be a 'vindication', and opposition to the deal was presented as 'whining' and 'moaning' in September 2014. By December 2014 the GAA's president, Liam O'Neill, was claiming that 'the Sky component of our media rights deal has worked really spectacularly for the organisation'.[35] Do these statements stand up?

Measuring success, or otherwise, of a TV deal for a sports organisation is an inexact science, but it is important to look at two aspects: viewership in Britain and viewership in Ireland, using measures overseen by the Broadcasters' Audience Research Board (BARB) and TAM Ireland (Television Audience Measurement Ireland Ltd), which oversee audience-measurement systems for the whole of the television-advertising industry. In respect of Ireland, fair comparisons of viewing figures are rendered less possible by the fact that, while Sky Sports 3 is measured in Ireland, viewers with Sky Sports 3 HD are not counted.[36] Allowing for this, it is clear that the home viewerships for matches shown on Sky Sports in Ireland were dramatically lower when compared with similar matches shown on TV3 in 2013 and when compared with similar matches on RTÉ in 2014. For example, when Sky Sports showed the Dublin–Monaghan All-Ireland football quarter-final in 2014, average viewership was 54,000. By contrast, the previous year's Donegal–Mayo All-Ireland football quarter-final on TV3 averaged 442,800 viewers, while viewership of the 2014 Dublin–Tipperary All-Ireland hurling quarter-final on RTÉ averaged 480,900. That 54,000 total was just about the highpoint of Sky Sports' performance. In the middle of the 2014 hurling summer, its coverage of the Tipperary–Galway All-Ireland hurling qualifier averaged 35,200, while just 10,400 watched the Armagh–Monaghan Ulster football championship match.

In the summer of a World Cup, the GAA chose to put showpiece games on Sky Sports, and the result was clear. Take Saturday 14 June 2014: Dublin versus Wexford in the Leinster hurling championship averaged 18,000 viewers on Sky Sports; later that evening Uruguay versus Costa Rica averaged 358,900 viewers on RTÉ. It should be noted that the average viewership on TV3 for GAA matches in 2013 was 288,900 over eleven matches – that is, more than ten times higher than the Sky Sports average for 2014.

Incidentally, and unsurprisingly, when games were shown simultaneously on both channels, RTÉ won hands down. Take, for example, the drawn 2014 All-Ireland hurling final, where Sky Sports averaged 15,600 viewers (with a peak of 26,300), while RTÉ averaged 577,000 viewers (with a peak of 935,000); or the 2014 Dublin–Donegal All-Ireland football semi-final: the Sky Sports average for the latter was 5,400 viewers (average share: 0.5 per cent), while RTÉ's average was 665,000 viewers (average share: 60.2 per cent).

These figures proved to be tellingly predictive of those that followed in 2015 and 2016. For example, for as high-profile a hurling championship game as Cork versus Clare in June 2015, the average viewership in Ireland on Sky Sports, which had exclusive rights, was 37,700. To put that number in context, on 18 June 2015 (to choose one night at random), the average viewership for *Oireachtas Report*, shown after midnight on RTÉ One, was 44,400. To choose another programme at random, a June Thursday afternoon 4.30 p.m. repeat showing of *Judge Judy* on TV3 drew an average viewership of 39,600. Basically, high-quality live hurling championship matches shown on Sky Sports in Ireland draw fewer viewers than repeats of *Judge Judy* and the post-midnight 'highlights' of Dáil debates in the middle of summer. The evidence is clear-cut: disastrous viewing figures for important championship matches have underlined just how extensively the GAA disenfranchised its own communities by shifting games to Sky Sports. These are people who, in many instances, have given or continue to give a lifetime of service to the association, and there is no hiding from a decline that approaches 90 per cent in terms of home viewership.

Turning to Britain, the average home viewership audience in Britain for matches shown on Sky Sports in 2014 was 32,000; this amounts to 0.25 per cent of all the people watching television at any given time in Britain, according to BARB ratings. The low point was the 8,900 who watched the Sligo–Cork All-Ireland football fourth-round match, while the high point was the average of 104,000 viewers for the drawn Tipperary–Kilkenny All-Ireland hurling final in 2014. The context of that high point is important: the final was the only match shown on Sky Sports 1 (the rest were shown on Sky Sports 3), and it was shown on a weekend in which there were no other events broadcast live on Sky to compete with it. The normal average audience for a Sunday afternoon slot on Sky Sports 1 is between 1 million and 1.8 million.

Figures are not available for facilitating a season-long comparison with Premier Sports as figures from that station appear only to have been collected from 2014. In the early rounds of the championship, Premier Sports drew audiences of between 8,000 and 12,000. The situation was then skewed by the arrival of GAAGO: Irish emigrants to Britain could not watch any of the twenty games (including the All-Ireland semi-finals and finals) shown by Sky Sports on GAAGO, but could watch all the games shown by Premier Sports on GAAGO. This was an arrangement unique across the 150 countries in which GAAGO broadcasts.

What we cannot do, either, is establish the extent to which the games drew their wider audience from among Irish emigrants as against newcomers. The GAA's annual report, *An Chomhdháil Bhliantúil 2015*, referred to 'young, English-born people, who have been arriving in substantial numbers at our UK clubs seeking to take up football and hurling. Many of these newcomers have no background in Gaelic games, but were simply enthralled by what they saw on TV'.[37] However, when requested, the GAA was unable to provide numbers relating to the new members drawn to the GAA by Sky Sports, and acknowledges that such claims are anecdotal. Subsequent years have brought no evidence of these 'substantial numbers', not least because other anecdotal evidence from Britain suggests that any Sky Sports-related influx is extremely difficult to discern.[38]

Showing the games on Sky Sports certainly brought new viewers to GAA matches. Newspaper pieces noted the viewership (and approval) of individuals as disparate as Queen Elizabeth and the soccer player Joey Barton. There were also summer-long newspaper articles noting Twitter commentary ('Watching the hurling on Sky Sports 3. My paddy cousins are feckin mad. What a mental game' and 'First time watching Hurling on Sky Sports 3. From what I can gather it is a sport that involves lots of guys having a pub fight on grass'). This was something that was favourably referenced in the GAA's 2014 annual report, which noted the 'excited Twitter reaction'.[39] That the GAA should have felt it necessary – or even appropriate – to refer favourably to commentary on Twitter as evidence of the success of the Sky Sports deal is most striking (not least given the expressed nationalist ambitions of its *Official Guide* and its perceptions of its own history); there appears to have been no consideration of the gross stereotypes that were perpetuated in numerous references to the 'Irishness' of the games.

SKY SPORTS VIEWERSHIP IN IRELAND

The most striking thing, of course, is how utterly predictable these figures were: indeed, they were completely in line with what happened, for instance, following the move of Heineken European Cup rugby from RTÉ to Sky Sports. Ratings show clearly that far fewer people watched Heineken Cup rugby in 2006–7 when it was shown in Ireland exclusively on Sky Sports than when it was broadcast free-to-air on RTÉ in 2005–6. A direct comparison can be made between the quarter-finals of the competition in successive years, played in the aftermath of successful international rugby seasons that saw Ireland win the Triple Crown and enjoy an unprecedented media profile. On Saturday 31 March 2007, Leinster played an away Heineken Cup quarter-final against London Wasps. The game was shown live on Sky Sports 1. The previous year, at the quarter-final stage, Leinster had played away at Toulouse, again on a Saturday afternoon, 1 April 2006. This game was shown free-to-air on RTÉ. There was a significant difference in viewership:

- 255,000 people watched the 2006 match on RTÉ, 47,000 people watched the match on Sky Sports in 2007.

- 27,000 children under fourteen watched the 2006 match on RTÉ, 2,000 children under fourteen watched the match on Sky Sports in 2007.
- 67,000 women watched the 2006 match on RTÉ, 9,000 women watched the match on Sky Sports in 2007.
- 111,000 people in rural areas watched the 2006 match on RTÉ, 9,000 people in rural areas watched the match in 2007.
- The decline in people watching the quarter-final was particularly pronounced in Connacht–Ulster, where the number of viewers fell from 45,000 for the 2006 RTÉ broadcast to 3,000 for the Sky Sports match in 2007.
- 19,000 farmers watched the 2006 match on RTÉ, 1,000 farmers watched the match on Sky Sports in 2007.
- 98,000 people over fifty-five watched the 2006 match on RTÉ, 14,000 people over fifty-five watched the match on Sky Sports in 2007.
- The overall share of all viewers watching television at that time fell from 33.2 per cent on RTÉ in 2006 to 5.5 per cent on Sky Sports in 2007.[40]

This collapse in viewership is not a phenomenon restricted to Ireland. In 2006 Sky Sports paid £220 million to cover English test, one-day and county cricket over a four-year period beginning in 2006. The only cricket that would be shown on free-to-air television would be a forty-five-minute highlights programme on Channel 5, the least watched of all the main English stations, and the highlights were timed to coincide with unshakeably popular soaps on other stations such as *EastEnders* and *Coronation Street*. In general, the viewing figures that followed for Sky Sports broadcasts of cricket matches were disastrous. For example, the estimated average viewing figure in 2006 was just 261,000; this was about one-third of the figure for those who had watched cricket on Channel 4 the previous year, and only one-sixth of the average figure for those who used to watch live test-match cricket on the BBC before 1998.[41] In essence, this is not a story of Irish exceptionalism; rather, a local manifestation of a much broader trend.

CONCLUSION

The basic facts of the impact of the sale of Gaelic games to Sky Sports cannot be disguised. Viewing figures for those showcase GAA games sold exclusively to Sky Sports were extremely low, and had collapsed by comparison with figures from earlier seasons when they were free-to-air. Further, the supposed new service for Irish emigrants in Britain not only already existed but did so in a more extensive way. More than that, Irish emigrants who wished to watch Gaelic games in Britain now paid much more than was previously the case.

The matter was discussed at the association's annual congress in 2016, when a motion from Dublin sought to outlaw the exclusive sale of All-Ireland championship games to Sky Sports. In advance of the debate on the motion, the GAA shifted the ground on which it based its arguments. In the course of shifting its ground, it made it absolutely clear that, in selling its games to Sky Sports, the GAA was doing so *only* for the money. The shift in the GAA's position on Sky Sports actually began with the publication of Director General Páraic Duffy's annual report for 2015. Duffy wrote: 'Any restriction that prohibits the GAA from engaging with all interested parties, including subscription TV providers, would seriously reduce our negotiating power…'.[42] In the end, the debate at the annual congress was not on the *merits* of the Sky Sports deal, of course; rather, it was simply on whether it was prudent to tie the hands of the GAA in advance of negotiations on the next deal. The argument against passing the motion was that there was a logic to keeping all available buyers in the auction in order to drive up the price. The result was that the annual congress decided to 'trust the leadership of the GAA to make the right decision' when it comes to the next broadcast deal.[43]

The decision on the next deal duly arrived in 2017. Despite the collapse in its viewing figures and the opposition from its own membership, GAA officials deemed the Sky Sports deal to have been a success, and announced that it would again sell the exclusive rights to almost one-third of senior All-Ireland championship matches to Sky Sports. This came as no surprise; to walk away would have entailed acknowledging that the initial decision was ill-judged. That the GAA now decided to break with its tradition of making media deals that lasted three years and decided, instead, to extend this new deal across the next five years was rooted in two basic desires: to sustain the illusion that the deal with Sky Sports is working well for the GAA, and to 'normalise' the idea that Gaelic football and hurling should be put behind an additional paywall and sold to pay-TV sports channels. That the 'new normal' was at odds with its own *Official Guide*, with the imagery of its advertising, with the legacy of its history, and with the words of its own officials, was simply ignored.

A Level Playing Field? Irish broadcast-sports rights and the decline of the national

RODDY FLYNN

T HE SYMBIOTIC RELATIONSHIP between RTÉ as the national broadcaster and 'official' national sports (i.e. sporting codes unique to Ireland or games involving the national team) has, until relatively recently, been taken for granted. In its various incarnations since 1926, RTÉ's deployment of sports coverage has constituted a key element in the station's construction and reinforcement of markers of national identity. However, the arrival of active competition from local and international players into the Irish broadcasting scene since the late 1980s has complicated the nature of the RTÉ–sports nexus. This chapter explores the implications of these changes and asks what the gradual leakage of national sports away from RTÉ means for that station's particular status. Can RTÉ still assert its position as a national broadcaster if it is no longer the 'natural' home of Irish sport?

The role played since 1926 by the Irish national broadcaster in a larger project to assert a coherent vision of nationality and nationhood as a legitimating identity for the nascent Irish state is well established in Irish cultural-studies literature. Taken together, state support for institutions emphasising a particularly Gaelic vision of identity points to a reasonably coherent project of 'nationing'[1] during the 1920s and 1930s. This is evident in the revival of the Tailteann Games between 1924 and 1932, the creation of the publishing board An Gúm, the official elevation of the Abbey to the status of national theatre (both in 1925), and the suppression of potential counter-narratives via the Censorship of Films Act (1923) and the Censorship of Publications Act (1929). The broadcaster's arrival in the midst of this project ensured that it would in some way be imbricated in it. Thus, while, for purely pragmatic (that is, financial) reasons, the Irish state initially expressed a preference for a privately run broadcaster, this was overridden by the need, in the words of the Special Dáil Committee on Broadcasting in 1924, to ensure that radio was used to minister to 'cultural progress'.[2] This faith in broadcasting's capacity to promote a national culture was widely shared. During the 1924 debates around the establishment of a national broadcaster, for example, the Radio Association of Ireland stressed how, 'With State control of broadcasting that great national spirit which has been the forerunner of all national prosperity in every country of the world will have ample opportunity of development.'[3] That 2RN, the original incarnation of the state broadcaster, might play a particular role in this regard was made explicit by Gaelic League founder Douglas Hyde's opening broadcast on 1 January 1926:

> A Nation is made from the inside, itself, it is made, first of all, by its language, if it has one; by its music, songs, games and customs... Éire is not completely saved yet, and will not be until the foreign influence is wiped out.[4]

Hyde's manifesto, with its stress on language, culture and sports, found expression in the early 2RN schedules, even if the paucity of funds voted to the radio service constrained active production of new content to promote the national culture. The station relied instead on already existing content to promote a vision of nationhood, with a strong emphasis on the Irish language and music. Sporting events also came to constitute a key element of this 'national' programme, reflecting Bairner's assertion that the Gaelic Athletic Association (GAA) 'and Gaelic games in general have played an important part in consolidating a sense of Irish national identity'.[5]

Pine[6] suggests that 2RN was ahead of its time (or at least its contemporaries) in its inclusion of live sports commentaries within the schedule. This may be a little overstated. Although the live relay of the August 1926 All-Ireland hurling semi-final is frequently cited as the first live relay of a field game in Europe, radio listings suggest that, as was usual on Sundays, 2RN shut down at 11 a.m. It appears that 2RN's actual first broadcast of a field game was *not* of a GAA match but of a Five Nations rugby game: Ireland versus Scotland at Lansdowne Road in February 1927. It would be another seven months before the first live broadcast of a GAA match occurred: the All-Ireland football final between Kerry and Kildare in September 1927. Nonetheless, thereafter GAA matches became a particularly prominent part of the Irish broadcast firmament. From 1928 onwards the semi-finals and finals of both codes of the men's game were fixtures in the annual broadcast schedule. As Luke Gibbons has asserted, 'both radio and the press contributed substantially to creating a nationwide audience for Gaelic games, thus establishing the Gaelic Athletic Association as a truly national organisation'.[7] Furthermore, Gibbons argues that, far from simply relaying the public sporting events (and, by extension, performances of national identity) that were already 'naturally' popular, the national broadcaster instead acted as an agent of cultural change, placing a particular emphasis on those elements of popular culture that chimed with the prevailing vision of official cultural nationalism.

The early presence of rugby on Irish radio seems to confound the assertion by the first minister for posts and telegraphs, J.J. Walsh, that 'we resolutely refused to admit the broadcasting of foreign games'.[8] Bairner notes that, while in other British colonies 'it was enough to beat the British at their own games', Irish nationalists had gone 'one step further', engaging 'in sporting activities that were exclusive to them and, thus, helped to maintain their sense of having a separate and unique identify'.[9] Nonetheless, he also notes that, in practice

> British games are played enthusiastically throughout Ireland... Irish sports people are celebrating their national identity, albeit by playing sports that do not have their origins in Ireland. Indeed, rugby has given the Irish a particularly valuable vehicle for the promotion of sporting nationalism since it provides annual opportunities to play (and hopefully to beat) the English at one of their own games. Gaelic games, on the other hand, provide no such opportunities.[10]

In this regard, the fact that the Irish rugby team was something of a force to be reckoned with at the point when 2RN was launched

– winning the Five Nations Championship in 1926 and 1927 and, perhaps more importantly, defeating England 19-15 at Lansdowne Road in February 1926 – may have accounted for the willingness to countenance live relays of rugby from 1927 onwards. Given this, Walsh's comment almost certainly refers to the early absence of another 'foreign game' – soccer – from the airwaves, its de facto popularity notwithstanding. It was December 1935 before Radio Éireann (the successor to 2RN) carried a live relay of the sport (a friendly against the Netherlands at Dalymount Park), and not until 1938 were international soccer matches routinely covered.

Nonetheless, by the end of the 1930s, the national broadcaster was ineluctably associated with both coverage of the 'official' indigenous sports – that is, GAA – and also international games played by the national team. Radio Éireann and later RTÉ would become synonymous with coverage of Irish sporting events and, by dint of its direct control of the broadcaster, the state was in a position to determine and underwrite, per Gibbons, the terms upon which certain sports could be framed as central to Irish identity. Equally, those sports came to be understood as part of the DNA of the national broadcaster by the second half of the twentieth century.

THE MARKETISATION OF EUROPEAN BROADCASTING

The processes undermining this symbiotic relationship were scarcely felt until the 1990s. Although the central position of commercial players is taken for granted in the twenty-first-century European broadcasting firmament, state-owned, public-service-oriented broadcasters dominated until the 1980s. RTÉ's unproblematic identification as *the* home of Irish sports broadcasting in the 1980s was guaranteed by its de facto status as the only national broadcaster in Ireland until the end of that decade. Four decades later, commercial broadcasting accounts for a significant – indeed, usually a majority – share of the television audience in every European country. Within their national markets, even the best-resourced European public-service media (PSM) operators – the BBC in the UK, ARD and ZDF in Germany, and France 2 and 3 – are eclipsed in aggregate by their commercial counterparts. According to the European Broadcasting Union (EBU), by 2017 the operating revenues of the ten largest

European-based privately owned media conglomerates (including Sky, Liberty Global and Vivendi) were 80 per cent greater than the combined operating revenues of the sixty-five PSM attached to the EBU.[11] While the funding of those sixty-five PSM (across forty-six European markets) grew 2.9 per cent between 2013 and 2017, this was dwarfed by the 18.9 per cent revenue growth enjoyed by their ten largest private counterparts in Europe. (Even this was smaller than the 35.1 per cent growth enjoyed by the ten largest non-European media conglomerates in the same period.)

These market shifts are also evident in Ireland. Although the 18.5 per cent market share held by RTÉ's flagship television station in 2018 was still the single largest audience in Ireland (comfortably ahead of the nearest competition, the 12.5 per cent held by the Liberty Global-owned Virgin Media One), the market share of Irish public-service broadcasters has been cumulatively eclipsed by the plethora of Irish and international commercial channels that have emerged since the 1990s. The combined all-day market share of the two public-service television broadcasters RTÉ and TG4 was just over 28 per cent in 2018. Although another public-service broadcaster available in Ireland, the BBC, also has a 6 per cent market share, the remaining 66 per cent of audiences are accounted for by commercial broadcasters.[12]

The process of broadcast-market liberalisation and deregulation that swept across Europe from the 1980s onwards was politically legitimated by appeals to the notion of 'consumer sovereignty'. If audiences were the best judges of their own tastes, there was no reason to maintain the monopoly position of state-owned PSM. Ending their privileged position would allow new commercial market entrants to add choice to schedules. Certainly, the decision to licence new commercial channels in Ireland under the 1988 Radio and Television Act was overtly legitimated by the promise of new and diverse programme content. Yet, in practice in Ireland (as elsewhere), new market entrants primarily sought to win market share by acquiring content already popular on RTÉ. In September 2000 the Irish commercial channel TV3, founded in 1998, secured rights to the UK soap *Coronation Street* as part of a larger deal that saw the soap's producer Granada Television acquire a 45-per-cent stake in TV3. '*Corrie*' duly left RTÉ in January 2001, and contributed to a 50-per-cent rise in TV3's audience share over the following twelve months.[13] As Flynn notes, 'audiences were secured more by offering the familiar rather than the innovative'.[14]

Sports content – especially team sports with long-established and loyal fan bases – became a key element of such efforts to acquire new, or retain established, television audiences. Within months of acquiring *Coronation Street*, TV3 acquired Irish rights to both UEFA Cup and Champions League matches, hitherto exclusively enjoyed by RTÉ. Yet by this stage Irish viewers were well versed in the implications of competition for sports rights. Those living in multichannel regions of Ireland (mainly on the eastern seaboard) had long been accustomed to watching English soccer via the BBC's *Match of the Day* or ITV's *The Big Match*. However, in 1992 Sky Television secured exclusive rights to the new English Premier League, a reorganisation of top-flight soccer explicitly designed to maximise television revenues. Sky's 1992 bid of £304 million, however, far exceeded the counter-bids from the BBC and ITV, and the Premiership disappeared from free-to-air broadcasting, limited instead to those with the financial resources to pay for a Sky subscription.

The scale of the bid reflected the particular economics of Sky as a subscription broadcaster. For the BBC, the matches might have shored up its ratings and helped justify its existence as a public-service broadcaster, but the licence-fee revenues were not directly affected. For ITV, by contrast, the large audiences for soccer included key demographics attractive to advertisers, making the matches a critical element of the ITV revenue stream. From Sky's perspective, the deal meant exclusive access to content that was relatively cheap to stage, could fill the schedules for the bulk of the year, offered a built-in 'Who will win?' narrative, and promised a loyal fan base. Each new subscription generated by the Premiership was worth far more to Sky than the commercial revenue generated by ITV every time they sold an additional viewer to advertisers. That subscription broadcasters regarded such content as intrinsically more valuable than advertising-funded broadcasters was a lesson that RTÉ would learn a decade later in 2002.

The implications of the changing context for sports rights were not lost on Irish sporting organisations. While the Republic of Ireland soccer team achieved unprecedented success under manager Jack Charlton from 1986 onwards, the commercial manager of the

Football Association of Ireland (FAI), Donie Butler, had an even greater impact on the FAI's fortunes. Butler professionalised the FAI's financial basis following his appointment in 1986, quickly brokering a major sponsorship deal with Opel worth £400,000 and a swathe of other smaller commercial pacts. The impact was felt in television-broadcast and pitchside advertising revenues: just two international games against Spain and Germany in Lansdowne Road in 1989 netted the FAI in the region of IR£430,000.[15] When Ireland qualified for the Italia 90 World Cup, the FAI netted approximately IR£2 million from its share of the tournament television revenues.[16]

By 1993 the broader implications for RTÉ and Irish sports fans of increased commercial competition for sporting content were becoming more evident. In May that year, a Republic of Ireland World Cup qualifier against Albania in Tirana was not broadcast after the Albanian Football Federation (acting via a Dutch sports-rights agency) set an exorbitant broadcast fee that RTÉ refused to meet. Instead, the game was picked up by an early incarnation of Setanta Sports (in association with Tyrone Productions), which screened it via closed-circuit television to fee-paying audiences in forty venues around Ireland.[17] The longer-term significance of the heightened commodification of these games was clear. In 1994 RTÉ Television's then head of sport, Tim O'Connor, noted that

> Sky are actively seeking to buy the rights of the Republic of Ireland's European Championship matches away to Liechtenstein next June and away to Portugal the following November. Were we in RTÉ to lose one or both of those matches, the viewing public would want to know why. But what can I do if the price becomes too high?[18]

RTÉ managed to retain the rights for the Republic of Ireland's qualifying games for the 1996 European Football Championship and 1998 World Cup. However, when Star TV, the first private television channel established in Turkey, sought $2 million from RTÉ to screen Ireland's Euro 2000 play-off against Turkey in November 1999, then increased the asking price to $3 million, RTÉ (about to record a substantial loss of IR£16.6 million) had to demur, and the match was not screened in Ireland.

For its part, Sky Television had a strong incentive to acquire Republic of Ireland matches during the 1990s. Although its 1992

English Premiership acquisition encouraged a marked increase in Sky Sports subscriptions in Ireland, the absolute number remained low – just 12,000 of Cablelink's customers by early 1994.[19] Yet Sky's acquisition of other rights would impact Irish access to other sports in ways that lay entirely outside the control of Irish broadcasting and sporting institutions.

In 1996 the English Rugby Football Union broke ranks with the other members of the Five Nations Championship to agree an £87 million (sterling) deal with Sky for exclusive rights to live broadcasts of England's Five Nations home games between 1998 and 2002. Thus, Ireland's game against England at Twickenham in 1998 became the first Irish Five Nations match since 1927 not to be broadcast live on RTÉ. RTÉ did offer deferred coverage, but even this proved impossible in later years after Sky hiked the fee for delayed transmission rights. When the new Six Nations Championship (including Italy from 2000) looked set to be sold as a single package, there were concerns that every game might disappear from free-to-air television across Europe. However, before that could be addressed, July 2002 saw the question of Irish soccer rights thrown into the limelight.

In February 2002 the minister for arts and culture, Síle de Valera, faced criticism for her failure to use the powers afforded to her by a 1997 update to the EU's core media legislation, the 'Television Without Frontiers' directive. Mindful of the threat of pan-European media giants like Sky, Kirch in Germany and Silvio Berlusconi's Mediaset in Italy swooping in to secure major sporting events such as the Olympics and the World Cup for their respective suites of subscription sports channels, the European Commission amended the directive to permit member states to draw up lists of 'protected' sporting and cultural events that had to be made available to audiences on a free-to-air basis. De Valera defended her failure to use these listing powers – transposed into Irish law by the 1999 Broadcasting (Major Television Events Coverage) Act – by pointing to the discomfort of the GAA, the Irish Rugby Football Union and the FAI at the idea that their freedom to negotiate the sale of their broadcast rights in the open market might in any way be compromised. Although the 1999 Broadcasting Act did not require the approval of these institutions, the minister considered their consent politically vital, and felt unable to act. While the minister vacillated, Sky and the FAI negotiated: in July 2002 the FAI accepted Sky's offer of €7.5 million (far exceeding the €1.6 million offered by RTÉ) for four years of exclusive live television rights for Republic of Ireland home internationals. Public fury exploded at the prospect of having to pay an overseas broadcaster to watch the national team. Initially focused on the FAI, that opprobrium was increasingly directed at the government as the failure to use the 1999 Broadcasting Act became public knowledge. Politically obliged to respond, the government belatedly published a list of protected events including European Championship and World Cup qualifying matches, the All-Ireland hurling and football finals, the Irish Derby and the Irish Grand National. The state also amended the 1999 Broadcasting Act both to permit retrospective application of the list and to shift the focus of the legislation away from the broadcasting organisations and onto the sporting organisations selling the rights. The matter appeared to be over when RTÉ signed a €5 million deal with the FAI in 2005, securing live-broadcast rights of the team's home qualification matches up to the end of the 2010 World Cup qualifying campaign. Nonetheless, the whole affair established a 'new normal' with regard to public access to Irish soccer games: the senior team's sixteen friendly matches between 2004 and 2006 remained exclusively available on Sky, and thus effectively disappeared for most Irish television viewers.

The partial restoration of the status quo suggested by the FAI/Sky narrative proved temporary as a new Irish player joined the NTL cable platform in August 2004: Setanta Sports. Set up in 1990 to offer Irish sporting content to diasporic communities outside Ireland, Setanta enjoyed remarkable international growth in the 2000s. In April 2003 it won a contract to offer a sports service on the Freeview platform in the UK, and in May 2006 it broke Sky's monopoly to acquire two (of six) English Premiership rights packages for UK£392 million. Setanta's backers included London-based venture capital fund Doughty Hanson, which became directly involved in Irish broadcasting in 2006 when it acquired TV3 from then owners CanWestGlobal and ITV. Later in 2006, Doughty Hanson used TV3 as a vehicle to acquire a joint controlling share in Setanta Sports Holdings. Thus, by 2006 both TV3 and Setanta were – alongside Sky – well placed financially to compete with RTÉ for sports rights.

Even as the Celtic Tiger advertising market swelled its net profits, RTÉ found itself unable to stem the flow of sports events to commercial competitors. Having acquired UK rights to rugby's European Championship (or Heineken Cup) in 2003, Sky extended its exclusivity to Ireland from the 2006–7 season on, relegating RTÉ to deferred coverage two hours after the games ended. Setanta had already successfully gone head-to-head with RTÉ, securing Formula 1 rights in November 2004 and Irish live rights for midweek English Premiership games in 2006. Most damagingly for RTÉ, having screened every Rugby World Cup since 1987, in January 2006 it found its bid for the 2007 competition comfortably outbid by Setanta.[20] RTÉ remained hopeful it could still secure the national team's games in the tournament as they were protected for free-to-air broadcast under the 2003 Broadcasting Act. However, the games went instead to TV3 (then in the process of being taken over by Doughty Hanson).

The loss of the rugby rights was doubly damaging for RTÉ: a definitive loss of a national team event coincided with Irish rugby's move into the ascendant at provincial and national level. Sky's European Championship move immediately preceded a period when Irish provinces dominated the tournament (winning five times between 2006 and 2012). Similarly, having been the perennial underdogs during the Five Nations era (routinely coming last in the late 1990s), the Irish rugby-team's fortunes transformed after 2000, coming second five times from 2000 to 2007 and winning outright victory in the Six Nations in 2009. Broadcast rights for rugby had never been as important in either cultural or financial terms.

Worse followed. In spring 2005 RTÉ had to reach deep into its pockets to fend off a Setanta challenge for elements of the live rights package for the GAA football and hurling championships. The RTÉ head of sport, Glen Killane, legitimated the increased expenditure, describing the games as 'core…from a cultural as well as a sporting perspective'.[21] Though thwarted in its bid for championship games, Setanta acquired some rights to National League evening games, thus diluting TG4's exclusivity in that regard. However, even as the 2007 Rugby World Cup was screened on TV3, RTÉ saw its coverage of GAA games further undermined when those rights – by then split into twenty-five separate rights packages by medium, championship and code – came up for negotiation again in autumn 2007. Though

RTÉ retained key events, such as the later stages of the All-Ireland football and hurling championships, the straightforward identification of GAA games with RTÉ was further diluted when broadcast rights for earlier matches were shared with TV3 and Setanta.

THE ARRIVAL OF GLOBAL GIANTS

The gradual dilution of RTÉ's exclusivity with regard to indigenous sports and teams had occurred even though the broadcaster's finances were in rude health. However, the spectacular collapse of the Irish economy and, in consequence, the local media-advertising market after 2008 transformed the commercial Irish broadcast environment, further undermining RTÉ's capacity to compete for events. Both Setanta and TV3 were also affected, each forced to undergo significant retrenchment to survive. Although, in November 2010, TV3 secured upgraded 'Pack 2' GAA rights (including some of the championship quarter-finals), a month later it had to allow the 2011 Rugby World Cup rights revert to RTÉ.

This financial precarity left both TV3 and Setanta vulnerable to acquisition by even larger international media firms, the corporate horizons of which extended beyond broadcast television. The increasing bandwidth available via both cable and optical-fibre infrastructures increasingly saw these industries converge to become broadband-service providers that, on one level, were indifferent to the nature of the data – be it television programmes, voice telephony calls or online content – their networks carried. However, as Evens et al. note, 'sports rights have become a target for telecommunications firms and other "convergent" media players that regard ownership of premium rights as an important competitive advantage in the digital service market'.[22] After 2015 the new owners of Irish commercial television saw sports content less as a means for securing purely television audiences/subscribers than for securing new subscribers to their broadband platforms.

Though perhaps not immediately obvious, competition between three players – UPC (rebranded as Virgin Media Ireland in 2015), Sky and Eir – for dominance within the broadband market would increasingly shape the market for Irish sports rights and encourage the adoption of new market strategies by the main players. Subscriber take-up of television, voice telephony and broadband markedly increased in Ireland from 2009 following NTL's (UPC/Virgin Media Ireland's earlier corporate guise) significant post-2005 investment in network upgrades. In 2012 Sky Ireland began to reinvent itself as a broadband-service provider bundling television, data and voice services into a single package. While Sky maintained a significant lead over UPC in the Irish television-distribution market by 2015, UPC held 28.7 per cent of the fixed broadband market to Sky's 9.4 per cent. The largest player in that market, Eir, held a 35.4 per cent share.

At the start of 2015, Sky was the only commercial player simultaneously operating its own suite of channels alongside its own distribution system. In 2015 and 2016 Liberty Global acquired TV3 and the short-lived UTV Ireland respectively. Folded together, from August 2018 the channels adopted the Virgin Media brand. Eir, the latest incarnation of the former publicly owned telecommunications-infrastructure-and-service provider Telecom Éireann, had launched its own eVision television platform in 2013, thus bringing it into the 'triple play' television, voice telephony and broadband market. In 2015 Eir acquired Setanta, which had managed to regain partial access to sports rights – specifically, the Premier League and the European Rugby Cup – following a 2013 deal with British Telecom. By 2016 the Setanta brand had disappeared, replaced by Eir's sports channels, which were available free to Eir's broadband and mobile subscribers.

In 2014, as TV3 again landed exclusive rights to the 2015 Rugby World Cup, RTÉ's managing director, Glen Killane, had expressed disappointment at losing the event:

> … it just goes to show RTÉ has no God-given right to land every sports rights or competition. It's a very competitive environment; in this case it has gone to a domestic competitor. But we are facing far harder competition from international competitors with far deeper pockets, such as Sky.[23]

Yet though Sky continued to make inroads into sports content – most notably the hitherto unthinkable acquisition of fourteen GAA championship games previously held by TV3 (see chapter 11)

– it was the new market entrants who now most aggressively competed for sports rights. By the end of 2015, RTÉ faced three suites of channels – Sky, Virgin Media and Eir – that were integrated from above into three international television distribution and/ or broadband providers: respectively, Sky Television, the US-based Liberty Global and Eir. The contrast in their resources and those available to RTÉ were stark. RTÉ's turnover in 2018 (the most recent year for which the figure is available) was €339 million. By comparison, Comcast (the current owner of Sky) and Liberty Global (Virgin Media) recorded revenues of, respectively, $94 billion[24] and $11.9 billion[25] in 2018, while Iliad (Eir's principal owner) reached €4.9 billion.[26]

These players immediately made their sporting ambitions clear. December 2015 saw TV3's new CEO, Tony Hanway, declare that the company would deploy its substantial financial resources to target local sport. The 2018 to 2021 seasons of the Six Nations Rugby Championship, broadcast on the state-owned broadcaster without a break since 1927, were acquired by TV3 for €20 million in November 2015. Not everything went TV3's way, however. Eir's deal with BT Sport already gave it access to some European Rugby Champions Cup matches. In 2016 it replaced TV3 as the Irish rights holder for the 2019 Rugby World Cup in Japan (although a subsequent deal saw RTÉ sub-licence fourteen of those games, including Ireland's pool games, which were protected for free-to-air broadcasting). Eir also secured sole rights to what would be the Irish rugby team's first ever victory over the New Zealand All Blacks, in Chicago in November 2016. In July 2017 BT Sport acquired exclusive UK and Ireland pay-per-view rights to the European Rugby Championship, entirely displacing Sky. Eir extended its relationship with BT Sport to secure the right to screen the games on its Irish platform. Finally, in January 2018, Eir snatched three years' worth of Irish rights to rugby's Pro14 tournament away from Sky, which had exclusively broadcast it since the 2014–15 season.

By 2018 Virgin's primary focus was on soccer. In May 2018 TV3 again outbid RTÉ to secure exclusive Irish rights for virtually every UEFA Champions League and Europa League match for a three-year period from August 2018. The 327 matches secured for each year included exclusive rights to the Champions League final. In August 2018 TV3 (by then rebranded as Virgin Media) moved to establish a dedicated sports channel. As Eir had done with Eir Sports, the channel and its content were made available free to Virgin Media subscribers, thus directly deploying sports content to woo new subscribers to its broadband platform.

IMPLICATIONS FOR RTÉ?

Throughout these manoeuvres, RTÉ's capacity to mount credible bids for sports rights diminished. RTÉ's average annual expenditure on such rights declined from €21.4 million per annum between 2007 and 2012 to €15.5 million between 2013 and 2017.[27] It is unclear if this was a result of simply being outbid by competition (thus negating the need for such expenditures) or a reflection of RTÉ's declining financial resources. Certainly, the decline occurred against the backdrop of a permanent crisis for the public-service broadcaster. A collapse in advertising income saw the station's total revenues fall from €440 million in 2008 to €328 million in 2013, and it accumulated losses of €114 million between 2009 and 2012. Though just about breaking even in 2013 and 2014, more losses followed thereafter. The one-off sale of part of RTÉ's Donnybrook landbank saw the station record a €42 million surplus in 2017, but this was almost wiped out by the €36 million lost across 2015, 2016 and 2018.

Most notably, the decision not to bid at all for the rights for Ireland's soccer matches in the new UEFA Nations League in 2018 symbolised the extent of the station's capitulation. Furthermore, although the Nations League offered an alternative qualification route for the European Championship, the minister for communications declined to add the games to the list of free-to-air events protected under the 2003 Act. Thus, Ireland's opening Nations League match against Wales in September 2018 was the first competitive match in decades not to be screened live on free-to-air television. It, and the subsequent games in the league, were instead shown live on Sky Sports, while TV3/Virgin Media acquired both delayed coverage and highlights rights (and live rights to other higher-profile matches from League A of the competition).

Perversely, the most immediate consequence of RTÉ's inability to compete with transnational capital for sports rights is the further impoverishment of the station's finances. In March 2017, when RTÉ last held the rights for the Six Nations, coverage related to the championship accounted for thirteen of the top twenty most-watched programmes on RTÉ2 television that month.[28] More than one million viewers would tune in to RTÉ to witness Ireland's historic victory over the All Blacks at the Aviva Stadium in November 2018.[29] However, from 2018 those viewers and the associated advertising revenues ended up on Virgin Media's books during the 2019 Six Nations tournament. Ireland's Grand Slam victory over England on St Patrick's Day 2018 was watched by an average of 951,000 viewers (peaking at 1.3 million), and figures for the 2019 championship were higher still: an average of 979,400 viewers (peaking at 1.45 million), equivalent to more than two-thirds of all viewers, tuned in to watch Ireland's opening Guinness Six Nations match on Virgin Media One in February 2019.[30] RTÉ's notional replacement for the event – the Women's Six Nations – typically secured less than 20 per cent of the viewership achieved by Virgin Media across the five matches in the men's tournament.[31] Although the loss of some sports rights is not necessarily a zero-sum game – RTÉ could not conceivably cover every GAA championship and league game even with a dedicated sports channel – the loss of the higher-profile events undoubtedly impacts upon the station's bottom line.

In this context, and writing in the context of economic-welfare theory, Solberg[32] has argued that PSM should not spend limited financial resources acquiring sports rights that commercial broadcasters will acquire anyway. Solberg acknowledges that sporting events – perhaps especially those specifically associated with national sports and national teams – may have characteristics that constitute them as both public goods and meritorious goods in economic terms, but, nonetheless, he argues that the risk that the public will be denied access to such events is mitigated by their listing under the Television Without Frontiers directive. Indeed, spending finite financial resources on expensive sporting events means directing funding away from other, equally important, public-service content such as local drama and cultural programming. Solberg invokes the market-failure argument, suggesting that PSM should only seek to acquire those events that the market would not spontaneously make available.

Contra Solberg, while arguing in favour of free-to-air sports broadcasting in general, Evens et al. argue that PSM are 'uniquely placed to maximise the social and cultural value to be gained from sport',[33] and that commercial broadcasting is 'degraded by the intrusive commodification of audiences for advertisers'[34] as distinct from the manner in which PSM approach their audiences. For Evens et al., PSM still offer a

> forum for democratic debate and cultural exchange against a background of a deregulated global media system, inevitably influenced by market forces and dominated by large multi-national enterprises...Most significantly, PSBs treat people as citizens rather than consumers and in doing so they help to create and maintain a public sphere.[35]

Evens et al. are writing in a UK context, but there remains some validity in maintaining a distinction between the operations of PSM and commercial broadcasters in Ireland. RTÉ's commitment to news and current affairs far exceeds that offered by its competitors, and the station continues to invest more in indigenous television drama than any commercial channel. This PSM/commercial distinction is harder to maintain with regard to RTÉ and TG4's coverage of high-profile sporting events: extensively framed as it is by prominent sponsorship stings and advertising, the experience of watching sport on the Irish PSM may not be significantly less 'degraded' than on its commercial counterparts. Certainly, Virgin Media's success in retaining (indeed, expanding) audiences for the Six Nations does not suggest that Irish audiences are reluctant to watch such games outside the confines of the PSM.

This leaves the question of what, if anything, the loss of key sporting events – especially those in GAA, rugby and soccer – means for RTÉ's identity. A survey of indigenous-broadcast hours on RTÉ television in prime time from 2008 to 2017 points to both an absolute and relative decline in indigenous sporting content: from an average of 396 hours per annum between 2008 and 2012 to 318 between 2013 and 2017. Sport accounted for just under 20 per cent of all indigenous prime-time content in that first period, but just over 15 per cent in the second period. RTÉ increasingly looks to other programming genres to maintain the impression of being a national broadcaster. In 2008 sport constituted the second-largest genre of indigenous content; by 2017 it had fallen to fourth behind news, current affairs and entertainment. The subsequent loss of the Six Nations and the decision to eschew bidding for the UEFA Nations League will likely lead to sport's relative significance among RTÉ's indigenous content further declining.

CONCLUSION

According to Brown,[36] the traditional rationale for governments' ensuring the production and transmission of public-service-broadcasting content arises from the perceived social importance of the broadcasting media and their potential influence on values, attitudes and beliefs. Governments that promote PSB, therefore, place greater emphasis on viewers and listeners as social beings, citizens and voters than as consumers. The rationale for intervening in the broadcasting market is not on the basis of economic criteria but to achieve social objectives such as the promotion of education, equity, *national identity* and social cohesion.

For most of the twentieth century, the sense of nationality and nationhood constructed in post-independence Ireland was built around a supposed organic unity of people and institutions. From its inception, Irish broadcasting was instrumentalised for a conscious programme to project a specific – albeit arguably artificial and exclusionary – image of the Irish and Irishness. The high profile accorded to national sports and the national teams on the national broadcaster manufactured a mutually reinforcing identity between the two sets of institutions. As Marcus Free has pointed out with regard to both soccer and rugby, sports have long acted as analogues for 'collective imagining of national identity'.[37] However, while in its early decades the Irish state actively sought to influence which sports could and could not be considered part of that national imagining, the more recent acquiescence of the state with the marketisation of Irish broadcasting – through the failure to either sustain RTÉ's finances or update the listing of protected events – has undermined that influence. This may appear trivial: as long as the sports discussed above are universally available *somewhere*, the process of collective imagining, per Free, will continue to be worked through. However, there seems little doubt that RTÉ's status as a primary medium for that process is already under threat, and it is unclear what the long-term cultural impact of limiting access to national sporting events on market terms will be. That this uncertainty should prevail at a point when the Irish state is actively engaged in a process of 'nation-branding', under the auspices of programmes like the Creative Ireland programme, is particularly striking.

PART V

ഇ

Media, Geography and the Negotiation of National and Local Identities

CHAPTER THIRTEEN

'Talking broken biscuits': Irish Liverpool fans and The Anfield Wrap

CIARÁN RYAN

A CURSORY GLANCE AROUND Irish airports on a Saturday morning will reveal numerous groups wearing similar replica jerseys and scarves signifying their favoured English Premier League (henceforth EPL) side. Irish interest in 'cross-channel' football (soccer) is not a recent phenomenon, and Irish media has long tapped into this enthusiasm through radio, television and newspaper coverage. Yet, with the exception of radio phone-ins, fan participation in sports media was quite limited until the early twenty-first century.

Alongside its north-west rival Manchester United, Liverpool Football Club (LFC) appears to be the most represented among those weekend mass exoduses.[1] The influence of these supporters is significant. For example, the final section in journalist Keith Falkiner's *Emerald Anfield: The Irish and Liverpool FC* (2010) is dedicated to giving the Irish-fan perspective.[2] Nonetheless, the majority of content produced around Liverpool matches is by the mainstream media. This consists of pre-match and post-match analyses from 'experts' (i.e. ex-players), interviews with current managers and players, and neatly filed newspaper and online reports, with increasingly bite-sized, digestible pieces of information (player ratings, vital statistics, and so on). Official club social-media accounts give some insight into the match-day experience. For example, Liverpool's YouTube channel runs a popular feature entitled 'Inside Anfield' that goes 'behind the scenes'. Nonetheless, these videos speak very little to the experience of actually going to the match itself, which is framed as more of a secondary activity to matters on the pitch.

New-media platforms have given football supporters options outside of traditional broadcasting and print journalism. One such example is the focus of this chapter: The Anfield Wrap (TAW), a podcast and corresponding website launched in 2011. Produced by Liverpool fans for Liverpool fans, the early podcasts were recorded in a room above a Liverpool bar, with the presenter and contributors audibly nervous. In the intervening years, The Anfield Wrap has transformed into a multi-award-winning multimedia operation with offices in the heart of Liverpool city centre. TAW, as it is frequently referred to, employs eleven people (at the time of writing), has a cast of close to fifty contributors, and produces two weekly free podcasts, numerous free articles and videos, and a host of weekly subscriber-only shows.

This research aims to determine the role TAW plays in sustaining globalised football fandom, specifically focusing on the experiences of Irish fans of this English Premiership club. It examines the extent to which these new-media texts can provide different connections with the club and city of Liverpool for the global football fan through the language, and perhaps more specifically, the local slang, used in the podcasts, as well as through the fan-based experiences of TAW's contributors. It is an outlet that an Irish interviewee (Dave) sees as different because 'they are fans, not ex-players. They do it for the love of it, especially at the start, rather than a pay cheque'.[3]

As part of ongoing research exploring the role of fan media in contemporary fan culture, semi-structured interviews were conducted with users and producers of The Anfield Wrap – eighteen thus far, carried out in person and electronically via Skype and email – together with a survey conducted among more than 500 respondents sourced primarily through social media (some printed copies were completed at a TAW live show). The survey sought to determine the level of engagement users had with TAW content, what was appealing about that content, and whether or not the respondents considered themselves to be fans of TAW. Interviewees were subsequently recruited from the completed surveys, where more detailed discussions about their attachment to TAW took place. Furthermore, this data is complemented by the analysis of

TAW's output and the interactions of its users through social media and at a live event in Dublin in 2017.

A TALE OF TWO COMEBACKS

Shortly after 8.30 p.m. on Wednesday 25 May 2005, an estimated 320,000[4] viewers in the Republic of Ireland heard the words 'It could be a humiliation now' from the mouth of Liam Brady. Brady and fellow former Irish international footballers John Giles and Eamon Dunphy formed the studio panel of experts that the state's public-service broadcaster RTÉ had assembled for its coverage of the Champions League final between AC Milan and Liverpool.

For Irish fans of Liverpool, RTÉ was the primary outlet for coverage before, during and after the match. A Liverpool side that had defied the odds to reach the final was trailing the Italian giants 3-0 at the break. Analyst John Giles added, '[Steven] Gerrard, as usual, in the big matches has disappeared, Bill [Herlihy, programme anchor]…Liverpool have come up against a real team on the night…it's a reality check…all over the pitch, they've been outclassed.' Most viewers would not have disagreed with Giles' assessment. Those who opposed it probably expressed their views privately within the domestic sphere, or perhaps more publicly and effusively in public houses. Platforms such as Twitter were not yet in existence, and simultaneous 'second screen' discussion of the match and its ongoing analysis was limited. On the bulletin-board website Boards.ie, a dedicated thread was established for the match, with a total of 532 posts logged between 25 May and 26 May, though only 242 of these took place within the actual timeframe of the match. Aside from this, there is very little to suggest that any other content was generated from the fan's perspective; the majority of mediated coverage of the event was from the mainstream media.

Liverpool would subsequently go on to produce what media outlets quickly dubbed 'The Miracle of Istanbul',[5] drawing the match 3-3 in regulation time before defeating AC Milan on penalties to win an unlikely fifth European Cup. The result has been the cornerstone of recurring discussions around the English club and its ability to stage seemingly remarkable comebacks on the European stage. This is something that official sources – and none as official as the club itself[6] – have intertwined with well-worn tropes around 'famous European nights' under the 'Anfield lights'.[7]

A more recent exemplar would be the Europa League quarter-final of April 2016, when an injury-time goal gave Liverpool a dramatic 5-4 aggregate victory over Borussia Dortmund. While eleven years previously the post-Istanbul media frenzy was primarily confined to television and newspaper reports, a plethora of new-media options were now available to sports fans. Indeed, the active creation, recycling and remixing of sports-media content from fans themselves – via memes, YouTube compilations, and so on – was evident in the aftermath of the Dortmund match. One example is the *When I'm Liverpool* video,[8] which mashes match highlights, music, video-game and pop culture into a frenetic and somewhat absurd ninety seconds. Unsurprisingly, given that it is one of the Internet's central hubs for memetic culture, the *When I'm Liverpool* videos (the Dortmund video is just one of a series) originate on Reddit but are spread quickly through platforms such as Twitter and YouTube. Furthermore, primarily through the likes of Twitter, fans were interacting throughout the match itself, sharing their reactions to the events that unfolded. Galily notes that the increasing prevalence of 'second screen' viewing experiences – that is, where the fan has the ability to watch television and simultaneously use another device to communicate with others about the event – has led to better social interaction around sporting fixtures.[9]

The Anfield Wrap straddles the line between professional media outlet and fan productivity. John Fiske argues that fans tend to be productive in terms of creating and distributing their own fan texts,[10] many of which borrow from or, indeed, subvert, the cultural phenomena that their fandom is based on (for example, the spread of slash fiction).[11] Writing during the nascent stages of fan studies, Fiske opined that fans often had the technical capabilities to craft works (for example, fan fiction) with production qualities as high as the official culture. In a digital era, new opportunities are available for the fan producer, and TAW offers a highly interactive and social mode of communication with its users. After the full-time whistle was blown on 14 April 2016, a cohort of TAW contributors descended on a Liverpool city-centre location to record their post-match show *The Pink*.[12] This show can be considered the most unfiltered of the TAW canon; usually recorded within thirty minutes of the final whistle, it carries much of the same spirit of the match-going experience, and seems far removed from the packages produced by the mainstream broadcasting networks. TAW's Craig Hannan, himself originally from County Antrim, considers the post-match podcast to be an online version of the post-match drink:

> I think people listen to that because it's almost their version of going to the pub and talking to their mates about it. Maybe they live in Ireland, or the States or Australia, and their mates don't support Liverpool or whatever. They're almost living it through us, if that makes sense?[13]

For listeners, the general impression is that TAW represents the fan's perspective. In the words of the contributors themselves, they are 'going the match'[14] – instead of locating themselves in the press box and delivering standardised match updates, their users are instead treated to often expletive-ridden and alcohol-fuelled audio, as well as complementary visual content, through TAW's social-media channels. This resonates with a subset of supporters who are becoming disillusioned with mainstream sports media. For instance, Irish supporter Dave positions TAW in opposition to the BBC's football stalwart *Match of the Day*:

> The discussions on TAW are obviously vastly different to, say, *Match of the Day* or the official LFC club channel [LFC TV], but I'm not sure that people of my generation who love football rely on these for their insight and opinions anymore. There has definitely been a huge surge in the amount of independent fan-led blogs and podcasts over the last few years, and TAW was a trailblazer in that regard. The nature of independent media outlets means that you can always be more emotive, more passionate, more critical, more biased, whatever. That's their USP [unique selling point], and I think that's why people have shifted to consuming football media in this way.

This is particularly evident in the edition of *The Pink* post-Dortmund; one of the main TAW contributors, John Gibbons, takes his trousers off in celebration, with accompanying footage shared via TAW's Twitter account.

The Pink is when TAW is at its most carnivalesque, to borrow from Bakhtin's concept of the carnival. Garry Whannel describes sport itself as a site for 'carnivalesque' behaviour,[15] drawing on Bakhtin's concept.[16] While Whannel does not specifically refer to the work of Bakhtin, the notion of the carnival has been fruitful in studies of football supporters going back to Giulianotti's work on Scottish fans at Italia 90.[17] Deriving this notion from French renaissance writer/satirist François Rabelais, Bakhtin celebrated medieval carnival as a periodically licensed popular celebration that was 'characterized by laughter, by excessiveness (particularly of the body and the bodily functions), by bad taste and offensiveness, and by degradation'.[18] Therefore, humour and chaos are central to the textual disruption that takes place in carnivalesque media texts. The language used in *The Pink* can be vulgar, offensive or haphazard, echoing 'what Bakhtin (1968) calls the language of the low to disrupt the official, polite meaning'.[19] Within seconds of the Dortmund episode commencing, expletives were fired about with abandon: 'Shove yer fucking drum up yer arse…go and take yer fucking drum back to Germany. Shove it up yer fucking arse and go and pity yourselves with nothing this season dickheads.' Perhaps this type of behaviour can be deemed a form of adolescent masculinity; after all, of the eight contributors to appear on this edition of *The Pink*, just one was female. Furthermore, of over 500 TAW listeners surveyed as part of this study, 96 per cent identified as male. Despite the impression that the above comment might give, TAW is quite varied in terms of its content; it regularly features segments on women's football and has a number of female contributors. These are generally well-received by its audience; however, TAW host Neil Atkinson does point out that this is not always the case:

> We like our audience broadly speaking, with exceptions as there would be anywhere…If you don't like The Anfield Wrap talking about homosexual issues in football, then there's the door…We got a fair bit of grief when we did something with Juliet Jacques about her book *Trans* [an account of gender transition] and we did ten minutes on the radio and there was a series of puce-faced grumpy men who came through TAW DMs [direct messages]. One of them even said that 'This is the kind of thing that will cost you listeners'… and I'm like, 'That's ok'.

What that means is that the people who are with us, and the people that bought Juliet's book, they're the people who are going to be at the show tonight. Can't wait to see them – lovely fellas, mostly fellas.[20]

By the time Liverpool managed perhaps their greatest-ever European comeback – overturning a three-goal first-leg deficit to beat Barcelona 4-0 at Anfield in May 2019 in the Champions League semi-finals – TAW had numerous ways of delivering content to its users. Post-match articles and ratings were issued within hours, along with the usual post-match podcast and *Post Match Pint*, TAW's post-match free video. *Post Match Pint* shares many of the same uncensored and disruptive characteristics of the podcast. Sitting with a pint of stout in front of him and flagged by two other contributors, host Gareth Roberts opens with this proclamation:

Get Innnnnnnnn! Liverpool 4, Barcelona 0. Who the fuck are you trying to kid? You come here in your fucking luminous kit, thinking you're fucking kings of the world. You're going home with the tails between your legs. Luis Suarez – fuck off. Phil Coutinho – fuck off. Messi – fuck off. All of yese – fuck off… This is why we're Liverpool Football Club. This is why we are romantic about our team. This is why we love our club because we do stuff like this.

To return to the idea of carnival, we should also take into consideration Bakhtin's connection between it and collectivity. For Bakhtin, the suspension of hierarchy during carnival promoted a type of communication that was not evident in everyday life. In sports-media terms, this collectivity can be seen when there are no divisions between the creators and the users of content. Most Irish fans of Liverpool were not in Anfield on the night of their dramatic comeback with Borussia Dortmund, but some felt more closely connected to the events through their engagement with the podcast. For example, one of the Irish respondents to this study, Jason, noted that, 'They know the club's history and all you have to do is listen to *The Pink* after the Dortmund game to know how much the club means to them.'[21] Global football fans can feel a cultural and geographic disconnect from teams they support worldwide where they may have no tangible association on geographic or family grounds; interacting with a more authentic fan experience can abate these tensions somewhat.

IRELAND, LIVERPOOL AND GLOBAL FOOTBALL FANS

In a sense, it seems strange to place Irish fans of Liverpool Football Club into a global category. As a port city in close proximity to Ireland, Liverpool boasts a population with a significant Irish ancestry;[22] the Irish diaspora in the city would become the largest ethnic group in the city in the nineteenth century. The club itself has been home to many Irish footballers, and its foundation is strongly connected to Ireland. Among those who emigrated to Liverpool from post-Famine Ireland was John McKenna, who left Monaghan when he was seventeen years old. Twenty years later, in 1892, he was pivotal in the establishment of Liverpool Association Football Club, assuming the position of secretary.[23] Those existing strong links to the city, coupled with the club's success in the twentieth century, made Liverpool an easy choice for many young Irish football supporters. Before the era of affordable air travel, football tourists boarded boats in Belfast and Dublin on Friday nights to ensure they would make the Saturday-afternoon kick-off at Anfield. Two new passenger ferries were brought in to cope with the demand in the late 1960s by B&I (British & Irish Ferries).[24]

Internationally, sports media played a highly significant role in developing a global fandom for English league football, starting with the arrival of the BBC World Service. The post-Second World War English football establishment was reluctant to allow any live broadcasting of games as it felt it would damage revenue sources, which essentially amounted to match tickets and refreshments sold at games. However, the Football League and the Football Association were quite eager to allow games to be carried on the BBC's World Service as it would not impact on match-day attendances. Wyllie et al. argue that the contemporary international reach of England's largest clubs needs to be understood not just in the context of the current economic and broadcasting power of the Premiership but also of a global popular acquaintance with British football fostered by the BBC World Service.[25] It could be argued that television had a more substantial influence in spreading the English football gospel to Ireland, beginning with the introduction of the highlights programme *Match of the Day* in 1964, which could be viewed by those able to receive BBC television on the east coast of Ireland. Elsewhere, Harris points out that the rise in Scandinavian support for English teams such as Liverpool was precisely a by-product of cheaply imported coverage of the old First Division from the late 1960s onwards. Others (see Goksøyr and Hognestad[26]) point out that the football pools, which emerged in Scandinavian countries as early as the 1920s,[27] played a significant role in spreading interest in English football. However, this was an almost mythological interest until the arrival of this imported footage. It can be argued, as Harris does, that the delocalisation of football fandom – now an integral aspect of how Premiership football clubs actively seek to generate profits – was originally something of an accident.[28]

For others, print media was the portal into English league football. Grant Farred reminisces on how his own 1970s boyhood love of Liverpool was not maintained through ever seeing them play football – either in the flesh or on television; rather, it was print-media sources that mediated his long-distance fandom, whether that was snippets in the local Cape Town newspapers or the outdated copies of *Shoot* magazine that he sourced.[29] This differed considerably from the Irish context, where the national daily newspapers all carried extensive content related to football matters in England, particularly stories and reports about the activities of Irish players in the English league and, to a lesser extent, the Scottish league. That has been less of a focus in recent years, as the proliferation of Irish players in the EPL has dwindled, yet there seems to be a consistent level of coverage of the league in the Irish press.

Other forms of print media, outside of the mainstream, have played a role in connecting football fans, and it would be wrong to suggest that online and social-media spaces are the first ways that football fans have demonstrated their own textual productivity.[30] In the 1980s football fans began to act beyond their role of mere consumers. Richard Haynes postulates that the explosion of a football-fanzine culture in the 1980s is an example of supporter resistance to an increasingly commercialised game.[31] Football fanzines offered an opportunity for fans to both laud and criticise their players, management and ownership, and to do so in a

colourful and subjective manner. Without a commercial agenda to
adhere to, and without any real editorial constraints, the football
fanzine provided uncensored views, and did not require any real
training or education to establish. Irish fans in the 1980s and 1990s
picked up fanzines on their trips to Liverpool matches as a way of
helping them develop a link with the city and its people. In a sense,
outlets like The Anfield Wrap can be considered a descendent of
that fanzine culture, albeit in a more professional manner – many
of those involved in the operation of the website and podcast have
formal journalism and media training and work experience. TAW
appropriates the term fanzine for its website, with the banner
reading 'The Anfield Wrap – Liverpool Podcast & Fanzine'.

AUTHENTICITY AND FOOTBALL FANDOM

Throughout this research study, one of the central discourses to have
emerged is that of authenticity. This is unsurprising in any fan-related
activity, where tropes of participation and resistance are placed in
symbolic opposition to ideas around passive consumerism. Garry
Crawford argues that such an approach can contribute towards the
establishment of quite rigid distinctions between different types of
supporters.[32] Similarly, many fans will draw distinctions between
those who attend matches and those who, instead, watch it on
television. Cornell Sandvoss notes that 'at the heart of the implicit
notion of authenticity employed by these fans is the assumption that
mediated and unmediated events are still separate and that the latter
arises out of the former.'[33] Drawing on Baudrillard and the concept
of hyperreality, Sandvoss expands that a more postmodern cultural
perspective will pay more heed to the increasingly simulated nature
of football, acknowledging the merging between television and its
object of representation. Despite this, there are still contestations
at local and global levels as to what constitutes the 'authentic'
Liverpool fan. Less than 25 per cent of the respondents to an initial
survey that was distributed as part of this study were from the
city of Liverpool; seventy-five of those who completed the survey
identified themselves as Irish, and they continually pointed to the
'real' fan experience offered by TAW, such as this Irish respondent:
'I would say that I identify with TAW more so than the official

[LFC] output. I feel like the official output is very neutral, very on message… Kind of "franchise". TAW strikes the right balance of authenticity and objectivity.'[34] This was supported by data collected in follow-up interviews conducted in 2018 with Irish users of TAW, where it is placed in opposition to the mainstream media outlets by the respondents themselves:

> There's a lot of PC-ness in the mainstream media. I want to hear honest, passionate debate and insight to something I genuinely follow and love. TAW contributors do this for me. [Stephen]

> The direction of the club, the ambition it should have, the relationship with fans locally and beyond, getting more young fans in the stadium, affordable ticket prices, rail seating, Hillsborough – they tackle all these issues with sincerity and I agree with most of what TAW contributors have to say, so in a way my voice gets heard by supporting TAW. The mainstream media have other motives, sales, clicks, covering all teams. I'd question the motives of a lot of what they write. [Ross]

Since its establishment in 2011, TAW has firmly cemented its place as the leading fan-led podcast, with approximately 80,000 weekly listeners to its free podcast, with over 10,000 of these subscribing to The Anfield Wrap Player for additional content.[35] TAW is continually diversifying its output, with an increasing amount of video content emerging from 2018 onwards and plans announced in early 2019 for the launch of a paid video service as part of a new tiered pricing scheme. While Irish fans of TAW do not differentiate between themselves and the TAW creators, there is a difference in that those behind TAW are financially benefitting from their LFC fandom. In 2015 TAW made the decision to launch a subscription service, essentially to sustain the operation as a business and not just as a fan enterprise. This meant that, while the content already being produced remained free, a suite of new shows was launched (currently running at about sixty episodes per month) for subscribers at £5 per month. The subscription-service TAW Player has been quite a success, and has allowed TAW to invest in resources in staff and facilities. This is in marked contrast to the earlier do-it-yourself fanzine culture, and has also seen TAW's personnel flirt with the mainstream media, featuring on Sky Sports, BT Sport, BBC, and so on. These outlets have called on TAW personnel to contribute the fans' perspective on matters such as the retirement of Steven Gerrard and the 2018 Champions League final. One clip, aired prior to Christmas 2018 on Sky Sports, features ex-Manchester United player Gary Neville interviewing various TAW contributors outside Anfield, where he says to Neil Atkinson, 'You're a better pundit than me, you are!'[36] Furthermore, sponsorship of content has seen TAW co-opt the revenue sources of traditional media. The weekly free podcast features a geo-targeted advert at the outset of the show, and the 2018–19 season saw TAW partnering with a betting company as chief sponsor, mirroring a trend evident in sports broadcasting in the UK. These developments, along with suggestions of exclusivity – for example, subscribers get access to a private Facebook group – could be brought into question when considering the motivations of TAW's producers. Neil Atkinson, the host of TAW, feels that the switch has not diluted his fandom or passion for presenting and producing shows:

> If anything it's more enjoyable. As soon as it stops being great, it doesn't work anymore. I got to love Liverpool; I got to love supporting Liverpool; I've got to want to enjoy the shows we're doing. If I'm not going to enjoy doing them, then how are the guests going to, and how are the listeners? Win, lose or draw – and that's important – if I'm not enjoying this, how is anyone else? This is our leisure time.[37]

Discourses of authenticity in football fandom are frequently tied up in contestations around spectatorship,[38] location and lineage.[39] For many Irish fans, their links to the city and club are quite arbitrary. Liverpool's sweeping success in the 1970s and 1980s was a major factor for a number of respondents in choosing to support the club. That, combined with their favourite Irish players day-jobbing with Liverpool in the old First Division, was a selling point for fans like Ross: 'Liverpool were the team of the day and my mates, who were a year or two older, got me into them. Ronnie Whelan's goal in Euro '88 left me in awe. The fact that he also played for Liverpool secured my support.'[40] For others, it was an opportunity to express their difference from others:

...in 2002, just after the World Cup. I had just turned eight. I got into football during the tournament and then obviously needed a club team to support. Pretty much everyone in my class in school supported [Manchester] United, but my friend Rob liked Liverpool, and I think I was into the idea of being a bit different. That was it really, no family ties – my dad supports [Manchester] City. [Dave][41]

The interview data suggest that international fans come to supporting Liverpool for a myriad of reasons. Often, it is to sustain a connection with peers or family who have an existing relationship with the club. All of the Irish respondents related that their Liverpool fandom commenced in their childhood, without any significant knowledge of links between the city and Ireland. Nonetheless, what is also clear is that their awareness of the city, the football club and Liverpool's culture has grown over the life of their fandom.

TAW is acutely aware of its international fanbase. John Gibbons believes that anybody is welcome to support Liverpool as long as their investment in the club is genuine:

We don't make anybody apologise for not being from Liverpool. Rob Guttmann is one of the main guys since the start and he's originally from London. They don't have to repent for their sins on their first episode. We're not like Scouse separatists. We're inclusive. If you love the city and the football club, then sound...get involved.[42]

This stands in opposition to the view of the Liverpool-born Everton-supporting professional footballer Joey Barton, who stated the following when he appeared on TAW in 2017:

I've got a huge issue with people who don't support clubs from the city they were born, or if their Mum and Dad don't support them...I think it is a family thing; you shouldn't just be able to pick up and go 'Bang! We should be able to support that club'...what relation have they to Liverpool? Who cares?

Barton, a notoriously divisive figure in the professional era, was questioned by Atkinson, who drew on his own experiences of travelling around the world and meeting Liverpool fans, whom he felt clearly engaged with the culture of the club and the city. Nonetheless, the interview was a source of some controversy, particularly with Irish listeners. A posting on The Anfield Wrap subscribers' private Facebook group noted: 'So according to Joey, the last 28 years of my life supporting the reds have been pointless because I'm from Ireland and not Scouse.' What is evident here is not just chagrin with Barton but also an underlying self-awareness that tempers much global football fandom. This can be seen in something as simple as the insecurity that many Irish fans feel when using 'we' to identify with Liverpool in online and personal conversations. Another factor that should not be dismissed in this contested fandom is criticism that Irish fans of EPL clubs tend to receive from other Irish football supporters, particularly those who support League of Ireland teams solely. This discourse is sometimes played out mockingly[43] or in a more serious, self-reflexive manner.[44] The League of Ireland has been woefully under-resourced and under-supported,[45] and in one possible 'lost in translation' moment, former Republic of Ireland manager Giovanni Trapattoni claimed that there was no league in Ireland, such was its insignificance in public discourse.[46]

The podcasts that TAW produce do not just discuss football. Local popular culture and social issues such as food banks feature, and global fans felt TAW played a significant role in increasing their awareness of socio-economic relations in a city they may only visit a handful of times a year or a handful of times in their lifetime:

> I feel closer to the club and city from listening to it. When I go over it gives me a better insight to the city and the people and where to go when I'm there…which bars to avoid and the culture of attending a match…and a better grasp of Scouse. [Robbie]

The term 'Scouse' as a way of describing the Merseyside accent or dialect points to Liverpool's port heritage. The word is shared with a type of meat stew (derived from 'lobscouse') that was commonly eaten by Scandinavian sailors who docked at ports such as Liverpool. As a cheap dish to prepare and eat, it would also become popular with poorer locals in the nineteenth century (many of them Irish immigrants), and thereafter be used as a term to describe these people by outsiders. In a sense this encapsulates the peculiarities of Liverpool as a place: a port city that has been influenced by both those who have traversed it and immigrated to it. This has led to the city often distinguishing itself from other parts of the UK, and also being front and centre in a north/south divide, particularly in the early 1980s, when locally there was a sense that it was abandoned by Westminster. This peaked in the aftermath of riots in 1981 when Margaret Thatcher's then-Chancellor Geoffrey Howe proposed a 'managed decline' of the city.[47] This sense of difference spills over into football discourse, whereby many Liverpool fans revel in what they see as a general dislike for the club from many factions, most notably the mainstream media. Towards the end of the 2018–19 Premier League season, an injury-time own goal led to Liverpool beating Tottenham Hotspur 2-1 in an important match for Liverpool's title aspirations. In the subsequent TAW free podcast, Gareth Roberts saw this as an ideal opportunity to emphasise his joy that this could cause discomfort to those outside Liverpool fandom:

> I honestly think it was the best possible way to win a football match, in the context of everything. It's done everybody's head in. I've really enjoyed this morning, just reading all the media reports, because they're just all fuming…I absolutely love it. I love it when the media is fuming. I love it when the world doesn't want us to win and we win, and that's exactly what happened.

Global fans of Liverpool choose the club for many different reasons, as previously outlined. Many of these fans were unaware of perceptions of Liverpool as a city, politically or socio-economically, prior to becoming a fan. Perhaps that does not change over the life of their fandom. However, it could be suggested that outlets like TAW play a role in developing a sense of uniqueness around the city and the club, and developing a defiance around supporting a team that regularly appears around the top of polls about the EPL's most disliked teams. Countless episodes of TAW refer to this, and a narrative built in the climax of the 2018–19 league season that the supporters of every other club in the league wanted Manchester City to win the EPL title.

A LINGUISTIC EXCHANGE

While the Liverpool fans partaking in this study did not tend to comment on the Irishness of Liverpool, one area they did focus on was language. The phonologist Patrick Honeybone speaks of the Liverpool English dialect, or Scouse as it has been referred to in popular parlance.[48] Unique phrases, expressions and pronunciations are very much part of the local culture, and this is something the football club itself has embraced. Back in 1988, when Liverpool were preparing for the FA Cup final, such differences were depicted in the song 'The Anfield Rap', where the two Liverpudlians in the squad – John Aldridge and Steve McMahon – took centre stage. One couplet that was left to Irish international Aldridge went: 'No they don't talk like we do, do they do la/ We'll have to learn 'em to talk propa'. In more recent times, a clip of current manager Jürgen Klopp saying 'Boss tha' was recirculated through the club's social-media channels. TAW contributors created their own hierarchy when speaking with me, and referred to it as 'layers of Scouseness'. As TAW contributor Paul Senior expanded: 'I grew up in Liverpool. There's no escape. People can tell I'm from Liverpool straight way but there is another gear. There's a sense of poetry to Scouse…it's funny, it's quirky.'[49] Just like the song from 1988, there is an element of playing up on this sense of difference through language, with Neil Atkinson admitting there is a sense that they are showing off when producing TAW content:

> There is an underrated Liverpudlian love of language, and of phrases and jokes…there is an element of us showing off, for want of a better term. You want to be the fella who has the best line, the funniest joke, the fastest joke.[50]

Regular listeners to the podcast feel they develop a clearer understanding of the city through these localised accounts. Gone are the polished and standardised accents and vocabulary of the mainstream broadcasters, replaced with language that is quite specific to the city. In the survey, many global respondents signalled words they associated with Liverpool because of their interactions with TAW. Somewhat ironically, the most pinpointed word was 'wool', derived from the term 'woolyback'– a way of describing those from outside Liverpool who see themselves as being from Liverpool, similar to what Sarah Thornton termed 'poseurs' (imposters) in her study on 1990's club cultures.[51] 'Wool' appeared fourteen times in the data I collected from Irish listeners to the podcast, and despite its connotations, learning the slang helps Irish supporters feel more like insiders. However, the application of such language is something that must be treated carefully, lest one be considered a 'wool'. Some of the local phrases to have emerged during the podcast have taken on a notoriety, with one even making it onto the front of a TAW piece of merchandise:

> I coined a phrase on the show that was 'sent for the [Liverpool] *Echo*', and it was something that would be said when I was playing football…Rob [Guttmann, TAW contributor], who is not Scouse but he's lived here for so long, found it hilarious but when we said this when we were playing five-a-side, no one blinks…and then, because it's alien to some of the listeners, it's now on tee shirts. [Paul Senior][52]

Aside from those phrases that form part of everyday Liverpudlian language, TAW has developed its own lexicon, with phrases that are not particularly unique to the city or the football club but to the podcast itself. One of the subscribers developed a Neil Atkinson bingo card with well-used phrases by the charismatic presenter, including well-worn Atkinson phrases such as 'talking broken biscuits', 'buy goals', 'their heads've gone', and 'it's the absolute business'. Others in the subscriber group have shared stories of how they have subconsciously adopted the phrases and used them in their everyday and working lives. The ability to recognise and utilise the language of the podcast further bolsters this sense of insidership that regular listeners have, and it provides them with connections that other media are not capable of making. Furthermore, their desire for attainment and application of such language demonstrates a fandom that goes beyond Liverpool FC.

'FANS OF FANS'

Another way that TAW generates revenue and promotes its work is through live shows, which have taken place around the world.

Sometimes, they coincide with Liverpool pre-season tours, where a ready-made audience will be there. However, the first live show took place in the Irish coastal town of Bray in 2013. Those involved with TAW quickly realised that people were interested in coming out and seeing and meeting them, as TAW's John Gibbons explains:

> We were nervous a bit – The Anfield Wrap Live, it's quite a cocky thing to do really. It's quite 'Who do you think you are?' especially from Liverpool where being full of yourself is the worst thing that you can possibly do. We got [the journalist] Guillem Ballague over, we brought [the journalist] Tony Evans over, and we brought The Tea Street Band over. You're overcompensating. We quickly realised that people were paying €10 to come say 'hello' and tell you they like The Anfield Wrap …We feel more comfortable now making the shows about us because people just want to say hello and they want to have a laugh, and they want to have fun and enjoy being with other Anfield Wrap listeners…people come up and say they're made up: 'I've been listening since the start and I'm really proud how it's gone.' That's really unique. If you think about it from a business, how many people are saying 'I bought Coca-Cola really young and I'm made up now…they're doing really well lads'…that's not happening.[53]

Gibbons' comments are demonstrative of an underexplored type of fandom. What started with Liverpool fans producing content now has fans of those fans. Despite the furore they create around events such as 'transfer deadline day', it is hard to imagine that somebody would proclaim to be a 'fan' – as opposed to a 'viewer' or 'consumer' – of Sky Sports. Only the most ardent of journalism students would admit to being a fan of a particular sports-page journalist. Yet respondents to this study readily claimed to be fans of TAW and its output. That fandom was intensified for those who felt they had been with the podcast since its inception in 2011. There was a sense that the contributors were people that they personally knew, and this was heightened through social-media exchanges (primarily through Twitter) with these various contributors. In one interview, an Irish respondent indicated that the audience reaction at the live shows was perhaps too Irish-centric, almost suggesting that they should have had a better understanding of TAW and its dynamics:

> I've been to Bray 2013; another show in Lafayette in Dublin soon after and last year there was an event in The Hangar. Enjoyed most of it. Felt that the crowd didn't get exactly what the lads wanted to do…[There were] too many Irish-based questions for me and also too many footy-related questions when the crowd has been asked to provide non-footy questions for the panel. [Stephen]

Stephen's response suggests that there are underlying tensions among Irish fans of TAW and Liverpool FC. There are fans who want to immerse themselves in the culture and language of TAW without having to focus on their own identity as Irish supporters of the club. Others, however, feel that the Irish influence needs to be embraced, judging by some of the questions asked at The Hangar event. For instance, questions were asked about non-footballing aspects of Irish culture (including bars that the TAW personnel might attend), whereas others more specifically enquired about the view in Liverpool regarding Irish supporters of the club. This negotiation of place and fandom is a complex subject matter for Irish fans of Liverpool FC within the local/global fan nexus. Most decided, or were influenced by family members, to support Liverpool in childhood, with limited knowledge of the club's history and players or, indeed, of the city's culture and past. In some cases, as discovered during this research, something as trivial as the colour of the jersey was reason enough. While TAW will not be the reason for individuals deciding to support Liverpool, it has the potential, at a micro level, to solidify that fandom for its users through shared experiences and language.

Media have always played a role in feeding fan activity, inundating their users with information. The specificity of The Anfield Wrap, coupled with its distinctive approach, provides an outlet where the Irish football fan can perhaps not seem like an alien; it provides them with an outlet where they traverse the complex tapestry of fandom, can communicate with other fans, and sustain a fandom that has been part of their lives since childhood.

'Feel the build-up, feel connected': Mediated sport and the second-generation-Irish audience in Britain

DAN DWYER

THE IMPORTANCE OF SPORT in the formation and maintenance of an Irish cultural identity within Irish emigrant populations both from a historical perspective and in studies of the contemporary Irish diaspora has been well established in recent years.[1] Understandings of diaspora point to the porousness of national boundaries and the complexities of cultural identities among migrants and their descendants, while, as emphasised in the introduction to this collection, the interconnection of sport and media can be seen as a powerful cultural force in the creation of collective identities.[2] This chapter derives from an ongoing doctoral study of the Irish in Britain as a media audience in which interviews with participants self-identifying as Irish were analysed using a constructivist-grounded-theory approach in order to understand connections between their media-audience practices and Irish identity. The chapter focuses on the role of mediated Irish sports content in the audience practices of three second-generation-Irish participants from the study for whom regular use of Irish-themed and Irish-produced media content is predominantly motivated by an interest in sport.[3] The analysis reveals media-audience practices that have strong continuities with childhood exposure to Irish sports-media content accessed by the immigrant generation in Britain or during trips to Ireland. In adulthood these practices often require that extra effort be expended to bypass technological barriers or attend public broadcasts of Irish sporting occasions. This, alongside the significance the participants ascribe to Irish sports content on British media, points to how mediated Irish sport can validate and enhance a second-generation-Irish identity in Britain.

THEORETICAL CONTEXT

Identity is understood in contemporary sociology as dynamic, evolving and changing, but as John Sugden and Alan Tomlinson point out in their analysis of football culture, the postmodern tendency towards 'anything goes' is usefully tempered by emphasising the structural constraints on the range of possible identities available; they are not simply the free choice of the individual.[4] The combination of increased global migration along with technological advances that eased transnational communication towards the end of the twentieth century opened up new ways of understanding media audiences, which, until then, had been investigated primarily within the boundaries of nation states. Using insights from George Marcus on the difficulties, in the modern world, of mapping traditional notions of community onto specific localities, David Morley makes the case for a complex understanding of identity that can be constructed simultaneously across a number of different locales both within and without a national territory. Identity can just as easily form in the spatial or the virtual realms, and diasporic cultural spaces are increasingly part of migrants' everyday lives.[5] The engines of these spaces are what Arjun Appadurai calls the symbolic 'mediascapes' of native, host and diasporic media and the actual patterns – or 'ethnoscapes' – of geographical mobility that allow minority populations to link themselves with wider constituencies.[6] In a survey of the international research that conceptualises immigrants and their descendants as diasporic media audiences, Andy Ruddock concludes that media can be understood as resources that help members of a diaspora mediate the different worlds they inhabit, understand their own ethnic identity, negotiate dual identities, and maintain 'collective identities that geography and governance repress'.[7]

Contemporary data on the Irish in Britain reveal a complex diasporic community with multifarious intergenerational and intra-

generational differences.[8] Theorisations of diaspora can, as Breda
Gray suggests, engage critically with the 'boundary work' carried out
by Irish migrants as they deal with questions of identity, authenticity
and the 'normative assumptions [of] family, kinship and community'
in their daily lives.[9] Mary Hickman's work on the second-generation
Irish in the British education system shows how they had long been
rendered invisible in British society within a narrative of assimilation
into a 'homogenous' British nation that gave way to a multicultural
society during the post-war period. This problematises the common
view that the public invisibility of the Irish in Britain was a result
of the political troubles in the North of Ireland and the related
violent episodes in Britain during the 1970s. In Hickman's analysis,
the British state had incorporated the Irish into British society via
the English Catholic Church over the previous century, ensuring
that expressions of Irish identity had a low public profile. However,
this did not prevent engagement with Irishness in the privacy of the
family home or on the regular trips to, and extended periods spent
in, Ireland common to many Irish immigrant families.[10] Studies of
second-generation-Irish identity in Britain would show how a dearth
of acknowledgment of Irish narratives in the public discourse could
result in 'an individual search process' that sought out knowledge
and understanding of Irish history in diverse media, including books,
websites and films.[11]

PARTICIPANTS

Taking its cue from the international audience research mentioned
above, the study was designed as a set of semi-structured qualitative
interviews with what Ann Gray has called 'ethnographic intentions'
to allow participants articulate their use of media and its relation
to a sense of Irishness in their own terms.[12] The call for participants
was published in the Irish diasporic newspapers *The Irish World* and
The Irish Post print editions and social-media sites, pinned on the
noticeboards of Irish centres in Liverpool, Manchester, Birmingham
and London, and posted periodically over a six-month period in
2016 to a range of groups and individuals involved in supporting
the Irish diaspora in Britain via the social-media platforms
Facebook and Twitter.[13] It was worded with the purpose of finding

participants who self-identified as Irish and who felt that their use of Irish and/or Irish-themed media content was an important part of their everyday lives. Thirty interviews have been conducted to date, and the interview transcripts were coded and analysed using the constructivist-grounded-theory approach developed by Kathy Charmaz which, taking a postmodernist perspective on grounded theory, suggests that researchers must acknowledge the realities of their prior engagement with the topic and their subjectivity in interpreting the data provided by those participating in the study.[14] The interviews conducted with two male and one female participant provide insights into second-generation-Irish engagement with mediated Irish sport in Britain, and are the focus of this chapter. Jack, Liam and Laura were all born to Irish parents who emigrated from Ireland to England in the 1960s and 1970s, and all grew into adulthood strongly identifying as Irish there.[15]

Jack, in his early thirties, was born and raised in Liverpool and lives there now. He had come across the study because he had visited St Michael's Irish Centre in the city on the day of the All-Ireland football final in 2016, in which Mayo, the county his parents had come from and a place he had visited regularly as a child, had played Dublin in a drawn game. His enthusiasm for this sporting event, due to be replayed some days afterwards, was evident throughout the interview, as were his engagement with mediated sports content generally and his vivid memories of broadcast Irish sport. When asked to outline his everyday media habits, he described his sourcing of sports news through websites and smartphone apps originating both in Ireland and in Britain and switching his car radio between a BBC sports channel and the sports coverage of Ireland's public-service broadcaster RTÉ during his daily commute to and from his place of work:

> I've always had that [RTÉ] on the long-wave frequency...so I'm pulled between that and BBC 5 Live and again it's just to kind of keep up to date cos whenever I kind of go back over to Ireland and I speak to uncles either over there in person or via phone I think it's nice to be able to have some kind of knowledge as to what the current affairs are and what have you... [Jack][16]

Liam, who is in his early fifties and has recently moved to Ireland having spent his life up to then in London, also pointed to sport as the main motivating factor in his engagement with media.

> Sport is my passion and that's why…in the morning the first thing I do is Independent.ie then, the *Mirror* […] then the BBC for the sports news so I'm taking in all the media, you know I'm taking in Irish media and English media, I suppose, you know cos that's where I am, I'm both places you know but it's, it's again […] it's more […] the sport. [Liam]

The third participant, Laura, also from London and now in her early forties, accesses a broad range of Irish media content alongside her passionate interest in Gaelic games. She emphasised the social side of the live sports broadcast in Irish pubs around London:

> I'd always look at 'The *Indo*' for sport […] I was quite into GAA, I didn't play it, I didn't play camogie, but I was always from a young age…we'd go and see the games, cos it was a social thing […] you'd look forward to the summer and the championship. [Laura][17]

All three participants expressed an interest in Irish sport that was initially developed in childhood and young adulthood. Liam, born a mile from what is now the Emirates Stadium, remembers being taken as a child to soccer matches around London and to Gaelic games played at Wembley Stadium.[18] Like Laura, he has memories of his parents buying newspapers from Ireland sold in London – such as the regional *Connaught Tribune* and *Western People*, and the national *Irish Independent* – to keep up with Gaelic-games coverage. He and Laura continue to go to the *Irish Independent* website for sports coverage today, and he also remembers the accessing of Irish radio in London:

> There was a park, Gladstone Park, and that was quite high and before the days of satellite TV, that's where the lads used to go to listen to the Irish games, the Sunday game, cos they could pick up the long wave, so I remember late summers going… and people with transistor radios on top of the hill desperately trying to get a signal…Gladstone Park in north-west London

[…] cos London's a basin and to get the signal you have get up to the top of the basin, so that's what they were aiming for. [Liam][19]

Jack also pointed to his exposure to Gaelic-sports coverage on Irish radio as a child in Liverpool, and identifies RTÉ's main radio channel by a name not officially used for it in Ireland since the mid-1960s: 'I listen to what we call Radio Éireann but what I think is your RTÉ…One? That's what I was, we were, brought up with, for the Gaelic-football commentaries [Jack].' While well aware that this name – by which the station would have been known to his parents in Ireland at the time they emigrated – has fallen out of use in contemporary Ireland, Jack points out that this is how he and his siblings refer to the station to this day. Jack feels that he grew up with what he calls a 'time-capsule impression of Ireland', which leads him to make particular assumptions about Ireland based on his parents' memories, and that it is through access to Irish media that he gains an understanding of contemporary Ireland that can challenge that impression:

> I'm still learning lessons…not everyone in Ireland thinks like that or even thought like that back then when they came over…so that's been quite kind of refreshing…from media, from reading articles and seeing people explain their own experiences and how they're completely different from what I thought Ireland was like…we only saw a kind of sliver of it…that kind of balances me out a little bit. [Jack]

SEEKING OUT IRISH SPORTS CONTENT

Reflecting the 'individual search process' identified in the second-generation Irish in Britain, these participants also described particular efforts taken to access Irish sports content there over the years, and how sources of Irish content have increased over time due to new technologies.[20] Jack described how he deliberately took out a subscription to Sky Sports in Liverpool with the intention of allowing it to lapse as soon as was possible and keeping the satellite dish, to which he then connected a box he suspects is illegal in order to receive Irish broadcast television at his home. Through this he receives the Irish channels RTÉ and TG4, which he uses for watching Irish sports content and, in particular, Gaelic games throughout the summer. He checks Irish and British sports news via social-media apps on his smartphone throughout his typical day, and this includes GAA news directly from established Irish media personalities and newer Irish sources he has come across, such as Joe.ie.[21] He explains how recent developments in media technologies have helped him to feel more connected to Ireland and as 'informed' as someone living there:

> I'd have probably felt more…connected…just through the development of technology and the fact that you can keep in touch with people and events and stuff, sources of news much more easy now via your phone, via the set-top boxes, via the Internet that…I can be just as informed. [Jack]

Jack goes on to mention the digital access he now has to a local commercial FM radio station based in his parents' county of origin that just a few years ago he could only access if he was physically there, and stresses the sense of immediacy he feels when listening to its GAA coverage and how this enhances his identity:

> I can listen on an app on my phone to Midwest Radio and feel the build-up to the All-Ireland, like as if I was there, and as soon as you turn that on you feel connected, whereas before you had that kind of technology, you would feel a little bit removed and there's more of an effort…to maintain that sense of Irishness. [Jack]

Liam – who as a young adult worked alongside Irish immigrants on building sites in London and later ran an Irish pub there – has a detailed knowledge of the efforts put in to access live sports content in public settings.

> They used to bring over videos…to tape *The Sunday Game* on videotape and go to the pubs on a Monday…the guy who was behind it had a bank of videotapes and he would sell them to the pubs…a lot of the lads for them it would be part of the weekend, and…the pubs would be mad to get the tapes first cos they would show it throughout the whole of Monday…

and then in the evening as well...that was a big thing...[Then]
when satellite TV came in I was running a bar and I remember
I realised that Ireland were playing Germany in a friendly pre-
USA...you see the pubs didn't open all day then, they only
opened at seven o'clock...So this match was on at 2 o'clock
in the afternoon and I saw that Sky was sharing the satellite
with German TV and they were showing it on the German side
so I stayed open...well, let's say the bar wasn't open but the
pub was open [laughs], and obviously the commentary was
in German but the match was on...I tried to get some radio
commentary but it was out of sync so I didn't bother in the
end...so they watched the match and then people went to the
pub afterwards and they're all sitting down thinking they were
going to watch the match live and of course people had already
watched... and told them the score! [Liam][22]

Liam built on the knowledge of satellite television he developed
in the Irish community in London, and since he moved to the rural
west of Ireland has earned a living from fitting satellite dishes. He
pointed out that he often gets calls now from Irish people in London
looking for advice on how to access Irish television content there.

NEGOTIATING IRISH IDENTITY

Speaking about his Irish identity growing up in London, Liam made
the following observation about how his second-generation-Irish
schoolmates developed different allegiances around soccer as they
grew into adulthood:

I knew a guy at school who would have been doing Irish
dancing and that, so, you know, it was around, but... it wasn't
forced down our throat... but then as I grew older... a lot of
my friends became more English, if you know what I mean,
more following the soccer... so half the group followed Ireland
and especially when Ireland actually started, under Jack, started
getting a bit better, and then half would follow England... even
though, they came from the same demographic...most of them
would have been of Irish descent. [Liam]

Sugden and Tomlinson wrote of how the tensions between individual angst and collective constraints are both expressed and resolved through supporting a national team in a global competitive sport such as soccer.[23] Such tensions are all the greater for the second-generation Irish in Britain, where 'simultaneous, compatible loyalties made sense if you were second generation Irish in England, but did serve to differentiate and position the individuals in the eyes of others'.[24] Jack articulates his negotiation of such tensions through his memories of Irish sport being televised on British media, which gave him the sense as a teenager that an Irish identity could be normalised for a second-generation-Irish person like him in Britain:

> I have vivid memories of Channel 4 having Gaelic sport…they only had it for a couple of years but I remember being made up with that…felt good to see TV like [that] at home, I didn't have to go to pubs or clubs to watch it. [Jack][25]

The use of British media to access Irish sports content that can help negotiate Irish identity in England is also revealed in Jack's discussion of the All-Ireland football final, which was to the fore of his mind at the time of the interview. The story of the 'Mayo curse', frequently used to add colour to media coverage of finals featuring the Mayo team in recent years, was one Jack had an awareness of from his Irish-media use. However, he was not fully familiar with the detail of the story until he came across a BBC-website article that filled in the gaps in his knowledge:

> There was a really good article a couple of weeks ago on the BBC website [about] the Mayo curse…and that was written from quite an interesting…somebody who had obviously total knowledge and experience of Ireland but they were writing it for a British audience, they explained a lot of the terms and they looked at the history, the propensity for Irish people to look at mysticism, like the Celtic tradition and sort of the whole…curses and things…something that was quite prominent in Ireland, going back years…I've noticed that quite a lot…Ireland presented through that kind of…talking to a British audience and that's quite interesting to me cos obviously that's the way I've predominantly experienced Ireland anyway. [Jack][26]

The somewhat romanticised view of Ireland articulated here connects with the 'time capsule' sense of Ireland Jack feels he had growing up, but he is also aware that this view is from a British media source and that it resonates with others he has come across on British media. The differences Jack perceives between representations of Ireland framed for a British audience and the more immediate sense of Ireland that he gets from accessing Irish media directly speaks to the 'boundary work' carried out by the Irish-media audience in Britain.[27]

MEDIATED SPORT IN PUBLIC SETTINGS

The specific importance of mediated Irish sport in public settings to an Irish identity in Britain is also clear from the interviews discussed here. Raney, writing on why audiences watch and enjoy mediated sports, points to Melnick's conception of the 'sports encounter', where sports events broadcast in a public setting can legitimise interpersonal interaction between strangers, and 'many fans...report being motivated by a larger sense of group affiliation...[a] sense of belonging and community can be felt on various levels'.[28] Live sports broadcasts – with their ongoing suspense and tension, and which are enjoyed in public settings and attended by first, second and more generations of Irish migrants – provide opportunities for connection to, and identification with, the wider diaspora. Laura touched on this communality with other Irish fans when she spoke of her regular trips to local pubs in London to watch Irish soccer in her twenties and the hurling and Gaelic football championships every summer:

> You had to make an effort to go to the local pubs to watch...everyone would go and watch...you know, if Mayo and Galway were playing, you'd have some kind of ding-dong with the Mayo bloke down the pub...friendly banter and all that and I suppose that was an interest and I always did that really. [Laura][29]

The 'friendly banter' that Laura speaks of can set Gaelic sport apart from the more antagonistic inter-club rivalries of British soccer. Anticipating the upcoming All-Ireland final replay, Jack also contrasted a 'jealousy' that he felt is often apparent in media coverage of fans of British soccer clubs with the 'camaraderie' of Gaelic fans of other county teams rooting for a county felt to be the underdogs.

All three interviewees interspersed their discussion of the contemporary Irish sports content they access with vivid memories of watching the Republic of Ireland soccer team in public settings during the early 1990s. That successful period for the Irish side in international competition coincided with a broader flowering of Irish culture around the world as the tentative Northern Ireland peace process signalled the beginning of the end of the Troubles and the Irish state embraced, at least symbolically, a global Irish diaspora.[30] This was reflected in the British media portrayal of Irishness at the time, which included popular British/Irish television drama co-productions such as *Father Ted* and *Ballykissangel*, and has been understood as changing from a conception of 'race', in which Irish assimilation was presumed, to that of 'ethnicity', where Irishness was celebrated as a distinct and 'high-status cultural icon'.[31] Jack watched the Republic of Ireland soccer team compete in the 1994 World Cup in a pub setting as a teenager, in the company of first-generation and second-generation fans, and remembers this as a pivotal moment in the validation of his sense of Irishness.

> That was massive, that was huge cos there was a pub in Manchester called The Grove...that was kind of my first exposure really to...sports drinking culture...I loved it... getting that kind of interesting experience...really helped a lot...watching Ireland on the BBC [and] on ITV in the pubs when they were playing, being covered and being talked of so highly, like being so well respected cos of course, Liverpool, it's pure soccer here and seeing all of these first- and second-generation-Irish lads...and seeing the kind of adoration that they had over in Ireland but also seeing that the respect they had in England that gave me a bit of an access point to my identity...cos I know a lot of those lads had nowhere near the same level of connection that I had so...if those lads can be kind of accepted, then I can. [Jack][32]

CONCLUSION

Paul Gilroy argues that the power of diasporic identity is not based on the essentialist concepts of blood or soil but on its being worked upon over time by individuals who draw on and mix the communal histories and struggles made known to them through family and migratory ties.[33] Contemporary engagement with Irish sports-media content among the second-generation Irish can have strong continuities with practices normalised in family settings during childhood and young adulthood. Knowledge of Ireland handed down from first-generation migrants to Britain – often via exposure to that generation's use of Irish media content as well as from trips to Ireland and contact with family connections there – can form the basis of a keenly felt Irish cultural identity among the second-generation Irish in Britain. That identity can be negotiated and enhanced through the seeking out of Irish media content in adulthood. The participants discussed here show that these generational continuities in audience practices can be particularly strong around sports coverage. The passionate interest in the GAA championship articulated in two of the accounts can be linked to childhood summer holidays spent in Ireland, when extended family members, some resident in Ireland and some in Britain, enjoyed the unfolding competition together. The accessing of similar content in adulthood by second-generation immigrants in Britain via media technologies old and new, in private and in public settings, can rekindle and sustain feelings of belonging to collective identities first experienced then.

While a cultural identity based on Irish ethnicity in Britain can often be the site of tensions around acceptance and belonging, such tensions can be alleviated by engagement with mediated Irish sports content. The celebratory and public nature of media broadcasts of Irish international soccer in Britain in the early 1990s was remembered by the participants discussed here as a pivotal moment in the public validation of their Irish identities in Britain. Going to pubs and clubs to see Republic of Ireland soccer fixtures and watch GAA championship matches was a practice all the participants continued to enjoy in the ensuing years. Similar validation and enhancement of their Irish identities was experienced during more mundane periods of everyday life when Irish-themed content appeared in the sports coverage of British media. Such coverage, framed for a British audience, can chime with the immigrant-generation's memory of Ireland, but also provide contextual information about Irish sport that may be presumed as understood by Irish media that focus almost exclusively on their audience in Ireland. British media coverage of Irish sport is rare, however, and the second-generation Irish discussed here seek out sports content directly from Ireland, often bypassing technological and legal barriers in the process. Everyday access to Irish media can deepen knowledge of, and strengthen connections to, Ireland as a place of familial origin while allowing a second-generation-Irish person in Britain to feel part of that 'imagined community' of Irish people that is, at any point in time, tuned into local, national or Internet-based media sources.[34] Although more GAA coverage has become available on pay-per-view and subscription-based television and Internet services in Britain in recent years, these developments were not mentioned by the participants discussed in this chapter. This may be due to the fact that the interviews with them took place not long after this content was first made available, but it may also relate to their age and class profiles.[35] In the wider study, some awareness and usage of these new sources of GAA content was evident in interviews conducted at the same time with younger, middle-class Irish immigrants, which may point to higher disposable incomes along with more openness to payment-based media services. It remains the case, however, that the participants discussed in this chapter have actively sought out free-to-air broadcasts and non-subscription Internet-based Irish sports content, and made it an integral part of their everyday media-audience practices.

This chapter discussed interviews with three second-generation-Irish participants who grew up in Britain at a time when Irishness had a low and often negative public profile. Accessing Irish media in Britain and keeping in touch with Ireland through family connections and regular trips there was a normal feature of their lives growing up in Britain. They all entered adulthood at a time when Irishness came to be publicly celebrated in Britain and across the wider world, often through mediated sports content broadcast in public settings. That time also coincided with advances in media technologies such as satellite television and the Internet, which would add new ways to long-established ones of accessing Irish media in Britain. Engaging with Irish and Irish-themed sports media in private and public settings has been a significant resource for the second-generation Irish in Britain in the negotiation of identity, and continues to validate and enhance their Irish identities there today.

James McClean's Poppy Protest and the Cultural Politics of Diasporic Non-assimilation

ANTHONY P. MCINTYRE

IN NOVEMBER 2018, on the pitch of an English Championship football club, Stoke City, a by-now-familiar narrative was playing out. Footballer James McClean, a Stoke City player hailing from Derry City, was being incessantly booed by a small contingent of both home and visiting supporters as Stoke City played Middlesbrough FC. The oftentimes vitriolic abuse from the stands also finds its twenty-first-century equivalent in the trolling and hate messages directed at McClean on social media. This is nothing new for the player; the debate and controversy surrounding McClean has been a late-autumn fixture of the football calendar in England since November 2012. McClean's annual refusal to wear the Earl Haig poppy, a (contested) symbol of remembrance for British and Commonwealth military personnel who have died in conflict, reignites a well-rehearsed debate that pits patriotism and national pride against the painful legacies of colonialism and the freedom of individual choice. McClean will not wear the symbol on the grounds that it commemorates those soldiers who were stationed in his home city of Derry, the site of one of the most traumatic legacies of the Troubles, Bloody Sunday, when British troops killed fourteen civilians in 1972. This is a divisive stand that foregrounds sport's capacity to embody cultural fracture points. Indeed, in this chapter I interrogate how, through this one sporting figure, a number of twenty-first-century societal tensions relating to Irish identity can be discerned: these include tensions regarding a sense of national belonging while living abroad as part of the Irish diaspora, the impact of social media on such diasporic self-expression, and the fraught relationship between Britain and Ireland at a time of heightened national anxiety – a relationship that has been under intense scrutiny since the June 2016 Brexit referendum and its political and social aftermath.

McClean is a rich figure for the mode of media analysis employed herein due to the fact that, through his celebrity persona and tendency to become embroiled in controversy linked to national affiliation, we can discern notable recent shifts with regard to Irish identity as it plays out both within Ireland (North and South) and across the Irish Sea in Britain. In this player's specific case, the conflicted identity of many Irish nationalists growing up in Northern Ireland who then relocate to the UK mainland is evident. McClean's celebrity status as a high-profile footballer also enables – due in no small part to the public deliberation his actions provoke – an investigation into the impact of shifts in technological-communications capability. Notably, this heightened public status enables a scholarly focus on the emergence and broad uptake of social media, and an analysis of the recalibrations occurring in the manifestation of regional identities within the UK. This latter point is, of course, further exacerbated in the context of the Brexit vote, a seismic political shift that has revealed a number of divisions within the UK that parse out along regional, national and socio-economic lines. I argue in this chapter that the different technological, societal and political points raised above have combined to unsettle the coordinates of Irish diasporic populations in the (mainland) UK, and further undermine what is for many an already precarious sense of belonging; and that, in accordance with many of the other chapters included in the present collection, sport provides a valuable lens through which to examine evolving social processes.

In order to develop this investigation of shifting diasporic subjectivities, this chapter first introduces the theoretical framework underpinning the analysis, before giving an overview of McClean's career and detailing the various controversies in which he has been involved. Notably, these include his ongoing refusal to wear a Remembrance poppy; his polarising position on declaring for the Republic of Ireland national football team despite representing Northern Ireland as a youth player; some notable social-media postings that highlight tensions involved in diasporic assimilation; and his representation within mainstream elements of the British media. Uniting all of these elements is McClean's performance of what I term 'diasporic non-assimilation'. Irish diasporic identities are, of course, pluralistic and encapsulate a range of attitudes toward the diasporic home nation. Diasporic non-assimilation signifies a reluctance to modify opinions and behaviours shaped by one's home in order to gain acceptance and avoid conflict upon relocation. While this is obviously a trait that can exist to a greater or lesser extent in diasporic subjects, and can, of course, strengthen or attenuate significantly in different social contexts, McClean is remarkably consistent in his performance of non-assimilation, as I demonstrate in this chapter, and the implications of this position animate this chapter.

SPORTING CELEBRITY

Scholarship on sporting celebrity has developed from and extended earlier writings on stardom that emanated from film and media studies. Key to the understanding of how celebrity might be understood is Richard Dyer's term 'structured polysemy', which he offered to explain how figures subject to intensive public focus can be interpreted in different ways by different audiences.[1] While Dyer's work focused on studio-era classical Hollywood, other foundational work on stardom emphasised its tendency to cross into other cultural realms. In this vein, Christine Gledhill describes the star as a 'social sign, carrying cultural meanings and ideological values, which express the intimacies of individual personality, inviting desire and identification; *an emblem of national celebrity*, founded on the body, fashion and personal style; a product of capitalism and the ideology of individualism, *yet a site of contest by marginalised groups*' (my italics).[2]

David Andrews and Steven Jackson, themselves building on the work of sociologists Leo Braudy and P. David Marshall, in their influential essay 'Sports Celebrities, Public Culture and Private Experience' emphasise the emblematic nature of sports celebrities as well as their abilities to channel cultural trends and anxieties. Drawing a distinction between sportsmen and women and the more familiar figure of the film or television star, the authors point to a perceived heightened authenticity that the former derive due to their status as 'real individuals participating in unpredictable contest… [with] the seeming visceral, dramatic immediacy of the sport practice provid[ing] the sports celebrity with an important veneer of authenticity, that sets him or her apart from celebrities drawn from other, more explicitly manufactured, cultural realms'.[3] For a sportsman such as McClean, whose tendency is to 'throw his body on the line' in his sporting performance, such claims to authenticity are key to his cultural relevance and purchase.[4]

Much of the scholarship listed above foregrounds the ways in which sporting celebrity symbolises the nation, as well as tensions within nationality. In McClean's case, as we consider someone technically born in the UK and within the island of Ireland who can claim Irish citizenship, but is currently living, one presumes, in the Midlands of England, some of those tensions are notably pronounced. The footballer's celebrity image is built upon an undeniable sporting prowess, but also clearly inflected by national and regional histories, as well as the protocols and technological infrastructures of twenty-first-century media environments. As such, an analysis of the footballer helps enrich our understanding of the complexities of contemporary Irish identity.

CAREER OVERVIEW AND CONTEXT

Prior to signing for Sunderland FC in the English Premier League in August 2011, McClean had played in both of the top-level leagues in Ireland. He initially played for Institute FC in the Irish Premier League (Northern Ireland) as well as in the League of Ireland (primarily based in the Republic of Ireland) for Derry City FC. He failed to secure a first-team place with Sunderland FC under Steve Bruce, the manager who had signed him, but became a regular player for the side once fellow Derryman Martin O'Neill took the helm. It was during this time that McClean first took his decision not to wear the Remembrance Sunday poppy in November 2012. He went on to play under O'Neill when he lined up for the Republic of Ireland during the manager's 2013–18 tenure, having first represented his country in 2012 under then-manager Giovanni Trappatoni. Since departing Sunderland, McClean has played in a number of sides in both the English Premier League, for West Bromwich Albion FC, and the English Football League Championship, for Wigan Athletic FC; at the time of writing he is under contract with Stoke City FC, a Championship club.

Any examination of McClean as an athlete but also as a media construction (in terms of his celebrity profile) would be remiss without an emphasis on the importance of the city of Derry to the footballer's identity. Indeed, it is as a 'son of Derry' that the player is most often understood in media profiles. As the second largest city in Northern Ireland and the one with a Catholic majority, Derry has long been understood as a fulcrum of Northern Irish nationalist identity. The ongoing debate about the city's name (officially Londonderry, but with Derry being the preferred term for the majority of its inhabitants) is itself a microcosm of the wider debates that divide Northern Irish political life. It is worth noting that Derry City resigned from the Irish Premier League (in Northern Ireland) in 1972, citing discrimination on the part of the Irish Football Association (IFA) as a reason for its withdrawal, and then joined the League of Ireland (in the Republic of Ireland) in 1985, becoming the only team situated in Northern Ireland to play in this league. This is essential in understanding the footballing identity of McClean – who, analogously, played for both Northern Ireland and the Republic of Ireland – as well as the political significance of the game in the city. Indeed, as sports scholar David Hassan has convincingly shown, soccer plays a vital role for Northern nationalists in 'the development of national pride and independence and in engendering a positive counter-hegemonic role for that community'.[5] The following details of McClean's career and public profile can be understood as deriving in essential ways from, and constituting a continuance of, the political nature of Derry football.

It is as a direct result of this civic background that the other prominent controversy of McClean's career developed. In tandem with the poppy debate, which I treat in detail below, one other controversy to have emerged during McClean's rise to prominence relates to his international career, and is also directly related to the player's upbringing in Derry. In common with most other players from the North of Ireland, due to his place of birth and under the regulations of the Belfast (Good Friday) Agreement, McClean has dual citizenship should he so wish, and is entitled to play for either the Republic of Ireland or Northern Ireland. McClean played for the under-21 Northern Ireland side on a number of occasions in what he freely admits was a self-serving move.[6] When offered the chance to play for the Republic of Ireland, the Derryman had no qualms in changing his affiliation. He was also part of a notable trend that, much to the consternation of the IFA, the governing body of football in Northern Ireland, saw McClean become the sixth player in a three-year period to switch affiliation to the Republic of Ireland.[7]

Nationalist footballers – players whose communities would identify as Irish rather than British, from the North of Ireland, and who declare for the Republic of Ireland senior team – have already attracted a significant degree of scholarly attention.[8] Hassan et al., in an article focusing on McClean's Ireland teammate Darron Gibson, have posited a variety of reasons as to why players from nationalist communities in Northern Ireland have chosen to declare for the Republic of Ireland rather than Northern Ireland:

> These include the nature of the communities in which players reside, family ties, political affiliations, personal and national identities (including social class), sporting pragmatism and, last but by no means least, the perception of the IFA held by some nationalists in Northern Ireland, which has rarely been favourable.[9]

Of particular note in a number of these players' justifications for their switch in affiliation is the sense that the home supporters at Windsor Park, the ground at which the Northern Ireland international football team plays, is heavily partisan to Ulster-loyalist ideology, most evident in the types of song the home crowds sing as well as in the playing of the British national anthem, 'God Save the Queen'.[10] McClean has spoken of the difficulties of this, and a further controversial decision on his part was to turn his back on the British flag as the British national anthem was played during a West Bromwich Albion game against Charleston Battery in the US. One further mediated development of this incident is the videos uploaded to YouTube celebrating, in song, the player's protest.[11]

A particularly useful figure with which to compare McClean is former Northern Ireland international and Celtic FC player Neil

Lennon, who similarly hails from a nationalist background. Lennon's international playing career was plagued by the animosity towards him by some Northern Ireland fans, which resulted in the player receiving a number of death threats, particularly once he signed with Celtic. Unfortunately, such animosity has followed the former player into management; one low point of a 2018–19 Scottish Premiership season marred by a number of instances of sectarian fan behaviour was an incident in which Lennon, at the time manager of Hibernian FC, had a pound coin thrown at his face by an opposing-team's fan. Such actions show that sectarianism is still part of the Northern Irishman's day-to-day life in Scotland.[12] While the abuse aimed at Lennon and the animosity towards McClean have notable contextual differences in terms of both their current national location and the stages these athletes are at in their respective careers, one striking similarity is the unwillingness of either of these men to be cowed by the threats and hostility they face, a trait admired by fans and key to the diasporic non-assimilation both players display. Lennon's post-match comment after the 2018 incident that he would like to 'meet the individual who threw the coin at me some day, because [he is] not happy about it at all' shows a confluence of stereotypical masculine traits of aggression and a pointed non-assimilation with regard to openly hostile elements of a diasporic homeland that can be detected in many of McClean's behaviours examined in the following sections of this chapter.[13]

SOCIAL MEDIA AND UNRULY NORTHERN NATIONALISM

While McClean has delivered some celebrated footballing perfor-mances, notably for the Republic of Ireland, the player's career on the pitch has often been overshadowed by his presence on social-media platforms and his tendency to unwittingly, or indeed intentionally, ignite controversy. As John Price and colleagues have noted in their study of the use of Twitter by professional footballers, 'The medium…provides an opportunity for players themselves to find their own voice and provide their views unfettered by media or club'.[14] I argue that this unfettered access, in tandem with the amplification provided by McClean's celebrity status, allows for a modelling of Irish-nationalist subjectivities that would previously have been under the radar of broadcast media.

McClean's postings might be better understood within the context of a wider media environment in which Irish emigrant populations increasingly look to digital-media formats such as podcasts and Facebook groups to access content that enables them to feel connected to home while living abroad; or in which their sense of what constitutes 'home' is being reshaped to fit the contours of their new lives.[15] Jarlath Regan's popular podcast *An Irishman Abroad* (2013–), in which the comedian interviews celebrity Irish figures who have left Ireland, attests to the popular appeal of formats that foreground celebrity adaptation to the vicissitudes of diasporic living. The celebrities Regan interviews tend to emphasise strategies for achieving success while finding a balance between fitting in with their new home and not losing an essential sense of Irish identity. In contrast, McClean's self-authored media presence, as well as actions such as turning his back on the British flag mentioned above, can be characterised by a recalcitrant refusal to adapt or temper views and actions that, while consistent with the norms of his home community in Derry, go against the grain of his diasporic home. For instance, in one tweet from February 2012, McClean calls out TV presenter Colin Murray for naming him as a 'fellow Northern Irishman' as he introduced a goal he had scored against Stoke City on *MOTD 2*, writing 'Colin Murray get it right will you its #Irish'. The tweet was the subject of press attention both in Ireland and in the UK, and provided an early example of how McClean's postings with regard to his nationalist Irish identity gained the young footballer significant cultural purchase.[16]

A little more controversial was a tweet from February 2013 where McClean revealed that he uses The Wolfe Tones' folk song 'Broad Black Brimmer' to motivate himself for big games, such as the one he was due to play against future club West Bromwich Albion the following day. This revelation was contentious on account of the fact that the chorus ends with the following lines:

> When Ireland gets her freedom,
> The one they'll choose to lead 'em,
> Will wear the broad black brimmer,
> Of the IRA.

Although the lyrics are contextualised historically – the title referring to a brimmed hat worn by Irish Republican Army (IRA) guerrillas during the War of Independence (1919–21) – the fact that the song makes reference to the IRA explicitly would usually be cause enough for someone with a high profile not to declare their admiration for it on social media. McClean, for his part, in a BBC interview, stressed the cultural normativity of listening to such songs: 'Look, I was an Irish lad growing up. Ninety-five per cent of the population, in Ireland, probably listened to The Wolfe Tones…and all of a sudden it's in the papers that I'm pro-IRA'.[17] The appeal of musical artists such as The Wolfe Tones has been identified as a central element of Irish diasporic first-generation and second-generation cultures, with a primary appeal being their 'emotive accounts of the historical struggle for Irish freedom'.[18] Arguably, the popularity of such folk songs and newer forms that build on this tradition lie in the carnivalesque 'rowdy world of subaltern excess and mayhem' that Irish studies scholar Joe Cleary identifies in the music of second-generation-Irish band The Pogues, a rowdiness clearly in evidence in the fan songs celebrating McClean's various actions alluded to earlier.[19]

One might argue that some of McClean's more controversial postings are a means for the diasporic subject to retain a home identity while being surrounded by the cultural dominance of the host nation. Instructive in this regard is a portion of an interview Darragh McGee and Alan Bairner conducted with nationalist players who declared for Northern Ireland. Eugene Ferry, a footballer who at the time played for both Derry City FC and Northern Ireland, made the following comment about how he talked to his friends in Derry regarding his interactions with Northern Ireland teammates:

> When I was home or talking to people around the community about Northern Ireland, I felt as though I had to call 'them' all 'orange bastards' and all. You feel like you sort of have to put that on even though it's not really what I think. These boys don't understand what it's like to sit and chat with Protestant boys and wouldn't understand if I explained so I just don't…I just tell them what I think they want me to say. [Interviewed 26 June 2009][20]

McGee and Bairner utilise Erving Goffman's writings on the performativity of self to argue that the nationalist footballer may in fact 'perform' nationalism in an attempt to avoid 'stigma' or a tainted sense of Irish identity. While this is a claim made in terms of a Derry player speaking in person to his hometown friends in a specific context, this can be extrapolated to analyse the tweet of McClean's given above. Diasporic non-assimilation here is a performative mode of embodying Irishness that would seem excessive, perhaps, to one comfortably ensconced in his or her own nation, but that serves as a psychic defence against a potentially overwhelming alien culture. A notable feature of McClean's early biography is that an early transfer to Lincoln City FC a few years prior to his move to Sunderland FC was called off due to the player's homesickness,[21] suggesting that such a psychic defence is necessary on the part of this sportsman.

This tension with regard to home – a sense of belonging and diasporic uprootedness, as well as the negotiation of one's public and private selves – is clearly in evidence in McClean's social-media postings. This aspect of the player's celebrity identity is congruent with Anne Jerslev and Mette Mortensen's observation that 'Celebrities on social media reconfigure the border line between the public and the private...one of the crucial fields of tension in celebrity culture'.[22] In addition to this blurring of the public and the private, recent developments in technology have led to the notion of home becoming similarly porous. As media scholar David Morley puts it, 'traditional ideas of home, homeland and nation have been destabilized both by new patterns of physical mobility and migration and by new communication technologies which routinely transgress the symbolic boundaries around both the private household and the nation state'.[23] I suggest that, for diasporic celebrities, the border between home and host nation is similarly reconfigured as they post within and beyond their new environs, in sometimes problematic or ideologically countervailing ways. However, as Morley further elaborates – referencing the trend for Indian call-centre workers serving the UK market often being held up as an example of modern communications signalling the 'end of geography' – such mediated 'dislocations and deterritorialisations are still deeply enmeshed with the complexities and vicissitudes of geography and history', and utopian claims to the existence of a deterritorialised geography are 'much more legible if one reads it as a set of secondary (or "shadow") geographies created through the history of imperialism'.[24] That is, Morley resists simplistic utopian readings of modern communicative technologies conquering spatial constrictions, emphasising how historical and geographical factors can still be discerned through such 'new-media' communications.

It is clearly evident that such a history of imperialism is intrinsic to McClean's social-media postings. Football itself has a highly ambivalent history in Ireland. Initially perceived as a 'garrison game' associated with British rule, Hassan argues that football has since come to constitute 'an opportunity to express [Northern nationalists'] support for the idea of Irish unification and engage in counter-hegemonic activity against the Northern Ireland State'.[25] Football and diaspora have a long-standing interconnection that historian Conor Curran has valuably charted in his study of the well-established routes of footballing emigrants from Ireland to the UK and beyond from the late nineteenth century.[26] As just one player in this long lineage, McClean's diasporic non-assimilation can be read as one manifestation of a wider exilic ambivalence experienced by migrants who have departed their homeland in order to make a living playing football.

POPPIES, PROTEST AND NEGOTIATING MEDIA EXPOSURE

As argued earlier, the most notorious aspect of McClean's public profile in the UK is linked with Remembrance Sunday. For each year he has played in the English Football League (2012–19), McClean has refused to follow domestic-club conventions and wear the Earl Haig poppy in the November games proximate to Remembrance Sunday. This action is in defiance of an increasingly conformist public pressure regarding the symbol that has seen a variety of public figures castigated for not wearing or somehow disrespecting the poppy. For instance, England cricketer Moeen Ali had been 'caught' not wearing one on his lapel in November 2017 in an official team photo and was subject to vitriolic abuse on social media. In previous years, public figures – such as newsreader Charlene White of ITV News London – were racially abused for refusing to wear the poppy.[27] Notably, the above are people who are of BAME (Black,

Asian or Minority Ethnicity) heritage, and, as indicated, the criticism of these public figures was often racist in expression, suggesting the link between narrow conceptions of nation that associate Englishness or Britishness with whiteness and nativism – currents in popular discourse that were heightened in the run up to the Brexit vote. It is in this context that McClean's high-profile (and, at this stage, predictable) refusal to wear the symbol year on year has to be understood.

With regard to the poppy itself, it is far from being the apolitical symbol that some (including the English Football League) have claimed. As scholars Daniel Fitzpatrick and John Kelly have astutely noted, the Remembrance poppy is an ideologically charged symbol that articulates a particular civic–military positioning and construction of nationalism that resonates deeply within Britain at a time when ideas of nationhood are in flux, a resonance that is highly ambivalent to settled diasporic communities within the UK.[28] The supposed apolitical symbolism of the poppy has been increasingly undermined in recent years due to a number of high-profile incidents. For instance, Manchester City manager Pep Guardiola's decision to wear a yellow ribbon in memory of Catalan politicians imprisoned for their actions promoting the region's independence forced Martin Glenn, the Football Association CEO, to reject any suggestion there was an equivalence between the poppy and the Catalan symbol. Similar to McClean's stance, in November 2018 Manchester United's Serbian player Nemanja Matic refused to wear the poppy, offering as justification the fact that his home town of Vrelo had been bombed in 1999.[29] As Martin Samuel – writing in the *Daily Mail*, a publication that consistently admonishes McClean for his poppy stance – put it when reflecting on the Guardiola incident, 'The FA presides over arguably the most cosmopolitan league in the world. Did it never occur to them there may be issues?'[30]

For his part, McClean has come under intense pressure, from both media and fans, for his continued refusal to wear the poppy. The player admits fan antipathy stoked by his stance encouraged his departure from Sunderland, and when he went to Wigan, he wrote an open letter to the club chairperson published on the club website outlining in detail his reasons for not wearing the poppy, explicitly outlining his experience growing up in Derry and how, in his words, 'for me to wear a poppy would be as much a gesture of disrespect for the innocent people who lost their lives in The Troubles – and Bloody Sunday especially – as I have in the past been accused of disrespecting the victims of WWI and WWII'.[31]

It seems that McClean's persistence in refusing to bow under pressure has led to a wider acceptance of his position in recent years. I would suggest that a turning point in public sentiment with regard to the player is in evidence in a remarkably favourable profile of the player aired on BBC's *Football Focus* in April 2017. There are a number of cultural threads that can be detected in the profile overall that speak to a shift in the perception of the footballer in particular, and of the nationalist community of the North of Ireland in general. Notably, the piece dwelt at length on the death of McClean's former Derry City teammate Ryan McBride, who died unexpectedly in March 2017 at the age of twenty-seven. The piece seems to be harnessing a specific male melancholia in order to soften the image of the 'hard man' McClean.[32] Similarly, and somewhat problematically, the interviewer's surprise at one point that the footballer is articulate and not angry ('so softly spoken') invokes well-established tropes depicting the Irish as atavistic, unenlightened and prone to a violent tribalism,[33] only in this instance to emphasise how McClean is *not like that really*, segueing, at this point in the feature, into a section dealing with charity work the player does for the Oxford Bulls, a team made up of youths who have Down's syndrome.

While media profiles such as that of *Football Focus*, examined above, seemed to indicate something of a softening of reaction to the player, McClean's move to Stoke City in the summer of 2018 meant that he had once again to clarify his stance on the Remembrance poppy to a new set of fans. Stoke-on-Trent was notoriously claimed as the 'Brexit capital of Britain' by former United Kingdom Independence Party leader Paul Nuttall, and is a city associated with post-industrial decline and apathy, commonly described as being 'left behind'. While many in Stoke have contested such a characterisation,[34] the city does seem to harbour some of the elements of 'restorative nostalgia' that cultural theorist Svetlana Boym identifies as constitutive of ideologies that seek to re-establish a perceived past glory.[35] This animating fixation on a better past that must be regained is congruent both with the pronouncements of Brexit ideologues and with some of the more fervent critics policing the wearing of the Remembrance poppy. As such, it was perhaps not surprising that the Irish player once again faced a hostile element of his home supporters, as well as a significant proportion of the visiting Middlesbrough fans, and again became embroiled in a public spat, having described these fans as 'cave men', sharing the following quote from IRA hunger striker Bobby Sands: 'They have nothing in their whole imperial arsenal that can break the spirit of one Irishman who doesn't want to be broken.'[36] McClean's tendency to invoke colonial history in his postings is again evidence of the player's unruly nationalism and his capacity to embody the fraught relationship between Britain and Ireland in his social-media postings.

CONCLUSION

As I have argued in this chapter, Derry footballer James McClean provides a useful example of how sport, in this case football, constitutes a means through which societal tensions are worked through. By analysing McClean as a media text using the protocols of cultural studies and applying insights generated from stardom and celebrity studies as well as media studies, I have shown how the Derry player's celebrity identity is a 'negotiated terrain of significance'[37] through which nationality, region and history are channelled. In particular, I have focused on how diasporic identity is intrinsic to this signification, with McClean's performance of diasporic non-assimilation a constant feature of his celebrity image, one shaped as much by his own recalcitrance in the face of a conformist media landscape in the UK as by his upbringing in the city of Derry, a city whose fraught history is inextricably bound up with the sport of football in significant ways.

Concluding Remarks

MARCUS FREE AND NEIL O'BOYLE

THE VARIETY OF CHAPTER themes and approaches in this book attests, above all, to its interdisciplinarity. As a foundational collection on sport, the media and Ireland, its primary aim was to bring together scholars from diverse backgrounds, with distinctive working assumptions, conceptual frames and methods, in order to map the field in an Irish context. It has been a collective, but not entirely collaborative, endeavour. Interdisciplinarity highlights enduring differences as well as shared interests.

For example, there is a fundamental difference between historian Conor Curran's use of sports media from the early twentieth century as source material for a piecing together of the career of Irish international footballer Charlie O'Hagan, and Seán Crosson's and Lance Pettitt's focus on the constructive role of broadcast sports media in making and reproducing hegemonic mythical narratives and celebrity personas respectively. Curran's work involves the painstaking detective method of the empiricist historian in search of facts, despite sometimes frustratingly contradictory evidence and mysterious gaps. Those chapters, like Crosson's and Pettitt's, that focus on representation as their primary concern more typically highlight the contingent and contested nature of representations in various media as constructive practices. Anthony McIntyre's chapter also reveals the distinctiveness of each medium as the aggressive social-media persona of James McClean's tweets appears to contrast with the 'softer' version of his persona in a carefully edited BBC broadcast profile that highlights his geographically and culturally specific perspective on the symbolism of the commemorative poppy. Mike Cronin's chapter highlights the fruitful interplay between distinct disciplinary perspectives. Cronin combines the historian's concern with establishing basic facts and the media-scholar's questioning of the media's roles in reproducing myths, especially in subsequent commemorations, in his comparison of media narratives, participants' contemporary testimony and retrospective memories, and an official inquiry into the hooligan violence at the old Lansdowne Road stadium in 1995.

Those with a more sociological, cultural-studies, geographical or gender-studies background might ponder issues that are not directly prompted by the authors here but which emerge through their juxtaposition and thus invite further consideration and research. For example, Charlie O'Hagan's remarkably geographically varied career and lack of precision as to what it entailed, even in his own writing, may be indicative of a disconnected, restless, migrant sensibility peculiar to sporting migrants. If other migrants either assimilate or yearn to return, here we seem to have a character who returns briefly but is happiest when on the move, and is facilitated in this, in a possibly unique way, by the transnational cultural phenomenon of football. O'Hagan was from Donegal, whose geographical and cultural position pre-partition and especially post-partition was complex, and he had served as a soldier in the First World War. His narrow focus on the details of maintaining the body as a 'machine' may be indicative of an apolitically narrow focus on optimising the functionality of the body in football. However, if so, it is remarkable for its contrast with the politically outspoken James McClean, from the bordering county of Derry, nearly a century later. The contrast is indicative of the impact of partition on football – specifically, the split between the Belfast-based Irish Football Association and the Dublin-based Football Association of Ireland – and on nationalist and unionist identities, but also of how social media has facilitated the articulation between an aggressively nationalist identity and a transnational media presence unfiltered by institutional media.

The chapters on women, media and sport (Katie Liston and Mary O'Connor, Ciarán Dunne, Niamh Kitching and Ali Bowes) highlight the enduring marginality of women within and from sports media. As Liston and O'Connor argue, while the Ladies Gaelic Football Association is one of the largest women's sporting organisations in Europe, and women in Ireland and elsewhere are becoming more involved in sport, 'women's access to the corridors of sporting power and their public visibility remains comparatively restricted'. Each chapter in this section, including the round-table discussion, stresses the ways in which academic research can both make visible that which is generally taken for granted – the implicit association of sport with masculinity, in society generally, and sports media specifically – and become a platform for critical intervention in media practices through an interactive dialogue with media practitioners. Indeed, the recording of the latter has been made available to broadcast journalists for this very reason. Crucially, too, while a quantitative increase in media coverage and women professionals in media sport is to be welcomed, this alone will not transform practices in media representation of women athletes. As the round-table discussion made clear, those seeking to promote, normalise and report on women's sport in Ireland continue to face a number of overlapping challenges, including limited funding, resistant organisational cultures (in both sport and media organisations), persistent accusations of tokenism as well as negative comparisons with male athletes (especially in team sports), and a lack of up-to-date information about women's events in newsrooms. At the same time, the participants also pointed to a number of encouraging signs, including increasing participation levels in women's sport generally, improved outreach programmes targeting young girls, growing levels of public interest in women's sport, encouragement from many male colleagues, and, perhaps most importantly, an abundance of new-media platforms on which to create and share original content and interact with audiences. Participants at the round-table also pointed to the recent creation of Ireland's first 'Women in Sport Calendar' as a crucially important step in giving visibility to the diversity of women's sport across the whole island.

In a different vein, the chapters on broadcasting sports rights (Paul Rouse and Roddy Flynn) also highlight the potential value of rigorous academic research and critical scrutiny both of sporting organisations and of the media themselves. If Flynn reflects on the role of public-service broadcasting in an increasingly commercialised media–sports nexus, Rouse focuses on the implications of this for sporting bodies – namely the Gaelic Athletic Association (GAA) – and how the drive for profit maximisation can potentially undermine communitarian goals. John Connolly and Paddy Dolan's chapter traces how the GAA felt the need to adjust to and embrace broadcast and other media over the course of the twentieth century, while Seán Crosson highlights the logical outcome of this in the televised *Laochra* 1916 commemoration in 2016. However, Rouse and Flynn highlight both the risks of losing audiences attracted to GAA and other sports through terrestrial television if rights are progressively sold to subscription services, and the enduring value of public-service broadcasting, or at least free-to-air commercial terrestrial television in creating and reproducing unfolding dramas and symbols of national inclusivity through their greater reach. The expressed preference of Dan Dwyer's British-born informants for freely accessed Irish-origin terrestrial sports broadcasts over subscription alternatives may have an economic dimension to it, but it is also illustrative of the desire to reproduce the memories of a fully collective, national experience that the fragmentation of broadcast rights and charging for access threaten to undo.

Perhaps there is a danger, though, of reproducing the concept of national identity as the sole or central point of entry into the interrelations between sport and media. Although Liverpool has long-standing Irish associations and, as a 'port city', associations with the rest of the world, Ciarán Ryan's Irish informants show little interest in the 'Irishness' of the city or Liverpool FC's associations with specific Irish players, instead being drawn to the idea of Liverpool as a self-contained place through the dialect in operation in The Anfield Wrap, even as the club's history and global status make it available to them as an object of imaginative investment.

We might also question the degree to which and the ways in which mediated mass sporting events are fully nationally inclusive. A key impact of the feminist movement has been the interrogation of gender as a social and cultural construct. While Liston and O'Connor summarise international research on constructions of femininity in representations of sportswomen, and Kitching and Bowes show how gender, class and national identity intersect in their case study of Leona Maguire, arguably other chapters might go further in exploring the intersections of articulations of masculinity and national identity in sports media and consumption. If the hooligans in the 1995 riot were not orchestrated by a far-right organisation, were they 'doing' masculinity by seeking out and engineering opportunities for ritualised violence? Was there an articulation of constructions of gender and national identity in the Irish media's choice of a bewildered boy as their emblematic image of contrastive Irish innocence on the night? Are Ryan's Irish fans of The Anfield Wrap attracted to the expression of unbridled, aggressive, working-class masculinity permissible in a non-broadcast podcast but not mainstream broadcasting?

This also raises questions about the impact of social media on sport more generally. For example, considerable attention has recently been given to the use of social media by sports supporters and athletes to express racist, homophobic and other offensive sentiments, thereby undoing the myth that sport is apolitical. To this we might add the WhatsApp messages at the centre of the Belfast trial involving Paddy Jackson and Stuart Olding. It is unquestionably the case that social media can act as a conduit and protective veneer for 'toxic' locker-room masculinity, but we cannot assume that their use in the context of sport is entirely negative. When it comes to the uses and abuses of new media, this collection leaves many areas un/underexplored. One relates to sports fans, who are increasingly celebrated as 'prosumers' for their comments, reviews, blogs, videos, and so on. However, another area of increasing interest to scholars relates to the use of social media by athletes, clubs and sporting organisations. For example, a recent study of Twitter use by football clubs finds evidence of an ambivalent attitude towards the platform.[1] On one hand, clubs celebrate the possibility of more open communication and engagement with fans, while on the other hand they recognise the increased risk of information leaks and offensive content, as well as the possibility that players might vent frustrations with managers and club directors on social media. For example, after he was let go by Queens Park Rangers in 2012, former club manager Neil Warnock publicly claimed that exchanges of tweets between players and the club's chairperson had undermined his position.

Readers will also note that despite the 'Ireland' of the title, and the ambiguity it entails, with the exception of McIntyre's James McClean chapter, the book lacks a North–South dimension. Indeed, though 'Northerners', both McClean and George Best (Pettitt's chapter) are emigrant figures, and the chapters dealing with them do not focus on media in Northern Ireland. This absence is admittedly problematic as so many print-media titles and broadcast services are largely geographically bounded by the border in their content, despite their technical availability across the island and the history of cross-border and cross-Irish Sea television consumption, particularly in the Republic.[2] Two of the contributors here, Katie Liston and

Niamh Kitching, have recently examined the problems posed for
Northern Ireland-born golfer Rory McIlroy when it was announced
that golf would feature in the 2016 Rio Olympics. Reared as a
Catholic and – unlike McClean – a vocal supporter of the Northern
Ireland football team, McIlroy moved progressively from declaring
that he felt more British than Irish towards declaring for Ireland
rather than Great Britain prior to the Olympics, but repeatedly
stressed that he had no firm 'national' identity or affiliation.[3] Liston
and Kitching are currently engaged in a sequel project focusing on
how 'national' newspapers dealt with a figure whose non-, or, at best,
reluctant alignment may be symptomatic of both his social-class
upbringing and golf's history as a generally individualistic sport in
which national identities have been less significant than in others.

In their chapter, Liston and O'Connor also highlight how sport is
gradually reflecting the changing composition of a still predominantly
white Irish population, with young athletes of immigrant parentage
appearing in greater numbers at representative level. As they suggest,
another as yet underexplored avenue of research might focus on
the ways in which conceptualisations of national identity intersect
with race and ethnicity in Irish sport and its representation. As an
illustration of some of the issues involved, in 2019 former Munster
and Ireland rugby international, and current Racing 92 player, Simon
Zebo hinted in a tweet that he had been subjected to racist abuse
at a game between Racing and Ulster in Belfast: 'I hope my ears
deceived me with some comments directed my way from the crowd.
#NotOn. Django wins in the end.'[4] Despite the coded nature of the
tweet (Django is presumably a reference to Quentin Tarantino's
2012 film *Django Unchained*), it sparked extensive commentary in
Irish media, including a retrospective piece by Johnny Watterson in
The Irish Times on intermittently reported instances of racist abuse
from supporters in various Irish sports that are rarely seen as a more
enduring reflection of implicit associations of 'Irish' identity with
whiteness.[5] That Zebo's tweet was phrased in coded, non-explicit
terms may indicate the reluctance of the son of an immigrant father
(from Martinique) to address racism directly in a largely, but by no
means exclusively, white population north and south of the border.

In 2017, when New Zealand-born rugby player Bundee Aki
was scheduled to qualify to play for Ireland through the residency
rule in that sport but expressed uncertainty as to whether or not he

would declare for Ireland (he also qualified for New Zealand and Samoa through parentage), former Irish player-turned-journalist Tony Ward described his behaviour as 'puke inducing'. Ward expressed a preference for foreign-born players of Irish descent who 'want to come back and play for Ireland by choice'.[6] The idea that Irish descendants would simply be 'coming back' suggests a conceptualisation of national identity in terms of blood lineage that supersedes migrant qualification through residency. Aki's equivocation may be reflective of the fluidity of national identity in international rugby and the contingency of national identity for players of Pacific-island origin or descent given the long history of migration between and from those islands.[7] This fluidity may be seen to conflict with an enduring nativism and localism in Irish sport. Alternatively, and ironically, his (albeit later) recorded words may be illustrative of his having learned to 'fit in',[8] to accommodate to 'native' Irish expectations of humility, of 'not getting above' or 'losing the run of yourself', rather than some mercenary quality or equivocation with respect to his host country:

> Ireland have quality players. Jeez, they have a lot of good players there. I can't parachute my way in there. I got to just put my head down and do what I want to do, perform week in week out, perform consistently. When the time arises it arises, but for the moment my focus is just [his club] Connacht.[9]

Such instances are illustrative of the impact of the media – and increasingly social media and its secondary reporting in mainstream media – in highlighting the cultural politics at play in sport and wider society in contemporary Ireland.

Another absence in the book is the consideration of any LGBTQI dimensions to the interrelations between sport and the media in Ireland and beyond. If gender is a theme that might have been addressed at greater length across the various chapters here, it is important to acknowledge that it should not be narrowly defined in binary heteronormative either/or, or masculine/feminine, terms. Sport is an arena in which homophobia and heteronormativity endure, despite what Eric Anderson terms the emergence of a more 'inclusive masculinity' in men's sport.[10] In an Irish context, Ed Madden's work demonstrates how gay athletes' reflexive engagement with media representation and homophobic stereotypes can constitute a form of 'cultural agency' that challenges normative assumptions.[11] In his account of the gay rugby club Emerald Warriors' engagement with media, from the earliest recruitment posters and advertising in *Gay Community News* to the club's later publicity and representation in mainstream Irish media, Madden traces the movement from the 'camp and playful modes of gender representation' in 'the early subcultural images' towards later 'publicity efforts' that 'tended to normalise gender representation in order to stabilise or obviate the queer potential of the gay team athlete'.[12] Madden nonetheless concludes that 'given the range of self-representation as well as the ongoing dominance of heteronormative masculinity in sport culture, the Emerald Warrior as gay male athlete still retains the potential to destabilise the very norms that he may at times reinforce'.[13]

It is our hope that the present collection, partial and limited though it is, will stimulate further research on the interrelationship of sport and media, especially in the Irish context. We offer it, therefore, as a starting point rather than an endpoint – as an account of the current 'state of play' rather than a determination of its future. Above all, we hope that it will be a helpful and encouraging resource for future scholars in the field.

Notes

Introduction

1 Erica Chenowith and Jeremy Pressman, 'This Is What We Learned by Counting the Women's Marches', *Washington Post*, 7 February 2017.

2 Anthony Crupi, 'Despite Another Ratings Slump, the NFL Remains TV's Top Dog', *AdAge*, 2 January 2018.

3 Laura Slattery, 'Sporting Fixtures Dominate Top 20 Most-watched TV Programmes of 2017', *Irish Times*, 9 January 2018.

4 Roman Horak and Georg Spitaler, 'Sport Space and National Identity', *American Behavioral Scientist*, vol. 46, no. 11 (2003), pp. 1506–18.

5 Mark Falcous, 'The Decolonizing National Imaginary: Promotional media constructions during the 2005 Lions tour of Aotearoa New Zealand', *Journal of Sport & Social Issues*, vol. 31, no. 4 (2007), pp. 374–93.

6 Michael Messner, 'Sports and Male Domination: The female athlete as contested ideological terrain', *Sociology of Sport Journal*, vol. 5, no. 1 (1988), p. 198.

7 Aidan Arrowsmith, 'Plastic Paddies vs. Master Racers: "Soccer" and Irish identity', *International Journal of Cultural Studies*, vol. 7, no. 4 (2004), pp. 460–79.

8 Marcus Free, 'Diaspora and Rootedness, Amateurism and Professionalism in Media Discourses of Irish Soccer and Rugby in the 1990s and 2000s', *Éire-Ireland*, vol. 48, nos 1–2 (2013), pp. 211–29; idem, '"From there to here": Narratives of transition, migration and national identity in Irish media representations of rugby union in the professional era', *European Journal for Sport and Society*, vol. 14, no. 3 (2017), pp. 205–25.

9 Marcus Free, 'Smart, Clued-in Guys: Irish rugby players as celebrities in post-Celtic Tiger Irish media', *International Journal of Media and Cultural Politics*, vol. 14, no. 2 (2018), pp. 213–30.

10 Sport Ireland's 2017 survey found that 1.9 per cent of the adult population attended a rugby event that year, compared with 6.6 per cent for Gaelic football and 4.3 per cent for soccer. Rugby did not even feature in the top twelve sports for participation. There was a participation rate of 4.1 per cent in soccer and 2 per cent in Gaelic football, the fifth and eighth most popular participation sports, respectively. Sport Ireland, *Irish Sports Monitor Annual Report, 2017* (Dublin: Sport Ireland), https://assets.gov.ie/16014/3abf58a4a5af41b9ab66065de65e15a3.pdf, pp. 14, 49 (accessed 22 May 2018).

11 Will Reilly, 'Ireland's Grand Slam Grabs Record Audience for TV3', Six Nations Rugby, 20 March, https://www.sixnationsrugby.com/en/news/33073.php (accessed 23 May 2018).

12 David Rowe, 'Mediating the Asian Olympics: The Summer Games – image projection and gaze reception', *International Journal of the History of Sport*, vol. 29, no. 16 (2012), pp. 2231–43.

13 Ibid., p. 2232.

14 Department of Transport, Tourism and Sport, *National Sports Policy Framework Public Consultation Paper* (Dublin, 2016), p. 43.

15 'Hugo MacNeill to Head Group Tasked with Ireland's World Cup 2023 Bid', *Irish Independent*, 20 February 2014.

16 'New Report Confirms Record-breaking Rugby World Cup 2015 Economic Impact', https://www.rugbyworldcup.com/news/163399?lang=en.

17 Steven Jackson and Jay Scherer, 'Rugby World Cup 2011: Sport mega-events and the contested terrain of space, bodies and commodities', *Sport in Society*, vol. 16, no. 3 (2013), p. 891.

18 Liam O'Callaghan, 'Professional Rugby and Irish Society, 1995–2015', in John Nauright and Tony Collins (eds), *The Rugby World in the Professional Era* (Abingdon: Routledge, 2017), p. 15.

19 Gerry Thornley, 'Size Matters as Irish Bid Falls Short in Stadiums and Cities', *Irish Times*, 1 November 2017.

20 For example, Thornley, 'Size Matters as Irish Bid Falls Short'; Alan Quinlan, 'Fears for Safety and of Empty Stadia in South Africa Should Have Given Ireland the Edge', *Irish Independent*, 1 November 2017. France won the bid following a vote by World Rugby Union member countries despite the recommendation of a committee established to assess the bids independently that South Africa should be awarded the tournament.

21 Department of Education and Skills, '23 February, 2018: Minister Bruton announces first schools to study P.E. as Leaving Certificate subject', https://www.education.ie/en/Press-Events/Press-Releases/2018-press-releases/PR18-02-23.html (accessed 3 August 2018).

22 Marcus Free and Clare Scully, 'The Run of Ourselves: Shame, guilt and confession in Post-Celtic Tiger Irish media', *International Journal of Cultural Studies*, vol. 21, no. 3 (2018), pp. 308–24.

23 Michael Cronin, Peadar Kirby and Debbie Ging, 'Transforming Ireland: Challenges', in Debbie Ging, Michael Cronin and Peadar Kirby (eds), *Transforming Ireland: Challenges, Critiques, Resources* (Manchester: Manchester University Press, 2009), pp. 1–17.

24 Holly Thorpe, 'Action Sports, Social Media, and New Technologies: Towards a research agenda', *Communication & Sport*, vol. 5, no. 5 (2017), p. 560.

25 William R. Smith and Jeffrey Treem, 'Striving to Be King of Mobile Mountains: Communication and organizing through digital fitness technology', *Communication Studies*, vol. 68, no. 2 (2017), pp. 135–51.

26 Clive Barnett, 'The Consolations of Neoliberalism', *Geoforum*, vol. 36, no. 1 (January 2005), p. 10.

27 Free and Scully, 'The Run of Ourselves', p. 319.

28 David Rowe, 'The Mediated Nation and the Transnational Football Fan', *Soccer & Society*, vol. 16, nos 5–6 (2015), pp. 693–709.

29 David Rowe, 'Sports and Media', Oxford Bibliographies, www.oxfordbibliographies.com/view/document/obo-9780199791286/obo-9780199791286-0169.xml (accessed 24 August 2018).

30 Allyson Chiu, '"Sandpapergate" Cheating Scandal Rocks Australian Cricket: "It beggars belief", says prime minister', *Washington Post*, 29 March 2018.

31 Kevin Myers, 'An Irishman's Diary', *Irish Times*, 8 October 2004.

32 Markus Stauff, 'Non-fiction Transmedia: Seriality and forensics in media sport', *M/C Journal: A Journal of Media and Culture*, vol. 21, no. 1 (2018), http://journal.media-culture.org.au/index.php/mcjournal/article/view/1372 (accessed 23 August 2018).

33 David Rowe, Jim McKay and Toby Miller, 'Come Together: Sport, nationalism and the media image', in Lawrence A. Wenner (ed.), *Mediasport* (London: Routledge, 1998), p. 133.

34 Emma Poulton and Joseph Maguire, 'Plastic or Fantastic Brits? Identity Politics and English media representations of "Team GB" during London 2012', *Journalism, Media and Cultural Studies*, no. 2 (November 2012), p. 11.

35 Gary Whannel, 'Television and the Transformation of Sport', *Annals of the American Academy of Political and Social Science*, vol. 625, no. 1 (2009), pp. 205–18.

36 Marcus Free, 'Antihero as National Icon? The contrariness of Roy Keane as fantasy embodiment of the "New Ireland"', in Philip Dine and Seán Crosson (eds), *Sport, Representation and Evolving Identities in Europe* (Bern: Peter Lang, 2010), p. 199.

37 Rowe, McKay and Miller, 'Come Together', p. 120.

38 Patrick F. McDevitt, 'Muscular Catholicism: Nationalism, masculinity and Gaelic team sports, 1884–1916', *Gender & History*, vol. 9, no. 2 (1997), p. 279.

39 Dónal Óg Cusack, *Come What May: The autobiography* (Dublin: Penguin Ireland, 2009).

40 Debbie Ging and Marcus Free, 'Gay in the GAA: The challenge of Dónal Óg Cusack's "coming out" to heteronormativity in contemporary Irish culture and society', in Rosie Meade and Fiona Dukelow (eds), *Defining Events: Power, resistance and identity in twenty-first-century Ireland* (Manchester: Manchester University Press, 2015), p. 218.

41 Ibid., p. 227.

42 Paul Ryan, 'Coming Out, Fitting In: The personal narratives of some Irish gay men', *Irish Journal of Sociology*, vol. 12, no. 2 (2003), pp. 68–85.

43 Kath Woodward, *Sex, Power and the Games: Genders and sexualities in the social sciences* (Basingstoke: Palgrave Macmillan, 2012), p. 41.

44 Marcus Free, '"He is my strength and my shield": The antinomies of Katie Taylor as female sporting celebrity in twenty-first-century Ireland', *Sport in Society*, vol. 18, no. 10 (2015), pp. 1147–65.

45 Tom Inglis, 'From Self-denial to Self-indulgence: The class of cultures in contemporary Ireland', *Irish Review*, no. 34 (2006), p. 37.

46 *Conor McGregor: Notorious* was the title of a 2017 documentary chronicling his exploits.

47 See, for example, Ben Kiely, 'Video: Spine-tingling 'fighting Irish' UFC promo featuring McGregor, Pendre and Holohan', https://www.sportsjoe.ie/mma/video-spine-tingling-fighting-irish-ufc-promo-featuring-mcgregor-pendred-and-holohan-8742 (accessed 27 August 2018).

48 Mike Cronin, 'Is It for the Glamour? Masculinity, nationhood and amateurism in contemporary projections of the Gaelic Athletic Association', in Wanda Balzano, Anne Mulhall and Moynagh Sullivan (eds), *Irish*

Postmodernisms and Popular Culture (Basingstoke: Palgrave Macmillan, 2007), pp. 39–54.

49 Debbie Ging, *Men and Masculinities in Irish Cinema* (Basingstoke: Palgrave Macmillan, 2012), p. 30.

50 Tom Inglis, *Global Ireland: Same difference* (Abingdon: Routledge, 2008).

51 Brett Hutchins and David Rowe, 'From Broadcast Scarcity to Digital Plenitude: The changing dynamics of the media sport content economy', *Television & New Media*, no. 10 (2009), pp. 354–70.

52 Ibid., p. 356.

53 Kirsten Frandsen, 'Sports Organizations in a New Wave of Mediatization', *Communication and Sport*, vol. 4, no. 4 (2015), pp. 1–16.

54 David Rowe, Andy Ruddock and Brett Hutchins, 'Cultures of Complaint: Online fan message boards and networked digital media sport communities', *Convergence*, vol. 16, no. 3 (2010), pp. 298–315.

55 Jeroen Stragier, Tom Evens and Peter Mechant, 'Broadcast Yourself: An exploratory study of sharing physical activity on social networking sites', *Media International Australia*, May 2015, p. 120.

56 Neil O'Boyle and Colm Kearns, 'The Greening of Euro 2016: Fan footage, representational tropes, and the media lionization of the Irish in France', *Television & New Media*, vol. 20, no. 1 (2019), pp. 96–116.

57 Barbara Barnett, 'Girls Gone Web: Self-depictions of female athletes on personal websites', *Journal of Communication Theory*, vol. 4, no. 2 (2017), p. 98.

58 Ibid.

59 Thorpe, 'Action Sports, Social Media, and New Technologies'.

60 See, for example, Martina Devlin, 'Two-tier Morality Means Girls Face an Impossible List of Dos and Don'ts', *Irish Independent*, 29 March 2018.

61 'Thousands Show Solidarity with Rape Victims at Rallies in Ireland', *Belfast Telegraph*, 31 March 2018.

62 Claire O'Boyle, 'Ulster Rugby Fans Fund Press Ad Calling on Club to Reinstate Rape Trial Players Jackson and Olding', *Belfast Telegraph*, 11 April 2018.

63 Jonathan Bradley and Lesley-Anne McKeown, 'Jackson and Olding Not Sacked Over Money Says Ulster Chief, as He Vows to Stay On', *Belfast Telegraph*, 17 April 2018.

64 Claire O'Boyle, 'Calls for Issues Around Sexual Consent to Be Taught in School', *Belfast Telegraph*, 5 April 2018.

65 Steven Jackson and David L. Andrews (eds), 'Olympic Celebrity: Introduction', *Celebrity Studies*, vol. 3, no. 3 (November 2012), p. 263.

66 See *Ireland 2023: Ready for the world*, Discover Ireland video, https://www.youtube.com/watch?v=TIK2LLho5Dw (accessed 26 August 2018).

67 Robert Milliken, 'Sport is Murdoch's "Battering Ram" for Pay TV', *Independent*, 16 October 1996.

68 Paul Du Gay, Stuart Hall, Linda Janes, Anders Koed Madsen, Hugh Mackay and Keith Negus, *Doing Cultural Studies: The story of the Sony Walkman*, 2nd edn (London: Sage, 2013).

69 Svetlana Boym, *The Future of Nostalgia* (New York: Basic Books, 2001), p. 41.

Chapter 1. Ex-professional Footballers and Sports Journalism: Charlie O'Hagan's careers as a migrant professional footballer and writer in the early twentieth century

1 *Football Sports Weekly*, 19 June 1926; Michael Joyce, *Football League Players' Records, 1888 to 1939* (Nottingham: Tony Brown, 2012), p. 220.

2 See, for example, Colin Millar, 'The Mysterious Career of Charles O'Hagan, Sevilla's First Foreign Manager', These Football Times, https://thesefootballtimes.co/2017/11/01/the-mysterious-career-of-charles-ohagan-sevillas-first-foreign-manager/ (accessed 21 December 2018).

3 'Residents of a House 133 in Buncranna', 1901 Census, http://www.census.nationalarchives.ie/pages/1901/Donegal/Buncranna/Buncranna__A_form_No__301_refused_/1181463/ (accessed 20 December 2018).

4 *Strabane Chronicle*, 3 April 1915.

5 'Residents of a house 133 in Buncranna'.

6 *Derry Journal*, 12 September 1910.

7 Joyce, *Football League Players' Records*, p. 220.

8 *Football Sports Weekly*, 21 August 1926.

9 Ibid., 19 June 1926; Millar, 'The Mysterious Career of Charles O'Hagan'.

10 Matthew Taylor, *The Association Game: A history of British football* (Harlow: Pearson, 2008), pp. 41–50, 67.

11 Tony Mason, *Association Football and English Society, 1863–1915* (Brighton: Harvester Press, 1980), p. 89.

12 Ibid.

13 *Football Sports Weekly*, 19 June 1926; Joyce, *Football League Players' Records*, p. 220.

14 Ibid.

15 Steve Emms and Richard Wells, *Scottish League Players Records. Division One, 1890–91 to 1938–39* (Nottingham: Tony Brown, 2007), p. 181; *Dundee Courier*, 2 April 1912; *Evening Telegraph and Post*, 3 December 1912.

16 *Evening Telegraph and Post*, 3 December 1912; *Strabane Chronicle*, 3 April 1915.

17 *Football Sports Weekly*, 19 June 1926.

18 *Derry Journal*, 4 June 1923.

19 *Stirling Observer*, 5 January 1914; *Daily Record*, 30 January 1915.

20 *Strabane Chronicle*, 3 April 1915.

21 *Football Sports Weekly*, 19 June 1926.

22 Ibid., 12 June 1926.

23 *Dundee Courier*, 4 March 1920.

24 *Football Sports Weekly*, 19 June 1926.

25 Ibid., 23 October 1926.

26 *Londonderry Sentinel*, 5 June 1923.

27 *Derry Journal*, 4 June 1923.

28 *Football Sports Weekly*, 19 June 1926.

29 Millar, 'The Mysterious Career of Charles O'Hagan'.

30 *Irish Independent*, 14 April 1924; *Belfast Newsletter*, 21 April 1924.

31 For a reassessment of this term, see Conor Curran and David Toms, 'Introduction to Going Beyond the "Garrison Game": New perspectives on Association football in Irish history', in Conor Curran and David Toms

(eds), *New Perspectives on Association Football in Irish History: Going beyond the 'garrison game'* (Abingdon: Routledge, 2018), pp. 1–9.

32 Martin Moore, 'The Origins of Association Football in Ireland, 1875–1880: A reappraisal', *Sport in History*, vol. 37, no. 4 (2017), pp. 505–28.

33 Neal Garnham, *Association Football and Society in Pre-partition Ireland* (Belfast: Ulster Historical Foundation, 2004), pp. 191–5.

34 Curran, *Irish Soccer Migrants*, pp. 25–7, 47.

35 Garnham, *Association Football and Society in Pre-partition Ireland*, p. 9.

36 Ibid.

37 Ibid.

38 Ibid.

39 See Conor Curran, 'The Role of the Provincial Press in the Development of Association Football in Pre-First World War Ulster: The cases of Donegal, Fermanagh and Cavan', in Ian Kenneally and James T. O'Donnell (eds), *The Irish Regional Press, 1892–2018: Revival, revolution and republic* (Dublin: Four Courts Press, 2018), p. 54.

40 *Ireland's Saturday Night*, 13 August 1904.

41 *Football Sports Weekly*, 29 August 1925.

42 Ibid., 3 April 1926.

43 Ibid., 4 February 1928.

44 Conor McCabe, '*Football Sports Weekly* and Irish Soccer, 1925–1928', *Media History*, vol. 17, no. 2 (2011), pp. 147, 156.

45 See, for example, Conor Curran, *The Development of Sport in Donegal, 1880–1935* (Cork: Cork University Press, 2015), pp. 202–19.

46 Conor Curran, *Irish Soccer Migrants: A social and cultural history* (Cork: Cork University Press, 2017), p. 2.

47 *Football Sports Weekly*, 21 August 1926.

48 Curran, *Irish Soccer Migrants*, pp. 274–6.

49 Anon., 'Lawrie Cumming', Northern Ireland's Footballing Greats, http:// nifootball.blogspot.com/2006/09/lawrie-cumming.html (accessed 13 March 2017).

50 David Fitzpatrick, *Irish Emigration, 1801–1921: Studies in Irish economic and social history* (Dundalk: Dundalgan Press, 1984), pp. 5–6.

51 *Ireland's Saturday Night*, 13 August 1904.

52 Anon., 'Lawrie Cumming'.

53 Mason, *Association Football and English Society*, p. 118.

54 Joyce, *Football League Players' Records*, p. 59.

55 Anon., 'Jimmy Dunne', Northern Ireland's Footballing Greats, http://ni football.blogspot.com/2006/11/jimmy-dunne.html (accessed 25 June 2016).

56 Mark Simpson, 'Appeal Over Belfast Man. Utd. Player John Peden's Grave', BBC News, http://www.bbc.com/news/uk-northern-ireland-26177699 (accessed 5 February 2016); Anon., 'Sid Reid', Northern Ireland's Footballing Greats, http://nifootball.blogspot.com/2007/10/sid-reid.html (accessed 25 June 2016); Garnham, *Association Football and Society*, p. 93.

57 Fra Coogan, 'Was Mickey Hamill Belfast Celtic's Greatest Player?', Belfast Celtic, http://www.belfastceltic.org/archive/hamill.html (accessed 5 February 2016).

58 Anon., 'Matt "Gunner" Reilly', Northern Ireland's Footballing Greats, http:// nifootball.blogspot.com/2008/01/matt-gunner-reilly.html (accessed 16 June 2016).

59 Anon., 'Tom Priestley', Northern Ireland's Footballing Greats, http://nifootball.blogspot.com/2007/10/tom-priestley.html (accessed 16 June 2016; Anon., 'Hugh Blair', Northern Ireland's Footballing Greats, http://nifootball.blogspot.com/2006/08/hughie-blair.html (accessed 16 June 2016).

60 Mason, *Association Football and English Society*, p. 119.

61 Nuala McCann, 'Patrick O'Connell: Barcelona FC saviour they called "Don Patricio"', http://www.bbc.com/news/uk-northern-ireland-29426450 (accessed 13 March 2017); Anon., 'Pat "Don Patricio" O'Connell', Northern Ireland's Footballing Greats, http://nifootball.blogspot.com/2008/02/pat-oconnell.html (accessed 13 March 2017).

62 Mason, *Association Football and English Society*, p. 120.

63 *Irish News and Belfast Morning Post*, 5 November 1908.

64 *Football Sports Weekly*, 19 June 1926.

65 Ibid., 19 June, 21 August 1926.

66 Ibid., 20 August 1927.

67 Ibid.

68 Ibid., 21 January 1928.

69 Ibid., 19 June 1926.

70 Ibid., 30 January 1926.

71 Ibid., 30 October, 6 November 1926, 8 January 1927.

72 Ibid., 31 July 1926.

73 Mason, *Association Football and English Society*, p. 109.

74 *Football Sports Weekly*, 31 July 1926.

75 Mason, *Association Football and English Society*, pp. 108–9.

76 *Football Sports Weekly*, 31 July 1926.

77 Ibid.

78 Ibid.

79 Ibid.

80 Ibid., 10 July 1926.

81 Ibid., 26 June 1926.

82 Conor Curran, *The Development of Sport in Donegal, 1880–1935* (Cork: Cork University Press, 2015), ch. 7.

83 *Football Sports Weekly*, 26 August 1926.

84 Ibid., 31 July 1926.

85 Ibid., 7 August 1926.

86 Mason, *Association Football and English Society*, p. 178.

87 *Aberdeen Press and Journal*, 4 July 1931.

88 See, for example, Anon., 'Charlie O'Hagan', Northern Ireland's Footballing Greats, http://nifootball.blogspot.com/2007/08/charlie-ohagan.html (accessed 20 December 2018); *Donegal News*, 4 July 1931.

89 For an analysis of this Irish football migration to the ASL, see Conor Curran, 'Unscrupulous Adventurers Who Are Domiciled in "The Land of the Almighty Dollar"? The migration of Irish-born soccer players to the American Soccer League, 1921–31', *Journal of Sport History*, vol. 45, no. 3 (fall, 2018), pp. 313–33.

90 *Football Sports Weekly*, 18 December 1926.

91 Ibid.

92 Curran, *Irish Soccer Migrants*, p. 251.

93 *Football Sports Weekly*, 13 August 1927.
94 *Aberdeen Press and Journal*, 4 July 1931.
95 Ibid.
96 *Football Sports Weekly*, 30 October 1926.
97 'Dublin City Council Honours Patrick O'Connell, Legendary Footballer and Manager', Dublin City Council, http://www.dublincity.ie/dublin-city-council-honours-patrick-o%E2%80%99connell-legendary-footballer-and-manager (accessed 21 December 2018).

Chapter 2. National Identity, Media and the Promotion of Gaelic Games

1 See, for example, Mike Cronin, *Sport and Nationalism in Ireland: Gaelic games, soccer and Irish identity since 1884* (Dublin: Four Courts Press, 1999); Neal Garnham, 'Accounting for the Early Success of the Gaelic Athletic Association', *Irish Historical Studies*, vol. 34, no. 133 (2004), pp. 65–78; Tadhg Ó hAnnrachain, 'The Heroic Importance of Sport: The GAA in the 1930s', *International Journal of the History of Sport*, vol. 25, no. 10 (2008), pp. 1326–37; William F. Mandle, *The Gaelic Athletic Association and Irish Nationalist Politics, 1884–1924* (Dublin: Gill and Macmillan, 1987); Patrick F. McDevitt, 'Muscular Catholicism: Nationalism, masculinity and Gaelic team sports, 1884–1916', *Gender & History*, vol. 9, no. 2 (1997), pp. 262–84; Liam O'Callaghan, 'Rugby Football and Identity Politics in Free State Ireland', *Éire-Ireland*, vol. 48, nos 1–2 (2013), pp. 148–67; Paul Rouse, 'The Politics of Culture and Sport in Ireland: A history of the GAA ban on foreign games, 1884–1971', *International Journal of the History of Sport*, vol. 10, no. 3 (1993), pp. 333–60.
2 See Raymond Boyle, 'From Our Gaelic Fields: Radio, sport and nation in post-partition Ireland', *Media, Culture and Society*, no. 14 (1992), pp. 623–36.
3 Norbert Elias, *What Is Sociology?* (Dublin: University College Dublin Press, 2012); Norbert Elias, *On the Process of Civilisation: Sociogenetic and psychogenetic investigations* [1939] (Dublin: University College Dublin Press, 2012).
4 Elias, *On the Process of Civilisation*.
5 Norbert Elias, *The Society of Individuals* (Dublin: University College Dublin Press, 2010), p. 165.
6 Changes in the structure of interdependency tend to also intensify we-feelings. What is important therefore is to illustrate and explain the specific dynamic rather than assume a mono-directional change.
7 Norbert Elias and John L. Scotson, *The Established and the Outsiders* (Dublin: University College Dublin Press, 2008).
8 John Connolly and Paddy Dolan, 'The Amplification and De-amplification of Amateurism and Professionalism in the Gaelic Athletic Association', *International Journal of the History of Sport*, vol. 30, no. 8 (2013), pp. 853–70; Mandle, *The Gaelic Athletic Association and Irish Nationalist Politics*.
9 Paddy Dolan and John Connolly, 'The Civilizing of Hurling in Ireland', *Sport in Society*, vol. 12, no. 2 (2009), pp. 193–208.

10 Paul Rouse, 'Michael Cusack: Sportsman and journalist', in Mike Cronin, William Murphy and Paul Rouse (eds), *The Gaelic Athletic Association: 1884–2009* (Dublin: Irish Academic Press, 2009), pp. 47–60.

11 *Celtic Times*, 19 February 1887.

12 Mandle, *The Gaelic Athletic Association and Irish Nationalist Politics*.

13 Gaelic Athletic Association, *Minutes of GAA Annual Congress* (Dublin: Gaelic Athletic Association, 1901).

14 *Gaelic Annual*, 1908–9, p. 36.

15 Ibid., p. 30.

16 O'Callaghan, 'Rugby Football and Identity Politics in Free State Ireland'.

17 The partition of Ireland made the issue of representing the 'nation' more complex, as did the structure of sporting organisations that emerged as a result. Some were organised on an all-Ireland frame, and others on a twenty-six-county basis. See Cormac Moore, 'Partition in Irish Sport', in Paddy Dolan and John Connolly (eds), *Sport and National Identities* (London: Routledge, 2017).

18 Gaelic Athletic Association, *Minutes of Central Council* (Dublin: Gaelic Athletic Association, 1927).

19 Gaelic Athletic Association, *Minutes of Annual Congress* (Dublin: Gaelic Athletic Association, 1930).

20 Paddy Dolan, 'Cultural Cosmopolitanization and the Politics of Television in 1960s Ireland', *Media, Culture & Society*, vol. 36, no. 7 (2014), pp. 952–65.

21 Gaelic Athletic Association, *Annual Congress Booklet* (Dublin: Gaelic Athletic Association, 1936).

22 Cormac Moore, *The GAA v Douglas Hyde: The removal of Ireland's first president as GAA patron* (Cork: Collins Press, 2012).

23 Raymond Boyle, 'From Our Gaelic Fields: Radio, sport and nation in post-partition Ireland', *Media, Culture and Society*, no. 14 (1992), pp. 623–36.

24 John Connolly and Paddy Dolan, 'Sport, Media and the Gaelic Athletic Association', *Media, Culture & Society*, vol. 34, no. 4 (2012), pp. 407–23.

25 Moore, *The GAA v Douglas Hyde*, p. 27.

26 Gaelic Athletic Association, *An Chomhdháil Bhliantúil* (Dublin: Gaelic Athletic Association, 1953), p. A13.

27 Gaelic Athletic Association Ulster Council, *Minutes of Annual Convention* (Gaelic Athletic Association, 1953).

28 Gaelic Athletic Association Ulster Council, *Minutes of Annual Convention of Ulster Council* (Gaelic Athletic Association, 1969), p. 5.

29 Gaelic Athletic Association Ulster Council, *Minutes of Annual Convention of Ulster Council* (Gaelic Athletic Association, 1972), p. 4.

30 John Horgan, *Irish Media. A critical history since 1922* (London: Routledge, 2001).

31 Raymond Boyle, 'Nation Shall Speak Peace Unto Nation: Television, sport and nationhood', MA thesis, Dublin City University, 1990.

32 Gaelic Athletic Association, *Minutes of Annual Congress* (Dublin: Gaelic Athletic Association, 1961).

33 See *Gaelic Sport*, March–May 1962, p. 49; *Gaelic Sport*, January 1969, pp. 40–1; *Gaelic Sport*, April 1971, p. 23.

34 Ibid., January 1969, p. 29.

35 Ibid., April 1971, p. 3.
36 Gaelic Athletic Association, *Our Games* (Dublin: Gaelic Athletic Association, 1972), p. 74.
37 Gaelic Athletic Association, *An Chomhdháil Bhliantúil* (Dublin: Gaelic Athletic Association, 1979), p. B15.
38 The complexity of this process cannot be comprehensively outlined in a section of a chapter such as this. For a more detailed and complete account, see Paddy Dolan, 'The Development of Consumer Culture, Subjectivity and National Identity in Ireland, 1900–1980', PhD thesis, Goldsmiths College, University of London, 2005.
39 Elias, *The Society of Individuals*.
40 Paddy Dolan, 'Developing Consumer Subjectivity in Ireland: 1900–80', *Journal of Consumer Culture*, vol. 9, no. 1 (2009), pp. 117–41.
41 Dolan, 'The Development of Consumer Culture, Subjectivity and National Identity in Ireland'.
42 Ibid.
43 Gaelic Athletic Association, *Report of the Commission on the GAA* (Dublin: Gaelic Athletic Association, 1971); Robert O'Connor and Brendan Whelan, *Attitudes of Young People to Games and Pastimes* (Dublin: Economic and Social Research Institute, 1971).

Chapter 3. Best on the Box: George Best, television and the making of celebrity

1   Gary Whannel, *Media Sports Stars* (London: Routledge, 2002), p. 51.
2   Malcolm Brodie, interview with author, Belfast, 30 November 2006. See also 'Now Best Shares Are Available', *Belfast News-Letter*, 21 June 1971. See also Whannel, *Media Sports Stars*, pp. 111–14. Whannel provides an excellent analysis of the role of the English press in narrativising Best's biography, functioning as a 'condensing' of cultural discourses about popular morality and gender both in his heyday and more recent times. For a handy edited collection of English journalism on Best, see Richard Williams (ed.), *George Best: A life in the news* (London: Aurum Press, 2006). Michael Parkinson's latest memoir on Best, *George Best: A memoir* (London: Hodder & Stoughton, 2018) is one of a long line of non-fiction books (some of which are listed in the bibliography) that, combined with Best as a figure of auto/biographical writing, could be the subject of another essay. My personal favourite is Gordon Burn's fascinating 'double' study, *Best and Edwards* (London: Faber & Faber, 2006), with Parkinson's earlier *George Best: An intimate portrait* (London: Arrow Books, 1975) a close second.
3   Apart from my own short essay, 'Northern Ireland's Telestar footballer', *Vacuum* 27 (Belfast: Factotem, September, 2005), pp. 5–6, little attention has been paid to how Best was written about or presented in the press or on Ulster TV in his native Belfast during the 1960s as a precursor to the wider UK and world media.
4   Whannel notes that Best and Muhammed Ali were 'the first sports stars whose fame was fuelled primarily by television'; idem, *Media Sports Stars*, p. 111. See also Chris Rojek, *Celebrity* (London: Reaktion Books, 2001).

5   Specifically, the following items were consulted: BBC, 'Miscellaneous Artists: George Best', WAC/TVART4 (1963–70); BBC, 'Gibson Memo to John Harris', 6 November 1969, WAC T53/323/2; BBC, 'Gibson Memo', 22 January 1970, WAC T53/323/1, pp. 1–3; BBC, 'Donaldson Memo to Sylvia Hewitt', Artists Bookings (1969), WAC T53/323/2, p. 1; BBC, *Audience Research Report: The world of Georgie Best* (1970), WAC T53/323/2, p. 1; *TV Post*, 28 March 1963, microfilm reel no. 179, London, BFI; UTV 'Film Library Catalogue: Best', Belfast, UTV. The BFI holds BBC, ITV and Channel Four material, much of which can be viewed on site by advance booking, and the BFI Player has other relevant 'orphan collection' material that, lacking clear rights ownership, can be made available. This includes the 1969 *For the Record* (BFI NFTVA) with Michael Parkinson.

6   Arthur Hopcraft, *Football Man* (London: Aurum Press, 2006), p. 14.

7   The first of these was George Best, *On the Ball* (London: Pelham, 1970).

8   Hopcraft, *Football Man*, p. 14.

9   See Eamonn McCann's obituary analysis, 'George Best (1946–2005)', *Socialist Worker*, December 2005, https://socialistworker.co.uk/art/7687/George%20Best%20(1946-2005) (accessed 19 June 2007).

10 Chas Critcher, 'Football Since the War', in John Clarke, Chas Critcher and Richard Johnson (eds), *Working Class Culture: Studies in history and theory* (London: Hutchinson, 1979), p. 167.

11 Rojek, *Celebrity*, p. 178.

12 Best, from a BBC interview in 1973, in *George Best: In his own words* (BBC, Audio CD, 2012).

13 See the argument made by Pettitt, 'Northern Ireland's Telestar footballer' (2005) and Alan Bairner, '(George) Best: Ulster Protestantism, conflicted identity and the "Belfast Boy(s)"', *Canadian Journal of Irish Studies*, vol. 32, no. 2 (fall, 2006), pp. 34–41.

14 Rojek, *Celebrity*, p. 45.

15 Williams, *George Best*.

16 Whannel, *Media Sports Stars*, pp. 109–14.

17 *Daily Express*, 2 March 1964. The Telstar telecommunications satellite was launched in 1962, linking Europe and North America. Emblematic of technology-led modernity, it was also the subject of a catchy, electronic, instrumental pop tune released by the Tornados in the same year.

18 Derek Hoby, *Sunday Express*, 27 December 1964.

19 Best, from a BBC interview, 11 February 1970, in *George Best: In his own words*.

20 Malcolm Brodie was the journalist writing in April/May 1966. On the access to Best and local presentation, see author's interview with Brodie (2006). Malcolm Brodie, *Belfast Telegraph*, 11 March 1961, p. 4. See also his 'The Best Story', *Ireland Saturday Night*, 12 March–26 April 1966.

21 Brodie, *Irish Sports News*, 19 April 1966.

22 *Belfast Telegraph*, 4 March 1966.

23 David L. Andrews and Steven J. Jackson, *Sports Stars: The cultural politics of sporting celebrity* (London: Routledge, 2001), p. 7.

24 Parkinson, *George Best*, p. 46.

25 Stanley Matchett, quoted in *Daily Mail*, 28 October 1969.

26 Best, quoted in Brodie, 'The Pink', 9 April 1966, p. 3.

27 Hugh McIlvanney, 'The World of Georgie Best' (programme billing), *Radio Times*, 5 February, 1970, p. 35.
28 BBC, *Audience Research Report*, p. 1.
29 BBC, 'Donaldson memo', p. 1.
30 McIlvanney, *The World of Georgie Best*, BBC script, p. 2.
31 McIlvanney, 'George Will Be Coaxed...But Never Pushed', *Radio Times*, 5 February 1970, p. 6.
32 BBC, *Audience Research Report*, p. 2.
33 Ibid., pp. 2–3.
34 McIlvanney, *The World of Georgie Best*, p. 7.
35 Ibid., p. 21.
36 This technique was picked up on, using extensive audio-interview archive and supplemented with dramatised 'reconstruction' sequences by Daniel Gordon in his 2014 film *Best: In his own words*, creating the impression that Best 'narrates' a documentary about his life post-mortem.
37 McIlvanney, *The World of Georgie Best*, p. 6.
38 Ibid., p. 14.
39 Ibid.
40 Ibid,. pp. 18–19.
41 Ibid., p. 17, my italics.
42 Ibid., p. 22. The music is Don Fardon's 7-inch single, 'Belfast Boy: Echoes of the cheers' (1970).
43 BBC, 'Gibson Memo', 22 January 1970, p. 1.
44 Ibid., p. 3.
45 BBC, 'Gibson Memo to John Harris', 6 November 1969.
46 *This Is Your Life*, 27 January 1971, transcribed from VHS viewing notes at BFI.
47 Mark Simpson, *Male Impersonators: Men performing masculinity* (London: Routledge, 2006), pp. 6–8.
48 As Parkinson notes acerbically, he interviewed Best first for the programme in 1971, but the BBC failed to retain a copy of the series; Parkinson, *George Best: A memoir*, e-book, para. 132.7.
49 Best, *On the Ball*; Parkinson, *George Best: An intimate portrait*; George Best (with Roy Collins), *Blessed: An intimate portrait* (London: Ebury Press, 2001); George Best (with Martin Knight), *George Best, Scoring at Half Time* (London: Ted Smart/Ebury Press, 2003).
50 Terry Wogan (1938–2016) was a hugely successful radio DJ and television presenter who was born in Limerick but emigrated to England, where he learned his trade before becoming associated with the BBC, first as a Radio 2 host, then as the presenter of a TV chat show that ran between 1982 and 1992 and as the off-screen, deadpan commentator for the Eurovision Song Contest.

Chapter 4. The Lansdowne Road Riot of 1995: Ireland, the English far right and the media

1 Raf Diallo, 'What Happened to Combat 18 After the '95 Lansdowne Road', Newstalk, https://www.newstalk.com/What-happened-to-Combat-18-after-the-95-Landsdowne-Road-riot (accessed 6 October 2018).

2 'The Boy in the Crowd on England's Night of Shame', *Irish Independent*, https://www.independent.ie/lifestyle/the-boy-in-the-crowd-on-englands-night-of-shame-29295056.html (accessed 5 April 2019).

3 For initial television news coverage, see 'How the Media Reacted to the 1995 Lansdowne Riot', Journal.ie, 6 June 2015, https://www.the42.ie/how-media-reacted-england-ireland-1995-2142885-Jun2015/ (accessed 5 April 2019).

4 On music, see Anton Shekhovtsov, 'Apoliteic Music: Neo-folk, martial industrial and "metapolitical fascism"', *Patterns of Prejudice*, vol. 43, no. 5 (2009), pp. 431–57.

5 For an overview, see Nick Lowles, *White Riot: The violent story of Combat 18* (London: Milo Books, 2011); Matthew J. Goodwin, *New British Fascism: The rise of the British National Party* (London: Routledge, 2011); and Nigel Copsey and John E. Richardson (eds), *Cultures of Post-war British Fascism* (London: Routledge, 2015).

6 Nicholas Goodrick-Clarke, *Black Sun: Aryan cults, esoteric Nazism and the politics of identity* (New York: New York University Press, 2001), p. 51.

7 See, for example, Anthony King, 'New Directors, Customers and Fans: The transformation of English football in the 1990s', *Sociology of Sport Journal*, vol. 14, no. 3 (1997), pp. 224–40; Anthony King, 'The Lads: Masculinity and the new consumption of football', *Sociology*, vol. 31, no. 2 (1997), pp. 329–46; and Raymond Boyle and Richard Haynes, *Football in the New Media Age* (London: Routledge, 2004).

8 Andrew Pierce, 'Riot Planned for Months by Far-right Group', *Irish Independent*, 17 February 1995.

9 Aidan Hennigan, 'Combat 18 May Have Engineered Riot', *Irish Press*, 17 February 1995.

10 Michael Lavery, 'Nazis Planned Dublin Trouble', *Evening Herald*, 16 February 1995.

11 Noel Spillane, 'Shocking Night of Thuggery', *Irish Examiner*, 16 February 1995.

12 *Sun*, 16 February 1995.

13 *Daily Mirror*, 16 February 1995.

14 *Daily Mail*, 16 February 1995.

15 *Today*, 16 February 1995.

16 *Times*, 17 February 1995; *Independent*, 17 February 1995.

17 *Hansard*, 16 February 1995, 254, Q1.

18 Seanad Éireann Debates, 16 February 1995.

19 Dáil Debates, 16 February 1995.

20 Sargent was convicted of murder in 1998 and sentenced to life imprisonment after stabbing to death a fellow Combat 18 member, Christopher Castle, as part of an internal feud.

21 See Lowles, *White Riot*, p. 173, *Daily Express*, 17 February 1995; *Sunday Express*, 19 February 1995.

22 *Sunday World*, 19 February 1995.

23 See 'Warning Signals Must Never Again Be Ignored', *Irish Times*, 5 April 1995.

24 'The Finlay Report', *Irish Times*, 5 April 1995.

25 'These Guys Were Morons...They Didn't Come to Watch Football', Journal. ie, 4 June 2015, https://www.the42.ie/interview-ger-canning-lansdowne-riot-1995-2142820-Jun2015/ (accessed 20 December 2018).

26 Stephen Tudor, 'The Lansdowne Road Riots: When football returned to the Dark Ages', Tifo, https://www.tifofootball.com/features/lansdowne-road-riots-football-returned-dark-ages/ (accessed 20 December 2018).

27 'Gary Pallister: Rioting fans let England down in 1995', RTÉ.ie, https://www.rte.ie/sport/soccer/2015/0605/706019-pallister-rioting-fans-let-england-down-in-1995/ (accessed 20 December 2018).

28 Lowles, *White Riot*, pp. 171–2.

29 Ibid., p. 183.

30 'Why Do England Fans Sing No Surrender?', BBC News, https://www.bbc.com/news/magazine-22688494 (accessed 20 December 2018).

31 For the arguments against Combat 18's involvement in the riot, in the context of those monitoring the para-political extremes, see Larry O'Hara, 'Combat 18 and the 1995 Dublin Riot Revisited', Notes from the Borderland, http://www.borderland.co.uk/component/k2/item/8-combat-18-the-1995-dublin-riot-revisited-don-t-believe-the-hype.html (accessed 20 December 2018). On Combat 18 membership on their frustration at missing the riot, see Lowles, *White Riot*, p. 179.

32 For a discussion of the rising Irish economy in the context of soccer, see Marcus Free, 'Keeping Them Under Pressure: Masculinity, narratives of national regeneration and the Republic of Ireland soccer team', *Sport in History*, vol. 25, no. 22 (2005), pp. 265–88.

33 See, for example, 'Hooligan Porn', in Steve Frosdick and Peter Marsh, *Football Hooliganism* (Devon: Willan, 2005); Jon Dart, 'Confessional Tales from Former Football Hooligans: A nostalgic, narcissistic wallow in football violence', *Soccer and Society*, vol. 9, no. 1 (2008), pp. 42–55; and Steve Redhead, 'Hit and Tell: A review essay on the soccer hooligan memoir', *Soccer and Society*, vol. 5, no. 3 (2004), pp. 392–403.

34 Colin War, *All Quiet on the Hooligan Front: Eight years that shook football* (Edinburgh: Mainstream, 1996), p. 192.

35 *Jason Mariner – Lansdowne Road Football Riot*, YouTube, https://www.youtube.com/watch?v=GFgIHYrcY9o (accessed 20 December 2018).

36 Paul Dodd and Iain McNee, *England's Number One: The great adventure of a serial soccer yob* (London: PIG Books, 1998).

37 'Soldiers Recruited by Violent Far-right', *Independent*, 8 March 1999.

38 'UDA Killer to Join English Neo-Nazis', *Guardian*, 3 September 2000.

Chapter 5. The Mediatisation of the GAA's Commemoration of the 1916 Rising: 'A New Ireland rises'?

1 This chapter has emerged from ongoing research conducted with colleagues contributing to the TRUTHS Research Project, funded by the Spanish Ministerio de Economía y Competitividad and FEDER. [INTRUTHS: FFI2017-84619-P. AEI/FEDER, UE.] An earlier version of this chapter appeared as 'Sport, Representation, and the Commemoration of the 1916 Rising: "A new Ireland rises"?', *Review of Irish Studies in Europe*, vol. 2, no. 2 (2018), pp. 40–54. All images from *Laochra* are courtesy of Tyrone Productions Ltd.

2 Frank McNally, 'Fairyhouse Grand National Meeting Re-enacts 1916 Race', *Irish Times*, 29 March 2016.

3 Apart from the Gaelic Athletic Association event discussed in this chapter, a further relevant event in this respect was the Football Association of Ireland's (FAI) 1916 commemoration. This consisted of a pre-match ceremony prior to a friendly game between the Republic of Ireland and Switzerland played at the association's main stadium (the Aviva) on 25 March 2016 when the FAI presented the rather extraordinary sight of seven children from Ballymun reading out the Proclamation of Independence dressed as 1916 rebels while carrying mock rifles.

4 The Gaelic Athletic Association (GAA) is the organisation responsible for the promotion of Gaelic games in Ireland.

5 See Crosson, *Sport and Film* (London: Routledge, 2013).

6 Judith Butler, *Gender Trouble: Feminism and the subversion of identity* (London & New York: Routledge, 1999), pp. xv–xvi.

7 See, for example, Elizabeth Butler Cullingford, *Ireland's Others: Gender and ethnicity in Irish literature and popular culture* (Cork, Cork University Press, 2001).

8 For further on this issue, see Rebecca Lynn Graff-McRae, 'Forget Politics! Theorising the political dynamics of commemoration and conflict', in Mary E. Daly and Margaret O'Callaghan (eds), *1916 in 1966: Commemorating the Easter Rising* (Dublin: Royal Irish Academy, 2007), pp. 219–38.

9 Department of Culture, Heritage and the Gaeltacht, 'Thousands Will Take Part in Special Events Nationwide to Mark Calendar Centenary of Easter Rising – Minister Humphreys', 23 April 2016, https://www.chg.gov.ie/thousands-will-take-part-in-special-events-nationwide-to-mark-calendar-centenary-of-easter-rising-minister-humphreys/ (accessed 13 February 2020).

10 Ernest Gellner, *Nations and Nationalism* (Oxford: Blackwell, 1983), pp. 37–8.

11 Michael Billig, *Banal Nationalism* (London: Sage Publications, 1995), p. 120.

12 See, for example, Andrew Higson, *Waving the Flag: Constructing a national cinema in Britain* (Oxford: Clarendon Press, 1995); Mette Hjort and Scott MacKenzie (eds), *Cinema and Nation* (London: Routledge, 2000).

13 Susan Hayward, *French National Cinema* (London: Routledge, 2005), p. x.

14 Seán Crosson, '"Shillalah swing time…you'll thrill each time a wild Irishman's skull shatters": Representing hurling in American cinema: 1930–1960', in Ruth Barton (ed.), *Screening Irish-America: Representing Irish-America in film and television* (Dublin: Irish Academic Press, 2009), pp. 148–64.

15 Seán Crosson, '"Ar son an Náisiúin": The National Film Institute of Ireland's All-Ireland films', *Éire-Ireland*, special issue on Irish sport, vol. 48, nos 1–2 (2013), pp. 193–212.

16 Neil Jarman, 'Commemorating 1916, Celebrating Difference: Parading and painting in Belfast', in Adrian Forty and Susanne Küchler (eds), *The Art of Forgetting* (Oxford, New York: Berg, 2001), p. 171. Jarman is here drawing on the work of Maurice Halbwachs.

17 Mike Cronin, 'Projecting the Nation through Sport and Culture: Ireland, Aonach Tailteann and the Irish Free State, 1924–32', *Journal of*

Contemporary History, vol. 38, no. 3 (2003), pp. 54–5; Paul Rouse, *Sport and Ireland: A history* (Oxford: Oxford University Press, 2015), p. 258.

18 Neil O'Boyle and Colm Kearns, 'Sporting Shades of Green: A comparative analysis of sponsored national mythmaking in Irish rugby and soccer', *Sport in Society*, vol. 20, no. 7 (2017), p. 972.

19 David Rowe, 'The Mediated Nation and the Transnational Football Fan', *Soccer & Society*, vol. 16, nos 5–6 (2015), p. 693.

20 William Murphy, 'The G.A.A. During the Irish Revolution, 1913–23', in Michael Cronin, William Murphy and Paul Rouse (eds), *The Gaelic Athletic Association, 1884–2009* (Dublin: Irish Academic Press, 2009), pp. 67–8.

21 Seán Moran, 'The GAA and the 1916 Rising: Playing a major part in our history', *Irish Times*, 5 March 2016.

22 Murray cited in Moran, 'The GAA and the 1916 Rising'.

23 Aogán Ó Fearghail, 'Réamhfocal ón Uachtarán', *Allianz Football League Roinn I and II Finals* (match programme) (Dublin: DBA Publications, 2016), pp. 8–9.

24 Róisín Higgins, '"I am the narrator over and above…the caller up of the dead": Pageant and drama in 1966', in Mary E. Daly and Margaret O'Callaghan (eds), *1916 in 1966: Commemorating the Easter Rising* (Dublin: Royal Irish Academy, 2007), p. 153.

25 Declan Kiberd, 'The Easter Rebellion: Poetry or drama?', papers from The 1916 Rising: Then and Now conference held at Trinity College Dublin, 21–2 April 2006, organised by the Ireland Institute and Dublin University History Society, http://www.theirelandinstitute.com/wp/1916-then-now/ (accessed 13 February 2020).

26 Higgins, '"I am the narrator over and above"', pp. 151–2.

27 Ibid., p. 152.

28 Ibid., p. 151.

29 Seán Crosson, *Sport and Film* (London: Routledge, 2013), pp. 93–8.

30 'Dublin's League Final Win Brings Record-breaking Viewing Figures for TG4', TG4, 25 April 2016, https://www.tg4.ie/en/information/press/press-releases/2016-2/20-04-16-1/ (accessed 13 February 2020). It should be noted that the league finals featured Dublin, Kerry, Cavan and Tyrone – all counties with very large followings, which undoubtedly contributed to both the attendance and viewership.

31 Roche, 'Staging 1916 in 1966', p. 310.

32 Rebecca E. Farrell, *Across the Water: Teaching Irish music and dance at home and abroad* (Lanham, MD: R&L Education, 2010), p. 54.

33 Diane Negra, 'Urban Space, Luxury Retailing and the New Irishness', *Cultural Studies*, vol. 24, no. 6 (2010), p. 836.

34 Ibid.

35 Ibid.

Chapter 6. From Team of Aliens to #TeamofUs: The evolution of Irish-rugby advertising, 2007–17

1 Neil O'Boyle, *New Vocabularies, Old Ideas* (Bern: Peter Lang, 2011), p. 170.

2 David Rowe, *Sport, Culture and the Media: The unruly trinity* (Buckingham: Open University Press, 2004), p. 72.

3 Ibid., p. 73.
4 William O'Barr, *Culture and the Ad: Exploring otherness in the world of advertising* (Boulder, CO: Westview Press, 1994); Katherine Toland Frith and Barbara Mueller, *Advertising and Societies: Global issues* (New York: Peter Lang, 2003); Mark Falcous, 'The Decolonizing National Imaginary: Promotional media constructions during the 2005 Lions tour of Aotearoa and New Zealand', *Journal of Sport and Social Issues*, vol. 31, no. 4 (2007).
5 Joseph Maguire, 'Sport, Identity Politics, and Globalization: Diminishing contrasts and increasing varieties', *Sociology of Sport Journal*, no. 11 (1994), p. 400.
6 Falcous, 'The Decolonizing National Imaginary: Promotional media constructions', p. 277.
7 The widely celebrated success of the Ireland women's field hockey team in reaching the 2018 World Cup final has rendered this assessment somewhat questionable, but while hockey is very much a 'major' sport in terms of international participation, within an Irish context it has never attracted the same attention from advertisers and the wider media that rugby has. Whether the World Cup run of 2018 will change this remains to be seen.
8 Liam O'Callaghan, 'Rugby Football and Identity Politics in Free State Ireland', *Éire-Ireland*, vol. 48, nos 1–2 (2013), p. 156.
9 Frank McNally, 'An Irishman's Diary: Patriot games – cricket or rugby? A choice no longer', *Irish Times*, 18 February 2015.
10 Maguire, 'Sport, Identity Politics, and Globalization', p. 411.
11 Declan Kiberd, *Inventing Ireland* (London: Vantage, 1996); Luke Gibbons, *Transformations in Irish Culture* (Cork: Cork University Press, 1996).
12 O'Callaghan, 'Rugby Football and Identity Politics in Free State Ireland', p. 149.
13 Kiberd, *Inventing Ireland*, p. 565.
14 Aidan Arrowsmith, 'Plastic Paddies vs Master Racers: "Soccer" and Irish identity', *International Journal of Cultural Studies*, vol. 7, no. 4 (2004), p. 466.
15 Jason Tuck, 'Making Sense of Emerald Commotion: Rugby Union, national identity and Ireland', *Identities: Global Studies in Culture and Power*, no. 10 (2003), pp. 495–515.
16 Marcus Free, 'Diaspora and Rootedness, Amateurism and Professionalism in Media Discourses of Irish Soccer and Rugby in the 1990s and 2000s', *Éire-Ireland*, no. 48 (2013), pp. 220–2.
17 Kieran Bonner, 'Exciting, Intoxicating and Dangerous: Some Tiger effects on Ireland and the culture of Dublin', *Canadian Journal of Irish Studies*, no. 37 (2011), p. 60.
18 Arrowsmith, 'Plastic Paddies vs Master Racers', p. 466.
19 Majella McSharry, 'Stuck in a Ruck: The impact of rugby on social belonging', in Perry Share and Mary P. Corcoran (eds), *Belongings: Shaping identity in modern Ireland* (Dublin: Institute of Public Administration, 2008), pp. 90–3.
20 Peter Nohrnberg. '"Building Up a Nation Once Again": Irish masculinity, violence, and the cultural politics of sports in *A Portrait of the Artist as a Young Man* and *Ulysses*', *Joyce Studies Annual 2010* (2011), p. 118.
21 Colm Kearns, interview with IRFU marketing official, 25 July 2016.

22 John Fanning, *The Importance of Being Branded: An Irish perspective* (Dublin: Liffey Press, 2006), p. 329.

23 Liam O'Callaghan, 'The Red Thread of History: The media, Munster rugby and the creation of a sporting tradition', *Media History,* no. 17 (2011), p. 183.

24 Ibid.

25 Colm Kearns, interview with Irish rugby fans, 6 February 2018.

26 As of August 2018, the features on Henshaw and O'Connell have attracted over 60,000 views each, and the one on Sexton has earned just shy of 100,000 views.

27 In Sexton's case, this is particularly notable as the caption locates us in Listowel, County Kerry (where the player spent time visiting his godparents during his childhood), rather than in the affluent south Dublin suburb Sexton actually grew up in. This can perhaps be viewed as a tacit admission that the latter is too closely linked with Celtic Tiger culture to be readily perceived as 'authentically' Irish. Ideas of what constitutes authentic or traditional Irish culture and identity have long been dominated by notions of the idealised rural, and the confident cosmopolitanism that emerged from Celtic Tiger Ireland must be seen to not entirely abandon this if it is to be perceived as representing Irish identity positively.

28 Free, 'Diaspora and Rootedness, Amateurism and Professionalism'.

29 'Ad of the Week: Vodafone Ireland's Who We Are is How We Play', *AdWorld.com,* 2 November 2017.

30 Mary Hannigan, 'Rugby, the People's Game? Not according to the people', *Irish Times,* 6 March 2018.

31 Gary Whannel, 'Television and the Transformation of Sport', *Annals of the American Academy of Political and Social Science,* vol. 625, no. 1 (2009), pp. 210–11.

32 Journalist Ewan MacKenna, a persistent critic of rugby's perceived elitism, has argued vehemently in this regard, citing his experience at the now defunct *Sunday Tribune* national newspaper as evidence, claiming that in 2010 journalists were paid to travel to Argentina to cover a tour of the Ireland rugby-team's reserves, while the paper's chief football writer had to cover his own travel to the 2010 FIFA World Cup. MacKenna claims that 'people in key positions in newspapers, television stations and whatever else, people on a boardroom level often tend to come from private rugby playing schools and I think they set the agenda: "this is our sport, this is our game". I think that's why it gets so much coverage. I think it's overblown how popular it is and I think they defend the players over the top.' See Team 33 (2015), *Football Manager Fun, Rugby v Soccer Coverage, Fantasy,* podcast, https://www.ivoox.com/en/football-manager-fun-rugby-v-soccer-coverage-fantasy-audios-mp3_rf_9111718_1.html (accessed 13 February 2020). A 2017 report produced by Sport Ireland supports the idea that, for all the attention it gains in the media, rugby remains relatively under-attended and participated in compared to other sports. Notably, it does not feature in the top ten most-participated-in sports in Ireland, and only 1.9 per cent of the population had attended a rugby match in the year of the report. See Sport Ireland, *Irish Sports Monitor Annual Report, 2017* (Dublin: Sport Ireland), https://assets.gov.ie/16014/3abf58a4a5af41b9ab66065de65e15a3.pdf, pp. 14, 49 (accessed 22 May 2018).

33 John Fanning, *The Importance of Being Branded: An Irish perspective* (Dublin: Liffey Press, 2006), p. 331.

34 Free, 'Diaspora and Rootedness, Amateurism and Professionalism', p. 228.

35 Colm Kearns, Interview with Irish rugby fans, 6 February 2018.

36 Marcus Free, 'Irish Rugby Players as Celebrities', Post-Celtic Tiger Irishness Symposium, Trinity College, Dublin, 25 November 2016.

37 Susan McKay, 'How the "Rugby Rape Trial" Divided Ireland', *Guardian*, 4 December 2018.

38 Hayley Halpin, 'Over 1.4 Million People Tuned in to See Ireland's Opening Six Nations Game on Saturday', Journal.ie, 4 February 2019, https://www.thejournal.ie/ireland-england-six-nations-viewers-4476726-Feb2019 (accessed 5 April 2019).

39 Susan McFarlene-Alvarez, 'Human Billboarding: Peopled publicity and a new space of "agency" in advertising', *Advertising & Society Review*, no. 15 (2014).

Chapter 7. Media Sport, Women and Ireland: Seeing the wood for the trees

1 Ruth Hall and Carole Oglesby, 'Stepping Through the Looking Glass', *Sex Roles*, vol. 74, nos 7–8 (2016), p. 271; Valerie Siebert, '"I'm Proud to be Strong!"', *Daily Mail*, 17 July 2015.

2 Cheryl Cooky, Michael Messner and Robin Hextrum, 'Women Play Sport, But Not on TV: A longitudinal study of televised news media', *Communication & Sport*, vol. 1, no. 3 (2013), pp. 203–30.

3 Ian Reade, Wendy Rodgers and Leanne Norman, 'The Under-representation of Women in Coaching: A comparison of male and female Canadian coaches at low and high levels of coaching', *International Journal of Sports Science & Coaching*, vol. 4, no. 4 (2009), pp. 505–20.

4 Women on Boards, *Gender Balance in Global Sport Report*, 2016, https://www.womenonboards.net/womenonboards-AU/media/UK-PDFs-Research-Reports/2016_Gender-Balance-in-Global-Sport.pdf (accessed 24 May 2019).

5 'Record-breaking Crowd Attends All-Ireland Final', RTÉ, https://www.rte.ie/sport/gaa/2018/0916/994137-record-breaking-crowd-attends-all-ireland-final/ (accessed 24 May 2019); 'TG4 Ladies Football Finals Weekend Audience Viewership', Ladies Gaelic Football Association, https://ladiesgaelic.ie/tg4-ladies-football-finals-weekend-audience-viewership/ (accessed 24 May 2019).

6 Chapter 10 in this collection features a round-table discussion involving two of these presenters (Jacqui Hurley and Sinéad Kissane) in conversation with the two authors here, as well as freelance sportswriter Cliona Foley (also presenter of women's sport podcast *Off the Bench*) and academic Niamh Kitching (co-author of chapter 9).

7 Joan Ballantine and Pauric McGowan (eds), *Women into Business in Northern Ireland: Opportunities and challenges* (Belfast: Ulster University Business School, 2018), https://www.businessfirstonline.co.uk/wp-content/uploads/2018/06/REPORT-Women-into-Business-in-Northern-Ireland-Final.pdf (accessed 13 February 2020).

8 Pat O'Connor, 'Private Troubles, Public Issues: The Irish sociological imagination', *Irish Journal of Sociology*, vol. 15, no. 2 (2006), p. 14.

9 'Laying the Tracks to Liberation: The original contraceptive train', *Irish Times*, 28 October 2014.

10 Katie Liston, 'Revisiting Relations Between the Sexes in Sport on the Island of Ireland', in Tatiana Landini and Francois Dépelteau (eds), *Norbert Elias and Empirical Research* (New York: Palgrave Macmillan, 2014), pp. 197–217.

11 John Horgan, *Irish Media: A critical history since 1922* (London: Routledge, 2001), p. 3.

12 'If Women's Sport Struggles for Coverage It's Not Because of Sexism – It's Because You Can't Make People Care', *Irish Times*, 11 August 2014.

13 Liston, 'Revisiting Relations Between the Sexes'.

14 Katie Liston, 'Sport and Gender Relations', *Sport in Society*, vol. 9, no. 4 (2006), pp. 616–33.

15 Ciaran Dunne, 'An Examination of the Photographic Coverage of Sportswomen in the Irish Print Media: A study of an Irish broadsheet newspaper', *Sport in Society*, vol. 20, no. 11 (2017), pp. 1780–98.

16 Marcus Free, '"He is my strength and my shield": The antinomies of Katie Taylor as female sporting celebrity in twenty-first century Ireland', *Sport in Society*, vol. 18, no. 10 (2015), pp. 1147–65.

17 Global Media Monitoring Project, *Global Media Monitoring Project Regional Report 2015* (Toronto & Newcastle: World Association for Christian Communication, 2015), http://cdn.agilitycms.com/who-makes-the-news/Imported/reports_2015/regional/Europe.pdf (accessed 12 February 2020), p. 4.

18 Michael Messner, Michele Dunbar and Darnell Hunt, 'The Televised Sports Manhood Formula', *Journal of Sport and Social Issues*, vol. 24, no. 4 (2000), pp. 380–94.

19 Mark Falcous, 'Sport/Media Complex', in David Levinson and Karen Christensen (eds), *Berkshire Encyclopaedia of World Sport* (Great Barrington, MA: Berkshire Publishing, 2010), p. 994.

20 Toni Bruce, 'Reflections on Communication and Sport: On women and feminities', *Communication & Sport*, vol. 1, nos 1–2 (2012), p. 126.

21 Murray Phillips, *An Illusory Image: A report on the media coverage and portrayal of women's sport in Australia 1996* (Canberra: Australian Sports Commission, 1997), p. 20.

22 Global Media Monitoring Project, *Global Media Monitoring Project Regional Report 2015*.

23 Lucie Schoch and Fabien Ohl, 'Women Sports Journalists in Switzerland: Between assignment and negotiation of roles', *Sociology of Sport Journal*, vol. 28, no. 2 (2011), p. 204.

24 Ciaran Dunne, 'Undervalued and Underreported: The coverage of sportswomen in the Irish print media', in Neil O'Boyle and Marcus Free, *Sport, the Media and Ireland: Interdisciplinary perspectives* (Cork: Cork University Press, 2020).

25 Janet Fink, 'Female Athletes, Women's Sport, and the Sport Media Commercial Complex: Have we really "come a long way baby"?', *Sport Management Review*, vol. 18, no. 3 (2013), p. 333.

26 Ibid.

27 Donna Woodhouse, Beth Fielding-Lloyd and Ruth Sequerra, 'Big Brother's Little Sister: The ideological construction of Women's Super League', *Sport in Society*. vol. 22, no. 12 (2019).

28 Adrian Yip, 'Deuce or Advantage? Examining gender bias in online coverage of professional tennis', *International Review for the Sociology of Sport*, vol. 53, no. 5 (2018), pp. 517–32.

29 Emma Wensing and Toni Bruce, 'Bending the Rules: Media representations of gender during an international sporting event', *International Review for the Sociology of Sport*, vol. 38, no. 4 (2003), pp. 387–96; Karen Weiller, Catriona Higgs and Christy Greenleaf, 'Analysis of Television Media Commentary of the 2000 Olympic Games', *Media Report to Women*, no. 3 (2004), pp. 14–21.

30 Elizabeth Daniels, 'Sex Objects, Athletes, and Sexy Athletes: How media representations of women athletes can impact adolescent girls and college women', *Journal of Adolescent Research*, vol. 24, no. 4 (2009), pp. 399–422.

31 Alina Bernstein, 'Is it Time for a Victory Lap? Changes in the media coverage of women in sport', *International Review for the Sociology of Sport*, no. 37 (2002), p. 425.

32 Margaret Carlisle Duncan and Cynthia Hasbrook, 'Denial of Power in Televised Women's Sports', *Sociology of Sport Journal*, no. 5 (1998), pp. 1–21.

33 Dunja Antunovic and Marie Hardin, 'Activism in Women's Sports Blogs: Activism and feminist potential', *International Journal of Sport Communication*, no. 5 (2015), pp. 305–22.

34 Angela Lumpkin, 'Female Representation in Feature Articles Published by *Sports Illustrated* in the 1990s', *Women in Sport and Physical Activity Journal*, no. 18 (2009), pp. 38–51; Cooky et al., 'Women Play Sport, But Not on TV', pp. 1–28; Galen Clavio and Andrea Eagleman, 'Gender and Sexually Suggestive Images in Sports Blogs', *Journal of Sport Management*, vol. 25, no. 4 (2011), pp. 295–304.

35 Andrew Billings, *Olympic Media: Inside the biggest show on television* (London: Routledge, 2008); Andrew Billings, James Angelini and Andrea Holt Duke, 'Gendered Profiles of Olympic History: Sportcaster dialogue in the 2008 Beijing Olympics', *Journal of Broadcasting & Electronic Media*, no. 54 (2010), pp. 9–23; Cooky et al., 'Women Play Sport, But Not on TV'; Mary Jo Kane, 'The Better Sportswomen Get, the More the Media Ignore Them', *Communication & Sport*, vol. 1, no. 3 (2013), pp. 231–6.

36 Bruce, 'Reflections on Communication and Sport', p. 128.

37 Sarah Fields, 'A Toothless Tiger? Sports, Title IX, and gendered bodies', in Joseph Maguire, Mark Falcous and Katie Liston (eds), *The Business and Culture of Sports*, no. 3 (New York: Macmillan, 2019), pp. 19–33.

38 Kari Fasting, Trond Svela Sand, Elizabeth Pike and Jordan Matthews (eds), *From Brighton to Helsinki: Women and sport progress report, 1994–2014* (Helsinki: Finnish Sports Confederation, 2014), http://d3mcbia3evjswv.cloudfront.net/files/IWG%20Final%20Report.pdf?mRdkO5No_atTOUY7MwR.XrKo7t3Ar78d (accessed 11 February 2020).

39 Women on Boards, *Gender Balance in Global Sports*.

40 Sport Ireland, *Sport Ireland Policy on Women in Sport* (Dublin: Sport Ireland, 2019), https://www.sportireland.ie/sites/default/files/2019-11/wis_policy.pdf (accessed 13 February 2020); Sport Northern Ireland, *Public Authority Statutory Equality and Good Relations Duties Annual Progress Report 2016–17*, http://www.sportni.net/sportni/wp-content/uploads/2013/09/Sport-NI_S75-Annual-Progress-Report-2016-2017-Final-Draft-Approved-22-02-2018.pdf (accessed 13 February 2020).

41 'Women's Sport Hasn't Been Visible Enough to Occupy That Same Spot in Our Hearts. It should, it can and it will', Journal.ie, 25 December 2018, https://www.the42.ie/20x20-sarah-colgan-sit-down-feature-4405601-Dec2018/ (accessed 13 February 2020).

42 'There Needs to Be a Change in Mindset in How We View the Role of Women in Sport', Journal.ie, 5 April 2017, https://www.the42.ie/patrick-odonovan-irish-womens-football-team-3325612-Apr2017/ (accessed 13 February 2020).

Chapter 8. Undervalued and Underreported: The coverage of sportswomen in the Irish print media

1 Ciaran Dunne, 'An Examination of the Photographic Coverage of Sportswomen in the Irish Print Media: A study of an Irish broadsheet newspaper', *Sport in Society*, vol. 20, no. 11 (2017), pp. 1780–98.

2 Antonio Gramsci, *Selections from the Prison Notebooks of Antonio Gramsci* (New York: International Publishers, 1971).

3 Toni Bruce, 'New Rules for New Times: Sportswomen and media representation in the third wave', *Sex Roles*, vol. 74, nos 7–8 (2016), pp. 361–76.

4 C. Packer, D.J. Geh, O.W. Goulden, A.M. Jordan, G.K. Withers, A.J. Wagstaff, R.A. Bellwood, C.L. Binmore and C.L. Webster, 'No Lasting Legacy: No change in reporting of women's sports in the British print media with the London 2012 Olympics and Paralympics', *Journal of Public Health*, no. 37 (2015), pp. 50–6.

5 Helen Caple, 'Competing for Coverage: Exploring emerging discourses on female athletes in the Australian print media', *English Text Construction*, vol. 6, no. 2 (2013), pp. 271–94.

6 Hans Schmidt, 'Women's Sports Coverage Remains Largely Marginalized', *Newspaper Research Journal*, vol. 37, no. 3 (2016), pp. 275–98.

7 Dunja Antunovic, '"Turned into the Women's Journal": Representations of women in Hungary's sports magazine', *International Review for the Sociology of Sport*, vol. 54, no. 1 (2019), pp. 63–85.

8 Kate Petty and Stacey Pope, 'A New Age for Media Coverage of Women's Sport? An analysis of English media coverage of the 2015 FIFA Women's World Cup', *Sociology*, vol. 53, no. 3 (2018), pp. 486–502; Amy Godoy-Pressland, '"No hint of bulging muscles": The surveillance of sportswomen's bodies in British print media', *Journalism*, vol. 17, no. 6 (2015), pp. 744–59.

9 Simone French, 'Still Not There: The continued invisibility of female athletes and sports in the New Zealand print media', *Media International Australia*, vol. 148, no. 1 (2013), pp. 39–50.

10 Nicolas Delorme and Nadège Testard, 'Sex Equity in French Newspaper Photographs: A content analysis of 2012 Olympic Games by *L'Equipe*', *European Journal of Sport Science*, vol. 15, no. 8 (2015), pp. 757–63.

11 Honorata Jakubowska, 'Are Women Still the "Other Sex": Gender and sport in the Polish mass media', *Sport in Society*, vol. 18, no. 2 (2015), pp. 168–85.

12 Bruce, 'New Rules for New Times', pp. 361–76.

13 Deirdre O'Neill and Matt Mulready, 'The Invisible Woman? A comparative study of women's sports coverage in the UK national press before and after the 2012 Olympic Games', *Journalism Practice*, vol. 9, no. 5 (2015), pp. 651–68.

14 See, for example, Bruce, 'New Rules for New Times', pp. 361–76, and Janet Fink, 'Female Athletes, Women's Sport, and the Sport Media Commercial Complex: Have we really "come a long way baby"?', *Sport Management Review*, vol. 18, no. 3 (2013), pp. 331–42.

15 Emma Sherry, Angela Osborne and Matthew Nicholson, 'Images of Sports Women: A review', *Sex Roles* vol. 74, nos 7–8 (2016), pp. 299–309.

16 Carlos Cortés, *The Children Are Watching: How the media teach about diversity*, Multicultural Education Series (New York: Teachers College Press, 2000).

17 Paul M. Pedersen, 'Examining Equity in Newspaper Photographs: A content analysis of the print media photographic coverage of interscholastic athletics', *International Review for the Sociology of Sport*, vol. 37, nos 3–4 (2002), pp. 303–18.

18 Alfonso Montuori and Hillary Stephenson, 'Creativity, Culture Contact, and Diversity', *World Futures*, vol. 66, nos 3–4 (2010), pp. 266–85.

19 David Croteau and William Hoynes, *Media/Society: Industries, images, and audiences* (California: Sage Publications, 2013).

20 Alina Bernstein and Edward M. Kian, 'Gender and Sexualities in Sport Media', in Paul M. Pedersen (ed.), *Routledge Handbook of Sport Communication* (New York: Routledge, 2013), pp. 319–27.

21 R.J. Barry Jones (ed.), *Routledge Encyclopedia of International Political Economy: Entries G–O*, no. 2 (London: Taylor & Francis, 2001), p. 669.

22 Katie Liston, 'Sport and Gender Relations', *Sport in Society*, vol. 9, no. 4 (2006), pp. 616–33.

23 Maria E. Len-Ríos, Shelly Rodgers, Esther Thorson and Doyle Yoon, 'Representation of Women in News and Photos: Comparing content to perceptions', *Journal of Communication*, vol. 55, no. 1 (2005), pp. 152–68.

24 Pedersen, 'Examining Equity in Newspaper Photographs', pp. 303–18.

25 O'Neill and Mulready, 'The Invisible Woman?', p. 665.

26 French, 'Still Not There', pp. 39–50.

27 Ellen J. Staurowsky, *Women and Sport: From liberation to celebration* (Champaign: Human Kinetics, 2016).

28 Sarah Shephard, *Kicking Off: How women in sport are changing the game* (London: Bloomsbury Publishing, 2016).

29 Irish Life Health, *Irish Life Health School's Fitness Challenge Barometer* (2018), https://www.irishlifehealth.ie/IrishLifeHealth/media/Irish-life-Health/pdfs/fitness-challenge/sfc-barometer-2018-web.pdf (accessed 16 February 2020), p. 4.

30 *Houses of the Oireachtas Joint Committee on Arts, Sport, Tourism, Community, Rural and Gaeltacht Affairs Fifth Report: Women in Sport* (2004), Houses of the Oireachtas, https://www.oireachtas.ie/documents/committees29thdail/jcastrag/reports/Women-In-Sport.pdf (accessed 13 February 2020).
31 Dublin Sports and Recreation Council, *The Increasing Invisibility of Women in Irish Sport: Images of sportswomen in Irish newspapers* (Dublin: Dublin Sports and Recreation Council 2007), p. 5.
32 Liston, 'Sport and gender relations', pp. 616–33.
33 Kevin Myers, 'An Irishman's Diary', *Irish Times*, 8 October 2004.
34 *Irish Times*, 11 August 2014.
35 Michael Moynihan, 'Does the Media Give Women's Sport Proper Coverage?', *Irish Examiner*, 24 September 2011.
36 Dublin Sports and Recreation Council, *The Increasing Invisibility of Women*, p. 5.
37 Mary Hannigan, 'Changing the Game: More coverage a step forward', *Irish Times*, 19 November 2015.
38 Gaelic football is an indigenous Irish sport played by men and women, but teams are not mixed. It is the most popular sport in Ireland in terms of participation. The Gaelic Athletic Association (GAA) oversees the organisation and running of Ireland's indigenous Gaelic games, incorporating the sports of Gaelic football, hurling (men only), camogie (women only) and handball. The GAA is the largest sporting organisation in Ireland, with over 2,200 clubs spread across thirty-two counties (six of which form Northern Ireland). Gaelic football for females is overseen by the Ladies Gaelic Football Association, and is officially known as ladies Gaelic football.
39 Sport Ireland, *Irish Sports Monitor Annual Report, 2017* (Dublin: Sport Ireland), https://assets.gov.ie/16014/3abf58a4a5af41b9ab66065de65e15a3.pdf (accessed 22 May 2018), pp. 14, 49.
40 Marcus Free, '"He is my strength and my shield": The antinomies of Katie Taylor as female sporting celebrity in twenty-first-century Ireland', *Sport in Society*, vol. 18, no. 10 (2015), pp. 1147–65.
41 Amy Godoy-Pressland and Gerald Griggs, 'The Photographic Representation of Female Athletes in the British Print Media During the London 2012 Olympic Games', *Sport in Society*, vol. 17, no. 6 (2014), pp. 808–23.
42 Sherry, Osborne and Nicholson, 'Images of Sports Women'.
43 Galen Clavio and Andrea N. Eagleman, 'Gender and Sexually Suggestive Images in Sports Blogs', *Journal of Sport Management*, vol. 25, no. 4 (2011), pp. 295–304.
44 Bruce, 'New Rules for New Times', p. 372.
45 Sherry, Osborne and Nicholson, 'Images of Sports Women', p. 300.
46 Croteau and Hoynes, *Media/Society*, p. 19.
47 Bengü Arslan and Canan Koca, 'A Content Analysis of Turkish Daily Newspapers Regarding Sportswomen and Gender Stereotypes', *Annals of Leisure Research*, vol. 10, nos 3–4 (2007), pp. 310–27.
48 Liston, 'Sport and gender relations', p. 618.
49 O'Neill and Mulready, 'The Invisible Woman?', p. 666.

Chapter 9. 'Top of the tree': Examining the Irish print-news portrayal of the world's best female amateur golfer

1 Holly Thorpe, Kim Toffoletti and Toni Bruce, 'Sportswomen and Social Media: Third-wave feminism, postfeminism, and neoliberal feminism into conversation', *Journal of Sport and Social Issues*, vol. 41, no. 5 (2017), pp. 359–83.

2 Kim Toffoletti and Catherine Palmer, 'Women and Sport in Australia – New Times?' *Journal of Australian Studies*, vol. 43, no. 1 (2019), pp. 1–6; Fiona McLachlan, 'It's Boom Time! (again): Progress narratives and women's sport in Australia', *Journal of Australian Studies*, vol. 43, no. 2 (2019), pp. 7–21.

3 Toni Bruce, 'New Rules for New Times: Sportswomen and media representation in the third wave', *Sex Roles*, vol. 74, nos 7–8 (2016), pp. 361–76.

4 John Fry, Daniel Bloyce and Ian Pritchard, 'Professional Golf – a License to Spend Money? Issues of money in the lives of touring professional golfers', *Journal of Sport & Social Issues*, vol. 39, no. 3 (2015), pp. 179–201.

5 Todd W. Crosset, *Outsiders in the Clubhouse: The world of women's professional golf* (Albany, NY: State University of New York Press, 1995).

6 'New World Order', *Golf World*, March 2019, pp. 9–11.

7 Kitrina Douglas and David Carless, *Women Professional Tournament Golfers: A research project undertaken for UK Sport* (London: UK Sport, 2006).

8 Mary Jo Kane, 'The Better Sportswomen Get, the More the Media Ignore Them', *Communication & Sport*, vol. 1, no. 3 (2013), pp. 231–6.

9 Toni Bruce, 'Assessing the Sociology of Sport: On media and representations of sportswomen', *International Review for the Sociology of Sport*, vol. 50, nos 4–5 (2015), pp. 380–4.

10 Jennifer McClearen, 'Introduction: Women in sports media: new scholarly engagements', *Feminist Media Studies*, vol. 18, no. 6 (2018), pp. 942–6; Jack Black and Beth Fielding-Lloyd, 'Re-establishing the "Outsiders": English press coverage of the 2015 FIFA Women's World Cup', *International Review for the Sociology of Sport*, vol. 53, no. 4 (2019), pp. 282–301.

11 Ciarán Dunne, 'An Examination of the Photographic Coverage of Sportswomen in the Irish Print Media: A study of an Irish broadsheet newspaper', *Sport in Society*, vol. 20, no. 11 (2017), pp. 1780–98.

12 See Kay Biscomb and Gerald Griggs, '"A splendid effort!" Print media reporting of England's women's performance in the 2009 Cricket World Cup', *International Review for the Sociology of Sport*, vol. 48, no. 1 (2013), pp. 99–111; Ali Bowes and Niamh Kitching, '"Battle of the sixes": Investigating print media representations of female professional golfers competing in a men's tour event', *International Review for the Sociology of Sport*, April 2019, DOI: 10.1177/1012690219842544, pp. 1–21; Kate Petty and Stacey Pope, 'A New Age for Media Coverage of Women's Sport? An analysis of English media coverage of the 2015 FIFA women's world cup', *Sociology*, vol. 53, no. 3 (2019), pp. 486–502.

13 Katie Liston and Niamh Kitching, '"Our wee country": National identity, golf and "Ireland"', *Sport in Society*, March 2019, DOI: 10.1080/17430437.2019.1584186, pp. 1–16.

14 Emma Wensing and Toni Bruce, 'Bending the Rules: Media representations of gender during an international sporting event', *International Review for the Sociology of Sport*, vol. 38, no. 4 (2003), pp. 387–96.

15 See Toni Bruce, 'Women, Sport and the Media: A complex terrain', in Camilla Obel, Toni Bruce and Shona Thompson (eds), *Outstanding Research About Women and Sport in New Zealand* (Hamilton, New Zealand: Wilf Malcolm Institute of Educational Research, 2008), p. 66; and later, Bruce, 'Assessing the Sociology of Sport'.

16 Marcus Free, '"He is my strength and my shield": The antinomies of Katie Taylor as female sporting celebrity in twenty-first-century Ireland', *Sport in Society*, vol. 18, no. 10 (2015), p. 1157.

17 Alan Bairner, 'Political Unionism and Sporting Nationalism: An examination of the relationship between sport and national identity within the Ulster Unionist tradition', *Identities: Global Studies in Culture and Power*, vol. 10, no. 4 (2003), pp. 517–35.

18 Andrew Billings, James Angelini and Susan Eastman, 'Wie Shock: Television commentary about playing on the PGA and LPGA tours', *Howard Journal of Communications*, vol. 19, no. 1 (2008), pp. 64; Andrew Billings, Caroline Craig, Robert Croce, Kristian Cross, Kathryn Moore, William Vigodsky and Victoria Watson, '"Just one of the guys?" Network depictions of Annika Sorenstam in the 2003 PGA Colonial Tournament', *Journal of Sport & Social Issues*, vol. 30, no. 1 (2006), pp. 107–14.

19 Kay Maas and Cynthia Hasbrook, 'Media Promotion of the Paradigm Citizen/Golfer: An analysis of golf magazines' representations of disability, gender and age', *Sociology of Sport Journal*, no. 18 (2001), pp. 21–36; Nicolas Apostolis and Audrey R. Giles, 'Portrayals of Women Golfers in the 2008 Issues of *Golf Digest*', *Sociology of Sport Journal*, vol. 28, no. 2 (2011), pp. 226–38.

20 Andrew C. Billings, James R. Angelini and Susan Tyler Eastman, 'Diverging Discourses: Gender differences in televised golf announcing', *Mass Communication and Society*, vol. 8, no. 2 (2005), pp. 155–71.

21 Billings et al., '"Just one of the guys?"'

22 Bowes and Kitching, '"Battle of the sixes"'.

23 Niamh Kitching, 'Women in Golf: A critical reflection', in Martin Toms (ed.), *Routledge International Handbook of Golf Science* (London: Routledge, 2017).

24 Stacey Mitchell, Jacquelyn Allen-Collinson and Adam Evans, '"Ladies present!": An auto/ethnographic study of women amateur golfers at an English provincial golf club', *Qualitative Research in Sport, Exercise & Health*, vol. 8, no. 3 (2016), pp. 273–86; David Nylund, 'Taking a Slice at Sexism: The controversy over the exclusionary membership practices of the Augusta National Golf Club', *Journal of Sport & Social Issues*, vol. 27, no. 2 (2003), pp. 195–202.

25 Niamh Kitching, Jonathan Grix and Lesley Phillpotts, 'Shifting Hegemony in "a Man's World": Incremental change for female golf professional employment', *Sport in Society*, vol. 20, no. 11 (2017), pp. 1530–47.

26 Crosset, 'Outsiders in the Clubhouse'.

27 Dunja Antunovic and Erin Whiteside, 'Feminist Sport Media Studies: State of the field', in Dustin Harp, Jaime Loke and Ingrid Bachmann (eds),

Feminist Approaches to Media Theory and Research (Basingstoke: Palgrave Macmillan, 2018), p. 112.

28 Susan Birrell, 'Feminist Theories for Sport', in Jay Coakley and Eric Dunning (eds), *Handbook of Sports Studies* (London: Sage Publications, 2000), pp. 61–76.

29 Specific to Ireland, see Free, 'Katie Taylor as a Female Sporting Celebrity' and Dunne, 'An Examination of the Photographic Coverage of Sportswomen in the Irish Print Media'. More broadly, see Kay Biscomb and Hilary Matheson, 'Are the Times Changing Enough? Print media trends across four decades', *International Review for the Sociology of Sport*, vol. 54, no. 3 (2017), pp. 259–81; for golf, see Bowes and Kitching, '"Battle of the sixes"'; Maas and Hasbrook, 'Media Promotion of the Paradigm Citizen/Golfer', and Apostolis and Giles, 'Portrayals of Women Golfers'.

30 Victoria Braun and Victoria Clarke, 'Using Thematic Analysis in Psychology', *Qualitative Research in Psychology*, vol. 3, no. 2 (2006), pp. 77–101.

31 Ruaidhrí Croke, 'Leona Notches Up Another Milestone', *Irish Times*, 2 February 2018.

32 Barry Lennon, 'Maguire Bides Time to Stay Top of the Tree', *Irish Independent*, 2 January 2018.

33 Croke, 'Leona Notches Up Another Milestone'.

34 Brian Keogh, '"The Dream Is to Be the Best Player in the World": Maguires on different paths but both have same lofty goals in the pro game", *Irish Independent*, 7 June 2018.

35 Brian Keogh, 'Maguire Eyes US Open Pro Debut', *Irish Independent*, 18 April 2018.

36 Brian Keogh, 'Maguire Switching Focus to Europe After Falling Short in Florida', *Irish Independent*, 20 October 2018.

37 Brian Keogh, 'Inside Lines: Maguire taking to tour life as a pro', *Irish Independent*, 19 June 2018.

38 Brian Keogh, 'McIlroy Forced to Grind It Out on Windy Opening Day in Boston', *Irish Independent*, 1 September 2018.

39 Philip Reid, 'Maguire Holds Nerve to Win Full Tour Card; Cavan woman wins at first hole of playoff after marathon five rounds of play', *Irish Times*, 21 December 2018.

40 Brian Keogh, 'Maguire Full of Confidence as She Chases European Card', *Irish Independent*, 15 December 2018; Philip Reid, 'Maguire Two Shots Off the Lead in Morocco', *Irish Times*, 18 December 2018.

41 Brian Keogh, 'Maguire Holds Nerve to Claim Tour Card in Tense Play-off', *Irish Independent*, 21 December 2018.

42 Billings et al., '"Just one of the guys"'.

43 Bowes and Kitching, '"Battle of the sixes"'.

44 Kenny Archer, 'Stephanie Meadow First Female Winner of Irish Golf Writers' Professional Award', *Irish News*, 15 December 2018; Kenny Archer, 'Sunny Stephanie Meadow Is Ready to Rise and Shine Again', *Irish News*, 22 December 2018; Philip Reid, 'Maguire in Touch as Law Leads in Style', *Irish Times*, 19 December 2018.

45 James O'Connor, 'Maguires Seal Sponsorship Double Ahead of Pro Debut', *Irish Examiner*, 7 June 2018.

46 John Harris, Lee Sangkwon and Mark Lyberger, 'The Ryder Cup, national identities and team USA', *Sport in Society*, vol. 20, no. 3 (2015), pp. 413–27.

47 Philip Reid, 'Attracting More Women is Crucial for Growth of Golf', *Irish Times*, 1 March 2018; Brian Keogh, 'Mickelson Says Sorry as McIlroy Calls Fallout "Massive Overreaction"' *Irish Independent*, 21 June 2018; 'Irish Quartet Get Set for Fulford Test', *Irish Independent*, 26 April 2018.

48 Brian Keogh, 'Power of One: Family golf is key to the future as Golf Ireland takes a positive step to make sport more inclusive', *Irish Independent*, 8 February 2018.

49 Philip Reid, 'Five Things to Watch for in 2018: Leona is primed for the challenge of the professional ranks', *Irish Times*, 2 January 2018.

50 Free, 'Katie Taylor as a Female Sporting Celebrity', p. 1156.

51 Lennon, 'Maguire Bides Time'.

52 O'Connor, 'Maguires Seal Sponsorship Double'; Philip Reid, 'Maguires Ready for Professional Debuts', *Irish Times*, 7 June 2018; Keogh, 'The Dream Is to Be the Best Player in the World'.

53 Reid, 'Five Things to Watch for in 2018'.

54 Reid, 'Maguires Ready for Professional Debuts'.

55 Keogh, '"The Dream Is to Be the Best Player in the World"'; Brian Keogh, 'Maguire Twins Ready to Make Big Impact in the Golfing World', *Belfast Telegraph*, 7 June 2018.

56 Niamh Kitching, *'Practice' Makes Perfect: Locating young people in golf club culture* (Limerick: University of Limerick, 2011).

57 Kathleen Lynch and Anne Lodge, *Equality and Power in Schools: Redistribution, recognition and representation* (London: Routledge Falmer, 2002).

58 Bruce, 'New Rules for New Times'.

59 Qualifying school is a series of qualifying tournaments in which a fixed number of players earn membership to a professional golf tour. In this case, to earn playing rights with the LPGA tour and entry into tournaments for the 2019 season, Maguire had to navigate a three-stage qualifying process in the US in November (she failed to make the final stage). To earn playing rights with the LET tour and entry into tournaments for the 2019 season, Maguire had to navigate a two-stage qualifying process in Morocco in December (in which she was successful in gaining a tour card).

60 Keogh, 'Mickelson Says Sorry'.

61 Brian Keogh, 'Rain Dance for Rose as McIlroy Sits Tight in Philly', *Irish Independent*, 10 September 2018.

62 Of the 542 words in the article, 418 were on Maguire: Ruaidhrí Croke, 'Leona Maguire's LPGA Hopes Ended by a Single Shot', *Irish Times*, 20 October 2018.

63 Of the 797 words in the article, only forty-five were on Maguire: Brian Keogh, 'McIlroy Forced to Grind It Out on Windy Opening Day in Boston', *Irish Independent*, 1 September 2018.

64 Crosset, 'Outsiders in the Clubhouse', p. 122.

65 Brian Keogh, 'Top 10 Finish for Leona Maguire at Hilton Head', *Irish Independent*, 8 March 2018.

66 Bruce, 'New Rules for New Times'.

67 Reid, 'Attracting More Women', *Sunday Independent*, 22 April 2018; anon., 'Connelly Success No More Than He Deserves', *Sunday Independent*, 22 April 2018.

68 Nathalie Koivula, 'Gender Stereotyping in Televised Media Sport Coverage', *Sex Roles*, no. 41 (1999), pp. 589–604.

69 See Wensing and Bruce, 'Bending the Rules'; Bruce, 'Women, Sport and the Media'; Ali Bowes and Alan Bairner, 'England's Proxy Warriors? Women, war and sport', *International Review for the Sociology of Sport*, vol. 53, no. 4 (2018), pp. 393–410.

70 Liston and Kitching, '"Our wee country"'.

71 Bowes and Kitching, '"Battle of the sixes"'.

72 Bruce, 'New Rules for New Times'.

Chapter 10. Women, Media and Sport in Ireland: A round-table discussion

1 In July 2018 Ireland's 4 x 100-metre women's relay team won silver at the World Athletics Championships (under 20s).

2 The appointees have the status of observers only, but with no right to vote.

3 O'Donoghue has had extensive civil service experience over many years. In April 2019 she was appointed to the Football Association of Ireland governance review group, formed after the fallout from revelations concerning the management of finances by the chief executive.

4 Sarah Keane was elected president of the Olympic Council (now Federation) of Ireland in February 2017, having previously served as CEO of Swim Ireland.

5 Sally Jones, 'Breaking Glass Ceiling Into Sports Broadcasting as a Woman Was Not Without Pitfalls', *Telegraph*, 16 May 2019.

6 Following publication of a picture of Harris in action, she was subjected to extensive misogynistic abuse online; see ABC News, https://www.abc.net.au/news/2019-03-20/tayla-harris-felt-sexually-abused-aflw-photo-trolls-seven/10919008 (accessed 29 May 2019).

7 A reference to a pilot programme established by a leadership group within the Ladies Gaelic Football Association (LGFA) in 2018. It was aimed at encouraging more girls/women to take up roles: as coaches, in the media, as administrators and as officials. Both Liston and Hurley are involved, as a member of the group charged with designing a leadership policy for the LGFA and as a mentor of a programme participant respectively.

8 These are nicknames for the Cork camogie/ladies Gaelic-football and Dublin ladies Gaelic-football teams respectively.

9 The England women's rugby team.

10 The Silver Ferns are the New Zealand women's netball team. The Black Ferns are the rugby team.

11 In April 2017 the Republic of Ireland women's soccer team held a press conference to complain about the substandard conditions they had been subjected to. See 'In Quotes: Irish women's soccer team press conference', *Irish Times*, 5 April 2017.

Chapter 11. The GAA and Sky Sports, 2014–17

1   I declare that I am a former employee of RTÉ where I worked as a reporter for the 'Prime Time' programme and I continue to do occasional work for RTÉ. I have also worked for the GAA and am a lifelong, active member.

2   Michael Moynihan, *GAAconomics: The secret life of money in the GAA* (Dublin: Gill & MacMillan, 2013. Kindle edition), ch. 16, loc. 1665.

3   'Sky Sports Buys Exclusive Rights to 14 GAA Matches', *Irish Times*, 1 April 2014.

4   Colm Keys, 'GAA Faces Backlash Over Sky Sports Deal', *Irish Independent*, 2 April 2019; and 'Gaelic Football and Hurling's Ruling Body Accused of Selling its Soul to Sky', *Guardian*, 15 April 2014.

5   *Limerick Leader*, 10 April 2014.

6   'GAA's Sky Deal is a Thundering Disgrace', *Limerick Leader*, 10 April 2014.

7   Paul Rouse, 'Dark Clouds Still Surround the GAA's Deal with Sky', *Irish Examiner*, 16 December 2016.

8   'Communications Committee to Meet GAA on Sky Sports Deal', Houses of the Oireachtas, https://www.oireachtas.ie/en/press-centre/press-releases/20140414-communications-committee-to-meet-gaa-on-sky-sports-deal/ (accessed 13 February 2020).

9   'GPA: Players won't be paid for Sky interviews', *Irish Independent*, 2 April 2014.

10 See, for example, Martin Breheny, 'RTÉ Hysteria Fails to Spark Sky Backlash', *Irish Independent*, 21 May 2014.

11 Seán Moran, 'Playoff Takes Uncertain Twist', *Irish Times*, 14 April 2007.

12 'Joint Committee on Transport and Communications – Tuesday, 15 April 2014', Houses of the Oireachtas, https://www.oireachtas.ie/en/debates/debate/joint_committee_on_transport_and_communications/2014-04-15/ (accessed 13 February 2020).

13 GAAGO is a paid-for service provided by the GAA and RTÉ (the precise ownership of the shared nature of this venture is not disclosed) showing GAA games to subscribers outside the Republic of Ireland via the Internet. Subscribers can watch games in high definition on a desktop computer, laptop, tablet or mobile device through video streaming. From 2014–17 GAAGO had rights to the 100-plus games, including studio presentation and analysis, televised by RTÉ, TG4, Setanta Sports and Sky Sports during the 2015 GAA season. This included any replays televised by those channels. Games available included all GAA championship and Allianz League matches as televised in Ireland, and selected club, under-21 and minor games. The cost of the service to consumers for the 2015 season was €160. Neither RTÉ nor the GAA were prepared to release the precise number of subscribers for GAAGO, except to say that it had subscribers in 157 countries by the end of 2014 and that its top three markets were North America, Britain and Australia.

14 Due to rights restrictions, games broadcast by Sky Sports (including All-Ireland quarter-finals, semi-finals and finals) are not available on GAAGO in Britain. Accordingly, the price for subscribers in Britain is €100.

15 See, for example, Martin Breheny, 'GAA Earn Just €356,000 in Extra Revenue from Sky Link-up', *Irish Independent*, 5 February 2015. In its annual financial report for 2014, the media income was negligible in the

context of the GAA's overall finances, at €10.44 million, compared with €10.9 million in 2013. See Ian O'Riordan, 'Dublin Claiming the Bulk of GAA's Development Funds', *Irish Times*, 5 February 2015.

16 'Joint Committee on Transport and Communications Debate – Tuesday, 15 April 2014'.
17 'Gaelic Games Exclusive to GAAGO in 2015', *Irish Echo*, 28 January 2015.
18 'Joint Committee on Transport and Communications Debate – Tuesday, 15 April 2014'.
19 For the precise number of Sky TV customers, see *Sky Annual Report 2014*, http://www.annualreports.com/HostedData/AnnualReportArchive/b/LSE_BSY_2014.pdf (accessed 13 February 2020).
20 When a deal announcing this coverage was unveiled by the then GAA president, Christy Cooney, in 2010 – along with deals to show games live on TV in Africa, Asia, Australia and America – he said, 'Our overseas units and their continued passion for our games form a vital strand of the GAA given the large and vibrant Irish communities that are dotted across the globe. I look forward to the provision of a service that will allow so many of our members and supporters follow top level action this coming summer and into the future'. See 'GAA International Viewing This Summer', Gaelic Sports Cast, 29 April 2010, http://www.gaelicsportscast.com/2010/04/29/gaa-international-viewing-this-summer/ (accessed 13 February 2020).
21 See Sky TV, http://www.sky.com/products/sky-tv/sports/.
22 See, for example, Richard Giulianotti and Roland Robertson, *Globalization and Sport* (London: Wiley-Blackwell, 2009), *passim*.
23 Wladimir Andreff, 'Globalization of the Sports Economy', *Rivista Di Diritto Ed Economia Dello Sport*, vol. 4, no. 3 (2008), p. 16.
24 See, for example, *Freeman's Journal*, 5 May 1888.
25 Seán Moran, 'GAA Boss Liam O'Neill Critical of RTÉ's Coverage of Association's New Deal with Sky', *Irish Times*, 3 April 2014.
26 'Joint Committee on Transport and Communications Debate – Tuesday, 15 April 2014'.
27 Ibid.
28 Paul Rouse, 'The Impact of Pay TV on Sport', Working Papers in History and Policy no. 4 (2012), History Hub, http://historyhub.ie/the-impact-of-pay-tv-on-sport (accessed 13 February 2020).
29 Seán Moran, 'Boothman Regrets Continuation of the Ban', *Irish Times*, 14 April 1997.
30 Moynihan, *GAAconomics*, ch. 16, loc. 1678.
31 Gaelic Athletic Association, *Official Guide: Containing the constitution and rules of the G.A.A., revised and corrected up to date, and published by authority of the Central Council* (Dublin: Gaelic Athletic Association, 2018), p. 215.
32 Ibid., p. 5.
33 'Sky Sports Buys Exclusive Rights to 14 GAA Matches', *Irish Times*, 1 April 2014.
34 The viewing figures quoted in this section have been sourced from official television-ratings agencies, broadcasters and public-relations firms. The ratings in Ireland are produced by TAM Ireland (Television Audience Measurement Ireland Ltd), which oversees an audience-measurement system for the whole of the television-advertising industry. TAM Ireland is

made up of the majority of commercial broadcasters operating in Ireland (RTÉ, Virgin Media Solutions, TG4, Channel 4, SKY Ireland, Viacom and Eir Sport) and the principal Irish media-buying agencies. It commissions Nielsen TV Audience Measurement to carry out the actual measurement service. Ratings in the UK are produced by the Broadcasters' Audience Research Board (BARB). BARB was set up in 1981 to provide the industry-standard television-audience measurement service for broadcasters and the advertising industry. It is owned by BBC, ITV, Channel 4, Channel 5, BSkyB and the IPA (Institute of Practitioners in Advertising). For BARB ratings, see www.barb.co.uk.

35 John Fogarty, 'Sky Deal Good for the GAA', *Irish Examiner*, 24 December 2014.
36 Sky has not released the number of Sky Sports HD subscribers in Ireland.
37 Gaelic Athletic Association, *An Chomhdháil Bhliantúil 2015* (Dublin: Gaelic Athletic Association, 2015), pp. 36–8.
38 I spoke to a small number of county-board officials, club officials and club players based in London, the Midlands and in Manchester. None knew of any player drawn to the GAA having been enticed by seeing the game on Sky Sports.
39 Gaelic Athletic Association, *An Chomhdháil Bhliantúil 2015*.
40 AGB Nielsen Media Research, 31 March 2007 and 1 April 2006.
41 Sean Ingle, 'Fall in Sky Ashes Viewing Figures Leaves English Cricket Facing Stark Choices', *Guardian*, 12 July 2015.
42 Gaelic Athletic Association, *An Chomhdháil Bhliantúil 2015*.
43 Paul Rouse, 'GAA's Money-driven Sky Sports Ambitions Would Alienate members', *Irish Examiner*, 3 March 2016.

Chapter 12. A Level Playing Field? Irish broadcast-sports rights and the decline of the national

1 See David Rowe, Graeme Turner and Emma Waterton, *Making Culture: Commercialisation, transnationalism, and the state of 'nationing' in contemporary Australia* (London: Routledge, 2018).
2 See Rex Cathcart, 'Broadcasting the Early Decades', in Brian Farrell (ed.), *Communications and Community in Ireland* (Cork: Cork University Press, 1984), p. 4.
3 Cited in ibid., p. 41.
4 Cited in Richard Pine, *2RN and the Origins of Irish Radio: Broadcasting and Irish society* (Dublin: Four Courts Press, 2002), p. 147.
5 See Alan Bairner, *Sport, Nationalism and Globalisation* (Albany, NY: State of New York Press, 2001), p. 79.
6 Pine, *2RN and the Origins of Irish Radio*, p. 172.
7 See Luke Gibbons, 'From Megalith to Megastore: Broadcasting and Irish culture', in idem, *Transformations in Irish Culture* (Cork: Cork University Press, 1996), p. 73.
8 Pine, *2RN and the Origins of Irish Radio*, p. 175.
9 Bairner, *Sport, Nationalism and Globalisation*, p. 72.
10 Ibid.
11 See Media Intelligence Unit, 'Funding of Public Service Media 2018' (European Broadcasting Union, 2018).

12 Media Live, http://www.medialive.ie/index.php?option=com_content&view=article&id=954:channel-share-of-viewing-2010-2017&catid=93&Itemid=349 (accessed 11 June 2019).

13 See John Horgan and Roddy Flynn, *Irish Media: A critical history*, 2nd rev. edn (Dublin: Four Courts Press, 2017), p. 210.

14 Roderick Flynn, 'Neo-liberalism and Irish Broadcasting', in Peadar Kirby, Luke Gibbons and Michael Cronin (eds), *Reinventing Ireland: Culture and the Celtic Tiger* (London: Pluto Press, 2002), p. 165.

15 See Andy Pollak, 'Making Hay While the Soccer Shines', *Irish Times*, 1 June 1990.

16 See Jill Kerby, 'Ready to Buy a Piece of World Cup Action', *Irish Times*, 11 April 1990.

17 See Peter Byrne, 'Threat of TV Blackout for NI Match', *Irish Times*, 21 October 1993.

18 See Dermot Gilleece, 'A Revolution in Sports Coverage', *Irish Times*, 3 October 1994.

19 See Dermot Gilleece, 'Choice Was Never Greater', *Irish Times*, 3 October 1994.

20 There was some speculation that it may have been as much as ten times greater than RTÉ's offer. See Cliona Foley, 'Panic in RTÉ as Setanta Close In', *Irish Independent*, 29 June 2006.

21 See Seán Moran, 'RTE Swing Three-year All-Ireland Series Deal', *Irish Times*, 3 March 2005.

22 See Tom Evens, Petros Iosifidis and Paul Smith, *The Political Economy of Television Sports Rights*, Palgrave Global Media Policy and Business Series (Basingstoke: Palgrave MacMillan, 2013).

23 Kirsty Blake-Knox and Joyce Fegan, 'TV3 Outbids RTÉ for Rugby World Cup 2015', *Irish Independent*, 15 April 2014.

24 Lauren Feiner, 'Comcast Stock Rises After an Earnings Beat', CNBC, https://www.cnbc.com/2019/01/23/comcast-earnings-q4-2018.html (accessed 11 June 2019).

25 'Liberty Global Form 10-K Securities and Exchange Commission (SEC) Filing for the Year Ended 31 December 2018', p. II-4, 27 February 2019, https://libertyglobal.gcs-web.com/static-files/dd8cfb84-17a6-40ff-bc0b-131f44a95d2b (accessed 11 June 2019).

26 Iliad, '2018: A Year of Transformation; 2019: A New Cycle of Growth and Innovation', press release, Iliad, 19 March 2019, https://www.iliad.fr/finances/2019/CP_190319_Eng.pdf (accessed 11 June 2019).

27 RTÉ annual reports, 2007–17.

28 Media Live, http://www.medialive.ie/index.php?option=com_content&view=article&id=923:2017-mar-top-tv-progs&catid=62&Itemid=336 (accessed 11 June 2019).

29 'Over 1 Million People Watched the Nail-biting Conclusion of Ireland's All Blacks Win', Journal.ie, 19 November 2018, https://www.the42.ie/ireland-all-blacks-tv-audience-rte-4347319-Nov2018/ (accessed 11 June 2019).

30 'Over 1.4 Million Viewers Tune in for Ireland's Six Nations Defeat to England on Virgin Media One', Irish Film and Television Network, http://iftn.ie/broadcast/news/?act1=record&only=1&aid=73&rid=4292511&tpl=archnews&force=1 (accessed 11 June 2019).

31 Media Live, http://www.medialive.ie/index.php?option=com_content&view=article&id=1012:february-2019-top-tv-programmes&catid=62:top-monthly-programmes&Itemid=336 (accessed 11 June 2019).

32 See Harry Arne Solberg, 'Commentary: Sports broadcasting: Is it a job for public service broadcasters? A welfare economic perspective', *Journal of Media Economics*, vol. 20, no. 4 (2007), pp. 289–309.

33 Evens et al., *The Political Economy of Television Sports Rights*, p. 3.

34 Ibid., p. 71.

35 Ibid., p. 72.

36 See Allan Brown, 'Economics, Public Service Broadcasting, and Social Values', *Journal of Media Economics*, vol. 9, no. 1 (1996), pp. 3–15.

37 See Marcus Free, 'Keeping Them Under Pressure: Masculinity, narratives of national regeneration and the Republic of Ireland soccer team', *Sport in History*, vol. 2, no. 2 (2006), pp. 265–88.

Chapter 13. 'Talking broken biscuits': Irish Liverpool fans and The Anfield Wrap

1 While there may not be data to indicate exact figures of Irish football fans travelling abroad weekly, various reports have estimated that Manchester United and Liverpool have a significantly larger Irish fanbase than other English Premier League clubs. See Seán Flynn, 'List of Ireland's Favourite Premier League Teams by City', Sports News Ireland, https://www.sportsnewsireland.com/soccer/soccer_irish/list-of-irelands-favourite-premier-league-teams-by-city-according-to-total-facebook-followers, 2017 (accessed 3 April 2019).

2 Keith Falkiner, *Emerald Anfield: The Irish and Liverpool FC* (Dublin: Hachette Books, 2010).

3 Interview with author, 2018.

4 Media Live, http://www.medialive.ie/index.php?option=com_content&view=article&id=683:2005-may-top-monthly-tv-progs&catid=62&Itemid=336 (accessed 13 December 2018).

5 Paul Wilson, Brian Oliver and Kaz Mochlinski, 'The Miracle of Istanbul', *Guardian*, 29 May 2005.

6 Steve Hunter, '10 Unforgettable European Nights at Anfield', Liverpool Football Club, https://www.liverpoolfc.com/news/features/328992-top-10-nights-liverpool-europe-anfield, 2018 (accessed 17 January 2019).

7 Jason Burt, 'Liverpool Have a Glorious Chance to Use the Power of Anfield to Take the Next Step', *Telegraph*, 23 April 2018.

8 While not the original upload, a copy is available to view on YouTube: https://www.youtube.com/watch?v=RrXaBZh9QsI (accessed 2 April 2019).

9 Yair Galily, 'When the Medium Becomes "Well Done": Sport, television and technology in the twenty-first century', *Television & New Media*, vol. 15, no. 8 (2014), pp. 717–24.

10 John Fiske, 'The Cultural Economy of Fandom', in L.A. Lewis (ed.), *The Adoring Audience: Fan culture and popular media* (London: Routledge, 1992).

11 Slash fiction originates in *Star Trek* fan-fiction works that sexualised the relationship between the characters Kirk and Spock (K/S). See Henry

Jenkins, *Textual Poachers: Television fans and participatory culture* (New York: Routledge, 1992).

12 The title *The Pink* is a firm nod to the traditional post-match publications that newspapers such as the *Liverpool Echo* quickly and cheaply assembled in order for fans to get an almost immediate press reaction. TAW has since retitled the programme *The Post Match Show*.

13 Interview with author, 2017.

14 Frequently, TAW articles and podcasts will refer to the match experience as 'going the match' or 'going the game', excluding the preposition 'to'. For example: James Dutton '10 Years Ago Today: Liverpool 2-1 Arsenal', The Anfield Wrap, https://www.theanfieldwrap.com/2014/11/10-years-ago-today-liverpool-2-1-arsenal/, 2014 (accessed 15 April 2019).

15 Garry Whannel, 'Television and the Transformation of Sport', *Annals of the American Academy of Political and Social Science*, vol. 625, no. 1 (2009), pp. 205–18.

16 M.M. Bakhtin, *Rabelais and His World*, trans. H. Iswolsky [1984] (Bloomington, IN: Indiana University Press, 1968).

17 Richard Giulianotti, 'Scotland's Tartan Army in Italy: The case for the carnivalesque', *Sociological Review*, vol. 39, no. 3 (1991), pp. 503–27.

18 John Fiske, *Understanding Popular Culture* (London: Routledge, 1989), pp. 81–2.

19 Bakhtin, *Rabelais and His World*, p. 110.

20 Interview with author, 2017.

21 Interview with author, 2018.

22 John Belchem, *Irish, Catholic and Scouse: The history of the Liverpool-Irish, 1800–1939* (Liverpool: Liverpool University Press, 2007).

23 Falkiner, *Emerald Anfield*, pp. 11–19.

24 Ibid., p. 188.

25 James Wyllie, Kath Woodward and David Goldblatt, 'Tuning in to Football on the BBC World Service', *Soccer & Society*, vol. 12, no. 1 (2011), pp. 11–20.

26 Matti Goksøyr and Hans Hognestad, 'No Longer Worlds Apart? British influences and Norwegian football', in Gary Armstrong and Richard Giulianotti (eds), *Football Cultures and Identities* (Basingstoke: Macmillan, 1999).

27 J.R. Norberg, 'Football, Football Pools and the Unexpected Arrival of Sports in Swedish Welfare Politics', *Soccer and Society,* vol. 10, no. 3 (2009), pp. 418–37.

28 Rex Harris, 'Globalised Football Fandom: Scandinavian Liverpool FC supporters', *Football Studies*, vol. 3, no. 2 (2000), pp. 5–23.

29 Grant Farred, 'Long Distance Love: Growing up a Liverpool fan', *Journal of Sport & Social Issues*, vol. 26, no. 1 (2002), pp. 6–24.

30 Fiske, 'Cultural Economy of Fandom'.

31 Richard Haynes, *The Football Imagination: The rise of football fanzine culture* (London: Arena, 1995).

32 Garry Crawford, *Consuming Sport: Fans, sport and culture* (London: Routledge, 2004).

33 Cornel Sandvoss, *A Game of Two Halves: Football, television and globalization* (London: Routledge, 2003), p. 144.

34 Survey response, 2017.

35 Nicholas Quah, 'In Liverpool, a Football Podcast has Grown Into a Real Media Company – Based Mostly on Listener Payment, Not Advertising', NiemanLab, 12 February 2019, https://www.niemanlab.org/2019/02/in-liverpool-a-football-podcast-has-grown-into-a-real-media-company-based-mostly-on-listener-payment-not-advertising/ (accessed 19 March 2019).

36 *Is this the Best Liverpool Team Ever?!: Gary Neville interviews Liverpool fans*, YouTube, https://www.youtube.com/watch?v=52iE8MyyvFo (accessed 16 April 2019).

37 Interview with author, 2017.

38 Richard Giulianotti, 'Supporters, Followers, Fans and Flaneurs: A taxonomy of spectator identities in football', *Journal of Sport and Social Issues*, no. 26 (2002), pp. 25–46.

39 Kevin Dixon, '"A Third Way" for Football Fandom Research: Anthony Giddens and structuration theory', *Soccer and Society*, vol. 12, no. 2 (2011), pp. 279–98.

40 Interview with author, 2018.

41 Ibid.

42 Interview with author, 2017.

43 See Conor Neville, 'The 10 Lies That Irish Premier League Fans Tell Themselves', Balls.ie, 10 September 2015, https://www.balls.ie/football/the-10-lies-that-irish-premier-league-fans-frequently-tell-themselves-268071, 2015 (accessed 15 April 2019).

44 See Paul Fennessy, 'Why Loving Football Is About So Much More Than Just "the League of Ireland v the Premier League"', Journal.ie, 22 February 2017, https://www.the42.ie/league-of-ireland-v-premier-league-opinion-3252695-Feb2017/ (accessed 15 April 2019).

45 Former Republic of Ireland manager Brian Kerr is among those who have campaigned for increased investment in the domestic league. The former Football Association of Ireland chief executive, John Delaney, famously referred to the League of Ireland as a 'difficult child' in 2014. See 'FAI Chief Executive John Delaney: League of Ireland "a difficult child"', RTÉ, 2 October 2014, https://www.rte.ie/sport/soccer/2014/1001/649276-delaney-defends-handling-of-league-of-ireland/, 2014 (accessed 3 April 2019).

46 Daniel McDonnell, 'Fury Over Trapattoni's "there is no league in Ireland" claim', *Irish Independent*, 10 September 2013.

47 Simon Parker, 'The Leaving of Liverpool: Managed decline and the enduring legacy of Thatcherism's urban policy', London School of Economics and Political Science, https://blogs.lse.ac.uk/politicsandpolicy/the-leaving-of-liverpool/, 2019 (accessed 2 April 2019).

48 Patrick Honeybone, 'New-dialect Formation in Nineteenth Century Liverpool: A brief history of Scouse', in Anthony Grant and Clive Grey (eds), *The Mersey Sound: Liverpool's language, people and places* (Liverpool: Open House Press, 2007).

49 Interview with author, 2017.

50 Ibid.

51 Sarah Thornton, *Club Cultures: Music, media and subcultural capital* (Cambridge: Polity, 1995).

52 Interview with author, 2017.

53 Ibid.

Chapter 14. 'Feel the build-up, feel connected': Mediated sport and the second-generation-Irish audience in Britain

1   Paul Darby, 'Gaelic Sport and the Irish Diaspora in Boston, 1879–90', *Irish Historical Studies*, vol. 33, no. 132 (2003), pp. 387–403; Paul Darby and David Hassan, 'Introduction: Locating sport in the study of the Irish diaspora', *Sport in Society*, vol. 10, no. 3 (2007), pp. 333–46; Frances Harkin, '"Where Would We Be Without the GAA?": Gaelic games and Irishness in London', *Irish Studies Review*, vol. 26, no. 1 (2018), pp. 55–66.

2   Stuart Hall, 'The Question of Cultural Identity', in Stuart Hall, David Held and Anthony McGrew (eds), *Modernity and its Futures* (Cambridge, Polity Press, 1992); David Rowe, Jim McKay and Toby Miller, 'Come Together: Sport, nationalism and the media image', in Lawrence A. Wenner (ed.), *Mediasport* (London: Routledge, 1998), pp. 119–33.

3   Second-generation Irish is a term used here for participants born in Britain to an Irish emigrant parent or parents and self-identifying as Irish or part Irish. For a useful discussion of the nuances of meaning around the term, see Catherine Nash, *Of Irish Descent: Origin stories, genealogy, & the politics of belonging* (New York: Syracuse University Press, 2008).

4   Olga Seweryn and Marta Smagacz, 'Frontiers and Identity: Approaches and inspirations in sociology', in Luďa Klusáková and Steven G. Ellis (eds), *Frontiers and Identities: Exploring the research area* (Pisa: Pisa University Press, 2006); John Sugden and Alan Tomlinson, 'Sport, Politics and Identities: Football cultures in comparative perspectives', in Maurice Roche (ed.), *Sport, Popular Culture and Identity* (Oxford: Meyer & Meyer Sport, 2000).

5   David Morley, *Home Territories: Media, mobility and identity* (London & New York: Routledge, 2000).

6   Ibid., p. 11.

7   Andy Ruddock, *Investigating Audiences* (London: Sage, 2007), p. 78.

8   See, for example, Liam Kennedy, Madeleine Lyes and Martin Russell, *Supporting the Next Generation of the Irish Diaspora* (Dublin: University College, Dublin, 2014).

9   Breda Gray, 'Thinking Through Transnational Studies, Diaspora Studies and Gender', in D.A.J. MacPherson and Mary J. Hickman (eds), *Women and Irish Diaspora Identities: Theories, concepts and new perspectives* (Manchester: Manchester University Press, 2014), p. 35.

10 Mary J. Hickman, *Religion, Class and Identity: The state, the Catholic Church and the education of the Irish in Britain* (Aldershot: Avebury, 1997).

11 Bronwen Walter, Sarah Morgan, Mary J. Hickman and Joseph M. Bradley, 'Family Stories, Public Silence: Irish identity construction amongst the second generation Irish in England', *Scottish Geographical Journal*, vol. 118, no. 3 (2002), pp. 201–17.

12 Ann Gray, *Video Playtime: The gendering of a leisure technology* (London: Routledge, 1992). For a discussion of interview-based studies with an ethnographic orientation, see Joke Hermes, *Re-reading Popular Culture* (Oxford: Blackwell, 2005).

13 The study is indebted to the enthusiastic support of many people engaged with the Irish community in Britain who helped spread the word about the project.

14 Kathy Charmaz, *Constructing Grounded Theory*, 2nd edn (London: Sage, 2014).

15 Participants' names have been changed.

16 In his interview, Jack expresses interest in Irish current affairs and history in addition to sport, but the latter was clearly articulated as the primary focus of his Irish-media use. Many participants in the wider study outlined the importance of the availability of RTÉ Radio One on the long-wave frequency, including those, like Jack, who pointed out how a long-wave radio receiver in their cars allowed them access on the move without the costs associated with streaming digital data on a mobile-phone network. RTÉ's 2014 decision to end the long-wave service met considerable resistance among the Irish in Britain, and an ongoing public campaign has forced the broadcaster to maintain the service until at least 2021.

17 The term '*Indo*' is a colloquialism commonly used in Ireland for the *Irish Independent* newspaper.

18 The GAA rented Wembley Stadium for an annual tournament from the late 1950s to the mid-1970s. See, for example, 'Mayo, Offaly, Kilkenny and Cork Teams Depart for Wembley 1970', RTÉ Archives, https://www.rte.ie/archives/2015/0722/716384-gaa-teams-head-to-wembley/ (accessed 5 March 2019).

19 Although Liam refers to long wave here, transmission of RTÉ Radio One on the 252kw long-wave frequency only commenced in 2004. Prior to this, the station would have been accessible in Britain via a medium-wave signal that became weaker the further it travelled from transmitters in Ireland. Hence, it would have been more easily accessible in a location such as Liverpool than in London.

20 Bronwen Walter et al., 'Family Stories'.

21 Joe.ie is an Irish-owned male-orientated lifestyle brand that aims to get its social-media content, which includes sports news and punditry, shared and consumed on social-media platforms. It is currently focused on building on its initial success in Ireland by expanding into the UK, where it has already garnered significant online attention. See Mark Paul, 'Digital Media Founder Seeks Maximum Return from Joe', *Irish Times*, 22 February 2019.

22 *The Sunday Game* is RTÉ's flagship television programme for coverage of Gaelic games, and was first broadcast in 1979. Liam also refers here to the World Cup qualifying rounds prior to the 1994 competition in the US.

23 Sugden and Tomlinson, 'Sport, Politics and Identities'.

24 Mary J. Hickman, Sarah Morgan, Bronwen Walter and Joseph Bradley, 'The Limitations of Whiteness and the Boundaries of Englishness: Second-generation Irish identifications and positionings in multiethnic Britain', *Ethnicities*, vol. 5, no. 2 (2005), pp. 177–8.

25 When Channel 4 was launched in 1982, part of its remit was to be distinctive and cover a wide range of subject matter that would appeal to tastes and interests not generally catered for at the time by ITV. Irish content was part of fulfilling this remit, and included the re-broadcasting of RTÉ's weekly chat show *The Late Late Show* on Monday afternoons in the early 1990s, as well as the coverage of Gaelic games Jack is referring to here. See *Channel 4 Annual Report 2016*, https://annualreport.channel4.com/downloads/The%20remit%20and%20model.pdf (accessed 19 March 2019).

26 The Mayo county team is said to have had a curse put on it by a local priest in the aftermath of its 1951 victory so that it would not win the competition again until all the members of that team had passed away. The story is largely dismissed by GAA players and commentators, however. The website article Jack refers to is Diarmaid Fleming, 'A Fresh Chance to Banish the Curse of Mayo', BBC, 16 September 2016, https://www.bbc.com/news/magazine-37378935 (accessed 13 February 2019).

27 Gray, 'Thinking Through Transnational Studies, Diaspora Studies and Gender', p. 35.

28 Arthur A. Raney, 'Why We Watch and Enjoy Mediated Sports', in Arthur A. Raney and Jennings Bryant (eds), *Handbook of Sports and Media* (Mahwah, New Jersey: Lawrence Erlbaum Associates, 2006), p. 323.

29 The Irish Setanta Group acquired the international rights to a range of live sports content in the early 1990s, including live GAA matches, which it licensed commercially to the Irish pub sector then expanding across Britain.

30 Breda Gray, 'The Irish Diaspora: Globalised belonging(s)', *Irish Journal of Sociology*, vol. 11, no. 2 (2002), pp. 123–44.

31 Martin Mac an Ghaill and Chris Haywood, 'Being Irish and Male in Britain', in Tom Inglis (ed.), *Are the Irish Different?* (Manchester: Manchester University Press, 2014).

32 England, Scotland, Wales and Northern Ireland all failed to qualify for the 1994 World Cup, which also meant there was more interest from the British media in the Republic of Ireland team during the competition than might otherwise have been the case.

33 Paul Gilroy, 'Diaspora and the Detours of Identity', in Kathryn Woodward (ed.), *Identity and Difference* (London: Sage, 1997).

34 Benedict Anderson, *Imagined Communities: Reflections on the origin and spread of nationalism*, rev. edn (London: Verso, 1991).

35 In 2014 the GAA sold the rights to a substantial number of matches to the Sky Sports subscription channel and also entered into a partnership with RTÉ to provide 'pay-per-view' and subscription-based access via an international Internet streaming service branded as GAAGO. The interviews discussed here were conducted in 2015 and 2016.

Chapter 15. James McClean's Poppy Protest and the Cultural Politics of Diasporic Non-assimilation

1 Richard Dyer, *Stars* (London: British Film Institute, 1979), p. 3.

2 Christine Gledhill, 'Introduction', in Christine Gledhill (ed.), *Stardom: Industry of desire* (London & New York: Routledge, 1991), p. xiii.

3 David L. Andrews and Steven J. Jackson, 'Introduction: Sports celebrities, public culture, and private experience', in David L. Andrews and Steven J. Jackson (eds), *Sport Stars: The cultural politics of sporting celebrity* (London: Routledge, 2001), p. 8.

4 While not celebrated for being the most technically gifted player, McClean has often gained plaudits for his physical approach to the game and the bravery he displays in his performances. See, for example, Daniel McDonnell, 'Is This the Tackle That Changed Trap's Mind About James McClean?', *Irish Independent*, 21 February 2012.

5 David Hassan, 'A People Apart: Soccer, identity and Irish nationalists in Northern Ireland', *Soccer & Society*, vol. 3, no. 3 (2002), p. 80.

6 *Football Focus* (BBC 1), 29 April 2017.

7 The players who preceded him were Darron Gibson, Shane Duffy, Marc Wilson, Daniel Kearns and Paul George. See William Nestor, 'Five Things You May Not Know About James McClean', Joe.ie, 11 November 2011, https://www.joe.ie/sport/five-things-you-may-not-know-about-james-mcclean-26580 (accessed 14 February 2020).

8 Scholarly works by Darragh McGee and Alan Bairner (2010) and a recent piece by David Storey (2016), as well as others cited below, thoroughly unpack the intricacies and nuances of footballing identity in Northern Ireland, connections between football and the Troubles, and the cultural politics of player declaration, and have been vital in my thinking through of this topic. See Darragh McGee and Alan Bairner, 'Transcending the Borders of Irish Identity? Narratives of Northern nationalist footballers in Northern Ireland', *International Review for the Sociology of Sport*, vol. 46, no. 4 (2010), pp. 436–55; David Storey, 'Which Boys in Green? Identity issues in Irish soccer', in Colin Howley and Susan Dun (eds), *The Playing Field: Making sense of spaces and places in sporting culture* (Oxford: Inter-Disciplinary Press, 2016).

9 David Hassan, Shane McCullough and Elizabeth Moreland, 'North or South? Darron Gibson and the issue of player eligibility within Irish soccer', *Soccer & Society*, vol. 10, no. 6 (2009), pp. 740–53.

10 Storey, 'Which Boys in Green?'

11 *James McClean Hates the Queen – Lyrics*, YouTube, https://www.youtube.com/watch?v=aLUEJoaNfCI (accessed 28 May 2017).

12 Irene A. Reid, '"An outsider in our midst": Narratives of Neil Lennon, soccer & ethno-religious bigotry in the Scottish press', *Soccer & Society*, vol. 9, no. 1 (2007), pp. 64–80.

13 Gavin McCafferty, '"Fizzing" Neil Lennon Wants Fan Who Hit Him with Coin to Be "Embarrassed and Humiliated"', *Irish Independent*, 1 November 2018.

14 John Price, Neil Farrington and Lee Hall, 'Changing the Game? The impact of Twitter on relationships between football clubs, supporters and the sports media', *Soccer & Society*, vol. 14, no. 4 (2013), p. 458.

15 The importance of such digital-media formats for Irish emigrants abroad has been shown in Diane Negra, Eleanor O'Leary and Anthony P. McIntyre, *Broadcasting Irish Emigration in an Era of Global Mobility* (Dublin: Broadcasting Authority of Ireland, 2018). See also Dan Dwyer's chapter in this collection.

16 Stuart McKinley, '"Colin Murray, get it right": James McClean Reveals Why He Snubbed Northern Ireland', *Belfast Telegraph*, 13 December 2012.

17 *Football Focus* (BBC), 29 April 2017.

18 Phillip Ullah, 'Rhetoric and Ideology in Social Identification: The case of second generation Irish youths', *Discourse & Society*, vol. 1, no. 2 (1990), p. 179.

19 Joe Cleary, *Outrageous Fortune: Capital and culture in modern Ireland* (Dublin, Field Day Publications in association with the Keough-Naughton Institute for Irish Studies at the University of Notre Dame, 2006), p. 277;

James McClean Hates the Queen – Lyrics, YouTube, https://www.youtube.com/watch?v=aLUEJoaNfCI (accessed 28 May 2017).

20 McGee and Bairner, 'Transcending the Borders of Irish Identity?', p. 452.

21 'McClean Pulls Plug on Lincoln Switch', RTÉ, 27 November 2009, https://www.rte.ie/sport/soccer/2009/1127/257906-mcleanj/ (accessed 14 February 2020).

22 Anne Jerslev and Mette Mortensen, 'Celebrity in the Social Media Age: Renegotiating the public and the private', in Anthony Elliot (ed.), *Routledge Handbook of Celebrity Studies* (London & New York: Routledge, 2018), p. 157.

23 David Morley, *Home Territories: Media, mobility and identity* (London & New York: Routledge, 2000), p. 3.

24 David Morley, 'Domesticating Dislocation in a World of "New" Technology', in Chris Berry, So-yŏng Kim and Lynn Spigel (eds), *Electronic Elsewheres: Media, technology, and the experience of social space* (Minneapolis & London: University of Minnesota Press, 2010), pp. 3, 5.

25 Hassan, 'A People Apart', p. 69.

26 Conor Curran, *Irish Soccer Migrants: A social and cultural history* (Cork: Cork University Press, 2017). See also Curran's chapter in this collection.

27 James Dawson, 'A Large Minority of Young People Will Not Wear a Poppy This Year', LADBible, 2 November 2017, https://www.ladbible.com/news/news-a-large-minority-of-young-people-will-not-wear-a-poppy-this-year-20171102, (accessed 14 February 2020).

28 John Kelly, 'Popular Culture, Sport and the "Hero"-ification of British Militarism', *Sociology*, vol. 47, no. 4 (2012), pp. 722–38; Daniel Fitzpatrick, '"Football Remembers": The invention of the poppy in British football', research paper delivered at Football, Politics and Popular Culture Conference, University of Limerick, 23 November 2017.

29 Alex Smith, 'Nemanja Matic Explains Why He Won't Wear a Poppy', *Irish Mirror*, 5 November 2018.

30 Martin Samuel, 'How the FA Tied Themselves in Knots over Pep's Ribbon', *Daily Mail Online*, 26 February 2018.

31 Michael Hann, 'Wearing a Poppy Is Only Meaningful If It's Voluntary', *Guardian*, 1 November 2016.

32 A useful account of the cultural power of male melancholia can be found in Tania Modleski, 'Clint Eastwood and Male Weepies', *American Literary History*, vol. 22, no. 1 (2009), pp. 136–58.

33 For a seminal account of this representational trope, see John Hill, 'Images of Violence', in Kevin Rockett, John Hill and Luke Gibbons (eds), *Cinema and Ireland* (London & New York: Routledge, 1987), pp. 147–52.

34 John Domokos, 'Stokies Strike Back: The Potteries people scotching their "Brexit Capital" rep', *Guardian*, 9 January 2018.

35 Svetlana Boym, *The Future of Nostalgia* (New York: Basic Books, 2001), p. 41.

36 Tom Embury-Dennis, 'James McClean Quotes Bobby Sands at "Cavemen" Who Booed Him for Not Wearing Poppy', *Irish Independent*, 5 November 2018.

37 P. David Marshall, *Celebrity and Power: Fame in contemporary culture* (Minneapolis & London: University of Minnesota Press, 1997), p. 47.

Concluding Remarks

1 John Price, Neil Farrington and Lee Hall, 'Changing the Game? The impact of Twitter on relationships between football clubs, supporters and the sports media', *Soccer & Society*, vol. 14, no. 4 (2013), pp. 446–61.
2 Edward Brennan, *A Post-nationalist History of Television in Ireland* (Basingstoke: Palgrave Macmillan, 2019).
3 Katie Liston and Niamh Kitching, '"Our wee country": National identity, golf and "Ireland"', *Sport in Society*, March 2019, DOI: 10.1080/17430437.2019.1584186.
4 See 'No Formal Complaint from Racing 92 in "Alleged Case of Verbal Abuse" Aimed at Simon Zebo During Match Against Ulster', RTÉ, 13 January 2019, https://www.rte.ie/sport/rugby/2019/0112/1022855-simon-zebo-racing-92-ulster/ (accessed 14 May 2019).
5 Johnny Watterson, 'Racism Remains a Perennial Problem in Irish Sport', *Irish Times*, 19 January 2019.
6 Tony Ward, 'I Have Found Bundee Aki's "Who will I play for approach" Puke-inducing', *Irish Independent*, 3 January 2017.
7 John Overton, Warwick E. Murray and Jo Heitger, 'Pass the Passport! Geographies of the Rugby World Cup 2011', *New Zealand Geographer*, no. 69 (2013), pp. 94–107.
8 Marcus Free, '"From there to here": Narratives of transition, migration and national identity in Irish media representations of rugby union in the professional era', *European Journal for Sport and Society*, vol. 14, no. 3 (2017), p. 217.
9 Gavin Cummiskey, 'Bundee Aki Has No Ireland Plans for Now', *Irish Times*, 12 April 2017.
10 Eric Anderson, *Inclusive Masculinity: The changing nature of masculinities*, 2nd edn (Abingdon: Routledge, 2011).
11 Ed Madden, 'Get Your Kit On: Gender, sexuality, and gay rugby in Ireland', *Éire-Ireland*, vol. 48, nos 1–2 (spring/summer 2013), p. 276.
12 Ibid., p. 249.
13 Ibid., p. 276.

Bibliography

Anderson, Benedict, *Imagined Communities: Reflections on the origin and spread of nationalism*, rev. edn (London: Verso, 1991)

Anderson, Eric, *Inclusive Masculinity: The changing nature of masculinities*, 2nd edn (Abingdon: Routledge, 2011)

Andreff, Wladimir, 'Globalization of the Sports Economy', *Rivista Di Diritto Ed Economia Dello Sport*, vol. 4, no. 3 (2008)

Andrews, David L. and Steven J. Jackson, 'Introduction: Sports celebrities, public culture, and private experience', in David L. Andrews and Steven J. Jackson (eds), *Sport Stars: The cultural politics of sporting celebrity* (London: Routledge, 2001)

— and Steven J. Jackson, *Sports Stars: The cultural politics of sporting celebrity* (London: Routledge, 2001)

Antunovic, Dunja, '"Turned into the Women's Journal": Representations of women in Hungary's sports magazine', *International Review for the Sociology of Sport*, vol. 54, no. 1 (2019)

— and Erin Whiteside, 'Feminist Sport Media Studies: State of the field', in Dustin Harp, Jaime Loke and Ingrid Bachmann (eds), *Feminist Approaches to Media Theory and Research* (Basingstoke: Palgrave Macmillan, 2018)

— and Marie Hardin, 'Activism in Women's Sports Blogs: Activism and feminist potential', *International Journal of Sport Communication*, no. 5 (2015)

Apostolis, Nicolas and Audrey R. Giles, 'Portrayals of Women Golfers in the 2008 Issues of *Golf Digest*', *Sociology of Sport Journal*, vol. 28, no. 2 (2011)

Arrowsmith, Aidan, 'Plastic Paddies vs. Master Racers: "Soccer" and Irish identity', *International Journal of Cultural Studies*, vol. 7, no. 4 (2004)

Arslan, Bengü and Canan Koca, 'A Content Analysis of Turkish Daily Newspapers Regarding Sportswomen and Gender Stereotypes', *Annals of Leisure Research*, vol. 10, nos 3–4 (2007)

Bairner, Alan, *Sport, Nationalism and Globalisation* (Albany, NY: State of New York Press, 2001)

—, 'Political Unionism and Sporting Nationalism: An examination of the relationship between sport and national identity within the Ulster Unionist tradition', *Identities: Global Studies in Culture and Power*, vol. 10, no. 4 (2003)

—, '(George) Best: Ulster Protestantism, conflicted identity and the "Belfast Boy(s)"', *Canadian Journal of Irish Studies*, vol. 32, no. 2 (fall, 2006)

Bakhtin, M.M., *Rabelais and His World*, trans. H. Iswolsky [1984] (Bloomington, IN: Indiana University Press, 1968)

Ballantine, Joan and Pauric McGowan (eds), *Women into Business in Northern Ireland: Opportunities and challenges* (Belfast: Ulster University Business School, 2018), https://www.businessfirstonline. co.uk/wp-content/uploads/2018/06/REPORT-Women-into-Business-in-Northern-Ireland-Final.pdf

Barnett, Barbara, 'Girls Gone Web: Self-depictions of female athletes on personal websites', *Journal of Communication Theory*, vol. 4, no. 2 (2017)

Barnett, Clive, 'The Consolations of Neoliberalism', *Geoforum*, vol. 36, no. 1 (January 2005)

Belchem, John, *Irish, Catholic and Scouse: The history of the Liverpool-Irish, 1800–1939* (Liverpool: Liverpool University Press, 2007)

Bernstein, Alina, 'Is it Time for a Victory Lap? Changes in the media coverage of women in sport', *International Review for the Sociology of Sport*, no. 37 (2002)

— and Edward M. Kian, 'Gender and Sexualities in Sport Media', in Paul M. Pedersen (ed.), *Routledge Handbook of Sport Communication* (New York: Routledge, 2013)

Best, George, *On the Ball* (London: Pelham, 1970)

— (with Roy Collins), *Blessed: An intimate portrait* (London: Ebury Press, 2001)

— (with Martin Knight), *George Best, Scoring at Half Time* (London: Ted Smart/Ebury Press, 2003)

Billig, Michael, *Banal Nationalism* (London: Sage Publications, 1995)

Billings, Andrew, James R. Angelini and Susan Tyler Eastman, 'Diverging Discourses: Gender differences in televised golf announcing', *Mass Communication and Society*, vol. 8, no. 2 (2005)

—, Caroline Craig, Robert Croce, Kristian Cross, Kathryn Moore, William Vigodsky and Victoria Watson, '"Just one of the guys?" Network depictions of Annika Sorenstam in the 2003 PGA Colonial Tournament', *Journal of Sport & Social Issues*, vol. 30, no. 1 (2006)

—, *Olympic Media: Inside the biggest show on television* (London: Routledge, 2008)

—, James Angelini and Susan Eastman, 'Wie Shock: Television commentary about playing on the PGA and LPGA tours', *Howard Journal of Communications*, vol. 19, no. 1 (2008)

—, James Angelini and Andrea Holt Duke, 'Gendered Profiles of Olympic History: Sportcaster dialogue in the 2008 Beijing Olympics', *Journal of Broadcasting & Electronic Media*, no. 54 (2010)

Birrell, Susan, 'Feminist Theories for Sport', in Jay Coakley and Eric Dunning (eds), *Handbook of Sports Studies* (London: Sage Publications, 2000)

Biscomb, Kay and Gerald Griggs, '"A splendid effort!" Print media reporting of England's women's performance in the 2009 Cricket World Cup', *International Review for the Sociology of Sport*, vol. 48, no. 1 (2013)

— and Hilary Matheson, 'Are the Times Changing Enough? Print media trends across four decades', *International Review for the Sociology of Sport*, vol. 54, no. 3 (2017)

Black, Jack and Beth Fielding-Lloyd, 'Re-establishing the "Outsiders": English press coverage of the 2015 FIFA Women's World Cup', *International Review for the Sociology of Sport*, vol. 53, no. 4 (2019)

Bonner, Kieran, 'Exciting, Intoxicating and Dangerous: Some Tiger effects on Ireland and the culture of Dublin', *Canadian Journal of Irish Studies*, no. 37 (2011)

Bowes, Ali and Alan Bairner, 'England's Proxy Warriors? Women, war and sport', *International Review for the Sociology of Sport*, vol. 53, no. 4 (2018)

— and Niamh Kitching, '"Battle of the sixes": Investigating print media representations of female professional golfers competing in a men's tour event', *International Review for the Sociology of Sport*, April 2019, DOI: 10.1177/1012690219842544

Boyle, Raymond, 'Nation Shall Speak Peace Unto Nation: Television, sport and nationhood', MA thesis, Dublin City University, 1990

—, 'From Our Gaelic Fields: Radio, sport and nation in post-partition Ireland', *Media, Culture and Society*, no. 14 (1992)

— and Richard Haynes, *Football in the New Media Age* (London: Routledge, 2004)

Boym, Svetlana, *The Future of Nostalgia* (New York: Basic Books, 2001)

Braun, Victoria and Victoria Clarke, 'Using Thematic Analysis in Psychology', *Qualitative Research in Psychology*, vol. 3, no. 2 (2006)

Brennan, Edward, *A Post-nationalist History of Television in Ireland* (Basingstoke: Palgrave Macmillan, 2019)

Brown, Allan, 'Economics, Public Service Broadcasting, and Social Values', *Journal of Media Economics*, vol. 9, no. 1 (1996)

Bruce, Toni, 'Women, Sport and the Media: A complex terrain', in Camilla Obel, Toni Bruce and Shona Thompson (eds), *Outstanding Research About Women and Sport in New Zealand* (Hamilton, New Zealand: Wilf Malcolm Institute of Educational Research, 2008)

—, 'Reflections on Communication and Sport: On women and feminities', *Communication & Sport*, vol. 1, nos 1–2 (2012)

—, 'Assessing the Sociology of Sport: On media and representations of sportswomen', *International Review for the Sociology of Sport*, vol. 50, nos 4–5 (2015)

—, 'New Rules for New Times: Sportswomen and media representation in the third wave', *Sex Roles*, vol. 74, nos 7–8 (2016)

Burn, Gordon, *Best and Edwards* (London: Faber & Faber, 2006)

Burt, Jason, 'Liverpool Have a Glorious Chance to Use the Power of Anfield to Take the Next Step', *Telegraph*, 23 April 2018

Butler, Judith, *Gender Trouble: Feminism and the subversion of identity* (London & New York: Routledge, 1999)

Caple, Helen, 'Competing for Coverage: Exploring emerging discourses on female athletes in the Australian print media', *English Text Construction*, vol. 6, no. 2 (2013)

Cathcart, Rex, 'Broadcasting the Early Decades', in Brian Farrell (ed.), *Communications and Community in Ireland* (Cork: Cork University Press, 1984)

Charmaz, Kathy, *Constructing Grounded Theory*, 2nd edn (London: Sage, 2014)

Chiu, Allyson, '"Sandpapergate" Cheating Scandal Rocks Australian Cricket: "It beggars belief", says prime minister', *Washington Post*, 29 March 2018.

Clavio, Galen and Andrea Eagleman, 'Gender and Sexually Suggestive Images in Sports Blogs', *Journal of Sport Management*, vol. 25, no. 4 (2011)

Cleary, Joe, *Outrageous Fortune: Capital and culture in modern Ireland* (Dublin, Field Day Publications in association with the Keough-Naughton Institute for Irish Studies at the University of Notre Dame, 2006)

Connolly, John and Paddy Dolan, 'Sport, Media and the Gaelic Athletic Association', *Media, Culture & Society*, vol. 34, no. 4 (2012)

— and Paddy Dolan, 'The Amplification and De-amplification of Amateurism and Professionalism in the Gaelic Athletic Association', *International Journal of the History of Sport*, vol. 30, no. 8 (2013)

Cooky, Cheryl, Michael Messner and Robin Hextrum, 'Women Play Sport, But Not on TV: A longitudinal study of televised news media', *Communication & Sport*, vol. 1, no. 3 (2013)

Copsey, Nigel and John E. Richardson (eds), *Cultures of Post-war British Fascism* (London: Routledge, 2015)

Cortés, Carlos, *The Children Are Watching: How the media teach about diversity*, Multicultural Education Series (New York: Teachers College Press, 2000)

Crawford, Garry, *Consuming Sport: Fans, sport and culture* (London: Routledge, 2004)

Critcher, Chas, 'Football Since the War', in John Clarke, Chas Critcher and Richard Johnson (eds), *Working Class Culture: Studies in history and theory* (London: Hutchinson, 1979)

Cronin, Mike, *Sport and Nationalism in Ireland: Gaelic games, soccer and Irish identity since 1884* (Dublin: Four Courts Press, 1999)

—, 'Projecting the Nation through Sport and Culture: Ireland, Aonach Tailteann and the Irish Free State, 1924–32', *Journal of Contemporary History*, vol. 38, no. 3 (2003)

—, 'Is It for the Glamour? Masculinity, nationhood and amateurism in contemporary projections of the Gaelic Athletic Association', in Wanda Balzano, Anne Mulhall and Moynagh Sullivan (eds), *Irish Postmodernisms and Popular Culture* (Basingstoke: Palgrave Macmillan, 2007)

Cronin, Michael, Peadar Kirby and Debbie Ging, 'Transforming Ireland: Challenges', in Debbie Ging, Michael Cronin and Peadar Kirby (eds), *Transforming Ireland: Challenges, Critiques, Resources* (Manchester: Manchester University Press, 2009)

Crosset, Todd W., *Outsiders in the Clubhouse: The world of women's professional golf* (Albany, NY: State University of New York Press, 1995)

Crosson, Seán, '"Shillalah swing time…you'll thrill each time a wild Irishman's skull shatters": Representing hurling in American cinema: 1930–1960', in Ruth Barton (ed.), *Screening Irish-America: Representing Irish-America in film and television* (Dublin: Irish Academic Press, 2009)

—, '"Ar son an Náisiúin": The National Film Institute of Ireland's All-Ireland films', *Éire-Ireland*, special issue on Irish sport, vol. 48, nos 1–2 (2013)

—, *Sport and Film* (London: Routledge, 2013)

Croteau, David and William Hoynes, *Media/Society: Industries, images, and audiences* (California: Sage Publications, 2013)

Cullingford, Elizabeth Butler, *Ireland's Others: Gender and ethnicity in Irish literature and popular culture* (Cork, Cork University Press, 2001)

Curran, Conor, *The Development of Sport in Donegal, 1880–1935* (Cork: Cork University Press, 2015)

—, *Irish Soccer Migrants: A social and cultural history* (Cork: Cork University Press, 2017)

—, 'The Role of the Provincial Press in the Development of Association Football in Pre-First World War Ulster: The cases of Donegal, Fermanagh and Cavan', in Ian Kenneally and James T. O'Donnell (eds), *The Irish Regional Press, 1892–2018: Revival, revolution and republic* (Dublin: Four Courts Press, 2018)

—, 'Unscrupulous Adventurers Who Are Domiciled in "The Land of the Almighty Dollar"? The migration of Irish-born soccer players to the American Soccer League, 1921–31', *Journal of Sport History*, vol. 45, no. 3 (fall, 2018)

— and David Toms, 'Introduction to Going Beyond the "Garrison Game": New perspectives on Association football in Irish history', in Conor Curran and David Toms (eds), *New Perspectives on Association*

Football in Irish History: Going beyond the 'garrison game' (Abingdon: Routledge, 2018)

Cusack, Dónal Óg, *Come What May: The autobiography* (Dublin: Penguin Ireland, 2009)

Daniels, Elizabeth, 'Sex Objects, Athletes, and Sexy Athletes: How media representations of women athletes can impact adolescent girls and college women', *Journal of Adolescent Research*, vol. 24, no. 4 (2009)

Darby, Paul, 'Gaelic Sport and the Irish Diaspora in Boston, 1879–90', *Irish Historical Studies*, vol. 33, no. 132 (2003)

— and David Hassan, 'Introduction: Locating sport in the study of the Irish diaspora', *Sport in Society*, vol. 10, no. 3 (2007)

Dart, Jon, 'Confessional Tales from Former Football Hooligans: A nostalgic, narcissistic wallow in football violence', *Soccer and Society*, vol. 9, no. 1 (2008)

Delorme, Nicolas and Nadège Testard, 'Sex Equity in French Newspaper Photographs: A content analysis of 2012 Olympic Games by *L'Equipe*', *European Journal of Sport Science*, vol. 15, no. 8 (2015)

Department of Transport, Tourism and Sport, *National Sports Policy Framework Public Consultation Paper* (Dublin, 2016)

Dixon, Kevin, '"A Third Way" for Football Fandom Research: Anthony Giddens and structuration theory', *Soccer and Society*, vol. 12, no. 2 (2011)

Dodd, Paul and Iain McNee, *England's Number One: The great adventure of a serial soccer yob* (London: PIG Books, 1998)

Dolan, Paddy, 'The Development of Consumer Culture, Subjectivity and National Identity in Ireland, 1900–1980', PhD thesis, Goldsmiths College, University of London, 2005

—, 'Developing Consumer Subjectivity in Ireland: 1900–80', *Journal of Consumer Culture*, vol. 9, no. 1 (2009)

— and John Connolly, 'The Civilizing of Hurling in Ireland', *Sport in Society*, vol. 12, no. 2 (2009)

—, 'Cultural Cosmopolitanization and the Politics of Television in 1960s Ireland', *Media, Culture & Society*, vol. 36, no. 7 (2014)

Douglas, Kitrina and David Carless, *Women Professional Tournament Golfers: A research project undertaken for UK Sport* (London: UK Sport, 2006)

Du Gay, Paul, Stuart Hall, Linda Janes, Anders Koed Madsen, Hugh Mackay and Keith Negus, *Doing Cultural Studies: The story of the Sony Walkman*, 2nd edn (London: Sage, 2013)

Dublin Sports and Recreation Council, *The Increasing Invisibility of Women in Irish Sport: Images of sportswomen in Irish newspapers* (Dublin: Dublin Sports and Recreation Council 2007)

Duncan, Margaret Carlisle and Cynthia Hasbrook, 'Denial of Power in Televised Women's Sports', *Sociology of Sport Journal*, no. 5 (1998)

Dunne, Ciarán, 'An Examination of the Photographic Coverage of Sportswomen in the Irish Print Media: A study of an Irish broadsheet newspaper', *Sport in Society*, vol. 20, no. 11 (2017)

Dyer, Richard, *Stars* (London: British Film Institute, 1979)

Elias, Norbert and John L. Scotson, *The Established and the Outsiders* (Dublin: University College Dublin Press, 2008)

—, *The Society of Individuals* (Dublin: University College Dublin Press, 2010)

—, *On the Process of Civilisation: Sociogenetic and psychogenetic investigations* [1939] (Dublin: University College Dublin Press, 2012)

—, *What Is Sociology?* (Dublin: University College Dublin Press, 2012)

Ellen J. Staurowsky, *Women and Sport: From liberation to celebration* (Champaign: Human Kinetics, 2016)

Evens, Tom, Petros Iosifidis and Paul Smith, *The Political Economy of Television Sports Rights*, Palgrave Global Media Policy and Business Series (Basingstoke: Palgrave MacMillan, 2013)

Falcous, Mark, 'Sport/Media Complex', in David Levinson and Karen Christensen (eds), *Berkshire Encyclopaedia of World Sport* (Great Barrington, MA: Berkshire Publishing, 2010)

—, 'The Decolonizing National Imaginary: Promotional media constructions during the 2005 Lions tour of Aotearoa New Zealand', *Journal of Sport & Social Issues*, vol. 31, no. 4 (2007)

Falkiner, Keith, *Emerald Anfield: The Irish and Liverpool FC* (Dublin: Hachette Books, 2010)

Fanning, John, *The Importance of Being Branded: An Irish perspective* (Dublin: Liffey Press, 2006)

Farred, Grant, 'Long Distance Love: Growing up a Liverpool fan', *Journal of Sport & Social Issues*, vol. 26, no. 1 (2002)

Farrell, Rebecca E., *Across the Water: Teaching Irish music and dance at home and abroad* (Lanham, MD: R&L Education, 2010)

Fasting, Kari, Trond Svela Sand, Elizabeth Pike and Jordan Matthews (eds), *From Brighton to Helsinki: Women and sport progress report, 1994–2014* (Helsinki: Finnish Sports Confederation, 2014), http://d3mcbia3evjswv.cloudfront.net/files/IWG%20Final%20Report.pdf?mRdkO5No_atTOUY7MwR.XrKo7t3Ar78d (accessed 11 February 2020)

Fields, Sarah, 'A Toothless Tiger? Sports, Title IX, and gendered bodies', in Joseph Maguire, Mark Falcous and Katie Liston (eds), *The Business and Culture of Sports*, no. 3 (New York: Macmillan, 2019)

Fink, Janet, 'Female Athletes, Women's Sport, and the Sport Media Commercial Complex: Have we really "come a long way baby"?', *Sport Management Review*, vol. 18, no. 3 (2013)

Fiske, John, *Understanding Popular Culture* (London: Routledge, 1989)

—, 'The Cultural Economy of Fandom', in L.A. Lewis (ed.), *The Adoring Audience: Fan culture and popular media* (London: Routledge, 1992)

Fitzpatrick, Daniel, '"Football Remembers": The invention of the poppy in British football', research paper delivered at Football, Politics and Popular Culture Conference, University of Limerick, 23 November 2017

Fitzpatrick, David, *Irish Emigration, 1801–1921: Studies in Irish economic and social history* (Dundalk: Dundalgan Press, 1984)

Flynn, Roderick, 'Neo-liberalism and Irish Broadcasting', in Peadar Kirby, Luke Gibbons and Michael Cronin (eds), *Reinventing Ireland: Culture and the Celtic Tiger* (London: Pluto Press, 2002)

Frandsen, Kirsten, 'Sports Organizations in a New Wave of Mediatization', *Communication and Sport*, vol. 4, no. 4 (2015)

Free, Marcus, 'Keeping Them Under Pressure: Masculinity, narratives of national regeneration and the Republic of Ireland soccer team', *Sport in History*, vol. 2, no. 2 (2006)

—, 'Antihero as National Icon? The contrariness of Roy Keane as fantasy embodiment of the "New Ireland"', in Philip Dine and Seán Crosson (eds), *Sport, Representation and Evolving Identities in Europe* (Bern: Peter Lang, 2010)

—, 'Diaspora and Rootedness, Amateurism and Professionalism in Media Discourses of Irish Soccer and Rugby in the 1990s and 2000s', *Éire-Ireland*, no. 48 (2013)

—, '"He is my strength and my shield": The antinomies of Katie Taylor as female sporting celebrity in twenty-first-century Ireland', *Sport in Society*, vol. 18, no. 10 (2015)

—, '"From there to here": Narratives of transition, migration and national identity in Irish media representations of rugby union in the professional era', *European Journal for Sport and Society*, vol. 14, no. 3 (2017)

—, 'Smart, Clued-in Guys: Irish rugby players as celebrities in post-Celtic Tiger Irish media', *International Journal of Media and Cultural Politics*, vol. 14, no. 2 (2018)

— and Clare Scully, 'The Run of Ourselves: Shame, guilt and confession in Post-Celtic Tiger Irish media', *International Journal of Cultural Studies*, vol. 21, no. 3 (2018)

French, Simone, 'Still Not There: The continued invisibility of female athletes and sports in the New Zealand print media', *Media International Australia*, vol. 148, no. 1 (2013)

Frith, Katherine Toland and Barbara Mueller, *Advertising and Societies: Global issues* (New York: Peter Lang, 2003)

Frosdick, Steve and Peter Marsh, *Football Hooliganism* (Devon: Willan, 2005)

Fry, John, Daniel Bloyce and Ian Pritchard, 'Professional Golf – a License to Spend Money? Issues of money in the lives of touring professional golfers', *Journal of Sport & Social Issues*, vol. 39, no. 3 (2015)

Galily, Yair, 'When the Medium Becomes "Well Done": Sport, television and technology in the twenty-first century', *Television & New Media*, vol. 15, no. 8 (2014)

Garnham, Neal, 'Accounting for the Early Success of the Gaelic Athletic Association', *Irish Historical Studies*, vol. 34, no. 133 (2004)

—, *Association Football and Society in Pre-partition Ireland* (Belfast: Ulster Historical Foundation, 2004)

Gellner, Ernest, *Nations and Nationalism* (Oxford: Blackwell, 1983)

Gibbons, Luke, 'From Megalith to Megastore: Broadcasting and Irish culture', in idem, *Transformations in Irish Culture* (Cork: Cork University Press, 1996)

—, *Transformations in Irish Culture* (Cork: Cork University Press, 1996)

Gilroy, Paul, 'Diaspora and the Detours of Identity', in Kathryn Woodward (ed.), *Identity and Difference* (London: Sage, 1997)

Ging, Debbie, *Men and Masculinities in Irish Cinema* (Basingstoke: Palgrave Macmillan, 2012)

— and Marcus Free, 'Gay in the GAA: The challenge of Dónal Óg Cusack's "coming out" to heteronormativity in contemporary Irish culture and society', in Rosie Meade and Fiona Dukelow (eds), *Defining Events: Power, resistance and identity in twenty-first-century Ireland* (Manchester: Manchester University Press, 2015)

Giulianotti, Richard, 'Scotland's Tartan Army in Italy: The case for the carnivalesque', *Sociological Review*, vol. 39, no. 3 (1991)

—, 'Supporters, Followers, Fans and Flaneurs: A taxonomy of spectator identities in football', *Journal of Sport and Social Issues*, no. 26 (2002)

— and Roland Robertson, *Globalization and Sport* (London: Wiley-Blackwell, 2009)

Gledhill, Christine, 'Introduction', in Christine Gledhill (ed), *Stardom: Industry of desire* (London & New York: Routledge, 1991)

Global Media Monitoring Project, *Global Media Monitoring Project Regional Report 2015* (Toronto & Newcastle: World Association for Christian Communication, 2015), http://cdn.agilitycms.com/who-makes-the-news/Imported/reports_2015/regional/Europe.pdf

Godoy-Pressland, Amy and Gerald Griggs, 'The Photographic Representation of Female Athletes in the British Print Media During the London 2012 Olympic Games', *Sport in Society*, vol. 17, no. 6 (2014)

—, '"No hint of bulging muscles": The surveillance of sportswomen's bodies in British print media', *Journalism*, vol. 17, no. 6 (2015)

Goksøyr, Matti and Hans Hognestad, 'No Longer Worlds Apart? British influences and Norwegian football', in Gary Armstrong and Richard Giulianotti (eds), *Football Cultures and Identities* (Basingstoke: Macmillan, 1999)

Goodrick-Clarke, Nicholas, *Black Sun: Aryan cults, esoteric Nazism and the politics of identity* (New York: New York University Press, 2001)

Goodwin, Matthew J., *New British Fascism: The rise of the British National Party* (London: Routledge, 2011)

Graff-McRae, Rebecca Lynn, 'Forget Politics! Theorising the political dynamics of commemoration and conflict', in Mary E. Daly and Margaret O'Callaghan (eds), *1916 in 1966: Commemorating the Easter Rising* (Dublin: Royal Irish Academy, 2007)

Gramsci, Antonio, *Selections from the Prison Notebooks of Antonio Gramsci* (New York: International Publishers, 1971)

Gray, Ann, *Video Playtime: The gendering of a leisure technology* (London: Routledge, 1992)

Gray, Breda, 'The Irish Diaspora: Globalised belonging(s)', *Irish Journal of Sociology*, vol. 11, no. 2 (2002)

—, 'Thinking Through Transnational Studies, Diaspora Studies and Gender', in D.A.J. MacPherson and Mary J. Hickman (eds), *Women and Irish Diaspora Identities: Theories, concepts and new perspectives* (Manchester: Manchester University Press, 2014)

Hall, Ruth and Carole Oglesby, 'Stepping Through the Looking Glass', *Sex Roles*, vol. 74, nos 7–8 (2016)

Hall, Stuart, 'The Question of Cultural Identity', in Stuart Hall, David Held and Anthony McGrew (eds), *Modernity and its Futures* (Cambridge, Polity Press, 1992)

Harkin, Frances, '"Where Would We Be Without the GAA?": Gaelic games and Irishness in London', *Irish Studies Review*, vol. 26, no. 1 (2018)

Harris, John, Lee Sangkwon and Mark Lyberger, 'The Ryder Cup, national identities and team USA', *Sport in Society*, vol. 20, no. 3 (2015)

Harris, Rex, 'Globalised Football Fandom: Scandinavian Liverpool FC supporters', *Football Studies*, vol. 3, no. 2 (2000)

Hassan, David, 'A People Apart: Soccer, identity and Irish nationalists in Northern Ireland', *Soccer & Society*, vol. 3, no. 3 (2002)

—, Shane McCullough and Elizabeth Moreland, 'North or South? Darron Gibson and the issue of player eligibility within Irish soccer', *Soccer & Society*, vol. 10, no. 6 (2009)

Haynes, Richard, *The Football Imagination: The rise of football fanzine culture* (London: Arena, 1995)

Hayward, Susan, *French National Cinema* (London: Routledge, 2005)

Hermes, Joke, *Re-reading Popular Culture* (Oxford: Blackwell, 2005)

Hickman, Mary J., *Religion, Class and Identity: The state, the Catholic Church and the education of the Irish in Britain* (Aldershot: Avebury, 1997)

—, Sarah Morgan, Bronwen Walter and Joseph Bradley, 'The Limitations of Whiteness and the Boundaries of Englishness: Second-generation Irish identifications and positionings in multiethnic Britain', *Ethnicities*, vol. 5, no. 2 (2005)

Higgins, Róisín, '"I am the narrator over and above…the caller up of the dead": Pageant and drama in 1966', in Mary E. Daly and Margaret O'Callaghan (eds), *1916 in 1966: Commemorating the Easter Rising* (Dublin: Royal Irish Academy, 2007)

Higson, Andrew, *Waving the Flag: Constructing a national cinema in Britain* (Oxford: Clarendon Press, 1995)

Hill, John, 'Images of Violence', in Kevin Rockett, John Hill and Luke Gibbons (eds), *Cinema and Ireland* (London & New York: Routledge, 1987)

Hjort, Mette and Scott MacKenzie (eds), *Cinema and Nation* (London: Routledge, 2000)

Honeybone, Patrick 'New-dialect Formation in Nineteenth Century Liverpool: A brief history of Scouse', in Anthony Grant and Clive Grey (eds), *The Mersey Sound: Liverpool's language, people and places* (Liverpool: Open House Press, 2007)

Hopcraft, Arthur, *Football Man* (London: Aurum Press, 2006)

Horak, Roman and Georg Spitaler, 'Sport Space and National Identity', *American Behavioral Scientist*, vol. 46, no. 11 (2003)

Horgan, John, *Irish Media: A critical history since 1922* (London: Routledge, 2001)

— and Roddy Flynn, *Irish Media: A critical history*, 2nd rev. edn (Dublin: Four Courts Press, 2017)

Hutchins, Brett and David Rowe, 'From Broadcast Scarcity to Digital Plenitude: The changing dynamics of the media sport content economy', *Television & New Media*, no. 10 (2009)

Inglis, Tom, 'From Self-denial to Self-indulgence: The class of cultures in contemporary Ireland', *Irish Review*, no. 34 (2006)

—, *Global Ireland: Same difference* (Abingdon: Routledge, 2008)

Irish Life Health, *Irish Life Health School's Fitness Challenge Barometer* (2018), https://www.irishlifehealth.ie/IrishLifeHealth/media/Irish-life-Health/pdfs/fitness-challenge/sfc-barometer-2018-web.pdf

Jackson, Steven and David L. Andrews (eds), 'Olympic Celebrity: Introduction', *Celebrity Studies*, vol. 3, no. 3 (November 2012)

— and Jay Scherer, 'Rugby World Cup 2011: Sport mega-events and the contested terrain of space, bodies and commodities', *Sport in Society*, vol. 16, no. 3 (2013)

Jakubowska, Honorata, 'Are Women Still the "Other Sex": Gender and sport in the Polish mass media', *Sport in Society*, vol. 18, no. 2 (2015)

Jarman, Neil, 'Commemorating 1916, Celebrating Difference: Parading and painting in Belfast', in Adrian Forty and Susanne Küchler (eds), *The Art of Forgetting* (Oxford, New York: Berg, 2001)

Jenkins, Henry, *Textual Poachers: Television fans and participatory culture* (New York: Routledge, 1992)

Jerslev, Anne and Mette Mortensen, 'Celebrity in the Social Media Age: Renegotiating the public and the private', in Anthony Elliot (ed.), *Routledge Handbook of Celebrity Studies* (London & New York: Routledge, 2018)

Jones, R.J. Barry (ed.), *Routledge Encyclopedia of International Political Economy: Entries G–O*, no. 2 (London: Taylor & Francis, 2001)

Joyce, Michael, *Football League Players' Records, 1888 to 1939* (Nottingham: Tony Brown, 2012)

Kane, Mary Jo, 'The Better Sportswomen Get, the More the Media Ignore Them', *Communication & Sport*, vol. 1, no. 3 (2013)

Kelly, John, 'Popular Culture, Sport and the "Hero"-ification of British Militarism', *Sociology*, vol. 47, no. 4 (2012)

Kennedy, Liam, Madeleine Lyes and Martin Russell, *Supporting the Next Generation of the Irish Diaspora* (Dublin: University College, Dublin, 2014)

Kiberd, Declan, *Inventing Ireland* (London: Vantage, 1996)

—, 'The Easter Rebellion: Poetry or drama?', papers from The 1916 Rising: Then and Now conference held at Trinity College Dublin, 21–2 April 2006, organised by the Ireland Institute and Dublin University History Society, http://www.theirelandinstitute.com/wp/1916-then-now/

King, Anthony, 'New Directors, Customers and Fans: The transformation of English football in the 1990s', *Sociology of Sport Journal*, vol. 14, no. 3 (1997)

—, 'The Lads: Masculinity and the new consumption of football', *Sociology*, vol. 31, no. 2 (1997)

Kitching, Niamh, *'Practice' Makes Perfect: Locating young people in golf club culture* (Limerick: University of Limerick, 2011)

—, 'Women in Golf: A critical reflection', in Martin Toms (ed.), *Routledge International Handbook of Golf Science* (London: Routledge, 2017)

—, Jonathan Grix and Lesley Phillpotts, 'Shifting Hegemony in "a Man's World": Incremental change for female golf professional employment', *Sport in Society*, vol. 20, no. 11 (2017)

Koivula, Nathalie, 'Gender Stereotyping in Televised Media Sport Coverage', *Sex Roles*, no. 41 (1999)

Len-Ríos, Maria E., Shelly Rodgers, Esther Thorson and Doyle Yoon, 'Representation of Women in News and Photos: Comparing content to perceptions', *Journal of Communication*, vol. 55, no. 1 (2005)

Liston, Katie, 'Sport and Gender Relations', *Sport in Society*, vol. 9, no. 4 (2006)

—, 'Revisiting Relations Between the Sexes in Sport on the Island of Ireland', in Tatiana Landini and Francois Dépelteau (eds), *Norbert Elias and Empirical Research* (New York: Palgrave Macmillan, 2014

— and Niamh Kitching, '"Our wee country": National identity, golf and "Ireland"', *Sport in Society*, March 2019, DOI: 10.1080/17430437.2019.1584186

Lowles, Nick, *White Riot: The violent story of Combat 18* (London: Milo Books, 2011)

Lumpkin, Angela, 'Female Representation in Feature Articles Published by *Sports Illustrated* in the 1990s', *Women in Sport and Physical Activity Journal*, no. 18 (2009)

Lynch, Kathleen and Anne Lodge, *Equality and Power in Schools: Redistribution, recognition and representation* (London: Routledge Falmer, 2002)

Maas, Kay and Cynthia Hasbrook, 'Media Promotion of the Paradigm Citizen/Golfer: An analysis of golf magazines' representations of disability, gender and age', *Sociology of Sport Journal*, no. 18 (2001)

Mac an Ghaill, Martin and Chris Haywood, 'Being Irish and Male in Britain', in Tom Inglis (ed.), *Are the Irish Different?* (Manchester: Manchester University Press, 2014)

Madden, Ed, 'Get Your Kit On: Gender, sexuality, and gay rugby in Ireland', *Éire-Ireland*, vol. 48, nos 1–2 (spring/summer 2013)

Maguire, Joseph, 'Sport, Identity Politics, and Globalization: Diminishing contrasts and increasing varieties', *Sociology of Sport Journal*, no. 11 (1994)

Mandle, William F., *The Gaelic Athletic Association and Irish Nationalist Politics, 1884–1924* (Dublin: Gill and Macmillan, 1987)

Marshall, P. David, *Celebrity and Power: Fame in contemporary culture* (Minneapolis & London: University of Minnesota Press, 1997)

Mason, Tony, *Association Football and English Society, 1863–1915* (Brighton: Harvester Press, 1980)

McCabe, Conor, '*Football Sports Weekly* and Irish Soccer, 1925–1928', *Media History*, vol. 17, no. 2 (2011)

McClearen, Jennifer, 'Introduction: Women in sports media: new scholarly engagements', *Feminist Media Studies*, vol. 18, no. 6 (2018)

McDevitt, Patrick F., 'Muscular Catholicism: Nationalism, masculinity and Gaelic team sports, 1884–1916', *Gender & History*, vol. 9, no. 2 (1997)

McFarlene-Alvarez, Susan, 'Human Billboarding: Peopled publicity and a new space of "agency" in advertising', *Advertising & Society Review*, no. 15 (2014)

McGee, Darragh and Alan Bairner, 'Transcending the Borders of Irish Identity? Narratives of Northern nationalist footballers in Northern Ireland', *International Review for the Sociology of Sport*, vol. 46, no. 4 (2010)

McLachlan, Fiona, 'It's Boom Time! (again): Progress narratives and women's sport in Australia', *Journal of Australian Studies*, vol. 43, no. 2 (2019)

McSharry, Majella, 'Stuck in a Ruck: The impact of rugby on social belonging', in Perry Share and Mary P. Corcoran (eds), *Belongings: Shaping identity in modern Ireland* (Dublin: Institute of Public Administration, 2008)

Messner, Michael, 'Sports and Male Domination: The female athlete as contested ideological terrain', *Sociology of Sport Journal*, vol. 5, no. 1 (1988)

—, Michele Dunbar and Darnell Hunt, 'The Televised Sports Manhood Formula', *Journal of Sport and Social Issues*, vol. 24, no. 4 (2000)

Mitchell, Stacey, Jacquelyn Allen-Collinson and Adam Evans, '"Ladies present!": An auto/ethnographic study of women amateur golfers at an English provincial golf club', *Qualitative Research in Sport, Exercise & Health*, vol. 8, no. 3 (2016)

Modleski, Tania, 'Clint Eastwood and Male Weepies', *American Literary History*, vol. 22, no. 1 (2009)

Montuori, Alfonso and Hillary Stephenson, 'Creativity, Culture Contact, and Diversity', *World Futures*, vol. 66, nos 3–4 (2010)

Moore, Cormac, 'Partition in Irish Sport', in Paddy Dolan and John Connolly (eds), *Sport and National Identities* (London: Routledge, 2017)

Moore, Cormac, *The GAA v Douglas Hyde: The removal of Ireland's first president as GAA patron* (Cork: Collins Press, 2012)

Moore, Martin, 'The Origins of Association Football in Ireland, 1875–1880: A reappraisal', *Sport in History*, vol. 37, no. 4 (2017)

Morley, David, *Home Territories: Media, mobility and identity* (London & New York: Routledge, 2000)

—, 'Domesticating Dislocation in a World of "New" Technology', in Chris Berry, So-yŏng Kim and Lynn Spigel (eds), *Electronic Elsewheres: Media, technology, and the experience of social space* (Minneapolis & London: University of Minnesota Press, 2010)

Moynihan, Michael, *GAAconomics: The secret life of money in the GAA* (Dublin: Gill & MacMillan, 2013)

Murphy, William, 'The G.A.A. During the Irish Revolution, 1913–23', in Michael Cronin, William Murphy and Paul Rouse (eds), *The Gaelic Athletic Association, 1884–2009* (Dublin: Irish Academic Press, 2009)

Nash, Catherine, *Of Irish Descent: Origin stories, genealogy, & the politics of belonging* (New York: Syracuse University Press, 2008)

Negra, Diane, 'Urban Space, Luxury Retailing and the New Irishness', *Cultural Studies*, vol. 24, no. 6 (2010)

—, Eleanor O'Leary and Anthony P. McIntyre, *Broadcasting Irish Emigration in an Era of Global Mobility* (Dublin: Broadcasting Authority of Ireland, 2018)

Nohrnberg, Peter. '"Building Up a Nation Once Again": Irish masculinity, violence, and the cultural politics of sports in *A Portrait of the Artist as a Young Man* and *Ulysses*', *Joyce Studies Annual 2010* (2011)

Norberg, J.R., 'Football, Football Pools and the Unexpected Arrival of Sports in Swedish Welfare Politics', *Soccer and Society*, vol. 10, no. 3 (2009)

Nylund, David, 'Taking a Slice at Sexism: The controversy over the exclusionary membership practices of the Augusta National Golf Club', *Journal of Sport & Social Issues*, vol. 27, no. 2 (2003)

Ó Fearghail, Aogán, 'Réamhfocal ón Uachtarán', *Allianz Football League Roinn I and II Finals* (match programme) (Dublin: DBA Publications, 2016)

Ó hAnnrachain, Tadhg, 'The Heroic Importance of Sport: The GAA in the 1930s', *International Journal of the History of Sport*, vol. 25, no. 10 (2008)

O'Barr, William, *Culture and the Ad: Exploring otherness in the world of advertising* (Boulder, CO: Westview Press, 1994)

O'Boyle, Neil, *New Vocabularies, Old Ideas* (Bern: Peter Lang, 2011)

— and Colm Kearns, 'Sporting Shades of Green: A comparative analysis of sponsored national mythmaking in Irish rugby and soccer', *Sport in Society*, vol. 20, no. 7 (2017)

— and Colm Kearns, 'The Greening of Euro 2016: Fan footage, representational tropes, and the media lionization of the Irish in France', *Television & New Media*, vol. 20, no. 1 (2019)

O'Callaghan, Liam, 'The Red Thread of History: The media, Munster rugby and the creation of a sporting tradition', *Media History*, no. 17 (2011)

—, 'Rugby Football and Identity Politics in Free State Ireland', *Éire-Ireland*, vol. 48, nos 1–2 (2013)

—, 'Professional Rugby and Irish Society, 1995–2015', in John Nauright and Tony Collins (eds), *The Rugby World in the Professional Era* (Abingdon: Routledge, 2017)

O'Connor, Pat, 'Private Troubles, Public Issues: The Irish sociological imagination', *Irish Journal of Sociology*, vol. 15, no. 2 (2006)

O'Connor, Robert and Brendan Whelan, *Attitudes of Young People to Games and Pastimes* (Dublin: Economic and Social Research Institute, 1971)

O'Neill, Deirdre and Matt Mulready, 'The Invisible Woman? A comparative study of women's sports coverage in the UK national press before and after the 2012 Olympic Games', *Journalism Practice*, vol. 9, no. 5 (2015)

Overton, John, Warwick E. Murray and Jo Heitger, 'Pass the Passport! Geographies of the Rugby World Cup 2011', *New Zealand Geographer*, no. 69 (2013)

Packer, C., D.J. Geh, O.W. Goulden, A.M. Jordan, G.K. Withers, A.J. Wagstaff, R.A. Bellwood, C.L. Binmore and C.L. Webster, 'No Lasting Legacy: No change in reporting of women's sports in the British print media with the London 2012 Olympics and Paralympics', *Journal of Public Health,* no. 37 (2015)

Parker, Simon, 'The Leaving of Liverpool: Managed decline and the enduring legacy of Thatcherism's urban policy', London School of Economics and Political Science, https://blogs.lse.ac.uk/politicsandpolicy/the-leaving-of-liverpool/, 2019 (accessed 2 April 2019)

Parkinson, Michael, *George Best: An intimate portrait* (London: Arrow Books, 1975)

—, *George Best: A memoir* (London: Hodder & Stoughton, 2018)

Pedersen, Paul M., 'Examining Equity in Newspaper Photographs: A content analysis of the print media photographic coverage of interscholastic athletics', *International Review for the Sociology of Sport,* vol. 37, nos 3–4 (2002)

Pettitt, Lance, 'Northern Ireland's Telestar footballer', *Vacuum* 27 (Belfast: Factotem, September, 2005)

Petty, Kate and Stacey Pope, 'A New Age for Media Coverage of Women's Sport? An analysis of English media coverage of the 2015 FIFA Women's World Cup', *Sociology,* vol. 53, no. 3 (2018)

Phillips, Murray, *An Illusory Image: A report on the media coverage and portrayal of women's sport in Australia 1996* (Canberra: Australian Sports Commission, 1997)

Pine, Richard, *2RN and the Origins of Irish Radio: Broadcasting and Irish society* (Dublin: Four Courts Press, 2002)

Poulton, Emma and Joseph Maguire, 'Plastic or Fantastic Brits? Identity Politics and English media representations of "Team GB" during London 2012', *Journalism, Media and Cultural Studies,* no. 2 (November 2012)

Price, John, Neil Farrington and Lee Hall, 'Changing the Game? The impact of Twitter on relationships between football clubs, supporters and the sports media', *Soccer & Society,* vol. 14, no. 4 (2013)

Raney, Arthur A., 'Why We Watch and Enjoy Mediated Sports', in Arthur A. Raney and Jennings Bryant (eds), *Handbook of Sports and Media* (Mahwah, New Jersey: Lawrence Erlbaum Associates, 2006)

Reade, Ian, Wendy Rodgers and Leanne Norman, 'The Under-representation of Women in Coaching: A comparison of male and female Canadian coaches at low and high levels of coaching', *International Journal of Sports Science & Coaching,* vol. 4, no. 4 (2009)

Redhead, Steve, 'Hit and Tell: A review essay on the soccer hooligan memoir', *Soccer and Society,* vol. 5, no. 3 (2004)

Reid, Irene A., '"An outsider in our midst": Narratives of Neil Lennon, soccer & ethno-religious bigotry in the Scottish press', *Soccer & Society,* vol. 9, no. 1 (2007)

Rojek, Chris, *Celebrity* (London: Reaktion Books, 2001)

Rouse, Paul, 'The Politics of Culture and Sport in Ireland: A history of the GAA ban on foreign games, 1884–1971', *International Journal of the History of Sport*, vol. 10, no. 3 (1993)

—, 'Michael Cusack: Sportsman and journalist', in Mike Cronin, William Murphy and Paul Rouse (eds), *The Gaelic Athletic Association: 1884–2009* (Dublin: Irish Academic Press, 2009)

—, *Sport and Ireland: A history* (Oxford: Oxford University Press, 2015)

Rowe, David, Jim McKay and Toby Miller, 'Come Together: Sport, nationalism and the media image', in Lawrence A. Wenner (ed.), *Mediasport* (London: Routledge, 1998)

—, *Sport, Culture and the Media: The unruly trinity* (Buckingham: Open University Press, 2004)

—, Andy Ruddock and Brett Hutchins, 'Cultures of Complaint: Online fan message boards and networked digital media sport communities', *Convergence*, vol. 16, no. 3 (2010)

—, 'Mediating the Asian Olympics: The Summer Games – image projection and gaze reception', *International Journal of the History of Sport*, vol. 29, no. 16 (2012)

—, 'The Mediated Nation and the Transnational Football Fan', *Soccer & Society*, vol. 16, nos 5–6 (2015)

—, 'Sports and Media', Oxford Bibliographies, www.oxfordbibliographies.com/view/document/obo-9780199791286/obo-9780199791286-0169.xııl (accessed 24 August 2018)

—, Graeme Turner and Emma Waterton, *Making Culture: Commercialisation, transnationalism, and the state of 'nationing' in contemporary Australia* (London: Routledge, 2018)

Ruddock, Andy, *Investigating Audiences* (London: Sage, 2007)

Ryan, Paul, 'Coming Out, Fitting In: The personal narratives of some Irish gay men', *Irish Journal of Sociology*, vol. 12, no. 2 (2003)

Sandvoss, Cornel, *A Game of Two Halves: Football, television and globalization* (London: Routledge, 2003)

Schmidt, Hans, 'Women's Sports Coverage Remains Largely Marginalized', *Newspaper Research Journal*, vol. 37, no. 3 (2016)

Schoch, Lucie and Fabien Ohl, 'Women Sports Journalists in Switzerland: Between assignment and negotiation of roles', *Sociology of Sport Journal*, vol. 28, no. 2 (2011)

Seweryn, Olga and Marta Smagacz, 'Frontiers and Identity: Approaches and inspirations in sociology', in Lud'a Klusáková and Steven G. Ellis (eds), *Frontiers and Identities: Exploring the research area* (Pisa: Pisa University Press, 2006)

Shekhovtsov, Anton, 'Apoliteic Music: Neo-folk, martial industrial and "metapolitical fascism"', *Patterns of Prejudice*, vol. 43, no. 5 (2009)

Shephard, Sarah, *Kicking Off: How women in sport are changing the game* (London: Bloomsbury Publishing, 2016)

Sherry, Emma, Angela Osborne and Matthew Nicholson, 'Images of Sports Women: A review', *Sex Roles* vol. 74, nos 7–8 (2016)

Simpson, Mark, *Male Impersonators: Men performing masculinity* (London: Routledge, 2006)

Smith, William R. and Jeffrey Treem, 'Striving to Be King of Mobile Mountains: Communication and organizing through digital fitness technology', *Communication Studies*, vol. 68, no. 2 (2017)

Solberg, Harry Arne, 'Commentary: Sports broadcasting: Is it a job for public service broadcasters? A welfare economic perspective', *Journal of Media Economics*, vol. 20, no. 4 (2007)

Sport Ireland, *Irish Sports Monitor Annual Report, 2017* (Dublin: Sport Ireland), https://assets.gov.ie/16014/3abf58a4a5af41b9ab66065de65e15a3.pdf

Stauff, Markus, 'Non-fiction Transmedia: Seriality and forensics in media sport', *M/C Journal: A Journal of Media and Culture*, vol. 21, no. 1 (2018), http://journal.media-culture.org.au/index.php/mcjournal/article/view/1372

Storey, David, 'Which Boys in Green? Identity issues in Irish soccer', in Colin Howley and Susan Dun (eds), *The Playing Field: Making sense of spaces and places in sporting culture* (Oxford: Inter-Disciplinary Press, 2016)

Stragier, Jeroen, Tom Evens and Peter Mechant, 'Broadcast Yourself: An exploratory study of sharing physical activity on social networking sites', *Media International Australia*, May 2015

Sugden, John and Alan Tomlinson, 'Sport, Politics and Identities: Football cultures in comparative perspectives', in Maurice Roche (ed.), *Sport, Popular Culture and Identity* (Oxford: Meyer & Meyer Sport, 2000)

Taylor, Matthew, *The Association Game: A history of British football* (Harlow: Pearson, 2008)

Thornton, Sarah, *Club Cultures: Music, media and subcultural capital* (Cambridge: Polity, 1995)

Thorpe, Holly, 'Action Sports, Social Media, and New Technologies: Towards a research agenda', *Communication & Sport*, vol. 5, no. 5 (2017)

—, Kim Toffoletti and Toni Bruce, 'Sportswomen and Social Media: Third-wave feminism, postfeminism, and neoliberal feminism into conversation', *Journal of Sport and Social Issues*, vol. 41, no. 5 (2017)

Toffoletti, Kim and Catherine Palmer, 'Women and Sport in Australia – New Times?' *Journal of Australian Studies*, vol. 43, no. 1 (2019)

Tuck, Jason, 'Making Sense of Emerald Commotion: Rugby Union, national identity and Ireland', *Identities: Global Studies in Culture and Power*, no. 10 (2003)

Ullah, Phillip, 'Rhetoric and Ideology in Social Identification: The case of second generation Irish youths', *Discourse & Society*, vol. 1, no. 2 (1990)

Walter, Bronwen, Sarah Morgan, Mary J. Hickman and Joseph M. Bradley, 'Family Stories, Public Silence: Irish identity construction amongst the second generation Irish in England', *Scottish Geographical Journal*, vol. 118, no. 3 (2002)

War, Colin, *All Quiet on the Hooligan Front: Eight years that shook football* (Edinburgh: Mainstream, 1996)

Weiller, Karen, Catriona Higgs and Christy Greenleaf, 'Analysis of Television Media Commentary of the 2000 Olympic Games', *Media Report to Women*, no. 3 (2004)

Wensing, Emma and Toni Bruce, 'Bending the Rules: Media representations of gender during an international sporting event', *International Review for the Sociology of Sport*, vol. 38, no. 4 (2003)

Whannel, Garry, 'Television and the Transformation of Sport', *Annals of the American Academy of Political and Social Science*, no. 625 (2009)

Whannel, Gary, *Media Sports Stars* (London: Routledge, 2002)

Williams, Richard (ed.), *George Best: A life in the news* (London: Aurum Press, 2006)

Woodhouse, Donna, Beth Fielding-Lloyd and Ruth Sequerra, 'Big Brother's Little Sister: The ideological construction of Women's Super League', *Sport in Society*. vol. 22, no. 12 (2019)

Woodward, Kath, *Sex, Power and the Games: Genders and sexualities in the social sciences* (Basingstoke: Palgrave Macmillan, 2012)

Wyllie, James, Kath Woodward and David Goldblatt, 'Tuning in to Football on the BBC World Service', *Soccer & Society*, vol. 12, no. 1 (2011)

Yip, Adrian, 'Deuce or Advantage? Examining gender bias in online coverage of professional tennis', *International Review for the Sociology of Sport*, vol. 53, no. 5 (2018)

Index